Transcendental Arguments in Moral The

Transcendental Arguments in Moral Theory

Edited by
Jens Peter Brune, Robert Stern and Micha H. Werner

DE GRUYTER

ISBN 978-3-11-062694-0
e-ISBN (PDF) 978-3-11-047021-5
e-ISBN (EPUB) 978-3-11-046989-9

Library of Congress Cataloging-in-Publication Data
A CIP catalog record for this book has been applied for at the Library of Congress.

Bibliographic information published by the Deutsche Nationalbibliothek
The Deutsche Nationalbibliothek lists this publication in the Deutsche Nationalbibliografie;
detailed bibliographic data are available on the Internet at http://dnb.dnb.de.

Printing and binding: CPI books GmbH, Leck

♾ Printed on acid-free paper
Printed in Germany

www.degruyter.com

Table of Contents

J.P. Brune, R. Stern, M.H. Werner
Introduction

Transcendental arguments are usually seen as a specific way to defend certain claims against fundamental sceptical doubts. According to most interpretations, their specific structure is characterized by the fact that they aim at defending some claim X by showing that the truth of X is a necessary condition for the possibility of Y, whereby Y is taken to be something that will not or even cannot be contested by the sceptic (Stern 2015), e. g. because it is part of what she herself already – albeit perhaps only implicitly – has claimed or accepted (Gethmann 1995). There is some discussion about the definition and the distinct features of transcendental arguments, though, and, correspondingly, about the precise extension of the concept. While Kant certainly did most to establish transcendental reasoning as a distinct way of philosophical argument (Walker 2006), transcendental arguments in the sense of our broad definition can already be found in ancient and medieval philosophy (Aristotle, *Met.*, 1005b35 – 1006a28, cf. Illies 2003, p. 45 f.; Thomas Aquinas *S. Th.*, 1 qu. 2 ad 1 obj. 3, cf. Siegwart 2010). Probably the most important reference point for the more recent discussion on transcendental arguments was Peter Strawson's *Individuals* (1959). During the decades of discussion following its publication, various versions of transcendental arguments have been categorized, evaluated, further developed, or put into different epistemological or metaphysical contexts. For the most part, the contributions to this discussion, especially those subsequent to Barry Stroud's influential paper on transcendental arguments (Stroud 1968), have not been overly optimistic regarding the potential of transcendental arguments. It is no contradiction that the project of radically "de-transcendentalising" (Rorty 1978; cf. Niquet 1991) philosophy has also lost some of its revolutionary momentum. It seems that many authors, proponents and critics of transcendental arguments alike, have turned to somewhat more moderate positions during the most recent years of discussion (cf. Brueckner 2010; the contributions in Stern 1999; Stern 2000, 2007; Strawson 1985; Walker 1989). The controversy may have reached a point where the limitations of transcendental arguments as well as those of the earlier objections against their possibility have become more clear. Why, then, do we add yet another volume to the list of publications on transcendental arguments?

Firstly, the overwhelming majority of examples that have been the object of systematic methodological discussion are drawn from contexts of theoretical, not practical philosophy. However, it is not completely obvious that the promises and problems of transcendental arguments in the context of theoretical philos-

DOI 10.1515/9783110470215-001

ophy are identical to those in moral philosophy. Arguments aiming at the refutation of external world scepticism may be confronted with different challenges than those that aim to vindicate some practical principle, at least if we do not take for granted certain forms of moral naturalism. Some authors explicitly claimed that some transcendental arguments in moral philosophy are not vulnerable to some of the objections that were made pertinent to those arguments in the discussion influenced by Stroud's classical paper. Based on a coherentist or pragmatist understanding of moral philosophy, they argue that the main point of transcendental arguments is not to defend knowledge claims about independent facts. Hence, they think, objections like those against transcendental arguments that aim at refuting external world scepticism are not relevant (e.g. Skidmore 2002).

Secondly and more importantly, in many contributions to moral philosophy that have been published since the "rehabilitation of practical philosophy" (Riedel 1972), we find a large variety of arguments that are either explicitly called transcendental arguments or that at least fall under some of the usual definitions of such arguments. Unsurprisingly, such arguments show up frequently in versions of (neo-)Kantian ethics, albeit in very different forms (Apel 1972; Darwall 2006; Gewirth 1978; Korsgaard 1996; O'Neill 1989), as well as in versions of (neo-)Hegelianism (Hösle 1990). However, we also find versions of transcendental arguments in moral philosophy inspired by Thomas Aquinas (Finnis 2011; Ricken 1983), and "hybrid" theories that try to combine elements from all those traditions (Illies 2003). However, we also find uses of transcendental arguments in realist, even in "robust" realist (meta-)ethical theories (cf. David Enoch's "indispensability arument" that, according to him, "may be thought of as a kind of a transcendental argument" Enoch 2011, 79, fn. 71). Some of those moral philosophers who make use of certain versions of transcendental arguments also tried to clarify their general structure (e.g. Illies 2003; Kuhlmann 1985) or even published more extensively on the general epistemological problems of transcendental arguments (e.g. Niquet 1991, 1994).

However, there seem to be room for a still more thorough methodological reflection on the uses of transcendental reasoning in recent contributions to moral philosophy. Philosophers from different traditions of moral reasoning may learn from each other by comparing their respective versions of transcendental arguments. They may also gain a more precise understanding of their own arguments and of the specific challenges to them by connecting to the more extensive discussion on transcendental arguments that we find in epistemology and metaphysics. On the other hand, experts on transcendental arguments who used to discuss mostly examples from theoretical philosophy may also gain valuable insights by widening their focus to arguments from moral philosophy.

At least this was the main idea behind a conference on *Transcendental Arguments in Practical Philosophy* held at Greifswald (Germany), organised by the University of Greifswald in cooperation with (and hosted at) the *Alfried Krupp Wissenschaftskolleg* in 2014 and funded by the *Deutsche Forschungsgemeinschaft (DFG)* and the *Alfried Krupp von Bohlen und Halbach-Stiftung*. Most of the essays collected in this book are revised versions of contributions to this conference. However, it comprises some papers that were not presented at Greifswald,and also does not contain all the presentations given at the conference. Rather, we selected papers from different theoretical backgrounds that would contribute something valuable to the understanding of transcendental arguments in moral philosophy and would fit in one of the following three sections: The first section contains essays that reflect on the general structure, the general prospects and problems of transcendental arguments but with a focus on examples from moral philosophy. The contributions to the second and third section present, defend or discuss more specific versions of transcendental reasoning in moral philosophy. Obviously, it would be impossible to do justice to the whole spectrum of ethical traditions within the confines of this volume. Hence, instead of trying the impossible, we focused on two strands of ethical theorising that can be assigned to the broader group of neo-Kantian approaches. While the focus of the second section is on transcendental reasoning based on the self-reflective structure of personal autonomy, rational agency, or human self-understanding, the third section discusses varieties of transcendental reasoning that are inspired by pragmatism, speech-act theory, and conceptions of intersubjectivity. All essays are prefaced with a short abstract, so that it does not seem necessary to give another introductory summary here.

All in all, we hope that the volume will shed still more light on a type of argumentation that continues to play a prominent role in practical philosophy. We also hope that it will promote mutual understanding and communication between branches of theoretical and practical philosophy as well as between different traditions and schools of philosophical reasoning. Without the generous funding by the *Deutsche Forschungsgemeinschaft (DFG)* and the *Alfried Krupp von Bohlen und Halbach-Stiftung,* and without the enthusiastic, proficient and professional support of Dr. Christian Suhm, Robert Lehmann, and all the other staff members of the *Alfried Krupp Wissenschaftskolleg* involved in organising the conference, this philosophical endeavour would not have been possible. To them we are deeply grateful.

Bibliography

Apel, Karl-Otto (1972): "The a Priori of Communication and the Foundation of the Humanities." In: *Man and World* 5. No. 1, pp. 3–37.
Aquinas, Thomas (1975): *Summa Theologiae.* Latin text and English translation. Cambridge: Blackfriars.
Aristotle (1999): *Aristotle's Metaphysics.* Santa Fe: Green Lion Press.
Brueckner, Anthony (2010): *Essays on Skepticism.* Oxford: Oxford University Press.
Darwall, Stephen L. (2006): *The Second-Person Standpoint: Morality, Respect, and Accountability.* Cambridge: Harvard University Press.
Enoch, David (2011): *Taking Morality Seriously: A Defense of Robust Realism.* Oxford: Oxford University Press.
Finnis, John (2011): *Natural Law and Natural Rights.* Oxford: Oxford University Press.
Gethmann, Carl F. (1995): "Retorsion." In: Jürgen Mittelstraß (Ed.): *Enzyklopädie Philosophie und Wissenschaftstheorie,* pp. 597–601.
Gewirth, Alan (1978): *Reason and Morality.* Chicago: University of Chicago Press.
Hösle, Vittorio (1990): *Die Krise der Gegenwart und die Verantwortung der Philosophie.* München: C. H. Beck.
Illies, Christian (2003): *The Grounds of Ethical Judgement: New Transcendental Arguments in Moral Philosophy.* Oxford: Oxford University Press.
Korsgaard, Christine M. (1996): *The Sources of Normativity.* Cambridge: Cambridge University Press.
Kuhlmann, Wolfgang (1985): *Reflexive Letztbegründung: Untersuchungen zur Transzendentalpragmatik.* Freiburg i. Br.; München: Karl Alber.
Niquet, Marcel (1994): *Nichthintergehbarkeit und Diskurs: Prolegomena zu einer revisionären Transzendentalpragmatik.* Frankfurt a. M.: Habilitationsschrift am Fachbereich Philosophie der Johann Wolfgang Goethe-Universität.
Niquet, Marcel (1991): *Transzendentale Argumente: Kant, Strawson und die sinnkritische Aporetik der Detranszendentalisierung.* Frankfurt a. M.: Suhrkamp.
O'Neill, Onora (1989): *Constructions of Reason: Explorations of Kant's Practical Philosophy.* Cambridge; New York: Cambridge University Press.
Ricken, Friedo (1983): *Allgemeine Ethik. Vierte überarbeitete und erweiterte Auflage.* Stuttgart; Berlin; Köln: W. Kohlhammer.
Riedel, Manfred, ed. (1972): *Rehabilitierung der praktischen Philosophie. Zwei Bände.* Freiburg i. Br.: Rombach.
Rorty, Richard (1978): "Epistemological Behaviourism and the De-Transcendentalisation of Analytic Philosophy." In: *Neue Hefte für Philosophie* 14..
Siegwart, Geo (2010): "Exerciter. Einige Unterscheidungen zur Retorsion im Ausgang von Sthlq2a1o3." In: *Metaphysische Integration: Essays zur Philosophie von Otto Muck.* Frankfurt a. M.: Ontos, pp. 65–89.
Skidmore, James (2002): "Skepticism about Practical Reason: Transcendental Arguments and Their Limits." In: *Philosophical Studies* 109. No. 2, pp. 121–141.
Stern, Robert (2015): "Transcendental Arguments." In: Edward N. Zalta (Ed.): *The Stanford Encyclopedia of Philosophy.* http://plato.stanford.edu/archives/sum2015/en triesranscendental-arguments/ (accessed April 20, 2016).

Stern, Robert (2007): "Transcendental Arguments: a Plea for Modesty." In: *Grazer Philosophische Studien* 74. No. 1, pp. 143–161.

Stern, Robert (2000): *Transcendental Arguments and Scepticism: Answering the Question of Justification*. Oxford: Oxford University Press.

Stern, Robert, ed. (1999): *Transcendental Arguments: Problems and Prospects*. Oxford: Oxford University Press.

Strawson, Peter F. (1959): *Individuals*. London: Methuen.

Strawson, Peter F. (1985): *Scepticism and Naturalism: Some Varieties*. London: Methuen.

Stroud, Barry (1968): "Transcendental Arguments." In: *The Journal of Philosophy* 65. No. 9, pp. 241–256.

Walker, Ralph C. S. (2006): "Kant and Transcendental Arguments." In: Paul Guyer (Ed.): *The Cambridge Companion to Kant and Modern Philosophy*. Cambridge: Cambridge University Press, pp. 238–268.

Walker, Ralph C. S. (1989): "Transcendental Arguments and Scepticism." In: Eva Schaper/Wilhelm Vossenkuhl (Eds.): *Reading Kant: New Perspectives on Transcendental Arguments and Critical Philosophy*. Oxford: Blackwell, pp. 55–76.

A Reflexions on the general structure and problems of transcendental arguments

Robert Stern

Silencing the Sceptic? The Prospects for Transcendental Arguments in Practical Philosophy

Abstract: This paper deals with the prospects of using transcendental arguments against scepticism in practical philosophy, focusing especially on Stroud's classic objections from 1968, and his claim that some form of idealism may be required in order to make them work. This might suggest one way in which such arguments are perhaps more effective in the practical case than the theoretical one, because anti-realism in ethics is less revisionary than in theoretical philosophy. But even in practical philosophy, people have often wanted to be more ambitious than this, where they have particularly appealed to retorsive transcendental arguments in order to "silence the sceptic". I argue, however, that such arguments either collapse into deductive transcendental arguments, or just make the sceptical position harder to rebut, in both the theoretical and practical cases. There is thus little to be gained from this strategy of dealing with scepticism.

Ever since Barry Stroud's classic 1968 article on transcendental arguments (Stroud 1968), the status of such argument in theoretical philosophy has remained rather embattled: though arguments of this sort continue to be produced, there is a sense that perhaps they flatter to deceive, and cannot really do the job that is required of them. On the other hand, it is often felt that transcendental arguments in practical philosophy are more promising, and more likely to succeed where theoretical transcendental arguments have failed.

I wish to suggest that there is one cogent ground for this optimism that the proponent of the practical transcendental argument is entitled to appeal to— namely that in this area, some sort of anti-realism or idealism is plausible, which makes it easier for the transcendental argument to achieve its goal. However, proponents of practical transcendental arguments have not always based their optimism on this consideration, and indeed have tried to use transcendental arguments to defend realism in ethics. But this then raises the question if there is any reason to think non-idealist practical transcendental argument are likely to be any more successful than their theoretical cousins. Proponents of such arguments have often suggested there is greater reason for optimism here, on the grounds that they can somehow "silence the sceptic" by forcing

DOI 10.1515/9783110470215-002

her to assume whatever it is she doubts or denies in what is called a "retorsive" manner, as it turns the sceptic's doubt back on herself; and this strategy is said to be particularly effective in practical philosophy.

By contrast, my aim in this paper is to suggest we have no such reason for optimism. I will begin by distinguishing these retorsive arguments from deductive transcendental arguments, and I will then consider how Stroud's challenge applies to each. I will then argue that in fact retorsive transcendental arguments collapse back into deductive transcendental arguments, so that it is really only in the latter form that the sceptic can be addressed, in a way that will have to be suitably modest.

1 Two types of transcendental argument: deductive and retorsive

I want to begin by distinguishing between two ways in which transcendental arguments have been presented, as this will help us better assess the prospects of this form of argument in relation to scepticism.

We can start by asking: what makes something a distinctively transcendental argument? I would say that it must contain a *transcendental claim*, which states that something is a necessary condition for the possibility of something else, where the necessity in question is less than logical and more than empirical.

Now, the first and perhaps most straightforward way a transcendental claim can be used against a sceptic is in a deductive argument, where it forms the second premise, and where the first premise is something the sceptic accepts, from which the transcendental claim is used to derive a conclusion which the sceptic doubts or rejects, thus giving us a transcendental argument of this form:

1. p (e.g. there is thought, consciousness or a way things appear)

2. q is a necessary condition for the possibility of p (where q is e.g. an external world, or other minds)

3. Therefore q

Clearly, at first sight, there are attractions to an anti-sceptical argument of this sort. First, they are meant to begin from premises that sceptic will accept, and therefore defeat the sceptic on her own terms. Second, they are deductive arguments, and so provide us with more certainty than inductive or abductive arguments. Third, they do not merely rebut the sceptic by questioning the sceptic's argument, but actually refute her, by proving what the sceptic doubts or questions. However, of course, transcendental arguments of this kind suffer from well-known problems, which I will come back to in the next section.

Before I do so, let me first bring out how these deductive transcendental arguments have been distinguished from what have been called "retorsive transcendental arguments" (to use terminology adopted by Gaston Isaye, Christian Illies, and John Finnis amongst other). The idea here is not to use the transcendental claim to show that the conclusion is true in a deductive manner, but rather to show that the sceptic's position is self-undermining in some way, as involving some sort of contradiction, for in doubting p, the sceptic is at one and the same time committed to the truth of p, as that commitment is a necessary condition for the possibility of doubt; and from the self-contradictoriness of doubting p its truth is then supposed to be established.

Here are some passages to this effect, taken first from Finnis, then from Illies, Karl-Otto Apel and Wolfgang Kuhlmann:

> Hence the work to be done by a retorsive argument exploiting operational self-refutation consists in drawing out the "implicit commitments" of the interlocutor, that is, the propositions entailed by "someone is asserting that....", that is, by the facts given in and by the interlocutor's statement. (Finnis 1977, p. 67)

> Essentially, this type of argument is designed to show that some judgement "r" is true because it cannot be rejected rationally. It does so by showing that any scepticism about r inevitably presupposes the truth of r by the implications of the very act or performance of sceptically regarding it. Thus, scepticism about the truth of r leads to a self-contradiction or inconsistency between what is *expressively* stated by the sceptic (the expressed judgement is "not-r") and what is *implicitly* expressed by his act of assertion (the implied judgement is "r"). Affirming r also presupposes the truth of r by the implications of it being a rational act. The affirmative judgement can therefore consistently be raised since the same truth is affirmed expressively and implicitly. Given that the original assumption can only be true or false, it follows that it must be true, since it is self-contradictory to judge it as false. (Illies 2002, p. 45)

> Everyone, even if he merely *acts* in a *meaningful* manner—for example takes a decision in the face of an alternative and claims to understand himself—already implicitly presupposes the logical and moral preconditions for critical communication. (Apel 1980, p. 269)

> Necessary presuppositions of meaningful argumentation (discourse) obviously must be secure against every argument, for if one were to argue against them, then the arguments would undermine themselves. (Kuhlmann 2016, p. 243)

Such arguments have been called "retorsive" from the Latin "retorquere", meaning to twist or bend back, referring to the way in which such arguments "turn back" the sceptic's own position against her. Of course, in some sense even the deductive transcendental arguments do this, as they are meant to start from a premise the sceptic accepts and then establish what she doubts on this basis. But retorsive transcendental arguments are meant to do more "bending back" than this, as they are meant to show the sceptic's position is self-contradictory and undermines itself, such that it cannot even be coherently articulated.

We thus seem to have two ways of using transcendental arguments, which are distinct from one another. I now want to consider if either way is to be preferred over the other, when it comes to dealing with familiar challenges to transcendental arguments—particularly Stroud's well-known objection.

2 Stroud's objection to transcendental arguments

In his famous 1968 paper, Stroud cast doubt on transcendental arguments from which they have struggled to recover ever since.

The nerve of Stroud's critique, as I understand it, is his attack on the transcendental claim which needs to play a role in both types of transcendental argument, namely that q is a necessary condition for the possibility of p, where Stroud argues that the sceptic can always plausibly weaken this claim to: believing q, or judging q, or it appearing that q is a necessary condition for p, from which q itself does not follow without some further appeal to verificationism or idealism—which are both objectionable positions in themselves, and anyway would render the transcendental argument redundant, as they contain enough to refute scepticism on their own. Stroud put the key move as follows:

> the sceptic can always very plausibly insist that it is enough [that] we *believe* that [q] is true, or [that] it looks for all the world as if it is, but that [q] needn't actually be true. (Stroud 1968, p. 24)

It is worth pausing, however, to ask two questions:
(a) how plausible is the "weakening move" to believing q etc, rather than q?
(b) does it matter which form of transcendental argument we are talking about —deductive or retorsive?

Let me begin by considering (a), the plausibility of the "weakening move".

In his 1968 paper, Stroud does not say much to justify this, and just gives two examples of transcendental arguments where it might apply (one by Strawson and one by Shoemaker): but this could perhaps seem a poor inductive base on which to condemn a whole class of arguments. Just because the weakening move might "very plausibly" apply to these examples, this would not seem to establish that it can be applied to transcendental arguments more generally, unless more is said.

However, Stroud does offer a more general argument elsewhere, in Stroud 1994. Here he suggests that to claim that some fact about the world is a necessary condition for the possibility of some other fact, we would need to "find, and cross, a bridge of necessity from the one to the other. That would be a truly remarkable feat, and some convincing explanation would surely be needed of how the whole thing is possible" (Stroud 1994, p. 159). So, the sceptic can "very plausibly insist" that q itself is not needed to make p possible, because she can question our confidence about the modal claim involved, forcing us to weaken it in the light of reasonable doubts we might have about such claims. Let me call this Stroud's modal argument for weakening.

How cogent is it, and does it apply more to one kind of transcendental argument than the other? First of all, in relation to the modal argument itself, it could be questioned using counter-examples. So take the Cogito, conceived of as a deductive transcendental argument:

1. I think

2. Existence is a necessary condition for the possibility of thinking

3. Therefore, I exist

Could the sceptic "very plausibly" weaken the second premise to "appearing to me that I exist" or "believing I am existing" as the necessary condition? In fact, this doesn't seem plausible at all or even coherent, as it is not clear how it could seem to me that I exist without already existing, while believing is itself a form of thinking, so cannot be a condition for the latter. (Of course, as Lichtenberg and others have argued, one might think the Cogito could be weakened in other ways: e. g. that the move from 2 to 3 does not work, as all 2 establishes is that something exists, not necessarily an I or subject—but that is a different issue.)

Second, at a more general level, there may also be a problem with Stroud's objection. I have argued elsewhere (cf. Stern 2007) that it isn't so strong, as it relies on the idea that modal claims are always easier to establish in relation to how we must think than how the world must be, as this is what Stroud uses to say that there is some special "bridge of necessity" that is required in the latter case that is not required in the former, which is why the transcendental claim can always be "weakened". But why think this is so? The thought seems to rely on an implausible Cartesianism about the structure of our beliefs and experiences as against our knowledge of the external world, as if we have privileged access to the modal structure of the former but not the latter.

But still, as I have also suggested previously (Stern 2007), one could claim there is a difficulty here which Stroud is right to pick up on: namely, that the dialectic with the sceptic makes it very unlikely that the transcendental claim can be used to do useful work. For, suppose you doubt the existence of the external world, because you have your doubts about perception as a source of knowledge; it then seems highly unlikely that you will be won round by a modal claim of the sort embodied in the transcendental claim. For, if you have doubts about perception, surely you will have even more doubts about such claims? So we either need to refute the sceptic sooner at the level of perception, or the transcendental argument will come too late.

So, it appears, albeit for reasons different from the ones offered by Stroud, the weakening move seems hard to resist. It may therefore be wiser to consider instead if it can somehow be accommodated in an adequate response to scepticism, either by deductive transcendental arguments or retorsive transcendental arguments or both. Let me consider each in turn.

3 Deductive transcendental arguments and practical scepticism

When it comes to deductive transcendental arguments, various sort of so-called "modest transcendental arguments" have been proposed, which are claimed to have some value against the sceptic, which do not take a retorsive form. So, for example, it is argued that by establishing that some belief is a necessary condition for a large number of our other beliefs, that makes the first belief justified on coherentist grounds, in a way that is compatible with Stroud's weakening move. But this is no longer a simple deductive transcendental argument, as it operates by adding an appeal to a theory of justification into the argument, rather than relying just on the transcendental claim itself to do the work: The transcendental argument establishes that our network of beliefs has a certain structure, but the basis on which we take those beliefs to be justified is the coherentist principle, that one is entitled to believe p if doing so renders your belief-system more coherent. (For further discussion of this "modest" approach, see Stern 2000.)

So could there be a deductive transcendental argument that would work on its own against the sceptic, while accommodating Stroud's weakening move? Stroud thought this could not work in the theoretical case, as the argument would then just tell us what we must believe or how things must appear to us —and we can't get from there to claims about the world, without verificationism or idealism, which many would find as problematic as scepticism itself. But perhaps in the case of *practical* philosophy, this is less of a worry: For after all, many people are anti-realists or idealists or constructivists in ethics, and indeed take this to be the common-sense view, rather than a revisionary one. If so, then there may be nothing wrong in ethics with combining a transcendental argument with idealism, to accommodate Stroud's criticism.

I think we can see how this option might work by looking at Christine Korsgaard's attempt to offer a transcendental argument for the value of humanity, which I have also discussed elsewhere (Stern 2011), so will be brief here. The transcendental argument that Korsgaard proposes is modelled on a position which she finds in Kant and which she outlines as follows:

> [Kant] started from the fact that when we make a choice we must regard its object as good. His point is the one I have been making—that being human we must endorse our impulses before we can act on them. He asked what it is that makes these objects good, and, rejecting one form of realism, he decided that the goodness was not in the objects themselves. Were it not for our desires and inclinations—and for the various physiological, psychological, and social conditions which gave rise to those desires and inclinations—we would not find their objects good. Kant saw that we take things to be important because they are important to us—and he concluded that we must therefore take ourselves to be important. In this way, the value of humanity itself is implicit in every human choice. If complete normative scepticism is to be avoided—if there is such a thing as a reason for action—then humanity, as the source of all reasons and values, must be valued for its own sake. (Korsgaard 1996, p. 122)

This argument can be laid out as follows:

(1) To rationally choose to do *X*, you must regard doing *X* as good.

(2) You cannot regard doing *X* as good in itself, but can only regard doing *X* as good because it satisfies your needs, desires, inclinations, etc.

(3) You cannot regard your desiring or needing to do *X* as making it good unless you regard yourself as valuable.

(4) Therefore, you must regard yourself as valuable, if you are to make any rational choice.

Consider this example. To rationally choose to eat this piece of chocolate cake, I must think that eating the cake is good in some way. How can I regard it as good? It seems implausible to say that eating the cake is good in itself, of intrinsic value. It also seems implausible to say that it is good just because it satisfies a desire as such: for even if I was bulimic it might do that, but still not be regarded as good. A third suggestion, then, is that it can be seen as good because it is good for me, as satisfying a genuine need or desire of mine. But if I think this is what makes eating the piece of cake good, I must value myself, as otherwise I could not hold that satisfying me is sufficient to make something good enough for it to be rational for me to choose to do it; so I must regard myself as valuable.

There are various issues that might arise with this argument. But focusing just on the Stroudian worry: Because this is an argument about value, there may be less concern that the conclusion is merely about how you must *regard yourself* as valuable, rather than *being* valuable in some more realist sense, as such anti-realism is more generally acceptable in ethics than in other areas. Thus, in this sense, we may think that transcendental arguments are more likely to be successful in practical philosophy than in theoretical philosophy, as the Stroudian weakening move can be taken on board with much less damage being done to our prior expectations concerning what we want a transcendental arguments to accomplish.

When it comes to deductive transcendental arguments, therefore, we seem to have two options in the face of Stroud's challenge:

(a) adopt a modest transcendental argument, that supplements the transcendental argument in some way with a further theory of justification
(b) focus on the practical case, where some form of anti-realism is acceptable

Thus, in this sense, we may think that transcendental arguments are more likely to be successful in practical philosophy than in theoretical philosophy, as the Stroudian weakening move can be taken on board with much less damage being done to our prior expectations concerning what we want a transcendental argument to achieve, as here we are not interested in defending a realist point of view.

4 Retorsive transcendental arguments and scepticism

However, even in the practical case, there are those who have thought we can do better, so this use of a deductive transcendental argument within an anti-realist context will not satisfy them. The question is, then, can we be more ambitious than this?

It has been argued that we *can* perhaps do better, by making use of retorsive rather than deductive transcendental arguments. For, using arguments of this retorsive kind, even if we allow Stroud his weakening move, it may seem we can still convict the sceptic of having contradictory beliefs, and from that conclusions satisfactory to the realist may still appear to follow. Optimism of this sort has been expressed by Finnis and Illies, and others. Without going into all the details of their arguments, I nonetheless want to question their optimism, essentially by proposing a dilemma for this form of transcendental argument:

(i) either arguments of this retorsive form collapse into deductive transcendental arguments, in which case they are no better off

(ii) or they do not, but then they have to abandon their use of a transcendental claim at all, and so cease to be transcendental arguments

The argument for this is as follows.

As we have seen, retorsive transcendental arguments are meant to be distinct from deductive transcendental arguments, in the sense of establishing that the sceptic must fall into self-contradiction. However, there are ways of convicting someone of self-contradiction that do not involve a transcendental claim, and so do not constitute a transcendental argument at all. For example, to deny the possibility of metaphysics is to make a metaphysical claim, so scepticism about metaphysics is self-contradictory. This may be a good way to refute metaphysical scepticism, but there does not seem to be anything *transcendental* about it, as it is not clear there is any *transcendental claim* involved or required. That is, it does not seem to hinge on the idea that making a metaphysical assertion is some sort of transcendental condition for denying metaphysics, but rather they turn out to be *one and the same thing:* to deny metaphysics *just is to do* metaphysics, as it is to purport to say something about the fundamental nature of the world, which thus amounts to doing metaphysics. And this seems true of many arguments against the sceptic that involve appeals to contradiction. For example, to completely doubt your own reason just is to reason, so you cannot do the former without self-contradiction, as to do the one just is to do the other. Or: to say all meaningful statements must be empirically verifiable is to make a statement that it not itself empirically verifiable, so verificationism is a self-contradictory position. However, as these arguments from self-contradiction do not employ any transcendental claims, I do not think we should count them as transcendental arguments.

So, for the retorsive approach to constitute a *transcendental argument*, it must do more that convict the sceptic of self-contradiction—it must do so on the basis of using a *transcendental claim*. So, to take a simple example of such an argument used against the sceptic who claims to doubt we have free will:

1. To doubt is to take oneself to operate in the "space of reasons" rather than the realm of causes

2. One cannot take oneself to operate in the space of reasons unless take oneself to possess free will

3. Therefore, to doubt is to take oneself to possess free will

4. Therefore, to doubt one has free will is to contradict oneself

Here, then, we have a transcendental argument that uses a transcendental claim (premise 2) to convict the sceptic of self-contradiction, and so have what appears to be a retorsive transcendental argument. In response, it seems, the sceptic can either give up doubting she is free, in which case she does not trouble us as we have hereby "silenced" her; or she can accept that her position is internally inconsistent, and so we can reject it.

However, there is a difficulty that then seems to emerge from this argument: namely, that it seems to establish the impossibility of doubts about freedom, without establishing that the doubting person actually *is* free—just that she cannot deny she is without contradicting herself by being committed to the opposite belief. But arguably this possibility itself amounts to a serious sceptical concern, as it seems to leave open the troubling possibility that a being could be unfree without being able to become conscious of this fact, as bringing it into consciousness would involve it in a self-contradiction, for the reasons outlined above.

I think this sort of worry is behind the following passage from Thomas Nagel, where he is responding to Putnam's famous refutation of brain-in-a-vat scepticism:

> Second, although the argument doesn't work it wouldn't refute skepticism if it did. If I accept the argument, I must conclude that a brain in a vat can't think truly that it is a brain in a vat, even though others can think this about it. What follows? Only that I can't express my skepticism by saying, "Perhaps I'm a brain in a vat." Instead I must say, "Perhaps I can't even *think* the truth about what I am, because I lack the necessary concepts and my circumstances make it impossible for me to acquire them!" If this doesn't qualify as skepticism, I don't know what does. (Nagel 1986, p. 73)

A similar sort of worry would seem to apply to the retorsive argument for free will: A being cannot express its scepticism or think that it is unfree, because to do so it must take itself to be free—but it seems that instead it could say "Perhaps I can't even *think* I am unfree, because to think this is to violate certain conditions on so thinking", where it does not seem to follow from this that the limits on my thinking will reflect the nature of the world. We have silenced the sceptic, but in a way that would seem to intensify the troublesomeness of her position, not to assuage it.

Now, an obvious response here is to say we need to look more closely at what it is that really *drives* the sceptic into self-contradiction, where one objection to what has been said could be that we are talking about *rational commitments* that the sceptic must accept, where this is what forces them into the self-contradictory position at the end: This is not just a psychological pressure that pushes the sceptic to hold two competing beliefs, but a strongly normative one, governed by the possession conditions for certain concepts, or the linguistic conditions for certain utterances.

Nonetheless, it is not clear this first response can be sufficient. For, the sceptic could allow that to think of oneself as doubting p, one must see oneself as in the space of reasons not merely causes, as a condition of seeing one's attitude to p as that of doubt: But still, by itself this does no more than tell us how our various concepts are structured, which may not reflect the world, unless we already presuppose verificationism or idealism, as Stroud suggested. Likewise, the norms governing meaning or speech may equally fail to reflect how things are.

We could, however, offer a more robust response: Namely, we could claim that the reason the sceptic falls into self-contradiction is that doubt requires the *actual ability* to operate in the space of reasons, which in turns requires actual freedom, so that no gap between the world and our conceptual scheme can be opened up.

But at this point, the retorsive transcendental argument would seem to have collapsed into a deductive transcendental argument, for now it would seem that convicting the sceptic of self-contradiction does not really need to play a role: instead, we can just re-formulate the argument as a deductive transcendental argument as follows:

1. You doubt that you are free

2. A necessary condition for doubt is operating in the space of reasons

3. A necessary condition for operating in the space of reasons is that you are free

4. Therefore, you are free

Here, the claim that the sceptic's position is self-contradictory seems to do no real work, as what establishes the conclusion is just the deductive transcendental argument.

It then seems that the only way to avoid this fate is to abandon the transcendental claim that plays a role in such arguments, and just argue straightforwardly for a contradiction in the sceptic's position, along the lines of the argument for the possibility of metaphysics sketched above. But, even if such an argument could be found, we would of course no longer have a transcendental argument of any sort—which was the second horn of the dilemma we started with in this section.

The only other option I can see, is to bring in the coherentist considerations we also mentioned earlier in relation to modest deductive transcendental arguments: namely, what the retorsive argument shows is that giving up a belief would greatly reduce the coherence of our belief-system, which gives us reason to hold it. This does not refute the sceptic in any strong sense, but does provide warrant for our belief provided we take coherence to be a test for truth. However, while I would be sympathetic to this response, it would seem to greatly reduce the ambitions of the retorsive approach, and bring it into line with the modest approach sketched previously.

Finally, it might be said that I am being too conservative in my conception of retorsive transcendental arguments by assuming that they should be judged by the criteria of theoretical philosophy, but where it could be suggested that the whole point of the use of such retorsive arguments is within a context where *practical reason* has been given a priority over *theoretical reason*, which amounts to the claim that if we must make certain assumptions as agents, this should be sufficient to satisfy us. Thus, as people sometimes say of Kant's arguments for freedom, if he can establish that freedom is something we must assume from "the practical standpoint" or "from the practical point of view", it is only a hankering for something more theoretically robust than this that can leave one dissatisfied, where "the priority of practical reason" over theoretical reason is meant to show this is a mistake.

An approach of this sort can be found in the following passage from Henry Allison:

> But while Kant does not preclude such a state of affairs [that our belief in freedom is illusory] on theoretical grounds, he does deny the *practical* possibility of accepting any such thesis on the grounds that it is not a thought on which one can deliberate or act. To take oneself as a rational agent *is* to assume that one's reason has a practical application or, equivalently, that one has a will. Moreover, one cannot assume this without already presupposing the idea of freedom, which is why one can act, or take oneself to act, only under this idea. It constitutes, as it were, the form of thought of oneself as a rational agent. (Allison 1997, p. 92)

However, this response seems to me to just raise the same problems but at a higher level: If theoretical reason leaves it open that free will could be an illusion, the fact that I must nonetheless assume that I am free as a precondition of seeing myself as a rational agent, seems the worst kind of sceptical nightmare: Either there is some argument from my rational agency to my freedom that will also satisfy the norms of theoretical reason, in which case there is no special or peculiar priority for practical reason here; or there is not, in which case if practical reason is nonetheless somehow forcing me to accept it, then I think we should view the priority thesis in this form with great dismay, and so do not think the proponent of a retorsive transcendental argument should take this path in their defense. (For an alternative view of the priority thesis, see Stern 2016).

5 Conclusion

Let me briefly finish with a passage from the work of C. S. Peirce, where he reflects on his relation to Kant:

> I do not admit that indispensability is any ground of belief. It may be indispensible that I should have $500 in the bank—because I have given checks to that amount. But I have never found that the indispensability directly affected my balance, in the least... when we discuss a vexed question, we hope that there is some ascertainable truth about it, and that the discussion is not to go on forever and to no purpose. A transcendentalist would claim that it is an indispensible "presupposition" that there is an ascertainable true answer to every intelligible question. I used to talk like that, myself; for when I was a babe in philosophy my bottle was filled from the udders of Kant. But by this time I have come to want something more substantial. (Peirce 1902 in Peirce 1931–60, vol 2 para 113)

Ironically enough, within the contemporary German tradition of using transcendental arguments in practical philosophy pioneered by Apel, Kuhlmann and others, Peirce is something of a hero and inspiration. However, as I think the quotation above suggests, Peirce seems to have shared some of the misgivings that I have expressed in this paper: that is, his concern is that arguments from indispensability of the retorsive kind, which show that we must base our thinking or inquiries on presuppositions, are not enough to establish the truth of those presuppositions, and so are not sufficient to warrant belief in them, but rather just their use as regulative ideas or "intellectual hopes". It seems clear that to try to do more, and argue from this indispensability to some sort of certainty regarding the truth of the belief, simply because we find we must assume it, is to go too far and make the mistake of one of those "transcendental apothecaries" who erroneously call for "a quantity of big admissions, as indispensible Voraussetzungen of logic" (Peirce 1902, p. 2.113). This does not mean that a modest form of retorsive transcendental argument, like a modest form of deductive transcendental argument, turns out to be valueless: for these presupposition arguments can show that if the sceptic, like us, wishes to engage in certain kinds of investigation and inquiry, she must accept certain positions as a starting point just as we must. But we should not fool ourselves into thinking (Peirce would argue) that we thereby get a kind of certainty regarding the truth of those presuppositions that otherwise we would be lacking.

Bibliography

Allison, Henry E. (1997): "We Can Act Only Under the Idea of Freedom". In: *The Proceedings and Addresses of the American Philosophical Association* 71, pp. 39–50, reprinted in Allison (2012): *Essays on Kant*. Oxford: Oxford University Press, pp. 87–98 [references are to the reprinted version].

Apel, Karl Otto (1980): *Towards a Transformation of Philosophy*, trans. G. Adey and D. Frisby. London: Routledge & Kegan Paul.

Finnis, John (1977): "Scepticism, Self-Refutation and the Good of Truth". In: P. M. S. Hacker/Joseph Raz (Eds.): *Law, Morality and Society: Essays in Honour of H. L. A. Hart*. Oxford: Oxford University Press, pp. 247–67. Reprinted as Finnis (2011): "Scepticism's Self-Refutation". In: *Reason in Action: Collected Essays*, Volume 1. Oxford: Oxford University Press, pp. 62–80 [references are to the reprinted version].

Illies, Christian (2003): *The Grounds of Ethical Judgement: New Transcendental Arguments in Moral Philosophy*. Oxford: Oxford University Press.

Korsgaard, Christine A. (1996): *The Sources of Normativity*. Cambridge: Cambridge University Press.

Kuhlmann, Wolfgang (2016): "A Plea for Transcendental Philosophy". In: Gabriele Gava/Robert Stern (Eds.): *Pragmatism, Kant, and Transcendental Philosophy*. Abingdon: Routledge, pp. 239–58.

Nagel, Thomas (1986): *The View from Nowhere*. Oxford: Oxford University Press.

Peirce, Charles Sanders (1902): *Elements of Logic*. Reprinted in Peirce (1931–60): *Collected Papers*. Ed. by Charles Hartshorne, Paul Weiss and A. W. Burks (Cambridge, Mass.: Harvard University Press), volume 2 [references are to the reprinted version].

Stern, Robert (2000): *Transcendental Arguments and Scepticism: Answering the Question of Justification*. Oxford: Oxford University Press.

Stern, Robert (2007): "Transcendental Arguments: A Plea for Modesty". In: *Grazer Philosophische Studien* 74, pp. 143–161.

Stern, Robert (2011): "The Value of Humanity: Reflections on Korsgaard's Transcendental Argument". In: Joel Smith/Peter Sullivan (Eds.): *Transcendental Philosophy and Naturalism*. Oxford: Oxford University Press, pp. 74–95. Reprinted in Stern (2015), *Kantian Ethics: Value, Agency, and Obligation*. Oxford: Oxford University Press, pp. 57–73.

Stern, Robert (2016): "Round Kant or Through Him? On James's Arguments for Freedom, and Their Relation to Kant's". In: Gabriele Gava/Robert Stern (Eds.): *Pragmatism, Kant, and Transcendental Philosophy*. Abingdon: Routledge, pp. 152–76.

Stroud, Barry (1968): "Transcendental Arguments". In: *Journal of Philosophy* 65, pp. 241–58. Reprinted in Stroud (2000): *Understanding Human Knowledge: Philosophical Essays*. Oxford: Oxford University Press, pp. 9–25 [references are to the reprinted version].

Stroud, Barry (1994): "Kantian Argument, Conceptual Capacities, and Invulnerability". In Paolo Parrini (Ed.): *Kant and Contemporary Epistemology*. Dordrecht: Kluwer, pp. 231–51. Reprinted in Stroud (2000): *Understanding Human Knowledge: Philosophical Essays*. Oxford: Oxford University Press, pp. 155–76 [references are to the reprinted version].

Boris Rähme
Ambition, Modesty, and Performative Inconsistency

Abstract: This chapter argues that the distinction between ambitious and modest transcendental arguments, developed and deployed by various authors in the wake of Stroud's influential critique of transcendental reasoning, may be pointless when applied to transcendental arguments from performative inconsistency that have moral statements as their conclusions. If moral truth is assertorically constrained, then any modest moral transcendental argument from performative inconsistency is convertible into an ambitious moral transcendental argument. The chapter provides an account of performative inconsistency and suggests an alternative to the widespread reading of transcendental conditionals in terms of an 'if-then'-sentences whose antecedents express a proposition to the effect that some *x* is possible and whose consequents express a statement to the effect that some *y* is actual.

1 Introduction

Call statements expressed by substitution instances of

(TC)   *y* is a necessary condition for the possibility of *x*

'transcendental conditionals'.[1] According to what is perhaps the standard account of transcendental conditionals, any given instance of (TC) is interpretable in terms of an 'if-then'-sentence whose antecedent expresses a proposition to the effect that some *x* is possible and whose consequent expresses a statement to the effect that some *y* is actual.[2] Despite its wide acceptance, this standard reading of transcendental conditionals is problematic. The first goal of this chapter is to bring out why it is problematic and to suggest an alternative reading. Section

---

1 The term 'transcendental conditional' is borrowed from Illies (2003, p. 31 and pp. 35–40). Stern (2000, p. 6–11 passim) uses 'transcendental claim' to refer to the relevant conditional statements. Admissible substituents for '*x*' and '*y*' in (TC) will be specified in section 2.
2 I use 'proposition' and 'statement' interchangeably. For ease of expression, I also use '<...>' as shorthand for 'the proposition that...'. For instance, '<humanity is valuable>' is to be read as 'the proposition that humanity is valuable', and '<*p*>' is to be read as 'the proposition/statement that *p*'; '*p*' takes declarative sentences as substituents.

DOI 10.1515/9783110470215-003

2 develops the alternative and sets out how it affects the inferential structure of transcendental arguments (henceforth, TAs). The second goal of this chapter is to argue that the much discussed distinction between ambitious and modest TAs, which has been developed and deployed by various authors in the wake of Stroud's influential critique of transcendental reasoning (Stroud 1968), may be pointless when applied to TAs from performative inconsistency that have moral statements as their conclusions. In what follows, I call TAs that have moral statements as their conclusions 'moral TAs'. Section 3 rehearses the distinction between ambitiousness and modesty, sketches an account of performative inconsistency and provides some justification for the following claim: if moral truth is assertorically constrained, then any modest moral TA from performative inconsistency is convertible into an ambitious moral TA from performative inconsistency. The concluding section 4 raises some open questions.

A caveat is in order. It may already be clear from my initial remarks that the discussion in section 3 will rely on a series of substantial metaethical assumptions. Jointly, these assumptions amount to a kind of (non-error-theoretic) moral cognitivism. Moral statements can be the conclusions of arguments; they are truth-apt; some of them are true; they can work together with non-moral truth-apt statements as premises in arguments (mixed inferences) and can occur as components of truth-apt logically complex (compound) statements whose other components, in their turn, may or may not be moral statements; they can be asserted (claimed to be true) and can be the contents of beliefs, which in their turn can be epistemically justified and criticised, i.e., rationally assessed with regard to the question of whether their propositional contents are true. Even though these assumptions may, arguably, lay good claim to expressing—in somewhat technical terms—important aspects of our performative self-understanding as participants in argumentative debates on moral questions, each of them can be, or has been, contested in the metaethical literature. Presumably, however, a philosopher who denies even just one of them will have little patience with moral TAs.[3] She will reject the philosophical project of devising TAs to moral conclusions—not because she will find particular fault with that kind of argument to that kind of conclusion but for the sweeping reason that,

---

3 Unless, that is, she assigns a kind of semantic value to moral statements that is different from truth but still allows for the collaboration of moral and non-moral (or more generally: normative and non-normative) statements as premises in arguments and as components of 'mixed' compound statements. This is what Habermas (1990, p. 56) seems to suggest when he distinguishes between "normative rightness" and "propositional truth" as the two dimensions of "validity" of prescriptive (more generally, normative) and descriptive statements, respectively. I think that this move creates more problems than it solves but cannot discuss the relevant issues here.

on her view, there are no sound arguments to moral conclusions to be had, be they transcendental or not. I submit, then, that each of the metaethical assumptions listed above is indispensable if a constructive and sustained discussion of moral transcendental arguments is so much as to get off the ground. Since my purpose in this chapter is to engage in precisely this kind of discussion, I assume for the sake of argument that the moral cognitivism outlined above is roughly correct.

2 Transcendental conditionals and transcendental arguments

It is sometimes said that TAs differ from other kinds of argument in that they either involve at least one transcendental conditional—i. e., at least one statement expressible by an instance of (TC)—among their premises or have a transcendental conditional as their conclusion (Stern 2000, pp. 6–7).[4] I take the disjunction to be inclusive since there is no obstacle to constructing arguments that have a transcendental conditional as their conclusion *and* involve transcendental conditionals among their premises. The relation expressed by '...is a necessary condition for the possibility of__' is usually, and plausibly, assumed to be transitive. If y is a necessary condition for the possibility of x, and z is a necessary condition for the possibility of y, it follows that z is a necessary condition for the possibility of x. Transitivity enables the construction of TAs from transcendental conditionals to conclusions that are themselves transcendental conditionals.[5] By contrast, given at least two transcendental conditionals that are inferentially connected via transitivity *and* a premise to the effect that the antecedent of the conditional initiating the transitive chain is true, one can proceed by repeated applications of modus ponens and detach, in the final step, the consequent of the last mem-

---

4 Franks (2005, p. 204, cf. p. 209) seems to hold that only arguments whose *conclusions* are transcendental conditionals deserve the title 'TA' (emphasis in the orig.): "[A]nything that might helpfully be called a transcendental argument should issue in some *conditional* to the effect that some *conditioned* would be impossible, if not for some *condition*." I find this point plausible insofar as it seems clear that the hard work regards arguing for transcendental conditionals rather than using them as premises in arguments.
5 Arguments of this sort would have to play a central role in pursuing the philosophical agenda envisaged by Stroud when he admits that by means of transcendental reasoning "we can come to see how our thinking in certain ways necessarily requires that we also think in certain other ways, and so perhaps in certain further ways as well" (Stroud 1994, p. 234).

ber of the chain.⁶ The latter is just a generalisation of the simple case in which we have one transcendental conditional, a premise to the effect that its antecedent is true, and a detachment of the conditional's consequent. In these regards, TAs exploit logical properties that are not at all peculiar to transcendental conditionals.

The preceding considerations already suggest that the mere presence of a free-standing (non-embedded) transcendental conditional among the premises or in the conclusion of an argument A does not *per se* make A a TA. Here is an example: Self-consciousness is a necessary condition for the possibility of agency. Whales are mammals. Therefore, self-consciousness is a necessary condition for the possibility of agency, and whales are mammals. An argument may also have a transcendental conditional as its conclusion and fail to be a TA: Self-consciousness is a necessary condition for the possibility of experience, or whales are fish. Whales are not fish. Therefore, self-consciousness is a necessary condition for the possibility of experience.⁷ The involvement of a free-standing transcendental conditional as a premise or conclusion distinguishes TAs from some, but not from all, non-transcendental arguments. Let us say, then, that an argument A is a TA *only* if the following inclusive disjunction is true: at least one of A's premises is—can reasonably be taken to entail—a transcendental conditional or A's conclusion is—can reasonably be taken to entail—a transcendental conditional.

To give substance to the idea that TAs differ from non-TAs in that they involve transcendental conditionals, restrictions will have to be imposed on what is to count as the right kind of inferential involvement. In addition, more will have to be said about what distinguishes transcendental from non-transcendental conditionals.

A useful way to start the discussion is to ask the following question: what, if anything, is the difference between y's being a necessary condition for the possibility of x and y's being a necessary condition of x?⁸ There are several suggestions in the literature as to what distinguishes transcendental conditionals from more familiar necessary-condition statements, such as the one expressed by 'handing in a paper is a necessary condition for passing the exam'. For the most part, these suggestions concern the subject matter of—and/or our epistemic position with regard to—the antecedent x of candidate transcendental condition-

---

6 Korsgaard's TA for the value of humanity, for instance, clearly employs the transitivity assumption in this way (Korsgaard 1996, cf. Stern 2011, p. 90).

7 Here and in what follows I use various *examples* of transcendental conditionals. I do not claim any of them to be true.

8 My thanks to Sorin Baiasu for having raised this question in conversation.

als. For instance, some philosophers follow Kant in saying that a given necessary-condition statement is a transcendental conditional only if it is to the effect that some y is a necessary condition for the possibility of experience. Others are more permissive and say that the possibility of experience is but one promising starting point of transcendental reasoning among others. What is important, according to these philosophers, is rather that for a proposed transcendental conditional to be plausible and philosophically useful, x has to be such that its being actual—a fortiori its being possible—cannot be rationally denied. Now, the thought goes, a good way to start searching for something that we cannot rationally deny is to reflect on what we presuppose as true in the very attempt to deny (assert the contradictory of) any given proposition. This latter thought —I will return to it in the next section—is what underlies the idea of TAs from performative inconsistency.

With the aim of complementing, rather than supplanting, these, and similar, approaches at characterising transcendental conditionals by imposing epistemological, dialectical, and topical restrictions on x, I here want to draw attention to two more formal points about (TC) and, accordingly, about its instances. First, (TC) can be read in two different ways:

(i) y [is a necessary condition for] the possibility of x.

(ii) y [is a necessary condition for the possibility of] x.

The square brackets are intended to indicate the following points. In (i), what y is said to be a necessary condition for, is the possibility of x. This reading of (TC) suggests that transcendental conditionals employ the same notion of necessary condition-hood that is employed in more familiar necessary-condition statements. If anything, it would then have to be the modal status of x—its being hypothesised as a possibility rather than as an actuality—that distinguishes transcendental conditionals from more familiar kinds of necessary-condition statement. Reading (ii), by contrast, takes the three-word string 'the possibility of' to be part of the expression that is used to refer to the relation which is stated to hold between x and y. This suggests the thought that transcendental conditionals employ a notion of necessary condition-hood that is distinct from and, presumably, intended to be stronger than the one employed in more familiar necessary-condition statements. Let us refer to the envisaged notion by 'necessary* condition'. In (ii), then, what y is said to be a necessary* condition for, is x, rather than the possibility of x. I will come back to readings (i) and (ii) shortly.

The second point to notice concerning (TC) is that, grammatically, 'x' and 'y' occupy positions which require substitution by expressions that can function as nouns (compare '*freedom of will* is a necessary condition for the possibility of *moral responsibility*', '*having free will* is a necessary condition for the possibility of *being a moral agent*'). Replacing '*x*' and '*y*' with declarative sentences yields results that are not grammatically well-formed. This is an obstacle to interpreting transcendental conditionals straightforwardly in terms of 'if-then'-statements. The latter, however, is desirable in that it would allow us to conspicuously represent the inferential roles, as premises and conclusions in arguments, that such conditionals are usually taken to be able to play. The obstacle to using instances of (TC) as premises in arguments can be brought out by considering the following widely used schematic representation of a TA:

$(TA_{schematic})$

1	(1)	x	premise
2	(2)	y is a necessary condition for the possibility of x	premise (transcendental conditional)
1, 2	(3)	y	(1), (2), ?

At line (1) we have to take '*x*' as occupying sentence position—otherwise we could not think of line (1) as a schematic *premise*. At line (2), however, both '*x*' and '*y*' occupy noun position. In the conclusion (3), in turn, '*y*' occupies sentence position. Syntactically, then, premises (1) and (2) do not connect in a way that makes them yield the conclusion (3).

The obstacle can be overcome by means of truth-talk, more precisely, by means of talk about the truth of propositions. For what follows, I restrict the range of admissible substituents for '*x*' and '*y*' in (TC) to one particular kind of noun-phrase, namely to instances of 'the truth of the proposition that...'.[9] This gives us the following schema of transcendental conditionals:

(TC1) The truth of the proposition that q is a necessary condition for the possibility of the truth of the proposition that p.

---

9 Against this move it might be objected that it illegitimately forces transcendental conditionals into a semantic mold, excluding by fiat that the point of a transcendental conditional may very well be ontological or metaphysical, rather than semantic. This worry is unfounded, however. The truth-talk employed here can be read as merely serving what Quine calls "semantic ascent". Ignoring Quine's misgivings about propositions, the following well-known sentence from "Philosophy of Logic"—with un-Quinean insertions in square brackets—makes the relevant point: "Here the truth predicate serves, as it were, to point through the sentence [proposition] to the reality; it serves as a reminder that though sentences [propositions] are mentioned, reality is still the whole point" (Quine 1986, p. 11).

(TC1) is bulky. However, it has the advantage that its schematic letters are in declarative-sentence positions—even if these positions are still embedded within noun constructions. Consider an instance of (TC1):

(Instance) The truth of the proposition that we have free will is a necessary condition for the possibility of the truth of the proposition that we are agents.

One begins to see how an interpretation in terms of an 'if-then' statement might be achieved. The truth of the proposition that we have free will is a necessary condition for the possibility of x iff what is the case if that proposition is true is a necessary condition for the possibility of x. What is the case if the proposition that we have free will is true is that we have free will. We can therefore take the statement that we have free will as the consequent of the 'if-then' statement that we are looking for. What about the antecedent? To answer this question I have to revert to the distinction between reading (i) and reading (ii) of (TC) outlined above.

According to reading (i), (Instance) is to be read as:

The truth of the proposition that we have free will [is a necessary condition for] the possibility of the truth of the proposition that we are agents.

This suggests an interpretation of (Instance) in terms of the following 'if-then' statement:

(Instance^i) If it is possible that we are agents, then we have free will.

Generalising from (Instance^i), we obtain this schematic 'if-then' statement as a reading of (TC):

(TC2) If it is possible that p, then q.

(TA$_{schematic}$) would then seem to be construable in terms of the following argument schema, in which 'p' and 'q' occupy sentence positions throughout:

(TA$_{schematic}^i$)

1	(1)	p	premise
2	(2)	If it is possible that p, then q.	premise (transcendental conditional according to reading (i))
3	(3)	If p, then it is possible that p.	premise (modal principle)
1, 3	(4)	It is possible that p.	(1), (3), MP
1, 2, 3	(5)	q	(2), (4), MP

Many authors writing on TAs seem to interpret transcendental conditionals along the lines of (TC2), and TAs along the lines of (TA$_{schematic}^i$) (see, for instance, Pihlström 2004, pp. 291–292, Giladi 2016, p. 213, fn. 2). However, there is a problem with (TC2) and its instances. Consequently, there is a problem with the schematic premise at line (2) of (TA$_{schematic}^i$). The problem is, quite simply, that regardless of whether we read the modal expression 'it is possible that' in the antecedent of (TC2) in terms of logical, logico-conceptual, or metaphysical possibility, instances of (TC2) would seem to be uniformly false. Arguably, logical, logico-conceptual and metaphysical possibility are the best candidates for interpreting the modality involved in the antecedent of (TC2). So this is bad news for (TC2). Recall

(Instance^i) If it is possible that we are agents, then we have free will.

According to a standard construal of logical possibility, it is logically possible that we are agents iff the statement that we are agents does not entail a contradiction, i.e., iff that statement is logically consistent. But the actual truth of <we have free will> is clearly not a necessary condition for the logical consistency of <we are agents>. What can maybe be said is that the logical possibility of the truth of <we have free will> is a necessary condition for the logical possibility of the truth of <we are agents>. That, however, is not the thesis expressed by (Instance^i). What can, perhaps, also be said is that the actual truth of <we have free will> is a necessary condition for the actual truth of <we are agents>. But again, this thesis is different from the one expressed by (Instance^i). On the logical-possibility reading, therefore, (Instance^i) seems to be false.

It is logico-conceptually possible (lc-possibile) that we are agents iff <we are agents> is logically consistent and there is no conceptual truth t such that <we are agents & t> is logically inconsistent. But the actual truth of <we have free will> is clearly not a necessary condition for the lc-possibility of the truth of <we are agents>. What can maybe be said is that the lc-possibility of the truth of <we have free will> is a necessary condition for its being lc-possible that we are agents. Moreover, it is not implausible to claim that the actual truth of <we have free will> is a necessary condition for the actual truth of <we are agents>. But these theses are both different from the one stated by (Instance^i). On the logico-conceptual-possibility reading, therefore, (Instance^i) seems to be false as well.

Finally, consider metaphysical possibility. The reasoning is analogous. It is metaphysically possible that we are agents iff it is not excluded by every way things might have been that we are agents. But our actually having free will is not a necessary condition for there being a way things *might* have been that does not exclude our being agents. What can here be said, at most, is that the metaphysical possibility of our having free will is a necessary condition for the metaphysical possibility of our being agents. Perhaps it is also correct to say that our actually having free will is a necessary condition for the actual truth of the statement that we are agents. But again, these plausible theses are both different from the one expressed by (Instance^i). Also on the metaphysical-possibility reading, therefore, (Instance^i) seems to be false.

Analogous lines of reasoning can be formulated with regard to any instance of (TC2). The problem is structural. It is quite generally not a good idea to claim that the truth of a nonmodal statement is a necessary condition for the truth of some logical, logico-conceptual or metaphysical possibility statement. These considerations would have to be made more precise. But even in their present form they provide strong reasons for the claim that it is a mistake to read (TC) along the lines of (i) and (TC2). The mistake is explainable by the surface grammar and the wording of (TC), which suggests (TC2) as the apparently most straightforward interpretation of (TC). Of course, it might be objected that the preceding considerations have no weight against (TC2) since the intended modality in its antecedent is neither logical nor logico-conceptual or metaphysical. However, this objection would have to be backed up by an account of what the intended sense of 'it is possible that…' in the antecedent of (TC2) is then supposed to be—and such an account does not seem to be forthcoming.

The rationale for using a transcendental conditional instead of a regular necessary-condition statement as a premise in an argument would seem to be the thought that transcendental conditionals are logically stronger than regular necessary-condition statements. (TC2) takes its lead from the wording and the grammar of (TC) and construes the envisaged additional strength of 'y is a necessary condition for the possibility of x' over 'y is a necessary condition of x' in terms of a modal weakening of the antecedent, i.e., of x. The underlying thought would seem to be this: if y is a necessary condition for the mere *possibility* of x, then y is *a fortiori* a necessary condition of x. As the above considerations show, however, it is very unclear how to understand the resulting 'if-then' statements. Consider reading (ii) of (Instance), then:

> The truth of the proposition that we have free will [is a necessary condition for the possibility of] the truth of the proposition that we are agents.

As already mentioned, the idea is to ignore surface grammar and treat the word group 'the possibility of' as qualifying the necessary-condition relation that is stated to obtain between the truth of <we are agents> and the truth of <we have free will>—rather than to treat it as expressing the modal status of the hypothesised truth of <we are agents>. This suggests the thought that instead of construing the envisaged additional strength of transcendental conditionals over regular necessary-condition statements in terms of a modal weakening of

x we can construe it in terms of a modal strengthening of the necessary-condition relation that is stated to obtain between y and x. The most obvious way to substantiate this idea is to think of the envisaged additional strength of transcendental conditionals in terms of a necessitation of ordinary necessary-condition statements. This would give us the following reading of (Instance):

(Instance^{ii}) Necessarily, if we are agents, then we have free will.

Generalising from (Instance^{ii}) we can interpret (TC) in terms of the following necessitated 'if-then' schema:

(TC3) Necessarily, if p, then q.

Relying on (TC3), (TA$_{schematic}$) can be reconstrued as follows:

(TA$_{schematic}^{ii}$)

1	(1)	p	premise
2	(2)	It is necessary that if p, then q.	premise (transcendental conditional)
3	(3)	If it is necessary that if p, then q, then if p, then q.	premise (modal principle)
2, 3	(4)	If p, then q.	(2), (3), MP
1, 2, 3	(5)	q	(1), (4), MP

(TA$_{schematic}^{ii}$) seems to get closer to adequately representing what someone who argues for <q> by means of a transcendental conditional rather than by means of an ordinary necessary-condition statement would seem to want to get at. Consider the instantiation of (TA$_{schematic}^{ii}$) with the example from above.[10] Line (1) introduces the premise that we are agents. Line (2) introduces the premise that necessarily, if we are agents, then we have free will. This expresses (at least a central part of) what the transcendental conditional '*freedom of will* is a necessary condition for the possibility of *agency*' comes to—if the proposed account is correct. Line (3) is an instance of the uncontentious modal principle that necessity implies actuality: if it is necessary that if we are agents, then we have free will, then if we are agents, we have free will. At line (4), the statement that if we are agents, then we have free will, is inferred by modus ponens from premises (2) and (3). At line (5) the conclusion that we have free will is inferred, again by modus ponens, from lines (1) and (4). The conclusion is reached by means

---

10 Again, what follows is meant to be an example of a TA. I do not claim that it is an example of a sound TA.

of an argument that purports to partly ground the claim that we have free will in a necessary-condition relation that, or so it is claimed at line (2), holds of necessity.

I think that the preceding considerations provide at least a partial answer to the question concerning the difference between y's being a necessary condition for the possibility of x and y's being a necessary condition of x. One difference is that y is a necessary condition for the possibility of x only if it is necessarily the case that y is a necessary condition for x. By contrast, some y can be a necessary condition of some x and fail to be necessarily a necessary condition of x.

The preceding considerations also suggest that it is a necessary condition for a given conditional's being of the transcendental variety that it be equivalent to, or at least entail, a statement the effect that some y is necessarily a necessary condition for some x. This feature distinguishes transcendental from *some* non-transcendental conditionals, but by no means from all. Whatever else can be said to set transcendental conditionals apart from non-transcendental conditionals (and thus TAs from non-transcendental arguments), it will have to be along the lines of the more substantial approaches that have usually been taken in the literature. That is, it will have to address questions concerning adequate subject matters of the antecedent x (x should presumably be about some basic and non-optional feature of our human practices), the epistemic and dialectical status of x (ideally, x should be in some sense epistemically evident, uncontentious or not rationally deniable), the kind of modality involved (presumably, it should be logical, logico-conceptual or metaphysical) and not least the precise nature of the consequence relation that each transcendental conditional states to hold of necessity between some antecedent x and some consequent y (presumably, transcendental conditionals should not be interpreted in terms of necessary material implication).[11]

3 Ambitious and modest transcendental arguments to moral conclusions

Much philosophical work that has either been carried out under the express title of 'transcendental reasoning/argumentation' or can reasonably be taken to fall under that description is driven by variations on two closely related but nonethe-

---

11 Reading transcendental conditionals in terms of strict (or necessary material) implication would commit one to the claim that every necessary truth is a condition for the possibility of the truth of any proposition whatsoever.

less distinct lines of thought. The first line of thought reflects our performative self-understanding as agents and participants in purposeful (collaborative) practices:

> Some of the practices we engage in put us in epistemic contact with the world and enable us to achieve knowledge of, or at least justified belief concerning, some of its aspects. Other practices put us in instrumental contact with the world, enabling us to operate on some of its aspects so as to shape them according to how we want or desire (those aspects of) the world to be. Some put us in communicative contact with each other, facilitating coordinated and collaborative action, the sharing of arguments, knowledge and information, the communication of emotions etc. By reflection we can come to know that, necessarily, if we engage in those practices and attain those achievements, then it is true that q. Given that we do engage in those practices and attain those achievements, it is (must be) true that q.

The second line of thought expresses a more cautious or modest take on what we are, do and achieve. It can be stated as an epistemologically reflected and attenuated version of the first one:

> We engage in practices that, we take it, enable us to achieve various goals. By reflection we can come to know that we cannot make rational sense of our taking ourselves to engage in those practices, and of our taking them to enable those achievements, unless we take it to be true that q. In other words: We cannot develop and/or maintain a rational self-understanding as participants in those practices unless we take it to be true that q. At the same time, engaging in those practices seems non-optional, inevitable, indispensable for us—or, as Habermas (1993, p. 163) puts it, without "functional equivalent in our form of life". Therefore, we have no choice but to take it to be true that q.

The distinction between ambitious and modest TAs developed in the course of the debates provoked by Barry Stroud's 1968 paper "Transcendental Arguments"[12] is, roughly, the distinction between TAs that instantiate the first, and TAs that instantiate the second of these two lines of thought. It is best illustrated by way of an example. Imagine a philosopher who wants to provide a TA in support of the statement that every event has a cause. An ambitious TA with regard to that statement would be a TA that has <every event has a cause> as its con-

---

12 Some important contributions to the discussion of ambitiousness and modesty are Brueckner (1996), Hookway (1999), Stern (2007), Stroud (1994), Stroud (1999).

clusion. A modest TA, by contrast, would here be a TA to the conclusion that it is in some sense inevitable, indispensable or unavoidable for us to believe <every event has a cause>.

It should be uncontentious that there is a significant difference between an argument A to the conclusion that q, and an argument A* to the conclusion that it is inevitable (indispensable, unavoidable) for us to believe <q>, quite independently of whether A and A* are TAs or not. A and A*'s conclusions differ, and that suffices for them to be distinct arguments. The more interesting point is that Stroud (1968, 1994, 1999) claims to establish that transcendental reasoning is viable, if at all, only insofar as it contents itself with modest TAs. All that one can reasonably hope to reach by means of TAs, according to Stroud, are conclusions to the effect that if we cannot but believe <p>, then it is inevitable for us to believe <q>. Of course, given a premise to the effect that we cannot but believe <p>, we can then infer that it is inevitable for us to believe <q>. But the inference from conclusions of the latter kind to <q> itself is blocked by the "simple logical observation that something's being so does not follow from its being thought or believed to be so" (Stroud 1994, p. 241)—not even from its being inevitably thought or believed to be so.

Stroud develops the distinction between ambitiousness and modesty, as well as his thesis that only modest TAs are viable, in the context of a discussion of epistemological scepticism. Leaving their merits in that context to one side, later on in this section I will sketch a line of thought that suggests that both the thesis and—in a sense—the distinction may be resisted when what is at issue are moral TAs from performative inconsistency. Before doing so, however, a closer look at the distinction between modesty and ambitiousness with regard to moral TAs is in order.

Does the distinction between ambitiousness and modesty sort *moral* TAs into two types? At first glance, this question would seem to have a straightforward affirmative answer. Consider the statement that humanity is morally valuable. A moral TA of the ambitious variety would here be a TA to the conclusion that humanity is morally valuable. A moral TA of the modest variety, by contrast, would here seem to be a TA to the conclusion that the belief that humanity is morally valuable is in some sense inevitable, indispensable or unavoidable for us.

However, the second part of this answer, which concerns modesty, is problematic. The problem generalises in that it casts doubt not just on the feasibility of modest moral TAs, i.e., of modest TAs to moral conclusions, but much more generally on the idea of TAs whose conclusions do more than just state that we are constrained to believe this or that proposition. As for the idea of modest moral TAs, the problem is this: no statement expressed by an instance of 'it is inevitable for us to believe that p', is a moral statement—regardless of whether the sentences substituted for 'p' express moral propositions or not.[13] To argue for the statement that humanity is morally valuable is to argue for a moral statement. To argue for the proposition that we are constrained to believe that humanity is morally valuable, by contrast, is to argue for a proposition that concerns our doxastic options—or rather, our lack of doxastic options—*with regard to* a moral proposition. If no statement expressed by an instance of 'it is inevitable for us to believe that p' is a moral statement, however, the distinction between ambitiousness and modesty does not divide the domain of moral TAs into two groups at all. It rather forces us to say that *if* any good TAs to moral conclusions are to be had, they are of the ambitious variety. And someone who follows Stroud in claiming that, generally, only modest TAs are viable will have to deny that there are any good moral TAs to be had.

It is perhaps helpful to redescribe the situation in the following way. We set out to construct a TA in support of the proposition that q, expressed by the sentence 'q', but—if Stroud's thesis is correct—we end up with an argument whose conclusion firmly embeds 'q' within the scope of the doxastic-predicament operator 'it is inevitable for us to believe that...'. It is apt to use the expression 'doxastic predicament' here because for all that a modest TA tells us it might be inevitable or indispensable for us to believe that q even if <q> is false. As long as we do not find a means to evacuate 'q' from the scope of the doxastic-predicament operator, we are stuck with a result that concerns the proposition we set out to argue for only insofar as it states that we have no choice but to treat it as true. Stroud (1994, p. 234) thinks that the prospects for finding such an argumentative evacuation measure look dim at best. However, independently of whether Stroud is right in the case of statements of the form 'it is inevitable for us to believe that p' or similar doxastic-predicament statements, there might be a way out of this putative impasse with regard to statements of the form 'it is performatively inconsistent to try to deny that p', at least where 'p' expresses a moral proposition. In the remainder of this section I try to indicate the way out.

To try to deny <p> is to try to assert the contradictory of <p>, and to deny <p> is to assert the contradictory of <p>. Denials are assertions, and attempts at denying are attempts at asserting. What, then, does it mean to say of an assertion

---

[13] Moral statements may here be thought of as propositions to the effect that some person (or all persons) morally ought to (or not to) act in some specified way; or as statements to the effect that it is morally permissible to act in some specified way; or as statements to the effect that some action or person or character trait is morally good or bad, valuable or valueless, right or wrong, virtuous or vicious.

attempt that it is performatively inconsistent? The standard response appeals to speech-act theory. Roughly, assertion attempts consist of an illocutionary component, expressible by the performative verb 'assert' in the first person singular present indicative, and a declarative sentence that expresses a proposition. The illocutionary component indicates the communicative mode in which the speaker intends the propositional content of her speech-act attempt to be understood and, accordingly, the kind of speech act that she (provided she is being sincere) intends her utterance to be—in our case she intends it to be an assertion. To say of an assertion attempt *v*, made by a speaker S, that it is performatively inconsistent is to say that the propositional content of *v* is—in a sense to be specified below—inconsistent with the illocutionary component of *v*. The idea is that if *v* is performatively inconsistent, then S's communicative intention in performing *v* remains unfulfilled. To say the same thing from the point of view of the addressees of *v*: if *v* is performatively inconsistent, then it is a mistake to take *v* in the way in which S intends it to be taken, i.e., as an assertion. Performatively inconsistent assertion attempts are unsuccessful assertion attempts in the sense that they do not result in assertions. If *v* is performatively inconsistent, then the statement that *v* is an assertion is false.[14] Note that, in the intended sense of 'successful' and 'unsuccessful', a successful assertion attempt may have a false propositional content and an unsuccessful assertion attempt may have a true one.

The vague gesture towards an inconsistency between the propositional content and the illocutionary component of *v* can be made more precise. To say that a given attempt *v*, made by a speaker S, to assert that *p*, is performatively inconsistent is to say that the propositional content of *v* (<*p*>) contradicts—or entails a proposition that contradicts—at least one of the performative presuppositions of *v*. The performative presuppositions of S's assertion attempt *v* comprise all, and only, those propositions that are logico-conceptually entailed (lc-entailed) by <S asserts that *p*>, i.e., all lc-entailments of <S asserts that *p*>.[15] Among the lc-entailments of <S asserts that *p*> a distinction can be drawn between propositions that are lc-entailed by <someone asserts something> (thus *a fortiori* by <S asserts that *p*>) and propositions that, while not lc-entailed by <someone asserts something>, are nonetheless lc-entailed by <S asserts that *p*>. Call the latter propositions 'local' and the former 'global performative presuppositions' of S's assertion

---

14 It is therefore better to avoid talk of performatively inconsistent assertions. This explains the cumbersome formulations in terms of assertion attempts.

15 <*q*> is logico-conceptually entailed by <*p*> iff <*q*> is either logically entailed by <*p*> or there is a conceptual truth *t* such that <*q*> is logically entailed by <*p* & *t*>. Note that unless <*p*> is itself a performative presupposition of S's attempt to assert <*p*>, the lc-entailments of <*p*> are not among the performative presuppositions of S's assertion attempt.

attempt *v*. We can then distinguish between two kinds of performative inconsistency. An attempt to assert <*p*> results in a *global* performative inconsistency iff <*p*> is logically inconsistent with at least one lc-entailment of <someone asserts something>. An attempt to assert <*p*>, made by the speaker S, results in a *local* performative inconsistency iff <*p*> is logically consistent with all lc-entailments of <someone asserts something> but logically inconsistent with at least one lc-entailment of <S asserts <*p*>>.[16]

If it is correct to say that an assertion attempt which leads to a local or a global performative inconsistency is unsuccessful in that it fails to result in an assertion, then global performative inconsistencies can be taken to indicate unassertability: <*p*> is globally unassertable iff any speaker's attempt to assert it would be performatively inconsistent, and <*p*> is locally unassertable iff some (but not any) speaker's attempt to assert it would be performatively inconsistent. In what follows, local performative inconsistency and unassertability will be irrelevant. Henceforth, I use 'performative inconsistency' and 'unassertablity' as shorthand for 'global performative inconsistency' and 'global unassertablity', respectively.

Assume that the present account of performative inconsistency is on the right track and assume, moreover, that we have been provided with a convincing argument R to the conclusion that a given attempt *v*, made by the speaker S, to deny <*p*> is performatively inconsistent. R would then entitle us to claim that the contradictory of <*p*> is unassertable. But what, if anything, would R entitle us to say with regard to the truth value of <*p*>? Instances of 'it is performatively inconsistent to try to deny that *p*' and of 'the contradictory of <*p*> is unassertable' closely resemble instances of 'it is inevitable to believe that *p*'. The latter express statements to the effect that we are in a doxastic predicament with respect to <*p*> —we cannot not believe <*p*>. The former express statements to the effect that we are in a dialogical or discursive predicament with respect to <*p*>—we cannot deny <*p*>. Unless we are given an additional argument to the conclusion that the truth conditions of <*p*> are among the truth conditions of <<not-*p*> is unassertable>—and thus of <it is performatively inconsistent to try to deny <*p*>>—R does not entitle us to say anything at all concerning the truth value of <*p*>.

---

16 The account of performative inconsistency suggested here is, prima facie at least, very different from the one proposed by the most persistent advocate of arguments from performative inconsistency in ethics (and elsewhere), i.e., by Karl-Otto Apel (cf. Apel 2001). However, I think that the present proposal is what Apel's account comes to when it is made precise enough to assess. For a more detailed discussion of the distinction between global and local performative inconsistencies, and of how the present account differs from Apel's, cf. Rähme (2016a) and Rähme (2016b).

A straightforward way to evacuate '*p*'—and thus <*p*>—from the scope of the dialogical-predicament operator 'it is performatively inconsistent to try to deny that...' would consist in making a case for the claim that the operator in question is factive (truth-entailing). If the present account of performative inconsistency is correct, instances of 'it is performatively inconsistent to try to deny that *p*' entail corresponding instances of '<not-*p*> is unassertable'. One way to show that the operator 'it is performatively inconsistent to try to deny that...' is factive would therefore consist in making a case for the claim that truth is constrained by assertability. Whilst assertability is unacceptable as a general constraint on truth (cf. Rähme 2010, ch. 5), it can, perhaps, be shown to constrain truth in the restricted case of moral statements.

To say that moral truth is constrained by assertability, or that moral truth is assertorically constrained, is to say that, as far as moral statements are concerned, assertability is a necessary condition for truth:

(AC_{moral}) If *p*, then it is assertable that *p* (where admissible substituents for '*p*' are sentences that express moral propositions).

The notion of assertability employed in (AC_{moral}) is weaker than the notion of *justified* assertability familiar from some epistemic accounts of truth and from assertability-condition semantics. If a statement fails to be assertable, then it fails *a fortiori* to be justifiedly assertable. By contrast, a statement can fail to be justifiedly assertable and nonetheless be assertable. With regard to the question of whether (AC_{moral}) is true, all I can offer here is an appeal to the plausibility of (AC_{moral}), or rather an appeal to the fact that (AC_{moral}) does at least not seem to be a wildly implausible constraint on moral truth. After all, moral statements are intrinsically related to the idea of guiding our own behaviour and assessing the legitimacy of the actions others. Statements that cannot even be asserted (claimed to be true), would seem ill-suited to that task. It is important to keep in mind here that (AC_{moral}) is restricted to moral statements. Accepting it does not commit one to the—some would say provably false—claim that all true propositions are assertable. Accepting (AC_{moral}) only commits one to the claim that there are no true *moral* statements that are unassertable.

Much more would have to be said, but let me venture the claim that the following argument schema, in which the range of admissible substituents for '*p*' is restricted to sentences that express moral propositions, captures the gist of moral arguments from performative inconsistency:

(Argument)[17]

1	(1)	It is performatively inconsistent to try to assert that not-p.	premise
2	(2)	to try to If it is performatively inconsistent assert that not-p, then it is not assertable that not-p.	premise
3	(3)	If not-p, then it is assertable that not-p.	premise, (substitution instance of (AC_{moral}))
1, 2	(4)	It is not assertable that not-p.	1, 2, MP
1, 2, 3	(5)	Not-not-p.	(3), (4), MT
1, 2, 3	(6)	p	(5), DNE

What remains to be explained is in what sense (Argument) can be considered a schematic TA. Consider the schematic premise (1). According to the account of performative inconsistency sketched above, an assertion attempt v is (globally) performatively inconsistent iff the propositional content of v contradicts (or entails a statement that contradicts) a proposition that is lc-entailed by <someone asserts something>. This can be restated as follows: an attempt to deny <p> is (globally) performatively inconsistent iff it is lc-necessary that if someone asserts something, then p. Given the account of transcendental conditionals and TAs sketched in section 2, this *allows for* the claim that (1) entails a transcendental conditional and thus for the claim that (Argument) is a schematic TA. Of course, even accepting both the present account of transcendental conditionals and the present account of performative inconsistency does not yet commit one to claiming that (Argument) is a schematic TA. But it is at least quite plausible to hold that global performative inconsistency and global unassertability occur where speakers attempt to assert the contradictories of statements that express necessary conditions for the possibility of the truth of <someone asserts something>.[18] If this is accepted, then (Argument) can be recast in a way that slightly expands on (TA$_{schematic}^{ii}$):

---

17 Recall that 'performative inconsistency' is to be read as 'global performative inconsistency'. Cf. Rähme (2016a) for a parallel line of argument that uses an *epistemic* constraint on moral truth couched in terms of possible justified belief.

18 This is how arguments from performative inconsistency are interpreted in Apel's transcendental-pragmatic version of discourse ethics (cf. Apel 2001).

(Argument*)

1	(1)	Someone asserts something.	premise
2	(2)	It is performatively inconsistent to try to assert that not-p.	premise
3	(3)	If it is performatively inconsistent to try to assert that not-p, then [necessarily, if someone asserts something, then p].	premise (account of global performative inconsistency)
2,3	(4)	Necessarily, if someone asserts something, then p.	(2), (3), MP
2,3	(5)	If someone asserts something, then p.	(4), necessity entails actuality
1,2,3	(6)	p	(1), (5), MP

A corollary of the preceding considerations is that if moral truth is assertorically constrained, then the distinction between modesty and ambitiousness becomes uninteresting with regard to moral TAs from performative inconsistency. If moral truth is assertorically constrained, then—where <p> is a moral proposition—any modest TA to the conclusion that it is performatively inconsistent to try to deny that p is convertible into an ambitious TA to the conclusion that p.

4 Conclusion

I have not discussed moral scepticism at all. That may seem odd for a discussion of moral TAs from performative inconsistency. The reason for the omission is this. Substantial philosophical commitments are unavoidable in spelling out the idea of moral (transcendental) arguments from performative inconsistency, and such commitments are in general not scepticism-resistant. The present account of moral TAs from performative inconsistency is therefore useless for someone who wants to refute—or even just find a justification for ignoring—the moral sceptic. I submit that the same holds for any account of performative inconsistency that is capable of justifying the claim that the inference from <it is performatively inconsistent to try to deny that p> to <p> is, under certain conditions at least, legitimate. Any such account will have to involve substantial theoretical commitments.

Of course, the main advocates of arguments from performative inconsistency in ethics, Karl-Otto Apel and those who work out the details of Apel's transcendental-pragmatic version of discourse ethics, often write as if merely pointing to a (putative) performative inconsistency in a given assertion attempt v were sufficient to establish the contradictory of the propositional content of *v*. But the distinction between modest and ambitious TAs gives good reason to pause. At any rate, the price of denying (or ignoring) that the step from <it is performatively inconsistent to try to deny that *p*> to <*p*> stands in need of independent justification is high. It amounts to leaving the presumed epistemic relevance of performative inconsistencies unexplained.

What is problematic about moral arguments from performative inconsistency is not so much that it is hard to see how they could be made to work. If global performative inconsistency reliably indicates global unassertability and if, furthermore, assertability is a necessary condition for moral truth, then at least in the domain of moral discourse there is a perfectly legitimate way to get from <it is performatively inconsistent to try to deny that *p*> to <*p*>. What is problematic about the idea of moral arguments from performative inconsistency is, rather, that it is not clear whether there *are* any moral statements whose attempted denial results in a global performative inconsistency. Put in terms of transcendental conditionals, it is not clear whether there are any necessary moral conditions for the possibility of the practice of assertion. My dummy example was <humanity is morally valuable>. It would be surprising, to say the least, to find out that <humanity is morally valuable> is lc-entailed by <someone asserts something>. I used <humanity is morally valuable> as an example of a moral statement because it is expressible in four words. Ultimately, moral TAs from performative inconsistency stand and fall with the respective theories of assertion on which they rely.

Bibliography

Apel, Karl-Otto (2001): *The Response of Discourse Ethics.* Leuven: Peeters.

Brueckner, Anthony (1996): "Modest Transcendental Arguments". In: *Philosophical Perspectives* 10, *Metaphysics*, pp. 265–280.

Franks, Paul W. (2005): *All or Nothing: Systematicity, Transcendental Arguments, and Skepticism in German Idealism.* Cambridge, MA: Harvard University Press.

Giladi, Paul (2016): "New Directions for Transcendental Claims". In: *Grazer Philosophische Studien* 93, pp. 212–231.

Habermas, Jürgen (1990): *Moral Consciousness and Communicative Action.* Cambridge, MA: MIT Press.

Habermas, Jürgen (1993): *Justification and Application: Remarks on Discourse Ethics.* Cambridge, MA: MIT Press.

Hookway, Christopher (1999): "Modest Transcendental Arguments and Sceptical Doubts: A Reply to Stroud". In: Robert Stern (Ed.): *Transcendental Arguments: Problems and Prospects.* Oxford: Oxford University Press, pp. 173–187.

Illies, Christian (2003): *The Grounds of Ethical Judgement: New Transcendental Arguments in Moral Philosophy*. Oxford: Oxford University Press.

Korsgaard, Christine (1996): *The Sources of Normativity*. Cambridge: Cambridge University Press.

Pihlström, Sami (2004): "Recent Interpretations of the Transcendental". In: *Inquiry 47*, pp. 289–314.

Quine, Willard Van Orman (1986): *Philosophy of Logic*. Second Edition. Cambridge, MA: Harvard University Press.

Rähme, Boris (2010): *Wahrheit, Begründbarkeit und Fallibilität. Ein Beitrag zur Diskussion epistemischer Wahrheitskonzeptionen*. Heusenstamm: Ontos.

Rähme, Boris (2016a): "Transcendental Arguments, Epistemically Constrained Truth, and Moral Discourse". In: Gabriele Gava/Robert Stern (Eds.): *Pragmatism, Kant, and Transcendental Philosophy*. New York, London: Routledge, pp. 259–285.

Rähme, Boris (2016b): "Performative Inkonsistenz für Fallibilisten". In: Michael Quante (Ed.): *Geschichte—Gesellschaft—Geltung. Deutsches Jahrbuch Philosophie 8*. Hamburg: Felix Meiner, pp. 605–619.

Stern, Robert (2000): *Transcendental Arguments and Scepticism: Answering the Question of Justification*. Oxford: Oxford University Press.

Stern Robert (2007): "Transcendental Arguments: A Plea for Modesty". In: *Grazer Philosophische Studien 74*, pp. 143–161.

Stern, Robert (2011): "The Value of Humanity: Reflections on Korsgaard's Transcendental Argument". In: Joel Smith/Peter Sullivan (Eds.): *Transcendental Philosophy and Naturalism*. Oxford: Oxford University Press, pp. 74–95.

Stroud, Barry (1968): "Transcendental Arguments". In: *The Journal of Philosophy 65*, pp. 241–56.

Stroud, Barry (1994): "Kantian Argument, Conceptual Capacities, and Invulnerability". In: Paolo Parrini (Ed.): *Kant and Contemporary Epistemology*. Dordrecht: Kluwer, pp. 231–251.

Stroud, Barry (1999): "The Goal of Transcendental Arguments". In: Robert Stern (Ed.): *Transcendental Arguments: Problems and Prospects*. Oxford: Oxford University Press, pp. 155–172.

Friedrich Reinmuth

On Pain of Self-Contradiction?

Obligatory Acceptance and Rejection in Alan Gewirth's dialectically necessary Method

Abstract: Claims that agents must accept or reject certain propositions "on pain of self-contradiction" play a key role in Alan Gewirth's dialectically necessary method. The aim of this paper is to investigate Gewirth's method with respect to the relation between such claims, entailment and self-contradiction. I will identify certain bridge principles connecting obligatory acceptance, rejection and entailment that seem to be presupposed by Gewirth. Contrary to what seems to be Gewirth's view, these principles, e.g., that one must accept simple and direct consequences of propositions that one must accept, do not follow from minimal rationality demands with respect to the avoidance of self-contradiction. Moreover, the bridge principles themselves appear to be rather problematic. Still, plausible dialogical versions of them can be developed. This dialogical treatment is not confined to the transfer of obligatory acceptance and rejection via entailment, but can be extended to primary acceptance with respect to the starting premises. It might seem questionable whether such a dialogical strategy is acceptable to a strict Gewirthian, since agents would have to accept certain propositions not "on pain of self-contradiction," but on pain of violating dialogical principles which would have to be justified independently. However, even Gewirth's demands with respect to the avoidance of self-contradiction go beyond what the rules of logic require. It seems that the dialectically necessary method cannot proceed without acknowledging a normative sphere of discursive practices.

In *Reason and Morality* (1978) Gewirth develops a well-known argument for the thesis that every (actual or prospective) agent must accept the so called "Principle of Generic Consistency (*PGC*)," namely, that he ought to act in accord with the generic rights of his recipients as well as of himself (1978, p. 135).[1] His argument proceeds by the so called "dialectically necessary method" and aims to show that any agent must accept the PGC since it follows from (propositions he must accept in virtue of) his being an agent (1978, pp. 42–47). The argument

---

1 There are different formulations of the PGC (cf. Beyleveld 1991, p. 415, n. 59).

DOI 10.1515/9783110470215-004

opens with an agent (who stands for any agent) having to accept that he acts for some purpose. It then proceeds in three stages to show that he also must accept the PGC. The first stage aims at establishing that he must accept that his freedom and well-being are necessary goods, the second stage that he must accept that he has rights to freedom and well-being and the third stage that he must accept that all other agents also have rights to freedom and well-being and that he must therefore accept the PGC (Gewirth 1978, p. 48; Beyleveld 1991, pp. 13–14; Steigleder 1997, pp. 253–254).

In the following, my aim is not to discuss the overall virtues of Gewirth's argument or the content of the propositions that the agent must accept or reject, but Gewirth's use of 'must' as applied to acceptance and rejection. It is thus (part of) the dialectically necessary method and not the contents it operates on that is under investigation. This investigation will be based on a reconstruction of the second stage of the argument, in which steps involving acceptance and rejection can be comparably easily identified. For each step, we will identify a bridge principle that connects simple and direct entailments with transfers between (obligatory) acceptance and rejection (1). It will emerge that these bridge principles do not follow from consistency demands, as seems to be Gewirth's view. Moreover, the bridge principles seem quite problematic. However, (prima facie) plausible dialogical versions of them can be developed. The dialogical treatment can also be applied to primary acceptance with respect to the starting premises of the argument (2). This dialogical "rescue strategy" might not be acceptable to a strict Gewirthian, since the agent would have to accept certain propositions not "on pain of self-contradiction," but on pain of violating discursive norms that go substantially beyond mere consistency demands. However, even consistency demands go beyond the requirements of logic. It seems that the dialectically necessary method has to presuppose normative discursive practices in any case (3).

1 Obligatory acceptance, rejection and entailment in the dialectically necessary method

Any discussion of Gewirth's use of 'must' as applied to acceptance and rejection has to be based on some understanding of Gewirth's argument. I first present the first two stages of the argument and try to develop a basic understanding of (obligatory) acceptance and rejection in the dialectically necessary method (1.1). To prepare a qualified discussion of moves that involve obligatory acceptance and rejection, a reconstruction of the second stage of Gewirth's argument is then put forward, which will present my understanding unambiguously and will allow us to use logical tools in our investigation (see Reinmuth 2014a, 2014b). Based on the reconstruction, we can identify bridge principles concerning the relation between (obligatory) acceptance, rejection and entailment, which will then be examined in the second part of the paper (1.2).

1.1 Outline of acceptance and rejection in the dialectically necessary method

In *The Community of Rights* (1996, pp. 17–19), Gewirth puts forward an "Argument for Human Rights," whose main part is a concise version of his argument for the obligatory acceptance of the PGC. Deleting sentences that seem to serve as commentary on the actual argument and numbering the sentences, we have for the first two stages:

Table 1: The first two stages of the argument

S1	Since the agent has at least a minimum of self-awareness, when he acts for some purpose there can be attributed to him a statement of the form (1) "I do X for end or purpose E."
S2	This is a statement form that logically must be accepted by every agent for himself […].
S3	From (1), the agent logically must accept (2) "E is good."
S4	For while the goodness in question need not be moral, and the ascription of goodness need not be definitive, it involves the agent's acceptance that the purpose for which he acts has for him at least some value sufficient to merit his trying to attain it.
S5	Now since freedom and well-being are the proximate necessary conditions of the agent's acting to attain any of his purposes and thus any goods, the agent, on the basis of his accepting (2), must also accept (3) "My freedom and well-being are necessary goods."
S6	Hence he must also accept (4) "I must have freedom and well-being," where this 'must' is practical-prescriptive in that it signifies the agent's advocacy or endorsement of his having the conditions he needs to have in order to act and to act successfully in general.
S7	On the basis of his accepting (4), the agent logically must also accept (5) "I have rights to freedom and well-being."
S8	That the agent logically must accept (5) on the basis of accepting (4) can be shown as follows.
S9	Suppose he rejects (5).

S10	Then, [S10a] because of the correlativity of claim-rights and strict 'oughts,' [S10b] he also has to reject (6) "All other persons ought at least to refrain from removing or interfering with my freedom and well-being."
S11	By rejecting (6), he has to accept (7) "Other persons may (i. e., It is permissible that other persons) remove or interfere with my freedom and well-being."
S12	And by accepting (7), he also has to accept (8) "I may not (i. e., It is permissible that I not) have freedom and well-being."
S13	But (8) contradicts (4).
S14	[S14a] Since every agent must accept (4), [S14b] he must reject (8).
S15	And [S15a] since (8) follows from the denial of (5), [S15b] every agent must reject that denial, [S15c] so that he must accept (5) "I have rights to freedom and well-being."

The first two stages of the argument try to establish that the agent must accept the proposition "I have rights to freedom and well-being" by steps that start from the agent having to accept the proposition "I do X for end or purpose E." The argument proceeds by trying to establish that the agent must accept further propositions, because they follow from propositions that the agent must accept (or from the negations of propositions he must reject).[2]

According to Gewirth, the dialectically necessary method "operates to trace what judgments and claims every agent logically must make from within this [i. e., his] standpoint" (1978, p. 44). Even though Gewirth sometimes speaks of "judgments he [the agent] necessarily makes or accepts" (1978, p. 45), he does not seem to exclude the possibility that agents at which the argument is directed fail to accept what they, according to Gewirth, must accept (Beyleveld 1991, pp. 119–120, 401, n. 5, passim). Thus, 'must' as applied to acceptance and rejection should be understood as expressing an obligation.[3]

With respect to this obligation, we can distinguish two kinds of obligatory acceptance: Primary acceptance of propositions that "give expression to the generic features that conceptual analysis shows pertain necessarily to his [the agent's] actions" (1978, p. 44), and transferred obligatory acceptance of propositions that follow in a direct way from propositions the agent has already had to accept (and the negations of propositions he has already had to reject). For Gewirth, the underlying reason for the agent having to accept the respective prop-

---

2 Gewirth also uses 'follow' with the qualification "from the agent's standpoint" (e. g., 2000, p. 492). This is not understood as meaning that logical entailment is agent-relative, but as meaning that the entailment holds under propositions the agent must accept (and under the negations of propositions he must reject).

3 According to Beyleveld (1991), p. 120, "the must is logically prescriptive."

ositions is that he is a rational agent who can grasp "entailments [that] are simple and direct" and avoids "self-contradiction in ascertaining or accepting what is logically involved in one's acting for purposes and in the associated concepts" (1978, p. 46). Gewirth holds that agents who fail to accept what they must accept do so "on pain of self-contradiction" (e.g., 1978, p. 48). According to Gewirth,

> where the entailments are simple and direct, there is no fallacy in making such entailment-transfers by attributing to the agent belief in or acceptance of certain propositions on the basis of their being entailed by other propositions he accepts. (1978, p. 46)

With respect to the agent's reasoning, Gewirth seems to assume a primacy of mental acts which can be given outward expression by linguistic acts, their "verbal counterparts" (1978, p. 43). However, the dialectically necessary method has to work with these outward linguistic acts (1978, pp. 42–47). We may thus view Gewirth's argument as showing through which discursive stages the agent must go to the final obligatory acceptance of the PGC.

In the context of the dialectically necessary method, the speech acts that count as acts of acceptance or rejection have to be alethic acts, such as assertion. For our purposes, we will assume that all affirmative alethic acts are acts of acceptance and all negative alethic acts are acts of rejection.[4] For all these speech acts we assume that their performance is not necessarily successful or correct. This seems in line with Gewirth, who assumes in his argument that the agent rejects a proposition he actually must accept—and which he thus, "on pain of self-contradiction," must not reject. In our reconstruens language, we will use '$A(.., .., ..)$' as a 3-ary predicate to describe that an agent accepts a proposition at a discursive stage. '$R(.., .., ..)$' will serve as a 3-ary rejection predicate. So, for example,

$A(a, p, d_6)$, and
$R(a, q, d_7)$

express that agent a performs the act of accepting proposition p at stage d_6 and the act of rejecting proposition q at stage d_7, respectively. We will view discourses as sequences of speech acts (Siegwart 2007, p. 45) and assume that discursive stages are discrete, that at most one speech act can be performed at a given stage and that a discursive stage immediately precedes at most one discursive

---

4 For the conception of (alethic) speech acts used in this paper, see Siegwart (2007), especially pp. 44–45, 47–48.

stage.[5] We will use '.. < ..' as a 2-ary predicate to express that one discursive stage immediately precedes another discursive stage. So, for example,

$$d_6 < d_7$$

expresses that stage d_6 immediately precedes stage d_7.

The verbs 'accept' and 'reject' are ambiguous between describing the performance of an act and describing being in a state. While we view Gewirth's argument as concerned with acts of acceptance and rejection the agent must perform at successive discursive stages, a discussion of self-contradiction should also deal with the states of acceptance and rejection. If we speak about the state of acceptance or rejection, we will indicate this by using the index 's'. We will assume that an agent $_s$accepts a proposition at a discursive stage just in case he has performed an act of acceptance at or before this stage and has not yet retracted that act of acceptance. Similarly, we will assume that an agent $_s$rejects a proposition at a discursive stage just in case he has performed an act of rejection at or before this stage and has not yet retracted that act of rejection.

1.2 Identification of bridge principles

We will now reconstruct the second stage of Gewirth's argument, more precisely, the steps from S6 to S15. The reconstruction will then be used to identify additional premises, or bridge principles, that connect (obligatory) acceptance and rejection with entailment. Of course, the reconstruction will document just one —possibly mistaken—understanding of the second stage of Gewirth's argument. It will do so, however, in a way that allows critics to pinpoint where I might have misrepresented Gewirth and us to identify where, relative to this understanding, additional premises are needed. For reasons of space, I will just present the reconstruens and then briefly comment on it:

Table 2: Reconstruens for S6 to S15

Add.	1	THUS $d_6 < d_7 \land d_7 < d_8 \land d_8 < d_9 \land d_9 < d_{10}$	from above
S6	2	THUS $\text{MA}(a, 4, d_6)$	from above
S9	3	SUPPOSE $\text{R}(a, 5, d_7)$	Assumption

---

5 The three stages of Gewirth's argument are not discursive stages, but consist of several discursive stages in which Gewirth argues that the agent has to go through certain discursive stages.

S10a	4	SINCE $E(6,5)$	Adduction
S10b	5	THUS $\mathbf{M}R(a,6,d_8)$	from 1 ('$d_7 < d_8$'), 3 and 4
Add.	6	SINCE $E(\text{neg}(6),7)$	Adduction
S11	7	THUS $\mathbf{M}A(a,7,d_9)$	from 1 ('$d_8 < d_9$'), 5 and 6
Add.	8	SINCE $E(7,8)$	Adduction
S12	9	THUS $\mathbf{M}A(a,8,d_{10})$	from 1 ('$d_9 < d_{10}$'), 7 and 8
S13	10	SINCE $E(8,\text{neg}(4))$	Adduction
S14a	11	THUS $\mathbf{M}A(a,4,d_6)$	from 2
S14b	12	THUS $\mathbf{M}R(a,8,d_7)$	from 1 ('$d_6 < d_7$'), 10 and 11
S15a	13	SINCE $E(\text{neg}(5),8)$	Adduction
S15b	14	THUS $\mathbf{M}R(a,\text{neg}(5),d_8)$	From 1 ('$d_7 < d_8$'), 12 and 13
Add.	15	SINCE $E(\text{neg}(\text{neg}(5)),5)$	Adduction
S15c	16	THUS $\mathbf{M}A(a,5,d_9)$	from 1 ('$d_8 < d_9$'), 14 and 15

The following key assigns the non-logical constants used in the reconstruens to expressions of Gewirth's language:

Table 3: Key for the reconstruens language

Expressions of the recon- struens language	Expressions of the reconstruendum language
Propositional connectives	
'$\mathbf{M}$___'	: 'it is (logically) obligatory that ___'
Predicates	
'.. $<$ ..'	: 'discursive stage .. immediately precedes discursive stage ..'
'$A(..,..,..)$'	: '.. accepts proposition .. at stage ..'
'$E(..,..)$'	: '.. simply and directly entails ..'
'$R(..,..,..)$'	: '.. rejects proposition .. at stage ..'
Operation symbols	
'neg(..)'	: 'the negation of ..'
Individual constants	
'4'	: '(4)' ("I must have freedom and well-being")

Expressions of the recon-struens language	Expressions of the reconstruendum language
'5'	: '(5)' ("I have rights to freedom and well-being")
'6'	: '(6)' ("All other persons ought at least to refrain from removing or interfering with my freedom and well-being")
'7'	: '(7)' ("Other persons may (i.e., It is permissible that other persons) remove or interfere with my freedom and well-being")
'8'	: '(8)' ("I may not (i.e., It is permissible that I not) have freedom and well-being")

As the logic of our reconstruens language we choose classical first-order logic. Since we want to focus on obligatory acceptance and rejection, we "skip" the reconstruction of the propositions that are (to be) accepted and rejected and simply use numerals to name these propositions. 'I' is replaced by 'a', a parameter or "temporary name" for some arbitrarily chosen agent.[6]

The reconstructed segment starts with an added inference. We assume that Gewirth presents the agent as moving through successive discursive stages. In a reconstruction of the full argument one would have to add a premise to the effect that there is a certain number of such stages that follow each other. S6 is rendered as an inference sentence, with the inference operator 'THUS' as main operator. The premises of this inference lie in the first stage of the argument, which ends with S6. We assume that the obligatory acceptance of (4) holds with respect to stage d_6 of the discursive stages the agent has to go through. The proposition of S6 is accordingly rendered as '$\mathbf{M}A(a,4,d_6)$', with '$\mathbf{M}$' as a unary propositional connective to represent 'must' (and 'logically must' and 'has to', which we will treat as stylistic variants) as applied to acceptance and rejection. S7 and S8 are treated as commentary that sums up the main result of the second stage of the argument and introduces the argumentative part. According to S7 and S8, the steps from S9 to S15 aim to show that the agent, as he must accept that he must have freedom and well-being (S6), must also accept that he has rights to freedom and well-being (S15c).

In S9 it is assumed that the agent rejects (5), the proposition he must accept according to S15c. The following steps up to S12 then try to establish that the agent would then also have to accept that he may not have freedom and well-being, which contradicts that he must have freedom and well-being (S13). It is

6 Compare the beginning of the argument in Gewirth (2000), p. 491: "Now, let us take any agent A, defined as an actual or prospective performer of actions in the sense just indicated."

not clear which argumentative purpose is served by S9 to S12 and how this part relates to the following steps. The assumption in S9 is apparently not discharged. This threatens the vertical intactness of the overall argument. On the other hand, the inferences that follow the adduction in S13 seem to rely only on premises that are established without having recourse to the assumption. We treat this segment as an "argumentative aside" that shows how the agent would fail if he rejected (5) and restart the numbering of stages after this segment. Nevertheless, we reconstruct this segment, because it contains relevant steps.

S9 is rendered as an assumption sentence, with 'SUPPOSE' as the main operator and the proposition '$R(a, 5, d_7)$'. S10a is interpreted as an adduction sentence in which a further premise for the inference in S10b is adduced. At least with respect to (5) and (6), "the correlativity of claim-rights and strict 'oughts'" can be understood as logical equivalence (Gewirth 1978, p. 66). Since Gewirth only needs that (5) is entailed in a simple and direct way by (6), S10a is rendered as 'SINCE $E(6, 5)$', with 'SINCE' as adduction operator and '$E(.., ..)$' as a 2-ary predicate for simple and direct entailment. S10b is rendered as an inference sentence in which it is inferred that the agent must reject (6).

S11 could be interpreted as the adduction of a conditional: Surely, if the agent rejects (or: must reject) (6), then the agent must accept (7). It can also be interpreted as an inference sentence, namely: hence the agent must accept (7), with "by rejecting (6)" serving as commentary that indicates that S10b serves as a premise. The latter option could be seen as malevolent as it introduces a gap. However, for our purposes, it seems preferable, since it locates the question of the legitimacy of the move from the (obligatory) rejection of (6) to the obligatory acceptance of (7) right within the reconstruens. So, S11 is rendered as an inference sentence with the proposition '$MA(a, 7, d_9)$'. With respect to S12, we also choose an inference reading, with the proposition '$MA(a, 8, d_{10})$'.

In both cases, the inferred propositions do not follow from the propositions that are available as premises. We reduce these gaps to moves that rely on simple and direct entailment by adding additional reasons. In the case of S11, we add the adduction of the premise '$E(neg(6), 7)$', where '$neg(..)$' is a unary operation symbol used to refer to the negation of a proposition. It seems safe to assume that Gewirth views the negation of (6), as logically equivalent to (7), which would also hold for a standard formalization in a usual deontic logic (if 'at least to refrain from removing or interfering' is understood as 'not to remove or interfere').

The entailment of (8) by (7) is intuitively and relative to a standard formalization not purely logical.[7] In order to reduce the gap in the move from S11 to S12 to the familiar kind, we nevertheless just add the adduction of 'E(7, 8)', noting that this entailment (relative to a standard formalization) just holds under further propositions.

With S13, we leave the segment from S9 to S12 and move back to the main argument. S13 is interpreted as an adduction sentence that provides a premise for the move from S14a to S14b. That (8) contradicts (4) can be understood as (8) entailing the negation of (4), so that we can render the adduced proposition as 'E(8, neg(4))'.

S14 is peculiar in that the part that seems to correspond to S6, i.e., S14a, does not just repeat that the agent must accept (4), but states that every agent must do so. With respect to the second part, S14b, it is then unclear whether the antecedent of 'he' is 'every agent' or 'the agent'. Despite the initial occurrence of 'since', S14a is not treated as an adduction sentence in which the universal proposition that every agent must accept (4) is adduced, since Gewirth argued for the weaker proposition that the agent must accept (4) in the first stage of the argument. It would seem malevolent to ascribe to Gewirth that he argued in detail for a weaker proposition, if he could just have adduced a stronger one. We neither treat it as an inference sentence in which the universal proposition is inferred, since that would complicate our reconstruction considerably. Since Gewirth only needs the instance inferred in S6 and since the universalization takes place in the third stage of the argument, we simply treat S14a as an inference of the proposition of S6, which is legitimate by the rule of repetition.

S14a "resets" the agent's discursive stage to d_6. The 'since' in S14a indicates that this sentence provides a premise for an inference in S14b. Accordingly, S14b is rendered as an inference sentence with the proposition 'MR($a, 8, d_7$)'. S15a is treated as an adduction sentence with the proposition 'E(neg(5), 8)'. Here and in the next sentence, we understand 'the denial of (5)' as 'the negation of (5)', i.e., as referring to the proposition that results from negating (5), and not as referring to the act of denying (5). The latter interpretation would make it difficult to speak of logical consequence between the denial of (5) and (8). With respect to the switch from 'the agent' to 'every agent', the situation in S15 is similar to that in S14. In line with our treatment of S14, we weaken the proposition of S15b to the needed instance, i.e., that the agent must reject the negation of (5). The

---

7 In a standard formalization in a usual multi-modal logic, one would have to add a proposition to the effect that it necessarily holds that if someone removes or interferes with the agent's freedom and well-being, the agent does not have his freedom and well-being.

'since' in S15a indicates that in S15b we have an inference with the proposition of S15a as a premise. Thus, altogether we have for S15b an inference sentence with the proposition '$MR(a, neg(5), d_8)$'. As the last move, from S15b to S15c, seems analogous to the move from S10b to S11, we add the adduction of the premise '$E(neg(neg(5)), 5)$'.

As it stands, the inferences of the reconstructed segment that involve entailment transfers of (obligatory) acceptance and rejection are not correct.[8] We will now identify additional premises that would make these steps correct. For each relevant step, the so called "associated conditional," the conditional that has the conjunction of the premises as its antecedent and the conclusion as its consequent, is (up to logical equivalence) the logically weakest proposition that closes the gap. However, each of these propositions covers only the particular case at hand, while Gewirth seems to presuppose general relations between obligatory acceptance, rejection and entailment that hold for all agents and propositions at all discursive stages. Therefore, we will start with generalizations of these conditionals. We will assume that with respect to the order of the stages, only the conjunct that concerns the stages relevant for a move has to be included. We then have:

a)　$\forall a \forall p \forall q \forall d_0 \forall d_1 (R(a, p, d_0) \wedge E(q, p) \wedge d_0 \prec d_1 \rightarrow MR(a, q, d_1))$ (Inference in S10b),

b)　$\forall a \forall p \forall q \forall d_0 \forall d_1 (MR(a, p, d_0) \wedge E(neg(p), q) \wedge d_0 \prec d_1 \rightarrow MA(a, q, d_1))$ (Inferences in S11 and S15c),

c)　$\forall a \forall p \forall q \forall d_0 \forall d_1 (MA(a, p, d_0) \wedge E(p, q) \wedge d_0 \prec d_1 \rightarrow MA(a, q, d_1))$ (Inference in S12),

d)　$\forall a \forall p \forall q \forall d_0 \forall d_1 (MA(a, p, d_0) \wedge E(q, neg(p)) \wedge d_0 \prec d_1 \rightarrow MR(a, q, d_1))$ (Inference in S14b),

e)　$\forall a \forall p \forall q \forall d_0 \forall d_1 (MR(a, p, d_0) \wedge E(neg(q), p) \wedge d_0 \prec d_1 \rightarrow MR(a, neg(q), d_1))$ (Inference in S15b).

a) through e) are (up to logical equivalence) the logically weakest general propositions that close the respective gaps. If we compare the inferences S15b and S10b, it seems safe to strengthen e) to

e)*　$\forall a \forall p \forall q \forall d_0 \forall d_1 (MR(a, p, d_0) \wedge E(q, p) \wedge d_0 \prec d_1 \rightarrow MR(a, q, d_1))$.

---

8 Of course, our reconstruction may be mistaken, but it seems doubtful that one could reconstruct the argument in a usual logical framework in such a way that the steps involving obligatory acceptance and rejection would be purely logical.

We now have identified universal propositions whose adduction would close the gaps in our segment, while, on the other hand, these propositions have to hold if the amended argument is to be sound. These universal propositions resemble so called "'bridge principles' connecting logical facts with norms for reasoning" (MacFarlane 2004, p. 1) as they are discussed in the debate on the normativity of logic. For classical consequence it holds that $A \vdash \neg B$ iff $B \vdash \neg A$ and that $A \vdash B$ iff $\neg B \vdash \neg A$. It seems safe to attribute to Gewirth that he endorses classical logic and that these relationships also hold for simple and direct entailments; in our reconstruens language:

(E1) $\forall p \forall q (\mathrm{E}(p, \mathrm{neg}(q)) \leftrightarrow \mathrm{E}(q, \mathrm{neg}(p)))$, and

(E2) $\forall p \forall q (\mathrm{E}(p, q) \leftrightarrow \mathrm{E}(\mathrm{neg}(q), \mathrm{neg}(p)))$.

Assuming (E1) and (E2), we can present the bridge principles more conspicuously as follows:

(BP0) $\forall a \forall p \forall q \forall d_0 \forall d_1 (\mathrm{R}(a, p, d_0) \wedge \mathrm{E}(\mathrm{neg}(p), \mathrm{neg}(q)) \wedge d_0 \prec d_1 \rightarrow \mathbf{M}\mathrm{R}(a, q, d_1))$ (equivalent to a) under (E2))

(BP1) $\forall a \forall p \forall q \forall d_0 \forall d_1 (\mathbf{M}\mathrm{A}(a, p, d_0) \wedge \mathrm{E}(p, \mathrm{neg}(q)) \wedge d_0 \prec d_1 \rightarrow \mathbf{M}\mathrm{R}(a, q, d_1))$ (equivalent to d) under (E1)),

(BP2) $\forall a \forall p \forall q \forall d_0 \forall d_1 (\mathbf{M}\mathrm{R}(a, p, d_0) \wedge \mathrm{E}(\mathrm{neg}(p), \mathrm{neg}(q)) \wedge d_0 \prec d_1 \rightarrow \mathbf{M}\mathrm{R}(a, q, d_1))$ (equivalent to e)* under (E2)),

(BP3) $\forall a \forall p \forall q \forall d_0 \forall d_1 (\mathbf{M}\mathrm{A}(a, p, d_0) \wedge \mathrm{E}(p, q) \wedge d_0 \prec d_1 \rightarrow \mathbf{M}\mathrm{A}(a, q, d_1))$ (identical to c)), and

(BP4) $\forall a \forall p \forall q \forall d_0 \forall d_1 (\mathbf{M}\mathrm{R}(a, p, d_0) \wedge \mathrm{E}(\mathrm{neg}(p), q) \wedge d_0 \prec d_1 \rightarrow \mathbf{M}\mathrm{A}(a, q, d_1))$ (identical to b)).[9]

In contrast to the other bridge principles, the antecedent of (BP0) does not state that the agent must accept or reject a certain proposition, but simply that he rejects it. It is thus not a principle that concerns the transfer of obligatory acceptance or rejection, but from rejection to obligatory rejection. This principle therefore faces its own problems (↓2.2). (BP1) and (BP2) specify sufficient conditions for obligatory rejection at a stage: An agent must reject a proposition if its negation is simply and directly entailed by a proposition he had to accept at the immediately preceding stage ((BP1)) or if its negation is simply and directly entailed

---

9 For an intuitionistic framework, we could also assume (E1), but only the left-right direction of (E2). In that case, a) would be entailed by, but not be equivalent to (BP0), and e)* would be entailed by, but not be equivalent to (BP2).

by the negation of a proposition he had to reject at the preceding stage ((BP2)). The remaining two bridge principles specify sufficient conditions for obligatory acceptance at a stage: An agent must accept a proposition if it is simply and directly entailed by a proposition he had to accept at the immediately preceding stage ((BP3)) or if it is simply and directly entailed by the negation of a proposition he had to reject at the preceding stage ((BP4)).

Together, the bridge principles specify what an agent must do at a stage with respect to any proposition for which it holds that either this proposition or its negation is simply and directly entailed by a proposition he had to accept or by the negation of a proposition he had to reject at the immediately preceding stage. He must reject any proposition whose negation is simply and directly entailed by a proposition he had to accept ((BP1)) and he must accept any proposition that is simply and directly entailed by a proposition he had to accept ((BP3)). Similarly, he must reject any proposition whose negation is simply and directly entailed by the negation of a proposition he had to reject (BP2)) and he must accept any proposition that is simply and directly entailed by the negation of a proposition he had to reject ((BP4)). In the next section, we will critically examine the bridge principles.

2 Criticism and a dialogical proposal

Contrary to what Gewirth seems to hold, there is no pain of self-contradiction if one does not accept what follows from propositions one must accept and the negations of propositions one must reject. In particular, the identified bridge principles do not follow from plausible non-contradiction principles. Moreover, the bridge principles themselves seem rather problematic (2.1). However, we will see that more plausible dialogical versions of them can be put forward. The dialogical treatment can also be extended to primary obligatory acceptance (2.2).

2.1 Self-contradiction, incompatible demands and clutter

As outlined above, Gewirth seems to presuppose that the agent must accept or reject propositions "on pain of self-contradiction" (↑1.1). But what constitutes a self-contradiction in terms of acceptance and rejection? For each agent a and discursive stage d, we let AP(a, d) be the set of propositions a ₛaccepts at d and RP(a, d) be the set of propositions a ₛrejects at d. For each agent a and stage d we let ANRP(a, d) be AP(a, d) ∪ {¬A | A ∈ RP(a, d)}, the union of AP(a, d) and {¬A | A ∈ RP(a, d)}. That an agent a is in a self-contradictory state at a stage d can then be understood as ANRP(a, d) being inconsistent (cf. Mackenzie 1989, p. 103). If ANRP(a, d) is inconsistent, a ₛaccepts and ₛrejects propositions at d such that from the ₛaccepted propositions and the negations of the ₛrejected ones there follows a contradiction. As Gewirth seems to tie self-contradiction to logical entailment, such a propositional understanding of being in a self-contradictory state seems acceptable (cf. Beyleveld 1991, pp. 105–108).

An agent can move into a self-contradictory state by performing acts of acceptance or rejection. An agent a contradicts himself at a stage d, if he accepts at d a proposition B such that ANRP(a, d) ⊢ ¬B. In this case, such B belongs to AP(a, d) and thus follows from AP(a, d) ∪ {¬A | A ∈ RP(a, d)} = ANRP(a, d) together with its negation. This form of contradiction also occurs if stage d_0 immediately precedes stage d_1 and a accepts at d_1 a proposition B such that ANRP(a, d_0) ⊢ ¬B. If he accepts such B at stage d_1, he cannot at the same time retract his acceptance or rejection of one of the propositions in AP(a, d_0) or RP(a, d_0). Therefore, ANRP(a, d_1) = ANRP(a, d_0) ∪ {B} will entail both B and ¬B. With respect to acts of acceptance and rejection, an agent contradicts himself in this way if he either accepts a proposition A and then accepts a proposition B such that A ⊢ ¬B, or if he rejects a proposition A and then accepts a proposition B such that ¬A ⊢ ¬B. Restricted to simple and direct entailments, suitable non-contradiction principles for moves from one stage to the next could be:

(NCP1) $\forall a \forall p \forall q \forall d_0 \forall d_1 (\text{E}(p, \text{neg}(q)) \wedge d_0 < d_1 \rightarrow \mathbf{M}\neg(\text{A}(a, p, d_0) \wedge$
$\text{A}(a, q, d_1)))$,

(NCP2) $\forall a \forall p \forall q \forall d_0 \forall d_1 (\text{E}(\text{neg}(p), \text{neg}(q)) \wedge d_0 < d_1 \rightarrow \mathbf{M}\neg(\text{R}(a, p, d_0) \wedge$
$\text{A}(a, q, d_1)))$.

An agent a also contradicts himself at d if he rejects at d a proposition B such that ANRP(a, d) ⊢ B. In this case, the negation of such B belongs to {¬A | A ∈ RP(a, d)} and thus follows from AP(a, d) ∪ {¬A | A ∈ RP(a, d)} = ANRP(a, d) together with B itself. This form of contradiction also occurs if stage d_0 immediately precedes stage d_1 and a rejects at d_1 a proposition B such that ANRP(a, d_0) ⊢ B. If he rejects such B at stage d_1, he cannot at the same time retract his acceptance or rejection of one of the propositions in AP(a, d_0) or RP(a, d_0). Therefore, ANRP(a, d_1) = ANRP(a, d_0) ∪ {¬B} will entail both B and ¬B. With respect to acts of acceptance and rejection, an agent contradicts himself in this way if he either accepts a proposition A and then rejects a proposition B such that A ⊢ B or if he rejects a proposition A and then rejects a proposition B such that ¬A ⊢ B. Suitable non-contradiction principles for moves from one stage to the next could be:

(NCP3) $\forall a \forall p \forall q \forall d_0 \forall d_1 (\text{E}(p, q) \wedge d_0 < d_1 \rightarrow \mathbf{M}\neg(\text{A}(a, p, d_0) \wedge \text{R}(a, q, d_1)))$,

(NCP4) $\forall a \forall p \forall q \forall d_0 \forall d_1 (\mathrm{E}(\mathrm{neg}(p), q) \wedge d_0 \prec d_1 \rightarrow \mathbf{M} \neg (\mathrm{R}(a, p, d_0) \wedge \mathrm{R}(a, q, d_1)))$.

These non-contradiction principles cover the injunction against self-contradiction in moves from one discursive stage to the next, restricted to simple and direct entailments and acts of acceptance and rejection. The bridge principles identified in section 1.2 are similarly restricted and also concern moves from one discursive stage to the next. If the pain for violating the bridge principles was self-contradiction, an agent who does not comply with one of the bridge principles should thereby also violate one of the non-contradiction principles. Moreover, this violation should not be by mere coincidence, but because the bridge principles are consequences of the non-contradiction principles.

If we strengthen our logic to include a standard regulation of '**M**' as deontic regulation, which we will assume for the following, we can indeed derive from our non-contradiction principles universal conditionals with the same antecedents as (BP1) through (BP4), respectively. From (NCP1) we can derive

(NCP1)^{B} $\forall a \forall p \forall q \forall d_0 \forall d_1 (\mathbf{M}\mathrm{A}(a, p, d_0) \wedge \mathrm{E}(p, \mathrm{neg}(q)) \wedge d_0 \prec d_1 \rightarrow$
$\mathbf{M} \neg \mathrm{A}(a, q, d_1))$,

a non-contradiction principle that has the same antecedent as the bridge principle

(BP1) $\forall a \forall p \forall q \forall d_0 \forall d_1 (\mathbf{M}\mathrm{A}(a, p, d_0) \wedge \mathrm{E}(p, \mathrm{neg}(q)) \wedge d_0 \prec d_1 \rightarrow$
$\mathbf{M}\mathrm{R}(a, q, d_1))$.

From (NCP2) we can derive

(NCP2)^{B} $\forall a \forall p \forall q \forall d_0 \forall d_1 (\mathbf{M}\mathrm{R}(a, p, d_0) \wedge \mathrm{E}(\mathrm{neg}(p), \mathrm{neg}(q)) \wedge d_0 \prec d_1 \rightarrow$
$\mathbf{M} \neg \mathrm{A}(a, q, d_1))$,

which has the same antecedent as

(BP2) $\forall a \forall p \forall q \forall d_0 \forall d_1 (\mathbf{M}\mathrm{R}(a, p, d_0) \wedge \mathrm{E}(\mathrm{neg}(p), \mathrm{neg}(q)) \wedge d_0 \prec d_1 \rightarrow$
$\mathbf{M}\mathrm{R}(a, q, d_1))$.

From (NCP3) we can derive:

(NCP3)^{B} $\forall a \forall p \forall q \forall d_0 \forall d_1 (\mathbf{M}\mathrm{A}(a, p, d_0) \wedge \mathrm{E}(p, q) \wedge d_0 \prec d_1 \rightarrow$
$\mathbf{M} \neg \mathrm{R}(a, q, d_1))$,

which has the same antecedent as

(BP3) $\forall a \forall p \forall q \forall d_0 \forall d_1 (\mathbf{M}\mathrm{A}(a, p, d_0) \wedge \mathrm{E}(p, q) \wedge d_0 \prec d_1 \rightarrow \mathbf{M}\mathrm{A}(a, q, d_1))$.

From (NCP4) we can derive

$(\text{NCP4})^{\text{B}}$ $\forall a \forall p \forall q \forall d_0 \forall d_1 (\text{MR}(a, p, d_0) \land \text{E}(\text{neg}(p), q) \land d_0 < d_1 \rightarrow$
$\mathbf{M}_{\neg}\text{R}(a, q, d_1))$,

which has the same antecedent as

(BP4) $\forall a \forall p \forall q \forall d_0 \forall d_1 (\text{MR}(a, p, d_0) \land \text{E}(\text{neg}(p), q) \land d_0 < d_1 \rightarrow$
$\mathbf{M}\text{A}(a, q, d_1))$.

However, the non-contradiction principles impose purely negative duties, they simply require the agent not to accept or reject a proposition if the respective antecedent condition is met, while the bridge principles require him in each case to accept or reject a proposition. Moreover, there is no logical way from the negative demands of the non-contradiction principles to the positive demands of the bridge principles. Assuming a standard regulation of '$\mathbf{M}$' as deontic obligation, none of the bridge principles identified in section 1.2 follows from {(NCP1), (NCP2), (NCP3), (NCP4)}.[10]

In general, there is no logical or conceptual way from the negative demands of non-contradiction principles to positive demands that require acceptance or rejection, since no agent can contradict himself merely by non-acceptance or non-rejection.[11] Positive demands to accept or reject propositions are not suitable to further the aim of consistency. Consider an agent a at a discursive stage d_0 which immediately precedes stage d_1. For two propositions A and B the following four cases correspond to the antecedents of the non-contradiction and bridge principles:

(i) $A \in \text{AP}(a, d_0)$ and $A \vdash \neg B$,

(ii) $\neg A \in \{\neg A \mid A \in \text{RP}(a, d_0)\}$ and $\neg A \vdash \neg B$,

(iii) $A \in \text{AP}(a, d_0)$ and $A \vdash B$,

(iv) $\neg A \in \{\neg A \mid A \in \text{RP}(a, d_0)\}$ and $\neg A \vdash B$.

---

10 This can be shown using a suitable semantics, for example, interpreting '$\mathbf{M}$' as '$\neg\text{CP}\neg$' in the (first-order fragment) of the semantics proposed in Reinmuth 2014b, pp. 456–459, and changing there the requirement that for every interpretation function it holds that every index i is an element of the extension of 'CP' for i to the requirement that the extension is not empty. This semantics corresponds to a standard regulation of '$\mathbf{M}$' as deontic obligation for which it holds that: (i) if $\vdash A$, then $\vdash \mathbf{M}A$, provided A does not contain closed molecular terms, (ii) $\vdash \mathbf{M}(A \rightarrow B) \rightarrow (\mathbf{M}A \rightarrow \mathbf{M}B)$, (iii) $\vdash \mathbf{M}A \rightarrow \neg\mathbf{M}\neg A$.
11 Harman 1984, p. 115, points out the gap between negative demands of inconsistency avoidance and positive demands of acceptance with respect to the acceptance of beliefs.

Restricted to simple and direct entailments and moves from one discursive stage in which the respective acts of acceptance or rejection are obligatory to the immediately following stage, (BP1) demands rejection of B in case (i), (BP2) demands rejection of B in case (ii), (BP3) demands acceptance of B in case (iii), and (BP4) demands acceptance of B in case (iv). Now suppose that one of the cases (i) through (iv) obtains and that a does neither accept nor reject any proposition at d_1. Then $ANRP(a, d_1)$ is identical to and thus co-consistent with $ANRP(a, d_0)$. Thus, if $ANRP(a, d_1)$ is inconsistent, so is $ANRP(a, d_0)$. So, while a may be in an inconsistent state at d_1, this will not be a result of his failure to accept or reject any proposition at d_1.

Now suppose we have case (i) or case (ii) and the agent rejects B. Then $ANRP(a, d_1)$ is identical to $ANRP(a, d_0) \cup \{\neg B\}$. In both cases it holds that $ANRP(a, d_0) = AP(a, d_0) \cup \{\neg A \mid A \in RP(a, d_0)\} \vdash \neg B$. Therefore, $ANRP(a, d_1) = ANRP(a, d_0) \cup \{\neg B\}$ is in both cases co-consistent with $ANRP(a, d_0)$. So, if $ANRP(a, d_1)$ is consistent, this will not be the result of a's rejection of B. Last suppose we have case (iii) or case (iv) and that the agent accepts B. Since in both cases it holds that $ANRP(a, d_0) \vdash B$, we have again that $ANRP(a, d_1) = ANRP(a, d_0) \cup \{B\}$ is in both cases co-consistent with $ANRP(a, d_0)$. So again, if $ANRP(a, d_1)$ is consistent, this will not be the result of a's acceptance of B.

In short, an agent's epistemic state does neither become "more consistent" if he rejects or accepts in accordance with our or with more broadly conceived bridge principles in the same spirit nor does his epistemic state become "less consistent" if he fails to do so by simply refraining from any acts of acceptance or rejection. The agent neither faces the "pain of self-contradiction" if he does not accept and reject in accordance with the bridge principles nor can acceptance or rejection in accordance with them alleviate any such pain. Moreover, for someone who endorses the non-contradiction principles, there are no unproblematic premises that would lead from them to the bridge principles since the bridge principles themselves are untenable as they stand.

In Gewirth's scenario, the agent must accept and reject certain propositions at certain stages. Suppose that a must accept a proposition A at stage d_0 and that d_0 immediately precedes d_1. Then A entails infinitely many propositions and the negation of infinitely many propositions. Some of these entailments are simple and direct, for example, A's entailment of $A \lor B$ for any simple proposition B, and A's entailment of $\neg(\neg A \land B)$ for any simple proposition B. So, it is safe to assume that there are distinct propositions Γ_0, Γ_1, Δ_0, Δ_1 such that Γ_0, Γ_1 and $\neg\Delta_0$, $\neg\Delta_1$ are simply and directly entailed by A.

$(NCP1)^B$ and $(NCP3)^B$, the non-contradiction principles that apply to our scenario, are then easily fulfilled—all a must do at d_1 is not to accept Δ_0 or Δ_1 or any other proposition whose negation is simply and directly entailed by A, and not to reject Γ_0 or Γ_1 or any other proposition that is simply and directly entailed by A. In contrast, a cannot comply with either (BP1) or (BP3) or both. (BP1) demands that he rejects Δ_0 at d_1 and that he rejects Δ_1 at d_1—and any other proposition whose negation is simply and directly entailed by A. Given that Δ_0 and Δ_1 are distinct propositions, (BP1) thus demands that a performs at least two different acts of rejection, one for Δ_0 and one for Δ_1, at the same stage. However, given that a can perform at most one act at a given stage, a cannot do that. Similarly, he cannot accept Γ_0 at d_1 and accept Γ_1 at d_1 as (BP3) demands. Last but not least, he cannot simultaneously perform acts of rejection and acts of acceptance as demanded by (BP1) and (BP3) together. Obviously, we can produce a similar scenario for the case that a must reject a certain proposition at a certain stage. In that case, the incompatible demands would come from (BP2) and (BP4).[12]

One might be tempted to change the bridge principles in such a way that they demand that the agent successively accepts and rejects all propositions he must accept and reject over the course of the following discursive stages. However, while there may not be infinitely many simple and direct entailments that involve the propositions an agent must accept or reject, there are surely enough to fill an average lifetime with accepting and rejecting the respective propositions. Thus, bridge principles that entail that agents must, for example, accept the multitude of propositions that are simply and directly entailed by propositions they must accept seem not like reasonable demands. Dutilh Novaes raises such an objection with respect to asserting the consequences of propositions one has asserted as a "a linguistic version of Harman's mind-cluttering objection" (2015, p. 594) and Harman's remark with regard to accepting everything that is implied by one's beliefs also holds true for our scenario: "it would be a terrible waste of time, leaving no room for other things" (1984, p. 108).

Apart from that, Gewirth does not need bridge principles that require agents to accept or reject every proposition standing in one of the relevant entailment relations to propositions they must accept or reject. His argument proceeds by trying to show that the agent must successively accept or reject one of the propositions that stand in the relevant entailment relations. Gewirth thus needs bridge principles that allow him to single out the proposition the agent must accept or reject at a certain stage.

---

12 One might want to point out that Gewirth assumes a primacy of mental acts (↑1.1) and insist that one can perform more than one mental act at a given stage or time. However, it seems doubtful if the number of mental acts one can perform at a given stage or time is at least as great as the number of propositions or beliefs one would have to accept and reject if the bridge principles were formulated for the acceptance and rejection of beliefs. So, arguably, the bridge principles would still lead to incompatible demands.

2.2 Sketch of a dialogical proposal

As noted above, the bridge principles identified in section 1.2 resemble those discussed in the debate on the normativity of logic. While such bridge principles are often discussed with respect to beliefs, Dutilh Novaes (2015) offers a discussion in relation to speech acts, arguing that such principles are more plausibly seen as relating to dialogical settings. We will follow her line. As Dutilh Novaes points out, dialogical versions of bridge principles in which the agent must accept or reject a proposition if asked to do so are immune to the clutter objection, because an interlocutor can only raise a limited number of such questions (2015, p. 605). Moreover, if an interlocutor has to ask with respect to the acceptance or rejection of specific propositions, the agent is not faced with incompatible demands that require him to simultaneously perform a multitude of mutually exclusive acts. We will now propose dialogical versions of the bridge principles which seem more plausible than the original ones and which could provide a starting point for the development of a dialogical version of Gewirth's argument.

First, we have:

(BPO) $\forall a \forall p \forall q \forall d_0 \forall d_1 (\text{R}(a, p, d_0) \wedge \text{E}(\text{neg}(p), \text{neg}(q)) \wedge d_0 \prec d_1 \rightarrow$
$\textbf{M}\text{R}(a, q, d_1))$.

As it stands, this principle is untenable not just because of the incompatibility and clutter objection. While we have only rejection in the antecedent, we have obligatory rejection in the consequent. If the agent rejects, by mistake, a logically true proposition, and thus a proposition whose negation entails the negation of every proposition, he would have to reject every proposition (as long as the entailment is simple and direct). Of course, what he should do in such a case is to retract his mistaken rejection. Moreover, (BPO) would make rejection self-justifying, which would be as strange as a self-justification of belief (for this and the previous point, see MacFarlane 2004, p. 9).

Revising a proposal of Dutilh Novaes (2015, p. 606) for a principle for granting in certain debates, we may recast (BPO) as follows, where '$\text{Q}_\text{R}(.., .., ..)$' is a 3-ary predicate to express that an agent is asked if he rejects a proposition or retracts his last act of acceptance or rejection and '$\text{C}_\text{R}(.., .., ..)$' is a 3-ary retraction predicate to express that an agent retracts his rejection of a proposition:

(BPO)$^\text{D}$ $\forall a \forall p \forall q \forall d_0 \forall d_1 \forall d_2 (\text{R}(a, p, d_0) \wedge \text{E}(\text{neg}(p), \text{neg}(q)) \wedge d_0 \prec d_1 \wedge$
$\text{Q}_\text{R}(a, q, d_1) \wedge d_1 \prec d_2 \rightarrow \textbf{M}(\text{R}(a, q, d_2) \vee \text{C}_\text{R}(a, p, d_2)))$.[13]

---

[13] Adapted to our scenario, the principle of Dutilh Novaes could be formalized by '$\forall a \forall p \forall q \forall d_0 \forall d_1 \forall d_2 (\text{E}(p, q) \rightarrow \textbf{M}(\text{A}(a, p, d_0) \wedge d_0 \prec d_1 \wedge \text{Q}_\text{A}(a, q, d_1) \wedge d_1 \prec d_2 \rightarrow \text{A}(a, q, d_2) \vee$

This rule seems quite "natural" for serious rational discourse. If an agent rejects a proposition and is then asked if he rejects a proposition whose negation is simply and directly entailed by the negation of the rejected proposition or retracts his previous rejection, it seems in order that he must either reject the proposition whose negation is entailed or retract his rejection.

In contrast to (BP0) and $(BP0)^D$, the antecedents in (BP1) through (BP4) do not state that the agent accepts or rejects a proposition, but that he must do so. If he must either accept or reject a proposition at a stage and is then asked with regard to his acceptance or rejection of further propositions, it seems reasonable to assume that he must not react by retracting his acceptance or rejection. If we therefore leave out the option of retraction, dialogical versions of the bridge principles (BP1) through (BP4) could be:

$(BP1)^D \quad \forall a \forall p \forall q \forall d_0 \forall d_1 \forall d_2 (\mathrm{MA}(a,p,d_0) \wedge \mathrm{E}(p, \mathrm{neg}(q)) \wedge d_0 \prec d_1 \wedge$
$\quad \mathrm{Q_R}(a,q,d_1) \wedge d_1 \prec d_2 \rightarrow \mathrm{MR}(a,q,d_2))$,

$(BP2)^D \quad \forall a \forall p \forall q \forall d_0 \forall d_1 \forall d_2 (\mathrm{MR}(a,p,d_0) \wedge \mathrm{E}(\mathrm{neg}(p), \mathrm{neg}(q)) \wedge d_0 \prec d_1 \wedge$
$\quad \mathrm{Q_R}(a,q,d_1) \wedge d_1 \prec d_2 \rightarrow \mathrm{MR}(a,q,d_2))$,

$(BP3)^D \quad \forall a \forall p \forall q \forall d_0 \forall d_1 \forall d_2 (\mathrm{MA}(a,p,d_0) \wedge \mathrm{E}(p,q) \wedge d_0 \prec d_1 \wedge \mathrm{Q_A}(a,q,d_1) \wedge$
$\quad d_1 \prec d_2 \rightarrow \mathrm{MA}(a,q,d_2))$, and

$(BP4)^D \quad \forall a \forall p \forall q \forall d_0 \forall d_1 \forall d_2 (\mathrm{MR}(a,p,d_0) \wedge \mathrm{E}(\mathrm{neg}(p),q) \wedge d_0 \prec d_1 \wedge$
$\quad \mathrm{Q_A}(a,q,d_1) \wedge d_1 \prec d_2 \rightarrow \mathrm{MA}(a,q,d_2))$.[14]

These dialogical bridge principles have a prima facie plausibility, but they have yet to be tested. In particular, it is to be asked if it is appropriate that agents incur positive duties to accept or reject propositions only because they had some duties at the preceding stage—independently of whether or not they actually fulfilled these previous duties.

The bridge principles concern the relationship between obligatory acceptance, rejection and entailment, i.e., transferred obligatory acceptance and rejection, but not primary acceptance. However, for the argument to succeed, it has to start with some propositions the agent must accept not because they are entailed by other propositions he must accept (or the negations of propositions he must reject), but on other grounds. It seems that these propositions are those that di-

---

$\mathrm{C_A}(a,p,d_2)))$', where '$\mathrm{Q_A}(..,..,..)$' is a 3-ary predicate to express that an agent is asked if he accepts a proposition or retracts his last act of acceptance or rejection and '$\mathrm{C_A}(..,..,..)$' is a 3-ary retraction predicate to express that an agent retracts his acceptance of a proposition.
14 For '$\mathrm{Q_A}(..,..,..)$' see n. 13.

rectly reflect generic features of agency (↑1.1). Gewirth claims with respect to (1), "I do X for end or purpose E":

> This is a statement form that logically must be accepted by every agent for himself, so that it serves to ground the categoricalness of the rights-principle generated by the argument. (1996, p. 17).

As we have seen above, the agent cannot be forced on pain of self-contradiction to accept (1), as non-acceptance cannot lead to contradiction (↑2.1). However, it seems plausible to demand that an agent who has warrants for the acceptance of a proposition must accept it if he has been asked to do so:

(PA) $\forall a \forall p \forall q \forall d_0 \forall d_1 (\mathbb{W}_A(a,p,d_1) \wedge \mathbb{Q}_A(a,p,d_0) \wedge d_0 \prec d_1 \rightarrow \mathbf{M}\mathbb{A}(a,p,d_1))$,

where '$\mathbb{W}_A(.., .., ..)$' is a 3-ary predicate to express that an agent has a warrant for the acceptance of a proposition at a stage.

Dialogical rules such as (PA) can provide a starting point for Gewirth's argument. So, for example, it should surely hold in a Gewirthian framework that any agent who performs action X for end or purpose E has a warrant for accepting (1). If the agent had to follow a rule such as (PA), he would thus be obliged to accept (1) if he was asked to do so.

3 Conclusion: reason and discursive integrity

It should be noted that we have at best provided a starting point for reworking Gewirth's argument in a dialogical framework in such a way that it establishes what it is supposed to establish. But what about the overall appropriateness of a dialogical treatment of the argument? Gewirth himself seems ambivalent: On the one hand, he wants to model how the agent must reason from his own standpoint, on the other hand, he seems to put himself in front of the agent and to show him that he must accept and reject certain propositions. The latter would be a dialogical setting. In fact, when he introduces the dialectical method, Gewirth explicitly speaks of "claims made by protagonists or interlocutors" (1978, p. 43) and refers to the Socratic dialogues.

However, one may doubt if a strict Gewirthian could follow a dialogical strategy. Micha Werner has pointed out that the conditions for the agent raising claims addressed to others are not met by Gewirth's "monologist and instrumentalist framework" (2002, p. 322; my translation). This diagnosis also fits the dialogical treatment offered here. Only if the agent addresses his acts of acceptance and rejection to someone (maybe himself), can he be asked if he accepts or rejects further propositions. This presupposes a dialogical practice of acceptance, rejection and questioning with its own principles, principles which can be subjected to scrutiny and whose justification can be questioned. However, for the Gewirthian, "an ethics of rational discussion" (Gewirth 1978, p. 359) can only be justified by recourse to the PGC. The Gewirthian order of justification is clearly this: Reason, which comprises "the canons of deductive and inductive logic" (1978, p. 22) has a "cogency and nonarbitrariness that provide a sufficient justification for relying on it" (1978, p. 23). Reason then provides the "ultimate justificans of the supreme moral principle [the PGC]" (1978, p. 25). In contrast to reason itself, its application to discourse is then subject to appraisal in terms of the PGC:

> It is the rules or criteria of deduction and induction that enter into the justification of the PGC; but what morality justifies is not these rules or criteria themselves but rather the way they are used and applied both in relations of interpersonal communication and in one's personal participation in intellectual operations. The 'syntactics' and 'semantics' of deductive and inductive rationality are the ultimate justificans of morality, while it is the 'pragmatics' of such rationality that morality justifies. (1978, p. 360)

However, dialogical principles that impose positive duties to accept or reject propositions do not follow from pure non-contradiction demands. They are genuinely normative principles that can force agents to act against what they deem to be their interests. Dialogical principles may be seen as principles of discursive integrity, but a Gewirthian who wants to develop a dialogical version of the argument will first have to establish that agents must follow such principles, that they must act with discursive integrity. Crucially, on pain of begging the question, he will have to do so without appealing to the PGC. It may be that "telling the truth when asked" is "directly in conformity with the PGC" (Gewirth 1978, p. 276), but principles such as (PA) can hardly be justified in this way if they are to serve as premises in an argument for the obligatory acceptance of the PGC. A Gewirthian who wants to follow the dialogical strategy will have to acknowledge "an ethics of rational discussion" (1978, p. 359) in order to establish the PGC that could only afterwards be subjected to it.

However, the need to establish normative requirements that are connected to discursive practices prior to the PGC does not just arise if one follows a dialogical approach. Talk of obligation or prohibition with respect to speech acts only makes sense relative to a conception of the respective speech acts and the rules (or conventions) that govern them. Such rules or conventions belong to discursive practices and the Gewirthian strategy of avoiding questions as to where the normative requirements concerning acceptance and rejection come from by simply invoking reason seems hardly tenable. This diagnosis would also hold if one granted Gewirth the justification of (some usual) logic and if his argument relied only on non-contradiction principles. Usual systems of logical rules consist of permissive rules that allow certain inferences and an interdiction principle that forbids all inferences that are not explicitly allowed by the permissive rules (Reinmuth, Siegwart 2016). Usual systems of logical rules do not forbid self-contradiction. They allow certain inferences and forbid others, but they are silent with respect to the propriety of the content of the propositions that are (not to be) inferred. For example, they allow one to infer $A \wedge \neg A$ from premises A and $\neg A$, and vice versa. Contrary to what Gewirth and his followers claim, the "logical 'ought'" (Beyleveld 1991, p. 104, passim) only occurs in propositions of the form: If an inference does not conform to any of the permissive rules specified, you ought not to perform that inference. That $\neg(A \wedge \neg A)$ is a logical truth (in many logics) does not imply on its own that agents must not accept contradictory statements—that is a normative demand that has to be argued for.

References

Beyleveld, Deryck (1991): *The dialectical necessity of morality. An analysis and defense of Alan Gewirth's argument to the principle of generic consistency.* Chicago: University of Chicago Press.

Dutilh Novaes, Catarina (2015): "A dialogical, multi-agent account of the normativity of logic". In: *Dialectica* 69. No. 4, pp. 587–609.

Gewirth, Alan (1978): *Reason and morality.* Chicago: University of Chicago Press.

Gewirth, Alan (1996): *The community of rights.* Chicago: University of Chicago Press.

Gewirth, Alan (2000): "The Justificatory Argument for Human Rights". In: James P. Sterba (Ed.): *Ethics. Classical Western texts in feminist and multicultural perspectives.* New York: Oxford University Press, pp. 489–494.

Harman, Gilbert (1984): "Logic and Reasoning". In: *Synthese* 60. No. 1, pp. 107–127.

MacFarlane, John (2004): "In What Sense (If Any) is Logic Normative for Thought?" Draft for presentation at the Central Division APA 2004. http://johnmacfarlane.net/normativity_of_logic.pdf, visited on 3/30/2016.

Mackenzie, Jim (1989): "Reasoning and logic". In: *Synthese* 79. No. 1, pp. 99–117.

Reinmuth, Friedrich (2014a): "Hermeneutics, Logic and Reconstruction". In: *Logical Analysis and History of Philosophy* 17, pp. 152–190.

Reinmuth, Friedrich (2014b): *Logische Rekonstruktion. Ein hermeneutischer Traktat.* Dissertation. University of Greifswald.
http://ub-ed.ub.uni-greifswald.de/opus/volltexte/2014/1996/.

Reinmuth, Friedrich; Siegwart, Geo (2016): "Inferential Acts and Inferential Rules. The Intrinsic Normativity of Logic". In: *Analyse & Kritik* 38. No. 2, pp. 417–432.

Siegwart, Geo (2007): "Alethic Acts and Alethiological Reflection. An Outline of a Constructive Philosophy of Truth". In: Geo Siegwart/Dirk Greimann (Eds.): *Truth and speech acts. Studies in the philosophy of language.* New York: Routledge, pp. 41–58.

Steigleder, Klaus (1997): "Gewirth und die Begründung der normativen Ethik". In: *Zeitschrift für philosophische Forschung* 51. No. 2, pp. 251–267.

Werner, Micha (2002): "Minimalistische Handlungstheorie—gescheiterte Letztbegründung: Ein Blick auf Alan Gewirth". In: Holger Burckhart/Horst Gronke (Eds.): *Philosophieren aus dem Diskurs. Beiträge zur Diskurspragmatik.* Würzburg: Königshausen & Neumann, pp. 308–328.

Niels Gottschalk-Mazouz

Claims as Departure Points for Transcendental Arguments: Understanding Argumentation as a Game

Abstract: The usual logical analysis of argument focusses on the content and form, and not on the performative aspects. But, as it is proposed here, it is the proponent's claiming (i.e. making a claim) that allows for an opponent in a dialogue situation to succeed with a transcendental argument. To work out this idea, a dialogical-logic inspired model of argumentation—as a fair game between a proponent and an opponent—is sketched. It is discussed what it means to play well, and to win in this game. It is also shown how, in different versions of transcendental arguments, the success of such arguments depends on the successful attribution of claiming. Such attribution relies on interpretation and on a —to some extent—shared praxis of interpretation. This does not require us to presuppose any common core of shared propositions, though; it is enough that we presuppose sufficiently large similarities in our beliefs and practices to make sense of ourselves as acting, reflecting and deliberating together. Only then, however, transcendental arguments can be successful.

I Claims

The notion of a claim, or of claiming, is sometimes seen as unproblematic, such that it can be used to explain rather than being itself in need of explanation. "An assertion is a speech act in which something is claimed to hold", writes Pagin (2014). Some proposition is claimed to be true, for example. Or to be morally right: I do not want to confine myself to veridical speech only, when it comes to the type of claims. Moreover, I do not want to confine myself to claiming as an all-or-nothing enterprise: So when you claim something, then you are not always so certain that you claim something to hold, 100%, full stop. It could also be only likely, or favourable, or a mere hypothesis. So we do not always claim with the full fervour of conviction, "aus vollster Inbrunst". Maybe we claim something because we believe it and think that we have good reasons for this belief. But, as I see it, belief comes in degrees, and justification can seem better or worse. So even if I claim something because I am convinced of it, I might be more or less convinced of it—and I take this to be a generic property of conviction as well as claims. Call this the intensity of a claim. The other aspect of the

DOI 10.1515/9783110470215-005

lack of full fervour of conviction is a modal one. E. g. sometimes we do claim something as *advocatus diaboli* or as a hypothesis to see whether it can be proven wrong or right, or because we think that there is at least something in this position such that it is worth exploring it, etc. In discourse, you might claim something that you do not straightforwardly believe. And we have a whole modal vocabulary to express these "not straight" modes of endorsement.

So we have type, intensity and mode of a claim. But there is also the evaluative scope of a claim: Quite general, in putting forth a claim, we can submit us to the judgement of others. This is not meant as factual agreement, but as a validity presupposition. Therefore, when I claim that for me, as a European, doing this-and-this is good, then this might mean the following: That Europeans profit from doing this-and-this, and since I am European I will profit. However, how do I know that other Europeans do also judge it as good what happens to them if they do this-and-this. But this is not the validity presupposition sense that I was talking about. In this sense, it is not us as the common recipients of some good that is meant but us as the community of evaluators. So if I claim that insofar as I am European, doing this-and-this is good, then this is ambivalent. It could mean that is we Europeans benefit from it, or that, whoever may benefit from it, we Europeans are those who evaluate this benefit. It is the latter that I will call the evaluative scope of the claim. Matthias Kettner, when he speaks of more or less universal reasons, speaks of the projectability of reasons, and the common property that the respective group shares that is seen as in charge when it comes to evaluating a reason he calls the "Projektionseigenschaft", the projection property, of this reason (Kettner 1998, p. 23).

Some claims—just as some reasons—are restricted in scope, some are not. However, and the same holds for reasons, claims are rarely those that I see only myself fit to evaluate. On one conference, one philosophy colleague countered a social theory of knowledge with the remark that only he himself would be knowing the colour of his underpants, and that the community has nothing to do with this his knowledge. Fair enough, there are these claims where—under contingent circumstances—this is so. But as a matter of principle, why should only he be in a position to evaluate the colour of something, and be it his underpants. Normally these narrow-scope claims would be claims of perceptual experience, that only I had, or feelings or pain or so. Universal claims, to the contrary, come with an unlimited scope. Here it is everyone who is in the position to evaluate the claim. Again, contingent circumstances may prevent one from doing so, but 'universal' means that there is no a priori limitation of the evaluating group.

Hence we end up with type, intensity, mode and evaluative scope as formal qualifications of claims. Now, as I see it (and have argued elsewhere, cf. Gottschalk-Mazouz 2000, pp. 264–266), we can transform every claim into a veridical binary straight universal one by making explicit the nature of the claim and its intensity and mode and scope, and then asserting it veridically, binary and straight and universally. I do not preclude other, so to say, coordinate systems apart from this one, to which other claims can be "reduced"; so I do not want to say that the veridical binary straight universal form is *the* basic form, but just that it is *a* basic form insofar as we can "project" other forms on this one. Such a transformation involves interpretation, of course, that ultimately has to be validated by the author of the original claim. But, just as asserting is "generally thought of being open, explicit and direct, as opposed e.g. to conveying something indirectly, without explicitly saying it" (Pagin 2014), so is claiming. In our normal conversations, we are well aware that when somebody is claiming something, *that* he is claiming, and that he is claiming *something*. Nevertheless, this explicitness is a matter of degree and perspective. More precisely, it is the contents as well as the form of a claim (along the four dimensions, type, intensity, mode and scope) that may be more or less explicit. This is so because of the more or less vague and divergent meanings of our sentences and their words on the one hand, and our practices on the other hand.

II Claims as departure points

When asking: "What are the most promising departure points for transcendental philosophy: Action? The capacity for action? Normative identity? Argumentation? Putting forth a normative aim?", one might expect that Discourse Ethic's answer will be: "Putting forth a normative claim!" But, for the Apel tradition of Discourse Ethics, this expectation has to be modified—because Apel in his seminal book started with veridical (and not normative) discourse (Apel 1973, p. 401). "Putting forth a claim", thus, would have made more sense. Anyway, I am prepared to argue that we should consider claims, or putting forth a claim (=claiming), as the most promising departure point for transcendental philosophy. At least for one type of problems that is prevalent in moral theory: convincing a sceptic to accept some normative claim. (And, similarly in epistemology, convincing a sceptic to accept some descriptive claim). The reason is that for this type of philosophical enterprise you need arguments. So identifying departure points for transcendental philosophy, in this respect, means identifying departure points of arguments.

I would like to suggest that the departure point for transcendental philosophy, insofar as it is focussing arguments, should be what seems to me to be the sound departure point of any argument: And that is a claim. But before we can further discuss which claim, or what kind of claim this might be, we should look at what a transcendental argument is (or is usually taken to be).

III Transcendental Arguments

As far as arguments in general are concerned, I would point to the Toulmin Scheme to explain what they are (cf. Toulmin 1958, p. 104). In this scheme, a certain piece of data can be brought under a rule (which itself is backed by some warrant) that (under normal conditions) allow to infer a certain conclusion. As far as transcendental arguments are concerned, we should try to figure out what the elements could be. The most peculiar item here is the rule. Robert Stern begins his Stanford Encyclopedia entry like this (2015):

> As standardly conceived, transcendental arguments are taken to be distinctive in involving a certain sort of claim, namely that X is a necessary condition for the possibility of Y—where then, given that Y is the case, it logically follows that X must be the case too.

So the scheme, he suggests, of a transcendental argument is something like:

(TA)   Y, X is a necessary condition for the possibility of Y, thus X.

While Y corresponds to Toulmin's data, what figures as a rule here is the necessity claim. I will scrutinize it later. First of all, I would like to discuss the nature of the elements. If we want to argue, or so I wrote, then we have to consider claims, not facts. So that Y is the case, cf. Stern, or that some rule holds, does not start an argument. Facts do not start arguments; they are strictly speaking not even parts of arguments. That is why they can not *be* departure points, but they can *figure in* departure points. Only if someone claims something to hold, in the above sense, an argument can start. So as candidates for departure points of transcendental arguments, we would naturally see 'Y' or 'X as a necessary condition for the possibility of Y'—if the single quotation denotes the resp. claim.

In the literature, we find various positions towards the nature of the necessity claim in (TA). Illies, in his book-length treatment, distinguishes explorational from retorsive transcendental arguments. Explorational transcendental arguments have a form similar to (TA), namely:

(ETA)   Y, Y only if X, thus X.

According to Illies, "Y only if X" shall be the same as "if Y then X" and the scheme (ETA) just the *modus ponens* (Illies 2003, p. 33). Now, this understanding of the second premise looks weaker than Stern's, because it would translate only to "X is a necessary condition for Y" and not "... for the possibility of Y". Let me call the first the weak version of the necessity claim, and the latter the strong version of it.

It is a general feature of transcendental arguments, Illies explains, that the necessity condition holds "in every possible world" (Illies 2003, p. 30), however. To me, this seems to rule out the weak reading. Later in his book, Illies tries to figure out what would be needed in an argumentation to convince the sceptic, or to put forth a transcendental argument as in Kant's transcendental deduction. There, he explains the "only if" shall be taken as a "rational necessity". It shall be neither contingent nor stipulative. "Y only if X" would then have to be read as "any coherent understanding of Y will include X". So we end up with the strong reading of the necessity claim.

We can call the explorational argument, in its weak or strong form, reflective because it answers to the question of how something, that we take for granted, is possible. But "possible" now not just so, but in which respect something is "only possible". We are not asking for the conditions of something to be real(ly the case). This would lead to sufficient conditions, and it is unclear whether we could enumerate all these conditions even for any single token ("case") Y. We are asking for a certain subset of these, those that are indispensable for any case of type Y. This is the necessity of the "only if" that we are after. It is strong in the sense that it denotes necessities that do not only hold in a certain case, but in every similar case (i. e. similar enough to also call it "Y"). For a single case Y it does not make sense, I want to suggest, to speak of necessary conditions. I mean, in a world of necessity, every condition is a necessary condition. It is only in comparison with other cases that it makes sense to use modal terms. What is meant, I propose here, with the necessity is that they are conditions that are required for every instance of Y (now taken as a type). In exactly this sense they are also conditions for the possibility of Y (which might also be a fair reading of Kant's "Bedingungen der Möglichkeit", 1998 B39 ff.).

According to Illies, there is not only the explorative, but also the retorsive type of transcendental arguments. The retorsive type does not start with just any Y and proceeds to some X, but shall be used to point out that the denial of some proposition, call it R, is pragmatically inconsistent. This is the case when denying R would presuppose R. For expressing this, he introduces 'R', in single quotes, as the speech act of asserting R (and 'Not-R' for the speech act of asserting Not-R, i. e. the negation of R) and writes (Illies 2003, p. 48):

(RTA*) R, Either R or Not-R

(RTA) 'Not-R' only if R, 'R' only if R, thus R

According to Illies, (RTA*) is merely preliminary because R does not figure as a premise, and Either R or Not-R is a logical law (the excluded third). So (RTA) is the core argument. In it, 'Not-R' only if R means that 'Not-R', the speech act of asserting Not-R, which is the same as denying R, is always unsuccessful. If we now find propositions R_i that are not only contingently undeniable but are so independently of who the speaker is or when he or she speaks, then we would have found necessary conditions of any possible claiming.

Stern seems to take it for granted that the argument (TA) starts with the premise Y. Illies agrees, as far as the explorational type is concerned. But for retorsive arguments, he writes, it is R that is the "starting point" of "the reasoning", whereas "the actual argument" begins only with Either R or Not-R. This creates the oddity that the reasoning shall start not with a premise but with the conclusion. Whereas the actual argument, for Illies, starts with a logical law, i.e. with a tautology, that again is not a premise but has to be presupposed for (RTA) to work.

I think that these suggestions are hard to evaluate if we do not take possible argumentation situations into account. Only then we can decide what are most promising departure points for transcendental arguments. I have stated above that it is the discussion with a sceptic that many moral theorists see as their main challenge. Now I will explain in more detail how it is most promising to understand this situation, and how transcendental arguments would look like that might be applied in it.

IV Argumentation as a game

There might be different setups, but for the purpose of discussing the argumentation with a sceptic, I suggest to pick up ideas of dialogical logic (Lorenzen/Lorenz 1978) and understand it decidedly as a game, i.e. the goal is not to discover some dialog-external truth but to play well and to win against the other player. If we imagine the argumentation situation as one of two persons, be it in my head or not, then it would be one of the persons who makes the first move. This can be the opponent (the sceptic) or the proponent. They do not need to take turns in making a move. In an argumentation game, as I see it, it will not do if only the proponent moves. But it may be fine if only the opponent moves. The game is asymmetric. The proponent wants to demonstrate to the opponent that he should accept a certain claim (or at least that he cannot successfully deny this claim). The opponent has the aim of not having to accept this certain claim (or, even better, to be able to uphold its denial).[1] Both players have the further aim of being able to hold on to those claims that they each consider to be valid outside of the game ("background"). Because of this, and because we usually care about the validity of our claims also outside of the game situation, this game can be classified as a "serious" game (cf. section VI). Because the game situation is open, i. e. we do not know exactly which rules apply and which backgrounds the players have, the proponent cannot win by just presupposing that the opponent endorses certain claims, logical laws etc. without reconfirming them with the opponent. So, a player can only suggest to play a game that presupposes some set of standard logical laws, or of definitions, of common sense truisms or empirical propositions. But it would amount to playing unfair if a player would just insist that every argumentation game has to be like this (even more so if it makes a move possible that allows him to win the game every time) or that it has to be played with a certain background. So, while any player might make any claim he wants in the game, he can use only those claims to convince the other player that have been endorsed by this other player. To sharpen the rules of the game, or to draw from the assumed background of the other player, a player can try to let the other player acknowledge claims. In any such case, technically speaking what is made is a concession request ("do you concede Z?") which is an essential element of the logic of dispute (Hegselmann 1985, p. 49). The response can be to concede it or not to concede it. Not to concede it comes is two flavours, one is to deny it (i. e. to concede Not-Z), the other is to reject the request. Denying means essentially rejecting the request and committing to Not-Z (which is OK since one can commit anytime to any proposition, with one consistency restriction, see below). So one reason for rejecting a request would be that one likes to commit to its negation. Other reasons might be that the request is not precise enough, or that it suffers from a presupposition mismatch. Every question presupposes something that might not be shared by the other, so we have to allow for rejection if we do not want to let commitments be forced upon players. Of course, after a rejection the other player might follow up with concession requests that are more precise or contain less or alternative presuppositions, etc. A disputable issue is whether one should require giving reason for a rejection. While in most argumentation situations we would expect our opponent to give us at least some clue, I do not see that every situation has to contain certain (which?) justification rules for the rejection of requests. The same goes for the justification of one's own claims. So while the

---

1 For both players, the moderate and the ambitious goals do coincide if the opponent acknowledges the law of the excluded third and the proponent is willing to make use of it if suitable.

player will under normal circumstances have some expectations and will see them met, there are no pre-argumentative rules to hold fixed such that they would constitute an argumentation situation. So I think that it is fair not to require any justification for any move of any player. Any player can always commit or not commit without penalty. This does not mean that the players cannot agree on adding certain rules in these respects, but again I do not think that we should see those rules as constitutive of every argumentation game.

Another respect in which the game situation is open is with regards to the forms of claims that are allowed in it. For the game itself it might be handy to restrict oneself to a certain form, a basic form, of claims only. But this is an issue that has to be settled just like any other rule. Furthermore, the problem is imminent whenever something from the background shall enter the game: Because outside of it, we normally do not restrict us to some "basic" claim form. Insofar as the form can be made explicit, it is possible to reconfirm in which way a certain claim is meant, so it is not self-destructive to leave the form of claims unregulated at the start of the game. Most probably, the exact rules of the game will vary according to the forms of claims that are being used. Rules of inference are usually taken to be different for different forms of claims. But this is something that does not need to bother us here, because we can leave that to the players.

While the game situation is open in many respects, it has to be a game situation though. For games like our argumentation game, this means that the players (and any observer, by the way) has to be able to determine what counts as a move; and to move in this particular game is making a claim. So, for the game of argumentation, as it is construed here, there is only one constitutive minimum requirement, and that is that we have to be able to make a claim, and decide whether a claim has been made. That is why, and here I follow Aristotle (Met. 1005b), players in an argumentation game have to accept the principle of noncontradiction. If we allowed for a player to claim Y and claim Not-Y (in the same respect etc., cf. Aristotle), then we would not be able to attribute any claim about Y to this player. So, the player would not make a move in the argumentation game. For our game this means that on an apparent contradiction by one player, the other player may demand that one or more commitments be taken back or modified such that the contradiction disappears, and it is clear again what moves have really been made. Apart from that, the practices of the players must be similar enough that they both realize when the other made a claim (and this more or less reliably, even though they may turn out to be wrong some of the time)—such that they can reassure themselves that they play *this* game and not some other, or no game at all—and that they better see themselves as involved in some other social practice.

I would see even the logical law of the excluded third as not essential (contrary to Aristotle, Met. 1008b). If it is approved by a player, then *ex-negativo* arguments are allowed to be put forward against him. In general, committing to additional rules by a player means to license its adversary to demand in additional situations that the player takes back a move. In terms of chances of winning (as defined by reaching the first aim), this makes a player worse off. But it makes a win appear more impressive, in the eyes of the adversary and the player itself) if he succeeds nevertheless. Moreover, winning is not everything (see below). Finally, if you are so keen on winning, you might try your luck with conditional commitments of the sort: If you commit to this law, I am doing so as well. Or to propose mutual commitment that overarch multiple games (in which you are sometimes opponent and sometimes proponent).

V Departure points of transcendental arguments in games

In transcendental argumentation games that instantiate ETA or RTA*/RTA, either the opponent or the proponent moves first.

a) If the opponent moves first, he might do so by endorsing some claim Y or R. For explorational arguments, this allows for an interesting continuation, because the proponent can then ask for the assertion of the conditional, and demonstrate that the opponent should assert X. For retorsive arguments, things are different. Since the opponent already endorsed R, it is pointless to enter an argumentation that shall convince him of R. The proponent would rather want to convince him that R is a *necessary* truth. But the opponent might also start with the attempt to deny R. Then the proponent can try to demonstrate that this attempt is failing. And again, what he might want to convince him of is that R is an undeniable, and in this sense: necessary truth.

As for the explorational type, the opponent may also start by endorsing the second premise, the necessity claim (which is a conditional). This would also be a promising start because the proponent can then look for good candidates for Y (i. e. the antecedents of it). If he finds any, he can ask the opponent whether he concedes it. Or wait until the opponent says or does something that looks like he would presuppose something that would work as Y (in this respect our argumentation game is interwoven with other practices) and then let him concede it.

But the opponent may, in the case of an explorational argument, also start with the denial of X, and we could then let him concede Y and then the conditional, and then ask him to decide between the denial of X (which would mean to take back at least one of the concessions) or the acknowledgement of X (which would mean to step back from the initial denial claim). So, as it seems, it would always be an inviting starting point if the opponent tries to deny the conclusion. The proponent would then try to prove him to be inconsistent, etc. This allows for more starting points than the argument schemes show. Moreover, any argument scheme can be embedded in other schemes, such that it becomes more or less futile to look for "the" starting point.

b) But the proponent can also start the argument. He can simply put forth the conclusion, as a bait for the opponent. As an opponent, he may then deny it or at least show that he is free to endorse it or not.

The proponent might also start with a concession request regarding any other claim that he sees fit, favourably with a request regarding any of the premises of the argument, or the rules, and work forward from there towards a complete argument.

Of course, how I set up the minimal rules, the opponent can just reject any concession requests and win nevertheless. Though that would make this game completely boring. And why should the opponent have decided to play this game, then? After all, no one is forced to play. This brings up the question of motivation, which I think is more complex as it may seem.

VI What does it mean to play, to play well, and to win?

It may be assumed that both the proponent and the opponent have some motivation to play the game. This can be a serious moral motivation, of the proponent, who wants to convince the other of the validity of some moral principle. Or it can be a more playful motivation of figuring out where certain claims will, or would, take us. The reward is always a gain in self-reflection, a better understanding of oneself—of one's beliefs and their subjective statuses as e. g. plausible, certain or undeniable—with the help of the other, be it in person or in my head, acting sincerely or as an *advocatus diaboli*. And a better understanding of the other. And of the unity or disunity in views on what argumentation is and on valid moral principles. Even if our views do not match, it will help us to plan and coordinate our actions accordingly, because we then have learned not only about ourselves, but also where we agree and disagree with the other, and we know that the other knows etc. etc.

Fair enough, the attribution of making a claim relies on not only the endorsement of something like the law of noncontradiction, but also on interpretation and ultimately on a to some extent shared praxis of interpretation, claiming and arguing. But, this does not require us to presuppose any common core of shared substantial propositions or further logical laws, though; for meaningfully playing the game of argumentation, and taking part in any other social practice that might be interwoven with it, it is enough that we presuppose sufficiently large similarities in our beliefs and practices to make sense of ourselves as acting, deliberating and reflecting together.

In the picture suggested here, some rewards already come from playing. I assume that players have mixed motives, they want to play well, and they want to win. To achieve the mentioned reflective-hermeneutic aims, you have to play well. Playing well means that a player should acknowledge requests that adequately meet his background, and that he should risk some of it in the argumentation. As for winning, there are different types of winning in this game. The opponent might just deny to commit to any interesting claim. This would be an "easy win" (or: an "empty win") for the opponent. But not well played. The opponent might also endorse the target claim (i. e. X or R) straightaway. This would be an "easy win" for the proponent. But again not well played. Apart from that there may be more interesting, or substantial, wins of the proponent or opponent if also parts of the argument are conceded. After all, this is how we usually characterize knowledge, as *justified* true belief, so apart from it to be true (which I do not discuss here) there is some value we see in justification of beliefs.

For a "full win" of the proponent in this game, he must be in a position where the opponent in the end has been conceding all the premises, and (at least: cannot deny) the conclusion. And, with that, the rules of logic that allow to proceed from the premises to the conclusion—such that the conclusion appears to really be a *conclusion.* A "full win" of the opponent, on the other hand, would mean that the proponent has to give up some part of his allegedly, successful argumentation (or at least its conclusion) with which he originally wanted to convince the opponent.

As I put it, even for a full win the proponent does not have to endorse all the claims himself—what makes him win is that the opponent endorses them. This might seem unsatisfactory, and indeed a win appears to be even stronger if the proponent can (and maybe has done so in the game) acknowledge all these claims himself. I would like to call such wins "epic" or "harmonic", because they allow to reassure both the proponent and, ultimately, also the opponent of some consistent and unrivalled scheme of right and wrong.

We can then, if we like, "run the argument" as often as we like, which would mean then would mean really going through it, from the perspective of the other, and arguing for the conclusion. To use the type-token distinction here: The argument type alone does not convince anybody. Convincing can only be an argument-token, more precisely: an argument-tokening (which points out not so much the objective instance but the intentional "performance" of a type; cf. Brandom 1998, p. 303). I would compare this to a chess game where, after the game is over, we can then follow the game using some notation, can comment on the moves, and can say from where on it was pretty much a lost case for one of the players or the like. We can mentally replay it, or we can actually replay it, with somebody else or with ourselves, to understand the game and see what happens when one varies the original game.

VII Apelian and Gewirthian openings

Within this framework, how can we understand the arguments that Apel and Gewirth offer to justify moral principles, as transcendental arguments?

With the above distinctions in mind, it is easy to see that Apel's first argumentative steps in his foundation of ethics in the 1973 version is explorational, as is Gewirth's. That is because Apel begins with *whatever* claim the sceptic makes, typically a (maybe binary straight and universal, in my vocabulary, but in any case:) veridical claim (Apel 1973, p. 401), and Gewirth begins with some particular claim (about agency—this is how he puts it what he is doing: "to follow out the implications of the concepts of action and agent"; Gewirth 1985, p. 748). So Apel's first move is broader and easier to do because he can pick on whatever claim the opponent makes, he takes it to be a veridical claim, and he does not have to let the opponent concede a particular claim. I will start with the discussion of Apel's proposal and then move to Gewirth's.

It is clear that Apel starts with taking a claim, say 'Y', of some fact Y, as the first premise. The necessity premise is not introduced as a claim of the opponent, nor is the conclusion. In the necessity conditional we have the reference to not *the fact* Y but to *the claiming of the fact* Y. Because of this internal reference we can call this type of argument a reflexive-explorational argument. It has this form:

(RE)   'Y', 'Y' not without X, thus X.

It differs from the scheme (ETA) mainly by the single quotation marks around the Y. It denotes the claiming of something, here: Y. So 'Y' means claiming Y, which is neither identical to the fact that Y nor the fact of claiming Y. I prefer the "not without" to the "only if" because it makes clear that the latter is necessary but (usually) not sufficient for the former, and the if...then-relation in formal logic is notorious for being not the lifeworld one. But it shall denote the same relation.

In the proposed game framework, what we have to get the opponent to acknowledge to succeed with our argument, is the claim *that he has just been making a claim Y,* and the claim *that making this claim Y is not possible without X,* and *that conceding the premises and the rules of inference make it (in the sense determined by be rules) logically necessary for him to accept X* (or at least, if he does not accept the law of the excluded third: ... *for him not to deny X*). While the first premise is already introduced as a claim, the second is not (nor is the conclusion). The Apel school is well aware that, for the first premise to appear as a claim, we need some notion of claiming (that also figures in the necessity claim). Let us put this aside for the moment and just assume that there is some notion available on the side of the opponent (who is making the claim Y) that the proponent can draw on. The proponent can then use in the argumentation with the opponent both Y and '.', i.e. the fact that Y (the opponent claimed this fact) and that he claimed something (whatever it is, indicated by the point between the quotation marks). If the first is used, I will call this the content route. If the second is used, I will call this the performance route. They do not exclude each other. On each route, the proponent would have to let the opponent acknowledge the appropriate conditional and then the conclusion. As I see it, Apel is going down the performance route, and Gewirth the content route.

Here is an example of, after the first concession request (which is a double request, hence the "and"), going down the performance route. Let (Ack) denote the acknowledgement of the concession request.

O: 'Y'

P: Y and '.'?

O: (Ack)

P: '.' not without X?

O: (Ack)

P: X?

O: (Ack)

Note that the last request (for X) is not redundant; before it we were in a situation where the opponent should acknowledge X, but does not have to. If he does not acknowledge it, however, he should (i.e. the proponent can demand him to) give up one of the commitments made earlier. If he does not do this, upon request, then something is wrong with the terminology, i.e. here with the "not without"—and requests could go in this direction.

Now, as for the initial claim Y, it does not matter whether the opponent claims Y or Not-Y because as it seems both of these claimings would be impossible without X. So we can easily form a twin reflexive-explorative argument.

(TRE)   'Y', 'Y' not without X, thus X.

'Not-Y', 'Not-Y' not without X, thus X.

So no matter what Y you claim (including its negation), X will be the case. But its performance seems strange, because we need to find an opponent willing to claim Y *and* Not-Y. (And grant the conditional and the rules etc.). So maybe we try it this way:

(TRE+)   'Y' or 'Not-Y', 'Y' not without X, 'Not-Y' not without X, thus X.

This twin explorative argument presupposes the law of the excluded third. Or so it seems, were not the quotation marks. But it fits to taking the binary veridical discourse as departure point (as in Apel 1973), because the proponent now just has to wait for whatever claim to be made and can then proceed. To perform this scheme, the opponent has just to acknowledge that he made some veridical claim (whatever it is), and the two conditionals (or at least the one that is triggered) and the rules of inference once acknowledged will allow the proponent to say that the opponent should endorse X.

Now, if the opponent made not just any claim as a start, but a claim about both of the conditionals to hold (notice that this involved a claim about claims, and their requirements), we could cut out the first disjunction. We would then get:

(TRE++)   'Y' not without X, 'Not-Y' not without X, thus X.

Now as it seems we are better off than in the reflexive-explorational case because we do not have to have the opponent acknowledge a claim to get started. But we have of course now a twin conditional proposition that is fairly abstract that we have to let us concede from the opponent (if we do not want to start with his asserting of other claims, that is), plus the rules of inference as always.

Anyway, its performance could look like this:

O: ' '.' not without X'

P: '.' not without X, and '.'?

O: (Ack)

P: X?

 O: (Ack)

The opponent starts with a claim about what a claim requires. Regarding (TRE++), if we had Y=X (call it R), then this would bring us to:

 (TRE+++) 'R' not without R, 'Not-R' not without R, thus R.

Which of course is equivalent to (RTA). The problem here is that I see no plausible performance of this scheme in real life. Suppose the opponent would start like this:

 O: 'R'

Then the following would be redundant, but reassures the proponent of winning:

 P: R?

 O: (Ack)

And the request: 'R' not without R? would seem strange, and it had to be followed by the above reassuring move that could have been done directly anyway.

  The opponent starting with 'Not-R' could even win the game, for he need not acknowledge: 'Not-R' not without R. If he wants to, however, the proponent can demand that he then retracts from Not-R. Both parts of the performance would together mirror what Apel called "Letztbegründung" (1978, p. 165): R cannot be justified without presupposing it, and it cannot be denied without self-contradiction. But all this works only if the opponent acknowledges something like: '.' not without X, and there is no way of getting around this proviso.

  Gewirth, in this picture, does stay on the explorational side. Here the proponent starts with a concession request towards a basic concept, say of being an agent, if the opponent is unwilling to claim straightaway that this concept is correct. The proponent then has to do the same with the conditional, and will go down the content route. This means that he will reconfirm what is required by the conditional (to make shure), will request the next conditional etc. It should be clear from how the game is construed that there is no strategy for the proponent that guarantees a win. Even though the proponent might think that there is no good alternative to understanding oneself as a such-and-such actor which presupposes this-and-that etc., the opponent is allowed to acknowledge them or not, just as well as the methodological standard that guide them and the overarching aim of appearing rational or a free actor in a certain Gewirthian, Kantian or whatever sense. And depending on the background of the opponent, a denial of acknowledgement by him may or may not be well played.

VIII Moves that always win?

The search for transcendental arguments is comparable to finding strong moves that always, or at least usually, win certain games (hermeneutic-pragmatic language games). In moral theory, the target claims of these games often contain moral oughts, and playing and (thereby) analysing them may be helpful for the (formal and material) explication of concepts of agency, justification, and morality. There are different kinds of (moral) sceptics around and maybe there is an argument for each of them, but I can see no one argument for all of them. The most promising departure points for us, in terms of winning, are those that connect best to the adversary's background. The most promising departure points for us, in terms of playing well however, are those that connect best to the own background. By playing and eventually discovering such strong moves, we can make explicit some of the most central elements in the network of our commitments and entitlements, to use Brandom's terms (1998, pp. 159 ff.). Some of them seem indispensable to us. We think that everybody else should agree. We even have no idea how things could be otherwise. But this still does not license us to claim an a priori win. Or so I have argued.

I have the impression that the Gewirth school is closer to this view of argumentation-as-game than the Apel school insofar as they see a transcendental argumentation as a substantial hermeneutic enterprise. On the Apel side, there is the idea prevalent that some central part of the argumentation is necessarily successful, and the resp. knowledge infallible. According to this idea, some propositions and necessity claims can be taken for granted, by explicating some implicit knowledge, preferably about requirements of claiming. Marcel Niquet however put forth a concise criticism of this idea of "self-explicating" practical knowledge (1999, pp. 12 ff.). It can be presented in three points (cf. Gottschalk-Mazouz 2000, pp. 44 f.): First, it cannot be apriori right what we obtain by any real-world explicatory mechanism because any real-world mechanism can fail. But how can it fail, as it is construed to render infallible knowledge, and how could we check for failure? Second, suppose that it works and we can generate and validate some proposition as a presupposition, according to some test for pragmatic self-contradictions that is. Then this presupposition is unmarked concerning its quality as necessary or contingent. It is just a proposition and we have no a priori criteria to separate those—the "self"-transformation works for both and gives us only the proposition, but no knowledge of its status. Third, we cannot circumvent this problem by running the test in different situations and then see which conditions hold universally and which not, because even then we do not know whether our necessities are really strict and not just obtaining due to some up to now empirically unknown, but, in every case looked at so far, fulfilled empirical conditions.

So, the transformation of some Y into some claim that Y and the acknowledgement of some necessity claim that Y not without X is something that should not be seen as intuitively clear or a priori. All the more a proponent should, in a transcendental argumentation, ask the opponent for the concession of those claims. Moreover, no argument, and a fortiori no transcendental argument, can take as its departure point some action, and be it the action of asserting, as such. And it cannot take any other fact in any other domain as a starting point, i.e. about being a person, having an/some identity, putting forth an aim or a normative aim, standing in relations to other persons, evaluating, cooperating, interacting etc. In those domains we might find hypotheses for our claims, but any inference from, e.g., apparently doing *phi* to attributing the claim of doing *phi*, or performing the action *phi*, is only abductive. In an argumentation situation vis-à-vis an adversary one cannot obtain premises directly from actions or any other real-world processes or states of affairs. This step requires interpretation, judgement and pragmatic fixation of meaning. To set up the argumentation game such that it allows the opponent to acknowledge or not to acknowledge what the proponent takes for granted means only playing fair. At least that is how I see it.

Bibliography

Apel, Karl-Otto (1973): *Transformation der Philosophie, Band II: Das Apriori der Kommunikationsgemeinschaft.* Frankfurt a. M.: Suhrkamp.

Apel, Karl-Otto (1978): "Einführung zu 'Der Ansatz von Apel'." In: Willi Oelmüller (Ed.): *Transzendentalphilosophische Normenbegründungen.* Paderborn: Schöningh, pp. 160 – 173.

Aristotle (1933): *The Metaphysics.* Trans. Hugh Tredennick. Cambridge, Mass./London: Harvard University Press.

Brandom, Robert (1998): *Making it Explicit. Reasoning, Representing and Discursive Commitment.* Cambridge, Mass./London: Harvard University Press.

Gewirth, Alan (1985): "Rights and Virtues". In: *Review of Metaphysics* 39, pp. 739 – 762.

Gottschalk-Mazouz, Niels (2000): *Diskursethik. Theorien, Entwicklungen, Perspektiven.* Berlin: Akademie Verlag.

Hegselmann, Rainer (1985): *Formale Dialektik.* Hamburg: Felix Meiner.

Illies, Christian (2003): *The Grounds of Ethical Judgement. New Transcendental Arguments in Moral Philosophy.* Oxford: Oxford University Press.

Kant, Immanuel (1998): *Kritik der reinen Vernunft.* Ed. by Jens Timmermann. Hamburg: Felix Meiner.

Kettner, Matthias (1998): "Neue Perspektiven der Diskursethik". In: Armin Grunwald/Stephan
     Saupe (Eds.): *Ethik in der Technikgestaltung. Praktische Relevanz und Legitimation.*
     Heidelberg: Springer, pp. 153–195.
Mittelstraß, Jürgen; v. Bülow, Christopher (Eds.) (2015): *Dialogische Logik.* Münster: Mentis.
Niquet, Marcel (1999): *Nichthintergehbarkeit und Diskurs. Prolegomena zu einer
     Diskurstheorie des Transzendentalen.* Berlin: Duncker & Humblot.
Pagin, Peter (2014): "Assertions". http://plato.stanford.edu/entries/assertion/ (visited on 2
     March 2016).
Stern, Robert (2015): "Transcendental Arguments".
     http://plato.stanford.edu/entries/transcendental-arguments/ (visited on 2 March 2016).
Toulmin, Stephen (1958): *The Uses of Argument.* Cambridge: Cambridge University Press.

Dennis Badenhop
Still Lonely: The Moral Solipsist after Transcendental Argumentation

Abstract: This paper argues that transcendental arguments have no significant role to play in moral epistemology. Proponents of respective arguments have a wrong idea about the epistemic grounds, which support basic egalitarian and universalist moral principles. They envision a *moral skeptic*, an amoralist, who shares with us all common non-moral beliefs, and must therefore be refuted based on a priori implications of 'thin' notions like agency, justificatory speech acts, or second-personal address. After rehearsing some common objections against the project of transcendental argumentation, I introduce as an alternative the figure of the *moral solipsist*, who accepts moral principles but denies their applicability to other human beings based on psychological ignorance. I then argue that 'thick' anti-solipsist reasoning provides a better role model for *all* pieces of moral reasoning that are usually considered fundamental, but will always be an instance of *empirical* reasoning, thereby leaving no room for the a priori refutation of an unspecified moral skeptic intended by transcendentalists.

In many philosophical debates there are three parties: attackers, defenders, and spoilers. As far as the project of transcendental argumentation is concerned, I am afraid I will have to side with the spoilers. The spoilers (e. g. Raz 1999; Rorty 2001; Williams 1976, Ch. 1) suspect that the project just outlined is beside the point. In this article, I wish to present a number of epistemological considerations that give further support to this suspicion. These considerations do not aim at a refutation of existing transcendental arguments, but challenge instead the way the epistemological problem is framed by transcendentalists. I have found it convenient to group these considerations under two headings: first, that of a comparison of transcendental arguments with rational intuitions, and second, that of a comparison of transcendental arguments with empirical intuitions (and empirical reasoning based on these). In the first part of the paper I will mainly call into question the assumption that the epistemic grounds of moral principles must be *argumentative*, rather than intuitive; I then question the assumption that the epistemic grounds of moral principles must be *transcendental*, rather than empirical. In the second, more important section, I will (re-) introduce the figure of the *moral solipsist*, who unlike the amoralist does not

DOI 10.1515/9783110470215-006

doubt the validity of common moral principles but refuses to apply these principles to individuals that we consider to be in the range of their application because of her partial or complete ignorance of these individuals' psychology. I will than attempt to make plausible the view that the moral solipsist can figure as the role model for *any* morally deviant personality and that dissuading her of her practical outlook will always be an instance of empirically informed discourse. As I see it, this provides a strong reason against the belief that transcendental arguments have any essential role to play in moral epistemology.

I Transcendental Argumentation, Intuitionism & General Epistemology

Transcendental arguments in the strict sense, in which I will understand them in this article, are arguments that derive from an uncontroversial premise through a number of a priori transitions some further proposition that is considered philosophically significant, e. g. a proposition stating the reliability of perceptual experience. A *moral transcendental argument* (MTA), according to this definition, is individuated by the fact that it has a moral principle as its conclusion and by the fact that all its intermediate steps are pieces of a priori reasoning. MTAs can be distinguished by their initial premise. Currently there are two kinds of MTAs, i) action-theoretic arguments that begin with the concept of agency or some closely related concepts like those of practical reason, identity, or integrity (cf. Gewirth 2000; Kant 2010; Korsgaard 1996, 2009; Nagel 1970), and ii) arguments from intersubjectivity that begin with the occurrence of some kind of intersubjective performance, like a justificatory speech act or a nonverbal kind of second-personal address (cf. Apel 1976; Darwall 2006; Forst 2010; Habermas 1983). In any case, an MTA can be visualized in a modus ponens form:

(1) p_1

(2) $N(p_1 \supset ... \supset p_n \supset MP)$

(C) MP.

Since (2) is supposed to be the result of a priori reasoning and thus independent of any contingent, empirical knowledge, it is a necessary truth. (1) is however not necessary, but merely uncontroversial, because it is of course possible for there to be a world without any rational beings and thus without agents or speech acts. Therefore, the conclusion (C) of the MTA cannot be N(MP). Still, if the first premise must be universally accepted in any world with rational agents, and an MTA is valid, it would be irrational for someone to reject MP, and this would presumably be a sufficient degree of necessity for the purpose of the MTA.

As can be guessed from what I said in the introduction, I do not believe that any existing argument in the literature fulfills these requirements. Rather than refuting particular arguments or groups of them, however, I will explain in this paper why I believe they fail.

One reason why MTAs do not work could be that they illegitimately rely on an obsolete notion of the apriori. For example, Richard Rorty's (2001) critique of the 'Platonists' in moral philosophy is motivated to a large extent by a rejection of any rationalist epistemology in favor of coherentism. In contrast to Rorty, I believe that recent works have sufficiently defended against empiricist attacks the thesis that at least some propositions can be known a priori in a robust, if somewhat more modest than the traditional sense, and that the transcendental project ought not to be easily debunked by rejecting rationalism altogether (cf. Bonjour 1998; Peacocke 2004).

The assumption that the notion of a priori justification is generally sound does not alone imply the possibility of transcendental arguments in ethics. It follows neither i) that basic *moral* principles are propositions a priori, nor ii) that the *practical* principles meant to figure in the second premise of MTAs are a priori, nor iii) that moral principles can be deduced from practical ones by means of a priori reasoning. Prima facie, practical and moral principles might be a posteriori (or worse, false) in contrast to other propositions, or they might be a priori but logically independent 'axioms' of conduct that can merely be known *intuitively*, but not argumentatively.

Many transcendentalists of course consider recourse to intuitions to be dogmatic. However, I get the strong impression that this opposition to intuitionism is largely unwarranted, even inconsistent, and that after a careful inspection of the matter we will have to sharply lower our expectations, this time not about the possibility for a valid MTA, but about their epistemic usefulness.

First, one may think that an argument for a moral principle has to be provided because holding it to be true would otherwise be unjustified. To give two examples, Gewirth and Korsgaard write:

> But how can we justify the basic principle itself? Here, by definition, there is no higher or more general moral principle to be appealed to as an independent variable. Is it the case, then, that justification comes to a stop here? This would mean that we cannot rationally adjudicate between *conflicting* moral principles... (Gewirth 2000, p. 489)

> ...the reflective mind must endorse the desire before it can act on it, it must say to itself that the desire is a reason. As Kant puts it, we must *make it our maxim* to act on the desire. (Korsgaard 1996, p. 94)

Both authors express the view that to rationally believe in a moral principle (Gewirth) or to rationally act on a desire (Korsgaard), one has to *actively provide a justification* for a belief or a kind of conduct. This does not follow. There is a difference between the status of a belief as *being justified* and the *process of justification* (Alston 1989, Ch. 1). As we can see in the common example of simple perceptual beliefs, it is reasonable to say that these beliefs can be held rationally by a perceiver without her having provided epistemic support for them inferentially. It is plausible because our sense perception is in general a very reliable belief-forming mechanism, and we might consider the same thing to be true for certain a priori intuitions. What the authors above implicitly presuppose for moral justification is a *strong form of internalism* like:

(J) For A's intuitive belief p_1 to be justified, A has to actively quote another justified belief p_2 that justifies p_1.

But this is too strong a requirement for a belief to be justified. Plausible is instead acceptance of something like the following:

(J') A's intuitive belief p_1 is justified, as long as A knows of *no reasons to the contrary.*

One response to J' could be to point out that the fact of profound dissent in the area of morality will always constitute strong reasons to the contrary and undermine justification for believing in fundamental moral principles. But this presupposes that the best interpretation of moral dissent is that this dissent is really about moral principles rather than something else. I will come back to this question later. Disregarding this issue for the moment, we can hold on to the assumption that it is not a requirement for an a priori justified moral belief that this belief be reached through a priori *reasoning.*

In the light of J', a second point can be made about the suspicion of dogmatism. Since undermining or defeating reasons may arise, it would be false to say that intuitions, both moral and non-moral, feature any of the common brands of epistemic immunity, i.e. infallibility, incorrigibility, or indubitibility. Most contemporary intuitionists agree that this holds for both empirical intuitions, that is, sense perceptions and a priori intuitions. Moreover, one can say about the latter that an apparent a priori intuition can be *misidentified* as such and that ongoing inquiry may demonstrate that this intuition was really empirically defeasible (cf. Peacocke 2004, p. 30). Therefore, it is not correct that any allusion to intuitions must automatically prompt hardheaded insistence on one's rules of conduct.

Third, the suggestion, discernable in many transcendentalists' contributions, to the effect that all justification must be inferential, is also inconsistent. This is so because for the transcendental argument to escape an infinite regress the transcendentalist must rely on conceptual intuitions for all the intermediate steps p_1, ..., p_n (or if some of these are again inferentially justified then their justification must ultimately rely on beliefs that are non-inferentially justified). This could be termed John Rawls' point: intuitions cannot be eliminated from the equation; they can merely be pushed to the edge of the stage.

To this one might reply that MTAs typically rely on intuitions, but at least not on *moral* intuitions. This however begs the question of why *moral* intuitions in particular should be considered dubious, if reliance on intuitions in general is not and cannot be eliminated. On the other side, the question is how transcendentalists could profit from this rejoinder. One idea might be that transcendental arguments are not the only, but at least the *more reliable* source of justification. It doesn't look, though, as if there are any common metaethical considerations that could support this point. Skeptical arguments with respect to ethical justification based on evolutionary considerations typically challenge the reliability of respective belief-forming mechanisms *in general* (cf. Street 2006). They do not target moral *intuitions* in particular, in contrast to argumentation. Moreover, even though I have not engaged in the refutation of any classical arguments here, one should at least grant the statistical point that many philosophers have not been convinced by existing MTAs and that this does not speak for their high reliability. On the other side, it seems that most people do accept that some moral principles akin to the ones that MTAs try to establish are correct, apparently in complete independence of these arguments. So one could hold that they believe them—with a high degree of confidence—*intuitively.*

Now, one could suppose that the transcendentalist would object to this last point and claim, quite in the spirit of the epistemic rule J', that because of *moral dissent* with respect to principles, a complementary justification is called for. However, I believe that since Kant transcendentalists have for the most part taken the opposite stance. For example, Kant himself famously expresses his conviction that "even the most consummate villain" (Kant 2010, Sect. III) believes in the Categorical Imperative; Korsgaard (cf. 2009, 8.4.5) reckons that tyrants, racists, and misogynists have ultimately inconsistent 'particular wills' because they tacitly acknowledge the command of universal respect; and Darwall makes a similar point with his example of Joseph Stalin (cf. 2006, pp. 138 ff.). From this perspective, it curiously looks as if transcendentalists are making a superfluous attempt to convince people of something they believe anyway, thereby somehow missing the point.

But one has to be careful here not to do injustice to the transcendental project. For one, although an MTA might be relatively ineffective, when it comes to installing a more benign moral outlook in evildoers and –thinkers this does not preclude the possibility of providing an *additional warrant* for a principle through a valid MTA. MTAs might then rather be of academic interest, but this fact is certainly non-prohibitory. Also, it has not yet been precluded that a valid MTA could eventually prove to be the *best reconstruction of the epistemic grounds* of our belief in moral principles, elucidating rather than supplementing these grounds.

To briefly summarize the points made in the discussion so far: nothing said above amounts to a proof of the impossibility of transcendental arguments in ethics. So far all that have been given are reasons why we ought to give up the idea that there is a strong epistemological requirement for providing such an argument and significantly lower our expectations as for their overall theoretical fertility.

The notion of an MTA, however, has yet another aspect. Since MTAs are designed to start with some single basic concept, like that of agency, a justificatory speech act, or of second-personal address, transcendentalists must presuppose that the epistemic ground of the resulting moral principle is *thin*. That is to say, the ultimate reason for believing MP solely lies in the one concept that figures as the starting point of the argument, in contrast to a wide array of facts about human life and society, respectively a *thick* description of these, *and* the rationale for believing them to be correct. This aspect is also reflected in the transcendentalist's hypothetical opponent, the 'amoralist'. The amoralist is obviously not designed to be skeptical about everything. Otherwise no MTA postulating the real occurrence of agents, speech acts, etc. in the world could possibly get off the ground. She is a *comparative skeptic* that by definition shares with us the entire network of ordinary beliefs about the world, *except* for the belief in moral principles. This is why, for the amoralist to be a consistent type, two premises must be made: i) that the truth of the targeted moral principles is completely *epistemically independent* of all non-moral facts, and ii) that none of the traditional skepticisms regarding the external world, induction, and, more importantly, other minds, can lay at the root of opposition to the basic moral truths. It is these last premises that I have come to find most incredible. In the following section I will explain why I believe they ought to be rejected.

II Moral Solipsism

In all examples that I know of, the moral principle in the conclusion of an MTA is designed to be *universal and egalitarian* in kind. Contingent on the particular features of the argument and the author's broader ethical outlook, there are obviously different ways to spell out such a principle and emphasize the key aspects of the targeted universalism and egalitarianism, e. g. as commanding ubiquitous mutual respect, equal concern for everyone's well-being, a general right to (public) justification, the treatment of everyone as an end in themselves, or some combination of these. As the exact formulation does not make a difference to what I am going to say about it, I will base my discussion on the following simple scheme:

(MP) *[I] All persons have [II] equal dignity.*

The question I would like to address arises with regard to the moral phenotype of agents who *apparently* act in gross violation of this or related fundamental principles. As explained in the last section, I understand the transcendentalist to assume that any extremely deviant personality is a *moral skeptic* aka amoralist who i) *denies* MP, while ii) otherwise *sharing* all our relevant non-moral beliefs and our faith in their justification. To these non-moral beliefs belongs, amongst other things, a clear idea of who is to count as a 'person' in the sense intended in MP.

But there is a fundamentally different interpretation of deviant phenotypes, where the respective agent i) *accepts* MP, while ii) doubting or denying our convictions with respect to the range of individuals that are to count as a 'person' in the intended sense. I call a personality that fits this second interpretation a *moral solipsist.* I choose this title because the obvious way in which somebody might quarrel with the extension of the term 'person' is by being skeptical about other peoples' *psychology.* This skepticism, as I conceive of it, allows for degrees and can be partial or complete. In the latter case the moral solipsist questions or is ignorant of other peoples' mentality altogether. This highlights that, taken to the extreme, she just *is* the other-mind-skeptic, the solipsist sans phrase, assessed for her implications for moral thought. So, in other words, while the moral skeptic denies MP because she doubts in part II that all persons have equal dignity, the moral solipsist accepts that all people have equal dignity, adding however, as she does for part I, that she is *the only real person.*

Two things about the moral solipsist come to mind. First, one may find the solipsist too grotesque a type to be of much utility in moral epistemology. Second, even if there was such utility, it does not look as if any trouble for the transcendental project could arise from it because it has only been stated that there are potentially two different standpoints behind various deviant moral phenotypes. Contrary to these thoughts, I want to show that the moral solipsist as a role model is very useful in the reconstruction of moral reasoning and moral learning. Furthermore, I want to suggest, though not prove, that once we have sufficiently described the solipsist and elaborated the epistemic means for a rational mitigation of his deficiencies, there are no possible agents left that could be called 'moral skeptics' to demand a transcendental refutation.

I wish to begin with a description of a rather simple example of intersubjective evaluation and the practical reasoning it involves, the relevance of which might not be initially transparent, but will, I hope, become clearer later, when I draw some more general conclusions from it.

Take the imperative: 'Help anyone else in pain if you can, unless seated comfortably!' If you ask yourself whether you could accept this imperative as a maxim or belief such that the respective ought statement is correct, your deliberation could proceed as follows. You could think that being seated comfortably constitutes only a small increase in well-being. You could then think that even a mild pain always outweighs a small comfort and that for this reason the imperative must be rejected.

But if the example is considered from the moral solipsist's perspective, she could obviously deny this conclusion. She could take the stance that no one else's pain matters to her and that she would always prefer her comfortable seating, adding—to her silent monologue—that she would only give up the latter in case the alleviation of her own pain was at stake. At this point, the moral solipsist could be pressured to reiterate her rationale for exclusively disvaluing her own pain in contrast to everybody else's. But her reply will come swiftly: It is only her, who is in *real pain*, while everybody else's pain is just a fake copy without interior design, i.e. *zombie pain*.

Eager to further test her position, the moral solipsist can now challenge herself with two common arguments. For illustration purposes she pictures two severely injured people, A and B, one of whom is herself and both of whom behave in such a way, i.e. screaming in agony and warping their faces, that they seem to be in pain. Now she considers, first, whether it is not true, as behaviorism claims, that there is nothing to pain but a certain pattern of behavior so that it simply does not make sense to consider A's pain, but not B's, as real, when both A and B display identical types of pain behavior. She rejects this presumption right away because she is too well aware of her own phenomenal states of consciousness to find an ontological reduction of these states to behavior in the least bit plausible.

The second argument the solipsist considers is linguistic. She is aware that there is a public language term 'pain', which she frequently uses when addressing zombies in a conversation (an event that she understands as some sort of simulation of and as such external tool for her inner monologue) and which she also employs in her individual practical deliberation. Now she wonders whether it is not an essential element in the possession conditions for 'pain' that she applies it not only to herself, but also to other humans that display the superficial indicators of pain, and whether it would not be a raw conceptual error not to do so. She finds that this is a *non sequitur.* For it would only be a clear conceptual error if there was a strict congruence between public language and her own conceptual understanding of the world. Since this is so far an unwarranted assumption, she holds it to be possible that the stereotypical term 'pain' is not a natural-kind term, but one that can refer to two different subspecies, namely I) her own genuine pain and II) others' zombie pain. However, she also accepts what I shall call the *principle of justified discrimination*, which states that if two entities superficially belong to the same kind, i.e. share the relevant set of properties, then for any distinction drawn between them there must be a further property or set of properties that one entity has but the second entity lacks that justifies this distinction. While she accepts this principle, it appears to her nevertheless that she has such a reason, which consists in the experiential quality of the first kind of pain. In the example, it is for A only A's pain that hurts, that is *felt* by A, while B's pain *looks* painful to A, but does not feel painful for A.

If we stop here for a moment, we can see that this constellation represents an instance of the classical problem of induction with respect to other minds, for which the behaviorist and the linguistic reply provide an insufficient solution. The solipsist's awareness of her own experiential states allows for a prima facie warranted discrimination between herself and other people, whereas the singularity of this awareness does not justify a generalized ascription of conscious mental states to other similar beings as a matter of induction.

Still, from another perspective the principle of justified discrimination can also point in another direction. First of all, it is noteworthy that the solipsist's experience of her own pain, a felt pain that hurts, is not only the basis for discrimination between her pain and others behavioral $PAIN^{BHV}$, but also the basis for her assessment of pain *as bad*. In this respect, it is noteworthy that the solipsist's $PAIN^{EXP}$ is bad because it has a specific *experiential quality*, whereas it wouldn't be correct to say that her pain is bad because it is experienced *by her.* The latter assertion would invalidly argue with indexicals. It would amount to the absurd claim that X_1 is of a different kind than X_2, because it is *this* X. It follows that if it could after all be established that $PAIN^{BHV}$ is really just $PAIN^{EXP}$, there would be no more room to discriminate between the two, thus, the solipsist had to admit that others' $PAIN^{BHV}$ is something *as intrinsically bad as* the solipsist's $PAIN^{EXP}$.

Are there any further reasons on the grounds of which the solipsist could accept the antecedent of the last sentence, the assumption that $PAIN^{BHV} = PAIN^{EXP}$? I think there are. Until now we have merely considered the *actual* occurrence of pain experiences registered by the solipsist and pain-related behavior with others. But there is also the question of what *explains* these occurrences of the experience and the behavioral patterns. Insofar as the solipsist has some basic knowledge about human life, she should now find that there is a strong *genealogical similarity* in the example between the occurrence of A's pain experience and B's display of pain-related behavior. For they are both offspring of the same human species and were raised in the same kind of human community, whose various members are themselves biologically related in numerous ways, and now suffer the same kind of injury. This is why the explanations for the two occurrences will essentially list the same brands of causes. The question that actually remains from this perspective is whether the solipsist has any good prima facie reason to assume some *additional cause* that further explains why among all humans she is the only one capable of conscious pain experiences.[1] To gain such a prima facie reason, the solipsist would have to assume that these experiences are either the result of a freak accident of nature or of some arbitrary intelligent design. But these explanations—in the former case there would be no explanation at all but recourse to mere chance, in the latter the otherwise superfluous assumption of a very biased divinity—are *worse* explanations than the one that does not list such an additional cause and posits homogeneity in A and B's cognitive capacities. So the other-mind problem is after all not a problem of induction, but of *abduction*, and this problem can easily be resolved because non-solipsism is an implication of the *best explanation* for the genesis of conscious (pain) experience, the alleviation or avoidance of which *matters*.

It is useful to describe in general terms some key features of the discussion above. 1. The root of the solipsist's refusal to believe that other individuals' pain is something worthy of care lays in her *undifferentiated psychology* of these individuals, i.e. in this most extreme case in the non-moral belief that they lack an 'inner' mental life altogether. 2. The initial cause of this deficiency is an *epistemic asymmetry* between the solipsist and all other subjects. After all, A can feel her own pain, but does not feel anybody else's pain. 3. To counter the solipsist's peculiar epistemic stance I didn't introduce a transcendental but an *empirical argument* that presupposes acceptance of a significant number of empirical beliefs about human beings. So there is nothing in the conclusion a hypothetical solipsist rationally 'must' believe, independently of this empirical knowledge.[2] 4. If

---

1 Neuroscientists would probably point out that it is also because of the interdependence of brain states and mental states that the zombie scenario is absurd. The latter argument, though, relies on expert neurological knowledge and potentially contestable claims in the philosophy of mind, whereas I would like to keep my argument more commonsensical.

2 Evidently, normal subjects usually do not need to work themselves through such an argument. It is plausible that most human beings for evolutionary reasons possess a natural empa-

the argument goes through, it implies *universal egalitarianism* with respect to the negative intrinsic value of pain. In the aftermath, the question of whether any-body else's pain is 'really' bad is closed.

One might suppose that this tale about the moral solipsist does not bear much affinity with the usual suspects from the moral cabinet of horrors, supremacists of the racist, misogynist, 'class-ist', or religious variety, in the light of which we feel the strongest inclination to provide convincing arguments for our basic uni-versalist moral principles. In this regard, it doesn't look at all as if their issue is a simple unsympathetic misappreciation of their victims' pain, so that the piece of reasoning articulated above could reform their practical stance or at least pro-vide the template for such a reform. But let's take a closer look.

Richard Rorty famously notes in his essay on human rights and human-rights violations that it is a fundamentally misleading reconstruction of the per-petrators' motivation to say that massacres, genocides, and other war crimes they take part in have been made possible by their rejection of the human rights agenda as such. Instead, they introduce a subdivision into the total class of hu-mans, a subdivision between good Serbs and bad Croats (Rorty's example), Ger-mans and Jews, or more generally between *real human beings* and *subhumans*. As a result, they do *not deny* that all (real) humans are fully entitled to well-being and the same system of rights and liberties, they merely limit the *scope of individuals* that this universal and egalitarian principle is applicable to (cf. Rorty 2001, p. 242). Rorty also seems to assume that the discussed mind-sets are essentially closed, coherent systems, as coherent as our non-discriminatory human right framework so that no rational procedure, especially not any foun-dationalist appeal to principles, could persuade supremacists to adopt our moral outlook. Instead of trying to convince these lost souls, he eventually recom-mends telling 'sad stories' about minorities to children, as a pragmatic method to manipulate them into a benign moral attitude.

Although I think that with respect to moral justification Rorty expresses a plausible critique of the transcendental project in particular, I also believe that he underestimates the prospects for reasoning in general. Initially, in line with what I said above, his main point of criticism is that none of the main fig-ures of moral deviance deny moral principles per se. Rorty, however, does not sufficiently acknowledge the fact that supremacists of all varieties can usually

---

thy, so that they can, as it were, perceptually intuit others' pain, abstractly or in concrete situa-tions. Important is here that because of the argument given, we can describe agents who lack natural empathy as epistemically *deficient* agents, instead of as a path to moral relativism.

be assigned a set of quite contestable beliefs. What does this belief-set include? We can plausibly imagine that discrimination of the supremacist's minority of choice might start all the way down at the level of sentience. He considers members of the target group too jaded to live up to his own refined appreciation of joys and sorrows. He does not question that they can experience pleasure and pain in the most primitive sense, in which all higher vertebrates can experience them. It is just that neither their suffering nor their feelings of happiness have the same *quality* as his own. Then there is the field of general intelligence, where he is of course strongly inclined to attribute himself and people of his liking superior reasoning abilities. Again, he will not in the least doubt that the others are immune to logic, or that they are responsive to reason in some minimal sense. This is why he would consider letting them perform simple tasks like domestic work or cotton picking under his supervision as a handy arrangement. But he is certain that with all complex matters, first and foremost discussions of the good and right social order, the possibility of their contributing anything significant is more hypothetical than real, which is why their exclusion from these discussion might not be mandatory in principle but surely for reasons of pragmatic sobriety. Finally, the supremacist will advance to the level of character, where he deplores as an irritating source of misery in the community of the decent the existence of such sneaky or dishonest or thievish or spineless pseudohumans. He may even possess an elaborate demonology about the—as Cicero would have put it—'in-name-only humans', stipulating as their sole motive the corrosion of the family of the pure and virtuous. In short, the supremacist despises these 'people' as paradigm examples of the *brute*, 'people' who are for the dimensions of happiness, intelligence, and virtue too *dull*, *dumb*, or *depraved*, respectively, to be mentioned in the emphatic description of humanity.

Needless to say that we know that all the supremacist's beliefs mentioned in the last paragraph are false. What we have to consider is not whether they are false, but *what* is wrong about them and *how* we know that they are false. As for the first point, we should observe that all these false beliefs about minorities fit the description of an *undifferentiated psychology:* the supremacist sees a fundamental sensible, intellectual, or moral emptiness in his opponent, where there is none, respectively where—ceteris paribus[3]—there is on average no smaller degree of intricacy in feeling, thought, and righteousness than among the individuals he considers superior. So the supremacist is an example of moral solipsism. To be sure, he does not deny other agents' mentality in its entirety, but he re-

---

3 Under unsuitable circumstances, e. g. in a slaveholder society, there might of course be stark differences between relevant groups because of contingent intervening social variables.

mains ignorant of crucial parts of it. It is worthwhile to stress that this is especially true with respect to demonologies. 'Demonizing the opponent' is essentially the psychological, oversimplifying elimination of the rich conglomerate of personal or communal interests that agents usually have, from an individualized theory of action, and putting a mysteriously underivative evil desire for destruction in its place.[4]

As for the second point, it can be granted that to a great extent the idea of a close affinity between rationality and morality has its merits. Pressing for consistency in a conversation (as unlikely as such an event might be in real life), one can point out to the supremacist solipsist that his discriminatory beliefs rely e. g. on selective perception, on overgeneralizing from too small samples, on negligence of intervening variables, and dubious hearsay. One can also explain how, as in the simple example of the complete moral solipsist, any inegalitarian or non-universalist *evaluations* are consistently undermined, in so far as these evaluations depend on false psychological beliefs. We should note that analogously to the previous example, our strategy will aim in this way to overcome an *epistemic asymmetry* between the supremacist's privileged access to his and his kin's—spectacular and laudable—character traits, and his epistemic access to the relatively more distant features of other groups.

On the other hand, it is evident that nowhere in this imagined dialogue will we allude to a minimal concept of agency or basic principles of intersubjective discourse and second-personal address, so that our pleading could from there onward continue as a piece of a priori moral reasoning. Reasoning starts here with a rich array of psychological facts that can in their entirety only be ascertained empirically. It is not through pure reason that the supremacist can be proven wrong. This implies on the downside that we can always depict him as a perfectly *rational* creature as long as we suppose an adequate amount of epistemic misfortune. We can then describe him as a subject who has fulfilled all his epistemic duties by gathering extensive knowledge about 'those people' loitering in his neighborhood (which is statistically significant, but unfortunately not representative), by discussing supremacist matters and seeking consensus with his peers (who are unfortunately all supremacists like him), by regularly studying pamphlets and all the articles on the *quasinews.ru* website. One may want to reiterate the unreliability of these methods of belief-formation. But the question is how we know about this unreliability, and the answer is again that their unreliability can only be established based on *completeness of the relevant empirical evidence*. It is simply not the case that the supremacist is unreasonable as

---

4 I thank Stephen Darwall for making me clarify this point.

such; it is for the *empirically enlightened* thinker that he must seem unreasonable.

It is apparent that the outlined patterns of reasoning do not yet give us the idea of the equal dignity of all (at least minimally) rational agents as envisioned as the conclusion of a transcendental argument. What we get is a constrained egalitarianism as a result of the impossibility of drawing, on psychological grounds, a moral line atop the usual ethnic, socioeconomic, or gender cleavages. This constrained egalitarianism would obviously leave enlightened supremacists enough room for a 'fair' contempt towards people who do not correspond to their original set of values, independently of their social background.

There is, however, another way in which greater humility could befall the supremacist. What I have just described is how the supremacist, taking pride in his superior sensitivity, intellect, and the righteousness of his kin, comes to see that these qualities aren't prevalent to a lesser degree in groups that he tends to discriminate against, and, that is, comes to see that the *extension of individuals representing his set of primary values* is different than expected. But what we can also plausibly imagine, however we fill in the details of his character, is that the supremacist will in time realize that the prime values he treasures also incur certain *costs*. This will inflict a certain ambivalence upon him. If he values the superior intellect, he cannot eventually fail to notice that being prudent and knowledgeable rids him of an enviable naivety, of taking a fresh look, or of the innocence of seeing things for the first time, while a higher intellect may also allow him to work more efficiently for the wrong causes. If the supremacist holds his refined taste and sensitivity in high regard, he will observe that through it he loses the simple pleasures or any higher resistance to stress and pain. Ultimately, he will have to learn to appreciate the enormous plurality of virtues, their partial mutual exclusivity, and how their status as virtues may vary with circumstances. If he strives for innovation and originality, he cannot preserve his cultural heritage at the same time. If he wants autarky and independence, he must sacrifice family and community. If he makes self-satisfaction and inner peace his priority, he cannot reach professional excellence.

This list could be prolonged indefinitely, but perhaps the crucial point has emerged. Starting with the belief in the superiority of a certain set of values, any supremacist is in the position to become aware of the inherent ambivalence of this evaluative outlook. As a consequence, he can come to value not only individuals that have the same way of life, but also individuals whose way of life is the focal point of a *different set of primary values*, which are recognized by him, but inevitably underrepresented in his way of life. Finally interpreting other agents as putting into practice such alternative sets of values will further advance the accuracy of his psychology (thus, reduce his solipsism), and allow him to see these agents, too, as deserving his respect and care.

Now, if the supremacist has progressed this far, it should seem plausible to him as well—not in the sense of the utmost rational urgency, but plausible—to reflect on the vagueness and uncertainty of virtue as well as the finite nature of his psychological and evaluative knowledge and conclude that there is a *strong moral prima facie reason* to treat indeed *all* individuals that fulfill minimum standards of agency, whether they embody his or any recognized alternative set of primary values, as if they merit respect. On the personal level, though, this prima facie reason may be overridden by closer acquaintance with people. After all there are subjects who are, e.g., depraved, and morality does not seem to prescribe treating these with the same kind of respect. Again due to all the uncertainties involved he could find that any conditionality imposed on a prima facie good will would probably lead agents like him and authorities to make too many wrong exceptions, since under more official circumstances close acquaintance with specific characters cannot be guaranteed. This is why he could find that, based on this prima facie *moral* reasoning, there is moreover a strong *legal reason* to constitutionalize this presumption of equality and make universal respect the *unconditional* principle of state authority and political institutions; and I tend to think that this *is* pretty much what is now intended with our common human-rights framework.

The bottom line of this long description of reasoning versus the solipsist aka supremacist is that the path towards moral universalism does not in these cases lead through an articulation of the thin notions of agency, practical discourse, or second-personal address, but through a comprehensive appreciation of the *patterns of moral and psychological complexity*. If this is accepted as a plausible route towards egalitarian universalism, we have to ask ourselves whether there are really any practical standpoints left that are fundamentally skeptical and do *not* fall into the solipsistic category, but belong to the 'amoralist' kind—and I must now admit that I cannot coherently imagine such a figure. The anti-solipsist patterns of moral reasoning outlined in this article seem to cover the essence of all common justifications that are of contemporary and historical importance and deserve the title 'fundamental'.

From this result, I am inclined to draw two conclusions. First, the main flaw of any attempts to provide an argument a priori for a universalist principle is not that these arguments will for general reasons be unavoidably invalid—which I have not attempted to show in this article—but rather that already at the outset adherents of this project have a false preconception of the *epistemic grounds* of these principles, which really lie in a complex set of facts about psychology, society, and ways of life. Second, as an appreciation of these facts is the upshot of an empirically informed process of moral learning, there is no rational procedure the application of which could by itself ascertain a moral phenotype that corresponds to the egalitarian universalism as envisioned in MP. It takes both reason *and* the right kind of experience to arrive at this ethical stance. This in turn does not refute, but makes thoroughly counterintuitive the metaphysical view of Kantian constructivists, traditionally in close alliance with transcendentalism, according to which ethical truth is constituted by the outcome of any such procedure. In this light, it may become necessary to either give up the notion of ethical truth or grant that ethical truth transcends practical reason. If—in the objectivist spirit, in which this paper has been written—the latter position is taken, it should be stressed that it is still far from the view that value is completely independent of the minds that conceive it. It should also be reemphasized that the complementary allusion to experience is far from suggesting a denial of the importance of sound practical deliberation or the reduction of moral insight to the telling of sad stories. Still, with a friendly glance on the melancholic, it seems to remain true that phenomenologically rich narratives are a rational equivalent to empirical reasoning, since they make intuitively intelligible the vast expanses of human equality, diversity, knowing, and not knowing, that are the groundwork for dignity.

References

Alston, William P. (1989): *Epistemic Justification. Essays in the Theory of Knowledge.* Ithaca: Cornell University Press.

Apel, Karl-Otto (1976): *Transformation der Philosophie Bd. 2. Das Apriori der Kommunikationsgemeinschaft.* Frankfurt a. M.: Suhrkamp.

Bonjour, Laurence (1998): *In Defense of Pure Reason. A Rationalist Account of "A Priori" Justification.* Cambridge: Cambridge University Press.

Darwall, Stephen (2006): *The Second-Person Standpoint. Morality, Respect, and Accountability.* Cambridge, Mass.: Harvard University Press.

Forst, Rainer (2010): "The Justification of Human Rights and the Basic Right to Justification. A Reflexive Approach". In: *Ethics* 120, pp. 711–740.

Gewirth, Alan (2000): "The Justificatory Argument For Human Rights". In: J. P. Sterba (Ed.): *Ethics. Classical Western Texts in Feminist and Multicultural Perspectives.* Oxford: Oxford University Press, pp. 489–494.

Habermas, Jürgen (1983): *Moralbewußtsein und kommunikatives Handeln.* Frankfurt a.M.: Suhrkamp.

Kant, Immanuel (2010): *Groundwork of the Metaphysics of Morals.* [Kindle eBook: MobileReference]. ASIN: B00FAY0UYW.

Korsgaard, Christine M. (1996): *The Sources of Normativity.* Cambridge: Cambridge University Press.

Korsgaard, Christine M. (2009): *Self-Constitution. Agency, Identity, and Integrity.* New York: Oxford University Press.

Nagel, Thomas (1970): *The Possibility of Altruism.* Princeton: Princeton University Press.

Peacocke, Christopher (2004): *The Realm of Reason.* Oxford: Clarendon Press.

Raz, Joseph (1999): "The Amoralist", In: J. Raz: *Engaging Reason. On the Theory of Value and Action.* Oxford: Oxford University Press, pp. 273–302.

Rorty, Richard (2001): "Human Rights, Rationality, and Sentimentality". In: P. Hayden (Ed.): *The Philosophy of Human Rights.* St. Paul: Paragon House, pp. 141–156.

Street, Sharon (2006): "A Darwinian Dilemma for Realist Theories of Value". In: *Philosophical Studies* 127, pp. 109–166.

Williams, Bernard (1976): *Morality. An Introduction to Ethics.* Cambridge: Cambridge University Press.

B **Uses and discussions of transcendental reasoning based on the self-reflective structure of personal autonomy, rational agency, or human self-understanding**

Sorin Baiasu
Constitutivism and Transcendental Practical Philosophy

Abstract: In her important Sources of Normativity, Christine Korsgaard offers a "transcendental argument" against scepticism about moral normativity (Korsgaard 1996, p. 123), and her more recent Self-Constitution claims that the Categorical Imperative is constitutive of acting (Korsgaard 2009, p. 76). The aim of this paper is to examine the prospects of this kind of transcendental practical argument. After I identify three unpromising versions (one which is too ambitious, one which is inconsistent and one which is empty), I formulate a fourth promising candidate. This is an argument which is more modest than the ambitious version, but can be made to work. To make it work, I argue, we need to introduce Kant's distinction between the necessity of analytic and the necessity of synthetic a priori judgements; perhaps even more challengingly, we need also to account for a necessity of the latter kind which is specifically practical.

1 Introduction

Constitutivism seems to be one of the more promising versions of constructivism.[1] It aims to justify substantial normative standards as constitutive of prac-

Acknowledgements. An early draft of this paper was presented to the 2014 Annual Conference of the European Consortium for Political Research in Glasgow in September; a revised version was presented to the "Transcendental Arguments in Practical Philosophy" conference organised by the Alfried Krupp Wissenschaftskolleg and the University of Greifswald in November 2014. A revised version was also presented to the Philosophy Research Seminar at the University of Durham in March 2015. Work on the preparation of these drafts was carried out while I was visiting at the University of Vienna as part of the ERC Advanced Research Project "Distortions of Normativity". I am grateful to the project's PI, to the University of Vienna and to Keele University for making that research visit possible. I am also grateful to the participants to the Glasgow, Greifswald and Durham events for great discussions. The paper published here is a revised version of my "Constitutivism and Transcendental Practical Philosophy: How to Pull the Rabbit Out of the Hat", initially published in Philosophia (2016) doi:10.1007/s11406-016-9746-3, https://creativecommons.org/licenses/by/4.0/

1 Thus, "the importance of constructivism [...] resides in the insight that the nature of practical truths should be explained in terms of the constitutive features of practical reasoning". (Bagnoli 2016) Of course, there are various accounts of what constructivism and constitutivism are. This

DOI 10.1515/9783110470215-007

tical reason. In this way, it can defend the constructivist commitment to avoiding realism and anti-realism in normative disciplines, such as ethics. Standards of action are not already given, independently from us, but are constitutive of practical reason; yet, they are not the result of arbitrary decisions, but are conditions, which make possible agency. Nevertheless, the nature of the justification, which constitutivism can offer in support of the normative standards it puts forward, is usually discussed from the perspective of the debate between realism and anti-realism. On the one hand, the claim is that there are normative standards independently from agents; on the other hand, the view is that normative standards depend in some sense on the agents, either because agents contribute to their construction or because they are constitutive of agency and could not exist without agents or for some other reasons.[2]

In this paper, I would like to focus on a related, but distinct, debate. My concern will not be whether the substantial normative claims asserted by the constructivist have some elements, which are not constructed, but real, given inde-

---

means, however, that on such accounts, certain versions of constitutivism would be incompatible with certain version of constructivism. For instance, on some accounts, Kant's version of constitutivism is quite different from Rawls's version of constructivism. (Krasnoff 1999)

[2] Commentators acknowledge the significance of constitutivism irrespective of its contribution to the realism/anti-realism debates, yet the focus continues to be on these debates. (Bagnoli 2016, esp. 7.3) The fundamental objection is that if the construction is not normatively constrained, then norms are arbitrary; if it is normatively constrained, then it relies on some normative constraints which are not constructed (for instance, Shafer-Landau 2003: esp. Ch. 2). Some debates focus on ethical intuitions, as such constraints, and the extent to which they can be taken as normative foundations. (Scanlon 1998: esp. Ch. 5; 2003) Some constructivists do not see a role for ethical intuitions in the construction of norms. (O'Neill 1989; Hare 1983) One way such constructivists respond to the fundamental objection is by claiming that constructed norms are constitutive features of practical reason. (Korsgaard 1996). Korsgaard's use of the language of transcendental arguments suggests to some that her position is realist. (Crisp 2006, esp. Ch. 2, Sect. 2; Larmore 2008, esp. Ch. 5, Sect. 5; Galvin 2011) The claim that to value ourselves presupposes as a necessary condition valuing humanity is criticised as presupposing that a condition of a thing's value is itself valuable. (Kerstein 2001; Ridge 2005; Coleman 2006). Whereas constitutivism may distinguish itself from non-naturalist realism (Shafer-Landau 2003) and naturalist realism (Firth 1952; Railton 1986) by regarding norms as the result of a process of construction undertaken from the first-person perspective (O'Neill 1989; Korsgaard 2003, 2009; Street 2010; Velleman 2009), a worry remains that it relies on moral assumptions it does not justify eventually. (Raz 2003; Timmons 2003) One reply here is that the objection misses the point of constitutivism, where the method is circular, but not in a vicious manner. (O'Neill 1992) A further objection is that constitutivism is unsuccessful in deriving norms of morality from features of rational agency. (Cohen 1996; Bratman 1998; Gibbard 1999; FitzPatrick 2005; Setiya 2007; Bagnoli 2009) Some such objections are formulated from a realist perspective, whereas others are formulated from an anti-realist standpoint. For the full discussion, see Bagnoli (2016, esp. 7.3).

pendently from us; instead, my concern will be more narrowly epistemic—whether those claims can be derived from premises, which are normatively less substantial than the normative conclusions themselves. Whether the premises or conclusions are constructed or independent from construction is, in this context, almost irrelevant; what is relevant is the extent to which an argument can enrich normatively its premises, so that we would start from some premises, which are normatively weaker, and end up with conclusions, which are normatively stronger.

Assuming that such a feat turns out to be possible, we could deal much more easily with sceptical arguments.[3] It is sufficient to start from premises sufficiently weak to be accepted by the sceptic and to derive in a justified way normatively stronger conclusions, in order to be able then to reject the sceptical position about the stronger, more substantial normative claims. I have said that my concern is with an issue, which is distinct from the debate between realism, anti-realism and constructivism, but related to this debate. This relation is easily noticeable in a particular case. Thus, if we start with merely descriptive premises and succeed in deriving normative claims through a constitutivist argument, then those normative claims constructed through the justification provided by the argument could no longer be suspected of secretly relying on some realist ground, on some normative component smuggled in, in the premises of the argument. In other words, a successful constitutivist argument could help constructivists show that it is possible to justify substantial normative claims in a non-arbitrary manner and without realist premises. Yet, as already mentioned, this is not my concern here.

Now, one of the prominent constitutivist positions in the literature is Christine Korsgaard's and, in this paper, I will focus on its articulation in her *The*

---

3 A clarificatory note is in order: I see the constructivist-constitutivist problem of deriving a substantial account of normative reasons from an account of the nature of action and agency as a particular case of the more general problem of deriving substantial conclusions from more abstract and formal premises. Nevertheless, there is a sense in which this second problem does not really make sense. The reason is the following. As we will see in Section 5 of this paper, I present such an argument as a valid syllogism. Yet, a valid logical argument can never derive more substantial conclusions from slender premises. Please replace with: Conclusions are already presupposed by the premises. The problems make sense if we regard them in the following way. Consider an argument with the premises A and A → B; if B is already part of A, then the conclusion B does not add anything to A; by contrast, if B is not already included in A, then the argument shows something substantial. To be sure, the conclusion is already included in the premises, but the point is that in the formulation of the second premise (A → B), we derive from B something which was not already in A, as opposed to simply making A more explicit.

Sources of Normativity (1996).[4] The articulation of the constitutivist position in this text is particularly important, since it suggests the kind of argument one would need, in order to move from normatively weaker premises to normatively substantial conclusions. Nevertheless, while a promising approach to this issue is suggested by Korsgaard, this suggestion is not explored further in her texts.[5] In this paper, I plan to examine this approach more closely and to suggest how it can work successfully.

In the next section, I will consider one recent objection to Korsgaard's constitutivism, an objection according to which, far from beginning from slender premises, she would start from a normatively substantial account of our essential identity and would then attempt to derive from it robust normative claims. I argue that this objection relies on an inaccurate interpretation of her position and, after a clarification, in Section 3, of some elements of the conceptual framework of the discussion, I present (in Section 4) what I take to be an accurate interpretation. Section 5 reconstructs the crucial argument of Korsgaard's constitutivism and Section 6 evaluates it. I conclude that more work would need to be done, in order for Korsgaard's argument to function as intended. One reason why this additional work might not seem a welcome complement to her position is due to an important implication: in order for Korsgaard's constitutivism to work, she would also need to adopt a metaphysical position she might not be keen to embrace. But let us begin with the objection to Korsgaard.

2 One Objection to Korsgaard's Constitutivism

According to Michael Smith,

> Constitutivism is the view that we can derive a substantive account of normative reasons for action—perhaps a Kantian account, perhaps a hedonistic account, perhaps a desire-fulfilment account, this is up for grabs—from abstract premises about the nature of action and agency. (Smith 2015, p. 187)

---

4 Since the paper focuses mainly on this text by Korsgaard, in what follows, references to this text will be made by indicating the page(s) referred to only.
5 My claim here is that, whereas Korsgaard talks explicitly about a transcendental argument in *Sources*, she abandons the expression in subsequent texts, perhaps also because it invites the criticism that she is getting close to moral realism. See also n3 above. Nevertheless, according to some authors, she continues to use transcendental arguments, even when she is not using this label for them—see n34 below.

Following this definition, therefore, constitutivism claims that we can get to a substantial account of normative reasons for action from an account of the nature of action and agency. Going from a view of action in general to a view of reasons for or against the performance of particular actions seems to involve the creation of something ex nihilo. As Eric Wiland notes, in relation to constitutivist arguments, "[t]hose who claim to extract reasons out of agency remind us of those who claim to pull rabbits out of hats". (Wiland 2012, p. 141)[6]

Smith thinks he is able to perform this trick, and he also claims to be able to distinguish his view from that of "another constitutivist", namely, Christine Korsgaard's (again, with reference to her 1996 text). According to him, Korsgaard commits "a grave mistake" when she identifies reasons "as the demands to which we are subject in virtue of our necessary identity". (Smith 2015, p. 193) Instead, we should regard reasons for action as connected with our function as agents. If we, with Korsgaard (as interpreted by Smith), think that reasons for action are those demands to which we are subject insofar as we are the kind of thing that we are essentially (that is, insofar as we share in the respective necessary identity), we will end up with deliberative dilemmas. (Smith 2015, p. 194) For instance, to use Smith's example, we may think of ourselves as essentially biological human beings facing the demands of reproduction. At the same time, however, we may also see ourselves as agents who have good reasons to help, and not interfere with, each other. The demands of reproduction, on the one hand, and, on the other, those of helpfulness and non-interference may be in tension or even irreconcilable conflict, in some circumstances.

Consider a particular person; as a human being, she will be a biological being necessarily, since, by definition, this identity is essential for human beings. Since the demand of reproduction is part of this identity, the particular person under consideration, as a human being, is, as a matter of fact, subject to this demand. Yet, according to Smith, this demand may come in contradiction with other demands, for which we may see ourselves as having good reasons. Hence, the starting point for a constitutivist account should not be some essential identity, but an account of ourselves as agents, since it is within the framework of such an account of agency that we can talk about commitments and our reasons for these commitments. Hence, according to Smith, the conflicting demands, which seem to be irreducible from the perspective of the presupposition of an essential identity, disappear when the starting point is an account of our-

---

6 Quoted in Smith (2015, p. 187). Smith addresses here Wiland's and David Enoch's objections to constitutivism (Enoch 2006), the former's being formulated against Smith's version of constitutivism, whereas the latter being broader in focus.

selves as agents and our reasons for commitment. For him, "only the demand relative to our function as agents is analytically tied to the concept of a reason for action". (Smith 2015, p. 19)

This suggests that there are at least two significant aspects of constitutivism, which must be considered. First, with which account of ourselves the constitutivist begins seems crucially important—on Smith's account, Korsgaard starts with an account of our essential identity, that is, an account of that without which we would be a different kind of being; yet, being essentially this or that kind of being, with this or that kind of demands upon us (say, biological human beings facing the demands of reproduction) leaves open the question whether being in this way is normatively permissible and desirable.

Secondly, how this account is connected with the normative claims the constitutivist derives seems equally significant, and here Smith specifies that the connection happens "analytically". As we will see, Korsgaard does not discuss this second important aspect of a constitutivist account and, at least if we interpret an 'analytic' connection in the standard way, Smith's specification of the link between the account of ourselves as agents and the normative conclusions identified as constitutive of action cannot pull any normative rabbit out of the constitutivist hat.

My paper focuses on this aspect of constitutivism, precisely because it is a significant, and yet not much examined, issue. Moreover, as already mentioned, I focus on Korsgaard's constitutivism, because, although she does not explicitly discuss the status of the connection between the initial account of agency, from which the constitutivist starts, and the later substantial normative account, with which he hopes to conclude, she does make a promising suggestion, which is worth pursuing. Nevertheless, to begin with, let us focus on the first important aspect of constitutivism and examine Smith's objection to Korsgaard. If this starting point is flawed in Korsgaard, then there is not much interest in exploring further the way in which a substantial normative account could be derived on this basis. I, however, think that Korsgaard's view on this is not flawed in the way Smith claims.

As mentioned above, on Smith's account, the problem with Korsgaard's constitutivism is that it is supposed to begin with an account of agency as given by our essential identity, by the kind of thing we essentially are. The problem is that demands stemming from this essential identity will be in tension or strong conflict with demands provided by reasons we have, as agents, to act in one particular way or another. Yet, as we will see in more detail in Section 4, Korsgaard's starting point is not an account of our essential identity, which would include some demands to which we would be subject as a matter of fact; Korsgaard agrees that our various identities and roles may provide various demands on us as a matter of fact, but she also regards us as beings that have the capacity to reflect on these demands, to distance ourselves from them and to question them. She thinks that, as self-reflective beings, we are beings that need reasons to act.

This characterisation of human beings as self-reflective beings that need reasons to act asserts the connection between agency and reasons. Hence, if there is some essential identity, which we must necessarily adopt and which forms the starting point for Korsgaard, then this is only an identity as beings who need reasons, since we can question any putative essential identity and try to determine whether to commit to its demand or not. Hence, Korsgaard begins from an account of human beings, which makes it possible for us to question our identities and roles and to justify our commitments to them.

In conclusion, Korsgaard's view, although admittedly dominated by an understanding of reasons in terms of identity, does not link reasons to some essential identity, which would make as subject to particular demands as a matter of fact. As human beings, as self-reflective beings who need reasons to act, we have an identity, but this identity does not impose specific demands—it questions them by reflecting on our commitments, by evaluating them and by endorsing them, if we have reasons to endorse them. According to Korsgaard:

> Circumstances may cause you to call the practical importance of an identity into question: falling in love with a Montague may make you think that being a Capulet does not matter after all. [...] What is not contingent is that you must be governed by *some* conception of your practical identity. For unless you are committed to some of your practical identity, you will lose your grip on yourself as having any reason to do one thing rather than another—and with it, your grip on yourself as having any reason to live and act at all. But *this* reason for conforming to your particular practical identities is not a reason that *springs from* one of those particular practical identities. It is a reason that springs from your humanity itself, from your identity simply as *a human being*, a reflective animal who needs reasons to act and to live. And so it is a reason you have only if you treat your humanity as a practical, normative, form of identity, that is, if you value yourself as a human being. But to value yourself as a human being is to have moral identity. (pp. 120 – 1)

There is here a clear distinction between a person's particular practical identities (such as, being in love with a Montague) and a person's identity as a human being (a reflective animal who needs reasons to act and to live). This distinction already suggests that Korsgaard begins with an account of ourselves as agents, as human beings who need reasons for our commitments, but this is not an account, which would regard us as subject to certain demands and reasons for action. On the contrary, as mentioned before, this account makes possible the process of questioning any specific identities and commitments. Moreover, our identity as human beings can itself become the object of reflection and commitment. It is only when we acknowledge that our identity as human beings (as a reflective animal who needs reasons to act and to live, and, hence, as an agent) is valuable that we acquire a moral identity. This moral identity, however, only makes sense from the perspective of reflection and, hence, from the perspective of our humanity.

Hence, our humanity is a capacity, which is not always acknowledged as valuable; we may continue our lives without acknowledging the value of reflection. When we treat this human identity as an identity we should be committed to, we acquire moral identity. But this moral identity is not an essential identity either, since not valuing your human identity is still compatible with your capacity for reflection and agency, and it is compatible with your being an agent, a human being. This, I think, answers Smith's objection to Korsgaard or at least makes this objection less urgent. Thus, to sum up, our identity as human beings makes it possible for us to question any putatively essential identity, whereas our moral identity is acquired when we do not simply acknowledge our reflective capacity and the need for reasons, but when we value them.

To be sure, there are here several questions, which are left open, such as: In what sense does Korsgaard claim that we "need" reasons to act and to live, given that she also acknowledges that we may not value our reflective capacity and agency? Is it really the case that our moral identity is not an essential identity —after all, if we needed our humanity, then should we not value it and, if so, then would moral identity not be a necessary part of our identity as agents? We will see that such questions will emerge in one form or another in the reconstruction and evaluation of Korsgaard's argument for normativity in Sections 4 and 5; in the next section, however, I turn to the second important aspect of constitutivism mentioned above: the connection between, on the one hand, the account of agency, which is the starting point for a constitutivist, and, on the other, the normative claims she thinks she is able to derive from that account of agency.

3 The Constitutivist Trick

Smith claims that the concept of an agent's reason for action "is not basic", but "gets analysed" in terms of the concept of desirability-relative-to-that-agent. The latter, in its turn, is not basic, but gets analysed in terms of the desires of that agent's idealised counterpart. Constitutivism enters the picture, Smith argues, when we ask ourselves whether the concept of ideality (the desires of the agent's idealised counterpart) is basic. He thinks the notion of the agent's idealised counterpart should in fact be that of an agent's functioning optimally as a desire-realiser. (Smith 2015, p. 189) Smith's version of constitutivism claims to be able to derive several conclusions from this notion of functioning optimally as a desire-realiser, some of them representing substantial reasons for action.

For instance, from an understanding of agents as desire-realisers, we can allegedly deduce the fact that agents who perform their function optimally must have and exercise the capacity to realise their desires, no matter what their content and know the world no matter what the world is like. From this, Smith claims, it follows that agents must possess coherence-inducing desires to help and not interfere, if agents are to perform their function optimally. We are also told there is an "analytic tie between facts about what is desirable-relative-to-an-agent and facts about the desires of ideal agents", as well as between "facts about an agent's reasons for action, on the one hand, and facts about which options that agent has and what is desirable-relative-to-that-agent, on the other". (Smith 2015, p. 193)

Smith offers a complex argument, but, for the purpose in my paper, the important point is the link between an account of an agent as desire-realiser and the substantial normative claims derived as constitutive of agency: how do we get from an account of agency to substantial normative conclusions? As we have seen, there are several steps for the derivation of the substantial normative claims made by Smith, and some are presented explicitly as made analytically. It is not clear what Smith has in mind when he talks about an implication's being drawn analytically, but the following standard account might clarify this notion sufficiently for the purpose of this paper.

The distinction between analytic and synthetic connections has a relatively long history. My attempt here is to work with a minimal conception of this distinction, which would be as uncontroversial as possible. According to Kant:

> In all judgements in which we think the relation of a subject to the predicate (I here consider affirmative judgements only, because the application to negative judgements is easy afterwards), this relation is possible in two ways. Either the predicate B belongs to the subject A as something that is (covertly) contained in the concept A; or B, though connected with concept A, lies quite outside it. In the first case I call the judgement *analytic*; in the second, *synthetic*. Hence (affirmative) analytic judgements are those in which the predicate's connection with the subject is thought by [thinking] identity, whereas those judgements in which this connection is thought without [thinking] identity are to be called synthetic. (A6 – 7/B10)[7]

---

7 In what follows, when referring to Kant's *First Critique*, I will do so by using the standard 'A/B' (first edition/second edition, in volumes 3 and 4 of the Akademie edition 1900 ff) convention. The translation used is listed in the Bibliography.

I am going to assume that we can regard claims in general as consisting of a subject and a predicate—the subject indicates that to which the claim attributes the predicate. For instance, the claim that 'desire-realising agents who perform their function optimally must have and exercise the capacity to realise their desires no matter what their content and know the world no matter what the world is like' can be seen as attributing a predicate (having and exercising the capacity to realise desires no matter what their content and knowing the world no matter what the world is like) to the subject (the desire-realising agents who perform their function optimally).

This subject itself can be understood as a claim (desire-realising agents perform their function optimally), which attributes a predicate (performing their function optimally) to the subject (desire-realising agents).[8] One example of an analytic judgement Kant offers is that all bodies are extended—we think the predicate of being extended as contained in the concept of a body. By contrast, the claim that all bodies are heavy does not make explicit a predicate (about the heaviness of a body) that we think as already contained in the subject (the notion of a body); hence, the claim must connect subject and predicate by linking them through a further element. This element can, in some cases, be given by experience. For instance, for 'This book is red', the truth of the claim depends on an experience of this book as red.

Hence, Kant claims, in the case of analytic judgements, the predicate is not different from the subject, in the sense that it is included in the subject. This is why Kant says that affirmative analytic judgements are those in which the predicate's connection with the subject is thought by thinking identity. By contrast, in the case of synthetic judgements, the claim attributes to the subject something that does not already exist in the notion of the subject. One implication of this is that an analytic judgement would not be able to make a substantial claim, a claim asserting about the subject something beyond what is already asserted by the subject. By contrast, a synthetic judgement will assert something beyond what the subject already includes.[9]

---

8 Again, the subject can be understood as a claim ('the agents are desire-realising') with a subject (agents) and a predicate (being desire-realising).

9 "Analytic judgements could also be called *elucidatory*. For they do not through the predicate add anything to the concept of the subject; rather, they only dissect the concept breaking it up into its component concepts which had already been thought in it (although thought confusedly). Synthetic judgements, on the other hand, could also be called *expansive*. For they do add to the concept of the subject a predicate that had not been thought in that concept at all and could not have been extracted from it by any dissection." (A7/B10–11)

An analytic claim or judgement is a claim which clarifies the concept of the subject by making explicit at least a part of it—it does not provide anything that is not already included in the concept of the subject (although, of course, a particular person may not be aware of the predicate as part of the subject and learns something new through the analytic judgement). By contrast, a synthetic judgement will assert something new—it will connect the concept of the subject to another concept, which is not already included in the subject.

One implication of this is that analytic judgements have a necessity, which is not to be found in synthetic judgements. To deny an analytic judgement is to deny that part of the concept of the subject (the predicate) is part of the concept of the subject, which is contradictory and, hence, impossible. If to deny an analytic judgement is to commit to impossibility, then the analytic judgement is necessary and, hence, Kant says, a priori. By contrast, synthetic judgements do not assert a predicate already included in the subject, so denying that the predicate applies to the subject does not commit us to an impossibility. Given the contingency of experience, analytic judgements cannot be based on experience, whereas synthetic judgements can:

> Thus the [analytic] proposition that bodies are extended is one that holds a priori and is not an experiential judgement. For before I turn to experience, I already have in the concept [of body] all the conditions required for my judgement. I have only to extract from it, in accordance with the principle of contradiction, the predicate [of extension]; in doing so, I can at the same time become conscious of the judgement's necessity, of which experience would not even inform me. (B11–12)

One of the crucial aspects of Kant's distinction is that, although he thinks all experiential judgements are synthetic, he does not think all synthetic judgements need to be experiential, that is, based on experience or a posteriori. The idea of a synthetic a priori judgement is what gives Kant hope that substantial judgements can be necessary and, hence, that cognition is possible. Insofar as we take cognition to refer to those claims, which are substantial and necessary, they can only be so if they are synthetic and a priori. Kant thinks the propositions of mathematics are synthetic and a priori. For Kant, a claim such as '7 + 5 = 12', for instance, is synthetic, although it is also a priori.[10]

---

10 "It is true that one might at first think that the proposition 7 + 5 = 12 is a merely analytic one that follows, by the principle of contradiction, from the concept of a sum of seven and five. Yet if we look more closely, we find that the concept of the sum of 7 and 5 contains nothing more than the union of the two numbers into one; but [in thinking] that union we are not thinking in any way at all what that single number is that unites the two. In thinking merely that union of seven and five, I have by no means already thought the concept of twelve; and no matter how long I

Kant's account of the distinction between synthetic and analytic propositions has been criticized in various ways. For the purpose of this paper, I cannot review the debates and defend any particular aspect. What I hope to do is to focus on a sufficiently unproblematic version of the distinction, while assuming that the distinction can still be used.[11] The first element of this simplified account is an assumption that declarative and imperatival propositions (whether affirmative or negative) can be understood as having two parts: a subject and a predicate. Secondly, there is a claim that, in the case of the analytic propositions, the link between subject and predicate is of identity.[12] If the distinction between analytic and synthetic propositions is to be exhaustive, then synthetic propositions would be those where the relation between subject and predicate is not one of identity.

One implication of this basic account of the distinction is already familiar: analytic propositions are not substantial claims: by linking subject and predicate, they do not assert anything more than what is already presupposed by the subject of the propositions. A second, already mentioned implication is that analytic propositions are necessary: their negation is a negation of a relation of identity and leads to a contradiction. As we know from standard modal logic, it is the negation of necessity that leads to impossibility, so analytic propositions are necessary, given that their negations lead to contradictions. Finally, given their necessity, analytic propositions are a priori, since a posteriori, experiential propositions are contingent and, hence, cannot be necessary.

---

dissect the concept of such a possible sign, still I shall never find in it that twelve. We must go beyond these concepts and avail ourselves of the intuition corresponding to one of the two: e. g., our five fingers, or (as *Segner* does in his *Arithmetic*) five dots. In this way we must gradually add, to the concept of seven, the units of five given in intuition". (B15) It should be noted that debates continue over synthetic or analytic nature of mathematical propositions.

11 See Robert Hanna's "The Return of the Analytic-Synthetic Distinction" (2012; reprinted in 2015).

12 This, as we have seen, is the way Kant presents the relation between subject and predicate for analytic propositions. The advantage is that there is no longer any need to specify how the predicate is supposed to be part of the subject (thought in the subject by the utterer, presupposed by the dictionary definition, implicit in the relevant linguistic community, etc.). The disadvantage is that this way of presenting analytic propositions is not entirely accurate. The predicate is not really identical with the subject, although, if identical, the proposition would still be analytic; but I understand this relation of identity as follows: it is impossible for the predicate to be denied of the subject (in the case of affirmative propositions). I will present this as an implication of identity, but in the context of my argument it is more basic in the understanding of the relation of identity for analytic propositions. Again, I allow this circular move here in order to avoid some of the debates concerning the analytic/synthetic distinction.

With this background in place, the worry of an anti-constitutivist, like Wiland, can be expressed more specifically in the following way. The issue is one of performing magic, because, if the premises from which the constitutivist starts already include the substantial account of normative reasons for action that the constitutivist claims to be able to derive (for instance, the desires to help and not interfere mentioned by Smith), then these premises are not really abstract or slender, although as we have seen in the definition of constitutivism, they should be so. If those premises do not already include this substantial account, then a substantial account cannot be derived from them analytically. If it is not derived from them analytically, then it should be derived synthetically and, yet, if it is to be derived synthetically, then the validity of the derivation will be either contingent (for instance, when based on experience) or necessary (in which case it becomes a synthetic a priori derivation).

What is specific for a substantial *normative* account, however, is its necessity: the claim that something *should* be the case (whether ethically, aesthetically or from some normative perspective) is stronger than the claim that that thing is the case and implies a specific requirement. Yet, in Smith's account, it is unclear how such a derivation is to be obtained and no indication that one of the premises in the argument would be synthetic a priori.

Smith does not examine the nature of the constitutivist argument, which is supposed to take us from some abstract premises about agency to some substantial normative conclusions, although he does present the argument in detail; nor does Korsgaard examine the nature of the constitutivist argument, although she does indicate a promising avenue, which I will investigate in the next three sections. This is the promise of a transcendental argument, which would take us from abstract premises to substantial normative claims. Transcendental arguments have been discussed in the literature and they are still a topic at issue. There is yet no overall agreement with regard to their role, their structure and how they are supposed to function. They are, therefore, perhaps most appropriate for the task of performing the magic expected from constitutivism.

4 Korsgaard's "Transcendental" Argument

Consider the following discussion of a transcendental argument offered by Christine Korsgaard in *The Sources of Normativity* (1996). First, according to her, we can assume that the human mind is "essentially self-reflective" (p. 92). This means that we have a capacity to turn our attention to our own mental activities, "to distance ourselves from them and to call them into question".[13] (p. 93) This threefold process of self-reflection, distancing and questioning enables us to have control over our actions: we can act only by motivational factors, which we decide to endorse or which we decide not to oppose. We can in this way control our incentives and, generally, any other factors that may prompt us to act. In order for such mental activities to be motivational, that is, in order for them to motivate us, we need to endorse them (or at least indirectly to endorse them by allowing them) to be determining grounds of our actions.

For instance, I may have a powerful desire to play computer games at the moment; upon reflection, distancing and questioning, I realise that, given an already made commitment to finishing this article by a certain deadline, I should continue to work. Hence, a mental activity, like my desire to play, will motivate me to act (and leave my work), if I endorse it or at least if I do not oppose it. The process whereby I decide whether to allow this desire to be a ground for my leaving my work for play may involve reflection on that desire, as well as reflection on other reasons I might have for or against it.[14]

Secondly, let us suppose I act; this happens if the questioning reflective process ends with an answer. I may conclude the questioning process with the outcome that I should act on one of the motivational mental activities (that particular desire or some other inclinations or predispositions). Given that I could also have acted on other motivational mental activities, the fact that I acted in this way and not in some other way indicates that I had a reason to endorse this motivation (even when this reason was that of *illustrating* an action which is performed in a particular way for *no* specific reason).

Hence, the conclusion of the reflective process is meant to provide me with a normative result: the obligation, permission or prohibition, which I have reason to endorse or to allow, is right.[15] For instance, I now have a reason to continue to work, rather than play computer games, *because* I have a previous commitment to completing my work by a particular deadline *and* leaving my work to play would make the completion of the project by the specific deadline less likely.

---

13 "...this sets us a problem that no other animal has. It is the problem of the normative. For our capacity to turn our attention on to our own mental activities is also a capacity to distance ourselves from them, and call them into question". (p. 93)

14 I do not think this process needs to be self-reflective, in the sense of being explicitly self-conscious; in other words, it need not involve my awareness that it is *me* who is thinking about my desires and similar mental activities; but it can be self-reflective simply in the sense that I reflect on *my* mental activities.

15 The sense in which they are right may be a precise one for the agent, but I need not specify at this stage a particular sense—say, a moral sense or an all-things-considered sense.

My reason provides a justification, which usually makes reference to a principle or value (carrying out what one committed oneself to do is good) and indicates what seems to me to be what I should do. 'Reason', therefore, is a "normative word", which "refers to a kind of reflective success". (p. 93) The same, Korsgaard says, goes for the words "good" and "bad". (p. 94)

Now, if reasons are the result of reflective success, the next question is how I can lead the reflective process to a successful conclusion. Given that the process of reflective questioning is one, through which I choose which motivational element to act on, the answer, according to Korsgaard, is that "the principle or law by which you determine your actions is one that you regard as being expressive of *yourself*". (p. 100) For instance, in deciding that I should complete what I committed myself to completing, I assume that the principle of keeping promises is valuable for me. This, in its turn, means that the principle functions as *my* principle of action, and, in this sense, it is expressive of me.

That this principle is expressive of me is another way of saying that I take it to be justified, that it is right to act in this way given the kind of person I am and the situation where I find myself. As an implication, we can say that I act based on an evaluative identity or, in other words, based on a view of myself which I value. It is under such a view that, according to Korsgaard, I find my life "to be worth living" and my actions, "worth undertaking". (p. 101)

One extreme illustration of this account that Korsgaard offers is a reaction against a "threat of a loss of identity". (p. 102) A loss of identity seems to be behind claims such as: "*I* cannot do this", when an action that seems morally abhorrent is suggested to a moral agent. For the agent feels that acting in that way would mean abandoning some fundamental principle, a principle without which she would not be the same person and without which perhaps her life would not be worth living. Hence, a person may be capable of sacrificing herself, when the alternative would be conceived as incompatible with the kind of person she is.[16] We should bear in mind, however, that, in many cases, our reasons for action derive from contingent and local identities. We belong to various groups and

---

16 As an illustration, consider the example of ethnologist and philosopher of culture Mircea Vulcanescu. He had been incarcerated for political reasons by the Romanian Communist regime in September 1946 in the Aiud Penitentiary. The conditions in prison were appalling and, with Vulcanescu, there were also other ill inmates (he himself had contracted tuberculosis, but was not allowed any treatment in spite of recommendations from the penitentiary's doctors); one of the inmates was so ill, he could not stand, and had to lie down on very cold concrete floor. To help him, Vulcanescu set himself on the floor, so that his ill cell colleague would lie on his body, rather than directly on the floor. Not doing anything when someone was in need was perhaps incompatible with Vulcanescu's personality to the point of self-sacrifice.

clubs, and our memberships change periodically, sometimes without any thoroughly considered reasons and sometimes even when, as in the extreme case presented above, they seemed to be aspects of our identities without which we could not exist.[17]

Thirdly, and as a result, one way to understand scepticism, Korsgaard says, is as "the fear that we might not find what Kant called 'the unconditioned'." (p. 94) Hence, one problem is to account for normative claims, which are not conditional on local and contingent identities. To account for such a claim, we can start with some contingent identities: we are born in a certain family or community, and sometimes into a profession or craft, we form ties to other persons, movements and ideas, and, as contingent, many of these identities can be shed. (p. 120) Yet, if all these identities can be shed and no identity has an unconditional character, then the sceptic may question whether there is anything more than contingent standards in morality.

In answer to this, Korsgaard suggests that what is *not* contingent is that an agent must be governed by *some* conception of practical identity, by *some* project. Without an identity, even a local and contingent one, there is no reason to do one thing, rather than another one and, hence, no reason to act at all. Yet, the commitment, or rather meta-commitment, to having *some* practical identity is not derived from one of the contingent identities: "it is a reason that springs from your humanity itself, from your identity simply as *a human beings*, a reflective animal who needs reasons to act and to live". (p. 121)

On Korsgaard's account, therefore, in order to answer the sceptical worry we need to account for an unconditional requirement (whether an obligation, per-

---

17 Two issues can be considered here and it might be worth distinguishing them explicitly. There is first the issue of the unconditionality of a normative requirement. Let us say that I enjoy drinking coffee and that I now feel a desire to drink coffee, which is based on the expectation of enjoyment. Given that I value drinking coffee, there is a normative requirement for me to bring about a situation where I drink coffee. One question here is whether all normative requirements are of this type, namely, contingent on some subjective factor, such as the preference for coffee, which is presumably based on the particular way I am made up physiologically, as well as on my particular circumstances. Let us now assume that there is at least an unconditional requirement, a requirement that is not conditional on subjective factors. For instance, Korsgaard thinks that there is an unconditional requirement that we are committed to some value. The second question is whether all normative requirements (conditional or unconditional) are requirements or duties to myself or whether there are also requirement and duties to others, where this question is not simply a question of whether I can conceive of such duties and requirements to others, but whether there are such justified standards. The question I discuss in relation to Korsgaard is the former, not the latter. When the sceptic doubts normativity, she doubts that there is anything that can obligate her unconditionally.

mission or prohibition[18]). Because such a requirement stems from reasons, which are provided by practical identities, the unconditional obligation will have to stem from a practical identity, which is necessary. We have seen that, as self-reflective beings, having *some* practical identity is necessary, if we are to be able to act. Hence, as agents, we are committed to the non-contingent requirement of having some practical identity. This non-contingent requirement is part of our identity as human beings; hence, it is part of our humanity. Identities which provide reasons (whether conditional or not) are evaluative, and, in order for them to be evaluative, we need to be committed to their validity. Given that the non-contingent requirement, to the validity of which we must be committed, is part of our humanity, it follows that we must be committed to our humanity or, in other words, "humanity [...] must be valued". Given that this is a non-contingent identity, it "must be valued for its own sake". (p. 122)[19]

This, according to Korsgaard, can answer the sceptic: if the sceptic is a human being and if he agrees with her argument, then the sceptic must value his humanity, if he is to act at all:

> Since you are human, you *must* take something to be normative, that is, some conception of practical identity must be normative for you. If you had no normative conception of your identity, you could have no reasons for action, and because your consciousness is reflective, you could then not act at all. [...] The argument I have just given is a transcendental argument. (p. 123)

Korsgaard's transcendental argument can therefore be summarised as follows: the sceptic doubts the possibility of an unconditional requirement—he doubts (what we can call) practical normativity; yet, human beings are reflective beings, who need reasons to act; reasons to act are provided by evaluative identities (identities we value) and, as evaluative identities, these identities are particular

---

18 Of course, an obligation requires that a particular action be performed, a prohibition requires that we refrain from performing a specific action, whereas a permission asserts that there is no obligation either to perform or to refrain from performing a particular action. What is common to these three claims is that the claims to the performance of the actions, to the refraining from the performance and to the possibility of performing or not performing are *unconditional*. In other words, the claims are not dependent on a further subjective condition for their validity.

19 Again, as mentioned before (see n14), this 'must' refers to an unconditional requirement, which is derived from non-subjective grounds. To act, a person must be committed to some standard (a norm or value reflected by her identity or project) and, as we have seen (towards the end of Section 2) this necessary commitment to some standard is what Korsgaard considers to be our identity as human beings. When the fact that a person is so committed to her humanity is also valued by that person, Korsgaard says the person has moral identity.

instantiations of the unconditional requirement that, as human beings, we be committed to some identity. Yet, as a human being, the sceptic must himself act and, in order to do so, must rely on some unconditional evaluation—her identity as a human being; but this contradicts the sceptic's initial doubt, which must therefore be rejected.

If this is a transcendental argument, as Korsgaard claims it would be, then how exactly is it supposed to work?

5 A Reconstruction of Korsgaard's Argument

Consider a standard account of explorative or deductive transcendental arguments:

1. X.

2. Y is a necessary condition for the possibility of X.

3. Therefore Y.[20]

What are X and Y in Korsgaard's argument? She relies on the fact that human beings act and that a necessary condition, which makes possible actions for human beings, is that they be committed to some evaluative identity. Yet, this commitment to some evaluative identity is unconditional. Hence, if the sceptic is an agent (if she acts), then she cannot deny practical normativity, that is, she cannot deny the unconditional requirement provided by such an evaluative identity.[21]

---

20 For instance, in Illies (2003) or Stern (2014).

21 Recall that Korsgaard would like to show that the sceptic should acknowledge a commitment to the unconditional standard of having some evaluative identity or, in other words, he should acknowledge his moral identity; she thinks she can show this through a transcendental argument, which would demonstrate that his moral identity is constitutive of agency. This commitment is not a demand, which we actually are subject to in virtue of our moral identity; it is a commitment she thinks we have good reason to hold. By contrast, the commitment to having some identity is a commitment, which we have insofar as we are human beings, yet, it does not specify any particular demand, which we should actually be subject to; instead, it questions any such demand through the need for reasons for action. This is in short the answer to Smith's objection discussed in Section 2.

Korsgaard's argument can therefore be understood as a deductive transcendental argument in the following way (call this CA_1 or the Constitutivist Argument$_1$):[22]

P$_1$. Human beings act.

P$_2$. A necessary condition for the possibility of a human being's action is a commitment to an unconditional principle or value (a standard).

C. Human beings are committed to an unconditional standard.

This interpretation seems to be confirmed by Korsgaard's reformulation of the transcendental argument:

> I might bring that out more clearly by putting it this way: rational action exists, so we know it is possible. How is it possible? And then by the course of reflections in which we have just engaged, I show you that rational action is possible if and only if human beings find their own humanity to be valuable. But rational action is possible, and we are the human beings in question. Therefore we find ourselves to be valuable. (pp. 123–4)[23]

So Korsgaard does start from our actions as human beings, then identifies the necessary condition which makes action possible and then asserts this necessary condition. Since this necessary condition is that of being committed to an unconditional standard of action, and since this unconditional standard is part of our evaluative identity as human beings, it follows that we are committed to our humanity. The sceptic, insofar as she is an agent (that is, insofar as she acts), cannot doubt that she is committed to an unconditional standard and, hence, cannot doubt that there is normativity.

---

22 This deductive transcendental argument can easily be put in the form of a retorsive transcendental argument as follows:

The sceptical agent (a sceptical human being who acts) doubts practical normativity.

A necessary condition for the possibility of agency is a commitment to a norm.

Hence, agential doubt of normativity implies normativity.

23 Korsgaard talks here about *rational* action, whereas so far we have talked about mere *action*; this is because Korsgaard has pursued her argument in terms of mere action too: "To act from such a conception [of the right and the good] is to have a practical conception of your identity. [...] [F]or if you do not allow yourself to be governed by any conception of your identity, then you have no reason to act [...] Does it really matter whether we act as our humanity requires, whether we find some ways of identifying ourselves and stand by them? [...] If you had no normative conception of your identity, you could have no reason for action, and because your consciousness is reflective, you could then not act at all. Since you cannot act without reasons [...] you must value your own humanity, if you are to act at all" (pp. 122–3). As we will see later in this paper, however, there may be a good reason for her introduction of the qualifying "rational".

Now, consider the first premise in CA₁: Human beings act. This is a factual statement and usually the truth of factual statements is contingent. Necessary conditions depend on the truths for which they are conditions, so the necessary condition of acting will depend on the contingent truth of acting. This also implies that the (necessary) condition, which makes possible the contingent truth, will be a contingent truth, affected by the contingency of that for which it is a condition. Specifically, the commitment to the unconditional standard of humanity will be made manifest when we act, and if acting is contingent, being committed to the unconditional standard of humanity will also be contingent. This leaves it open for the sceptic to say that, although acting in the way in which Korsgaard understands it may presuppose a commitment to an unconditional standard, there seems to be no compelling reason to perform actions in that way.

The contingent character of the standards associated with my actions is one of the important issues in the literature on Pyrrhonian scepticism. For, according to the Pyrrhonian sceptic, it is possible to act without being committed to a particular belief, let alone to an unconditional standard: "Holding to the appearances, then, we live without beliefs but in accord with the ordinary regimen of life, since we cannot be wholly inactive". (Sextus Empiricus 1996, p. 92) Moreover, the model of agency that this form of scepticism advances is significantly different from that suggested by Korsgaard; the Pyrrhonian sceptic does not seem to be prompted by some evaluative identity, but by a form of assent that, while considering appearances, neither asserts nor denies them: "...for the sceptic does give assent to the *pathé* that are forced upon him by a *phantasia*; for example, when feeling hot (or cold) he would not say 'I seem not to be hot (or cold)'". (Sextus Empiricus 1985, p. 90)

The extent to which this alternative conception of action is viable is a topic at issue, and it would take me too far away from the topic of this paper to try to explore it here in any depth.[24] The important point to be drawn from this very sketchy discussion of scepticism is that, as long as the claim of a commitment to an unconditional standard is premised on a contingent truth, the sceptic has the legitimate option to doubt normativity (where 'legitimate' simply means non-self-undermining), since by regarding action as contingent he can also regard any commitment to an unconditional standard as contingent too.[25]

---

[24] For some illustrations with very suggestive titles, see Burnyeat (1980) and Greco (2012).
[25] So, there are two sceptical theses: one, according to which the starting point is contingent; the second, according to which the derivation from the starting point to the conclusion is contingent. I can only consider the first one in this paper; the second continues to be debated in the literature and I do not need to solve it here for the argument in this paper.

But let us assume that action in the first premise of CA$_1$ is not contingent: Human beings act, but *necessarily*—for instance, agency is a necessary condition of humanity, so that, human beings can only act.[26] As Korsgaard puts it in a more recent text, in a formulation with a distinctively existential flavour: "Human beings are *condemned* to choice and action". (Korsgaard 2009, p. 1—emphasis in the original)[27] If we understand the first premise of CA$_1$ in this way, namely, if we take it to involve a claim to necessity, then the transcendental argument with which we started becomes:

P$_1$'.   Human beings necessarily act.

P$_2$.   A necessary condition for the possibility of a human being's action is a commitment to an unconditional principle or value (a standard).

C'.   Human beings are necessarily committed to an unconditional standard.

Let us call this CA$_2$. Compared to CA$_1$, CA$_2$ only introduces a claim of necessity in premise P$_1$', a claim which, given that CA$_2$ is valid, is preserved in the conclusion C'.

One worry about this argument is that the first premise specifies action as a necessary feature of humanity; this is worrying since action may be right, wrong or morally indifferent. Assuming we understand 'human being' in a classificatory, rather than evaluative, sense, we will say that a human being can perform any of these three types of action. In this case, CA$_2$ claims that, in order to perform an action (whether right, wrong or morally indifferent), a human being must be committed to an unconditional standard. It follows as a result, however, that this standard will not have a specific content—it is a necessary condition of action, irrespective of whether the action is right, wrong or morally indifferent. Yet, then, even if the argument is correct, it cannot challenge the sceptic's claim

---

26 When I talk about 'humanity', in this context, I have in mind that in virtue of which we are human beings—in this case, acting. Thus, insofar as he is a human being, that is, insofar as he has humanity, a person necessarily acts.

27 I do not mean to suggest that the only alternative, or even that the suggestion, in Korsgaard, would be that action is analytically presupposed by 'human being'; it is equally possible that some other notion is analytically contained by 'human being' and this notion is part of a synthetic a priori principle, in virtue of which human beings necessarily act. A similar claim seems suggested by Korsgaard's earlier *The Sources of Normativity* (1996).

about normativity.[28] Moreover, if the aim is not simply that of proving the sceptic wrong, but also that of providing guidance for moral action, then this type of argument has no chances to succeed, since what it tries to establish are necessary conditions of action, including wrong actions, rather than action-guiding standards.

This suggests the following solution: if the first premise is understood as a statement specifically about right actions, then there is a chance for an argument for normativity and for specific guidance. I have mentioned above that in some formulations of her transcendental argument, Korsgaard refers not only to action, but to rational action. This, I think, is precisely what can motivate this change from a talk about actions to a talk about rational actions: if we take seriously Kant's claim that an action performed under the guidance of pure practical reason or the will is a moral action, then to talk about rational action is to talk about moral action too.[29] In this case, the transcendental argument becomes:

P_1''.   Human beings necessarily perform rational actions.

P_2'.   A necessary condition for the possibility of a human being's performing rational actions is a commitment to an unconditional standard.

C'.   Human beings are necessarily committed to an unconditional standard.

I make haste to note that, compared to P_2, P_2' is unproblematic—it is just P2 restricted in scope from reference to actions in general to an application to rational

---

28 If we assume that, in order to act, we need to be committed to a standard, then my action (whether right or wrong) will indicate I am committed to that standard. Yet, it is unclear whether this is a genuine commitment. As we have seen, for Korsgaard, being committed to standard S is the result of reflective success: I find a reason, which is sufficiently convincing about the value of S. Yet, the fact that I need to be committed to some identity in order to act is not a standard about which I seem to have any choice and does not seem to require any commitment. Its unconditional character is the result of the necessity of acting and this necessity of acting is not understood in any normative sense.

29 This can be read as an implication of what, according to Henry Allison, is Kant's Reciprocity Thesis: "This is the claim that freedom of the will and the moral law are reciprocal concepts. Kant affirms this explicitly in both works [the *Groundwork* and the *Critique of Practical Reason*]; correlatively, he also insists in both works that, although the moral law (or, better, the bindingness of the moral law for all rational agents) expresses a synthetic a priori proposition, it would be analytic if freedom of the will were presupposed." (Allison 1986, p. 394) Given that freedom of the will is the freedom of the pure practical reason, rational action in this sense is also free action.

actions only. P2' may not be interesting, since it is weaker than P2, but, in the context of the discussion of P2, it is unproblematic as far as its content is concerned. Thus, since a necessary condition for performing actions in general is a commitment to an unconditional standard, a necessary condition for performing right actions will also be a commitment to that unconditional standard. I will call this version of the argument CA_3.

CA_3 seems able to avoid the problems of CA_1 and CA_2: it asserts a commitment to an unconditional standard as a necessity, and it refers to rational or right actions and their necessary condition. The problem with CA_3 emerges when we pay closer attention to the response this argument offers in fact to the sceptic. For this response does not seem any more able to answer the sceptic and to offer practical guidance than the response offered by CA_2 does. For recall that the unconditional standard that is the necessary condition for the performance of right/rational actions is that of following *some* principle or value. This, however, is not informative, since it seems *any* principle or value would do.

To be sure, the claim made by the unconditional standard is not that it is *sufficient* to follow a wrong principle in order to perform a rational action—this would be counterintuitive; the claim is only that the performance of a rational action presupposes as a *necessary* condition the commitment to some standard—and this does not exclude wrong principles and evil values. Hence, although the conclusion might not be counterintuitive, it is not substantial either.

Moreover, as in the case of CA_2, we might try to argue that, although CA_3 does not conclude with our commitment to a substantial standard, nevertheless it does conclude, against the sceptic, with our commitment to an unconditional (even if only formal) standard. Yet, once CA_3 is restricted in its first premise to rational or right actions, it can no longer function as an answer to the initial sceptical challenge concerning unconditional normativity. For the argument seems to presuppose that there is something called right action that human beings necessarily perform, whereas the sceptic doubts unconditional normativity in general. This seems to suggest a serious problem for any attempt to construct such a transcendental argument: if the aim is to show that there is normativity, then the sceptic cannot accept that we necessarily perform right actions, so the starting point must be a necessity of acting in a more general sense, not restricted to the normative domain. In this case, however, if the transcendental argument is supposed to show that the sceptic herself must be committed to an unconditional standard, then this implies that we must accept the possibility of deriving an 'ought' from an 'is'. I take this to be problematic.[30]

---

30 It might seem that there is no is-ought fallacy committed at this point: it might simply be a

Be that as it may, I would like to argue that constitutivist arguments may still be able to provide results, which are action-guiding, if the necessary condition for the performance of rational actions is formulated as a more substantial moral standard. In fact, this is what Korsgaard eventually plans to show, namely, that we should follow the Categorical Imperative[31], as a necessary condition for the performance of (rational) actions. (pp. 98–100)[32] Let us assume this new move succeeds and she can show that a commitment to the Categorical Imperative is the necessary condition which makes possible rational actions. The constitutivist argument, which is the focus of this paper, becomes:

P_1". Human beings necessarily perform rational actions.

P_2". A necessary condition for the possibility of a human being's performing rational actions is a commitment to the Categorical Imperative.

---

matter of deriving a robust 'ought' from rational/normative features of actions. A clarificatory note is therefore apposite: the objection is correct for the usual sense of the is-ought fallacy, but I take the fallacy in a more general sense; consider some rational/normative features of actions—f_1, f_2, ... f_n; if they belong to actions which are rational, then, when I attribute them to a rational action, I describe what a rational action *is*; the issue of going from f_1, f_2, ...f_n to a robust ought is the same as that of going from the way a rational action *is* to the way it *ought* to be, were it to be moral.

31 According to Kant, for limited rational agents like us, the moral law appears in imperatival form, as a command. Hence, for us, the moral law is a Categorical Imperative. I use capital letters for this expression to distinguish it from the maxims, which pass the test of Kant's Categorical Imperative, maxims that Kant sometimes calls categorical imperatives too. Korsgaard draws this distinction differently, calling the "moral law" what Kant usually calls the Categorical Imperative and, the "categorical imperative" what Kant usually takes to be a maxim: "Any law is universal, but the argument I just gave doesn't settle the question of the *domain* over which the law of the free will must range. And there are various possibilities here. If the law is the law of acting on the desire of the moment, then the agent will treat each desire as a reason, and her conduct will be that of a wanton. If the law ranges over the agent's whole life, then the agent will be some sort of egoist". (p. 99)

32 In her later *Self-Constitution: Agency, Identity and Integrity* (2009), Korsgaard no longer uses explicitly the idea of a transcendental argument, but can still be interpreted as formulating one (see, for instance, Guyer 2013). Her strategy, this time, is to introduce an additional argumentative step concerning self-constitution. Being committed to the Categorical Imperative is not simply a necessary condition for the possibility of good agency, but a necessary condition for the possibility of good self-constitution: "a commitment to the moral law is built right into the activity that, by virtue of being human, we are necessarily engaged in: the activity of making something of ourselves." (Korsgaard 2009, xiii)

    C".   Human beings are necessarily committed to the Categorical Imperative.

Let us call this CA_4; this seems to be the best version of the transcendental argument offered by Korsgaard, or at least a version which is better than $CA_{1\text{-}3}$. There is of course a longstanding debate on the extent to which the Categorical Imperative is in any sense a substantial or informative standard. As I have mentioned, there is also a question concerning the extent to which Korsgaard can successfully show that the Categorical Imperative is indeed a necessary condition for the possibility of morally right actions. I am going to set aside these important issues, in order to focus on the main topic of this paper: assuming the Categorical Imperative is action-guiding and assuming the sceptic does not doubt normativity per se, but the ability we have to formulate specific standards which have justification, does the constitutivist argument offer an answer to the sceptic?

4 An Evaluation of Korsgaard's Argument

First, I am going to assume that P_2" is correct[33], in order to focus on P_1". I am focusing on this premise, since it seems to make a very strong claim. It is unclear in what sense we can say that we necessarily perform rational actions. Any case of weakness of will or evil action shows the contrary. We could understand the claim as more limited—say, human beings necessarily perform *some* rational actions. But this interpretation would defeat the argument's purpose: we are interested in refuting the sceptic and getting practical guidance; if the conclusion of the argument will be that human beings are necessarily committed to the Categorical Imperative in some instances, then this would no longer be a commitment to an unconditional standard. If the validity of a standard were limited to certain instances, then the standard would no longer be unconditional.

    To be sure, there are instances where we may not be under the obligation of acting under the Categorical Imperative—say, when we are asleep.[34] But this is because when we are asleep we are not treated as responsible agents. This may suggest a better interpretation of P_1": Human beings necessarily perform rational actions, insofar as they are human beings. Although this may account for

---

33 Any moral theorist who is not a Kantian and who does not think that to act morally is to act rationally will challenge P_2".
34 This is an example inspired by Peter Steinberger's "The Standard View of the Categorical Imperative" (1999, p. 95)

situations where we may be justified in not treating one person as a responsible agent, it is still not enough to make the premise plausible. This is because even in cases where we can legitimately treat a person as morally responsible, it may still be possible for that person to act irrationally or against reason. Only if we take 'human being' to mean not simply a responsible being, but a responsible rational or morally good human being, can P_1" be more palatable.

Yet, on this interpretation of P_1", where 'human being' is taken in an evaluative sense, the claim is almost tautological: namely, the claim is that human beings, in the sense of responsible and rational, good beings, necessarily perform rational actions. It is unclear to me how, on this reading, the argument will help in any way with a response to the sceptic's challenge concerning unconditional normativity, since this seems to be already assumed. Nevertheless, the argument might provide a response to the question of moral guidance—it might be that the conclusion could provide an unconditional standard to which human beings, in the evaluative sense of the expression, must be committed. For recall that the two issues considered here in relation to the skeptical challenge is the commitment to an unconditional standard and the possibility of specifying the standard or standards to which we should be so committed—so while the argument cannot respond to the former issue, it might still be able to respond to the latter.

Let us now move on to P_2": A necessary condition for the possibility of a human being's performing rational actions is a commitment to the Categorical Imperative. As already said, I am going to assume this is correct; what I am interested in at this stage is the way in which it is correct. In particular, I am interested in the nature of the necessity involved in this claim. What does it mean to say that the commitment to the Categorical Imperative is a *necessary* condition which makes possible a human being's performing rational actions? Let us return to the analytic/synthetic distinction. P_2" is a judgement expressing a necessity and, as we have seen, necessities can be formulated in two ways[35]: either in the form of an analytic judgement or in the form of a synthetic a priori judgement.

Most recent Kantian philosophers have tried to provide accounts of some of Kant's insights, but without the metaphysics of transcendental idealism. A synthetic a priori judgement, on a standard interpretation, needs the Kantian metaphysics; insofar as such a judgement is synthetic, it can only be made a priori if

---

35 There seems to be no reason to think that there would be a third possibility for accounting for necessity that would be introduced by Korsgaard; she does draw a distinction in her *Self-Constitution* between three forms of necessity, but there is no explicit account of how we are to understand the notion of necessity she favours. See Korsgaard (2009, pp. 1–2).

the two parts of the judgement which are connected synthetically are connected either through an a priori intuition or through the idea of freedom. For instance, according to Kant, '7 + 5 = 12' is synthetic a priori because it is a substantial claim. As we have seen[36], we cannot derive the notion of twelve from the notion of the addition of the numbers 7 and 5. We get to this result by constructing through our a priori intuitions (either through a spatial or through a temporal representation, but in the case of this example, through a temporal representation of the numbers and their sum) the mathematical operation and its result.

Whether we regard an a priori intuition or an idea of reason as able to connect synthetically and a priori the parts of the judgement, we would need to accept at least parts of Kant's metaphysics. This is because space and time (as a priori intuitions) and freedom (as an idea of reason) could unify parts of a judgement only if we regarded them as structural elements of the mind, and this, I would argue, presupposes at least some important parts of transcendental idealism.[37]

If so, then one alternative is to regard P_2" as analytic and to understand the necessity of the commitment to the Categorical Imperative as the result of the fact that this commitment is already presupposed by the notion of performing rational or moral actions. In the same way in which a necessary condition for the possibility of being a bachelor is to be unmarried, a necessary condition for the possibility of performing rational actions is to be committed to the Categorical Imperative. To make this more palatable, we can rephrase the condition so that it is not expressed directly as a Categorical Imperative, but as, say, a principle of universalisability or of not treating others merely as ends for our purposes.

But this has problematic implications for CA_4. Thus, if part of being human (in the evaluative sense) is to perform rational actions and if performing rational actions means being committed to the Categorical Imperative, then CA_4 only makes explicit something that was already implicit in the evaluative sense of the notion of a human being. One possibility is for the sceptic to agree with this notion of a human being, but, then, she does not need an argument to accept a commitment to an unconditional standard. The other possibility is when she does not agree with the evaluative notion of human being, in which case CA_4 cannot help, since all CA_4 does is to make explicit something already included in the evaluative notion of human being.

---

36 See n12 above.
37 See also Baiasu (2011).

The only alternative left, then, is that P_2" would represent a claim to necessity provided by a synthetic a priori judgement. For instance, rational agency and the Categorical Imperative could be connected through freedom. Since the Categorical Imperative is a law of freedom and action presupposes freedom, we can perhaps assert P_2" as a synthetic a priori judgement. As a synthetic judgement, P_2" would assert something about the rational actions of good human beings, which would not already be included in these notions. If the necessary condition of rational action is a commitment to an unconditional standard, and if this commitment is not simply a commitment to something already presupposed by the notion of a morally good human being, then the argument can refute the sceptic and provide an action-guiding moral criterion. This would then be the path that would need to be followed by a constitutivist in order to offer a substantial account of normative reasons or standards of action and at the same time to refute scepticism about such an account by starting from premises that are sufficiently weak to be acceptable also to the sceptic.

5 Conclusion

In this paper, I have argued that constitutivism can represent a genuine avenue for constructivist attempts to formulate normative standards without realist metaphysical presuppositions and in a non-arbitrary, principled way. I have focused specifically on Korsgaard's constitutivism and on an epistemic aspect of the debate concerning constitutivism. More precisely, I discussed whether it is possible to construct substantial normative standards through an argument with premises, which are less substantial normatively. In general, supporters of constitutivism argue that such a justification of normative standards is possible and they present various arguments as illustrations of how such a justification is to be carried out, yet they do not examine the nature of such an argument. This leaves them open to the accusations that what they are trying to achieve is only possible by magic.

Unlike other supporters of constitutivism, Korsgaard makes an important suggestion about the nature of such an argument—she thinks a transcendental argument can perform the magic of pulling the normative rabbit out of the constitutivist's hat. If successful, such an argument would enable her to answer the sceptic who doubts the existence of unconditional practical standards. It would enable her to answer also the related question of the possibility of deriving robust practical norms from slender premises, which represents a version of the classical problem of empty formalism any Kantian moral theorist needs to face.

I began with an objection to Korsgaard's constitutivism in *The Sources of Normativity*, an objection according to which, in that text, Korsgaard's starting point is an account of persons as essentially defined in a way which attributes them, as a matter of fact, some demand. The objection, by Michael Smith, is in fact a quarrel in the family, as it is a supporter of constitutivism that formulates it. It is, therefore, not so much an objection to the promise of constitutivism, as to the particular version formulated by Korsgaard. However, we have seen that this criticism is unwarranted and very likely generated by Korsgaard's talk of reasons as deriving from specific identities and roles we are committed to in our everyday life. The criticism is unwarranted, because, although our identities and roles do come with particular demands, the source of our commitment to them is grounded in a more fundamental identity we have as reflective beings, who need reasons in order to commit to particular roles and projects, and in order to act. Korsgaard takes as starting point this more fundamental identity, which sets us the task of justification and reason-providing, rather than attributing to us a particular demand as already justified and normative.

After an excursus aiming to bring more clarity to the conceptual framework, in particular the analytic-synthetic distinction, I have presented in more detail Korsgaard's account of agency, I reconstructed her transcendental argument and I have evaluated the strongest version. The evaluation of the argument has shown that the crucial aspect of the argument is the premise, which links the starting point (the account of agency) and the conclusion (the commitment to the normative standard). This premise needs to be synthetic and a priori, if it is to enable the argument to function in the expected way. Yet, in order to be able to justify a synthetic a priori judgement, we need to adopt some form of transcendental idealism.[38]

Whereas such a commitment would still be compatible with the constructivist's intention to avoid metaphysical realism in practical philosophy and arbitrary decisions about the normative standard to be observed, it would go in a different direction than that intended by Korsgaard, who has been careful to avoid commitments to transcendental idealism. Quite independently of this, transcendental idealism has been criticised in various ways; one longstanding and reiterated criticism has been that it fails for offer a distinct metaphysical position and ultimately collapses into, and becomes indistinguishable from, traditional idealism with all its problems. While I think the latter criticism is unwarranted, all this

---

38 For a recent good discussion of some versions of transcendental idealism, see Richard Aquila (2015).

shows is that a viable constitutivism comes with what are standardly regarded as quite high costs.[39]

Bibliography

Allison, Henry E. (1986): "Morality and Freedom: Kant's Reciprocity Thesis". In: *The Philosophical Review* 95. No. 3, pp. 393 – 425.

Aquila, R. (2015): "The Transcendental Idealisms of Kant and Sartre". In: Sorin Baiasu (Ed.): *Comparing Kant and Sartre*. London: Palgrave Macmillan, pp. 217 – 256.

Bagnoli, Carla (2016): "Constructivism in Metaethics." In: Edward N. Zalta (Ed.): *The Stanford Encyclopedia of Philosophy*. http://plato.stanford.edu/archives/spr2016/entries/constructivism-metaethics/, visited on July 11 2016.

Bagnoli, Carla (2009): "The Mafioso Case: Autonomy and Self-Respect". In: *Ethical Theory and Moral Practice* 12. No 5, pp. 477 – 493.

Baiasu, Sorin (2016): "Is Kant's Metaphysics Profoundly Unsatisfactory?". In: *Kantian Review* 21. No 3., Forthcoming.

Baiasu, Sorin (2013): "Caird on Kant's Idealism: Traditionalist or Revolutionary?" In: *Collingwood and British Idealism Studies* 19. No. 1, pp. 19 – 45.

Baiasu, Sorin (2011): "Space, Time and Mind-Dependence." In: *Kantian Review* 16. No. 2, pp. 175 – 90.

Bratman, Michael E. (1998): "The Sources of Normativity". In: *Philosophy and Phenomenological Research* 58. No. 3, pp. 699 – 709.

Burnyeat, M. (1998): "Can the Sceptic Live His Scepticism?" In: Myles F. Burnyeat/Michael Frede (Eds.): *The Original Sceptics: A Controversy*. Indianapolis, Ind: Hackett, pp. 117 – 148.

Cohen, G. A. (1996): "Reason, Humanity, and the Moral Law." In: Korsgaard (1996), pp. 167 – 188.

Coleman, M. C. (2006): "Korsgaard on Kant on the Value of Humanity". In: *Journal of Value Inquiry* 40. No. 4, pp. 475 – 478.

Crisp, Roger (2006): *Reasons and the Good*. New York: Oxford University Press.

Enoch, David (2006): "Agency, Shmagency: Why Normativity Won't Come From What Is Constitutive of Action". In: *Philosophical Review* 115. No. 2, pp. 169 – 98.

Firth, Roderick (1952): "Ethical Absolutism and the Ideal Observer". In: *Philosophy and Phenomenological Research* 12. No. 2, pp. 317 – 45.

FitzPatrick, William J. (2005): "The Practical Turn in Ethical Theory: Korsgaard's Constructivism, Realism and the Nature of Normativity". In: *Ethics* 115. No. 3, pp. 651 – 691.

Galvin, Richard (2011): "Rounding up the Usual Suspects: Varieties of Kantian Constructivism in Ethics". In: *Philosophical Quarterly* 61. No. 262, pp. 16 – 36.

Gibbard, Alan (1999): "Morality as Consistency in Living". In: *Ethics* 110. No.1, pp. 140 – 164.

---

39 See also my texts Baiasu (2013 and 2016).

Greco, Daniel (2012): "The Impossibility of Skepticism". In: *Philosophical Review* 121. No. 3, pp. 317 – 58.

Hanna, Robert (2015): *Cognition, Content, and the A Priori: A Study in the Philosophy of Mind and Knowledge*. Oxford: Oxford University Press.

Hanna, Robert (2012): "The Return of the Analytic-Synthetic Distinction." In: *Paradigmi. Rivista Di Critica Filosofica* 30. No. 1, pp. 19 – 68.

Hare, Richard M. (1983): "Rawls' Theory of Justice." In: *Philosophical Quarterly* 23. Repr. (1989) *Essays in Ethical Theory*. Oxford: Clarendon Press.

Illies, Christian (2003): *The Grounds of Ethical Judgement: New Transcendental Arguments in Moral Philosophy*. Oxford: Clarendon Press.

Larmore, Charles (2008): *The Autonomy of Morality*. Cambridge: Cambridge University Press.

Kant, Immanuel (1996): *Critique of Pure Reason: Unified Edition*. Ed. by James W. Ellington, Tr. Werner S. Pluhar. Indianapolis, Ind: Hackett Publishing Company.

Kant, Immanuel (1900 ff): *Gesammelte Schriften*. Vols. 1 – 22 Preussische Akademie der Wissenschaften; Vol. 23 Deutsche Akademie der Wissenschaften zu Berlin; Vols. 24 ff. Akademie der Wissenschaften zu Göttingen.

Kerstein, Samuel J. (2001): "Korsgaard's Kantian Arguments for the Value of Humanity". In: *Canadian Journal of Philosophy* 31. No. 1, pp. 23 – 52.

Korsgaard, Christine M. (2009): *Self-Constitution: Agency, Identity, and Integrity*. Oxford: Oxford University Press.

Korsgaard, Christine M. (2003): "Realism and Constructivism in Twentieth-Century Moral Philosophy". In: *The Journal of Philosophical Research*. APA Centennial Supplement, pp. 99 – 122.

Korsgaard, Christine (1996): *The Sources of Normativity*. Cambridge: Cambridge University Press.

Krasnoff, Larry (1999): "How Kantian Is Constructivism?" In: *Kant-Studien* 90. No. 4, pp. 385 – 409.

O'Neill, Onora (1989): *Constructions of Reason*. Cambridge: Cambridge University Press.

O'Neill, Onora (1992): "Vindicating Reason" In: Paul Guyer (Ed.): *The Cambridge Companion to Kant*. Cambridge: Cambridge University Press, pp. 280 – 308.

Railton, Peter (1986): "Moral Realism". In: *Philosophical Review* 95. No. 1, pp. 163 – 207.

Raz, Joseph (2003): "Numbers, With and Without Contratualism". In: *Ratio* 16. No. 4, pp. 346 – 67.

Ridge, Michael (2005): "Why Must We Treat Humanity With Respect? Evaluating the Regress Argument". In: *European Journal of Analytic Philosophy* 1. No. 1, pp. 57 – 74.

Scanlon, Thomas M. (1998): *What We Owe to Each Other*. Cambridge, Mass.: Harvard University Press.

Scanlon, Thomas M. (2003): "Replies". In: *Ratio* 16. No. 4, pp. 391 – 423.

Setiya, Kieran (2007): *Reasons Without Rationalism*. Princeton, NJ: Princeton University Press.

Sextus, Empiricus (1985): *Selections from Major Writings on Scepticism, Man and God*. Ed. by Philip P. Hallie. Indianapolis, Ind: Hackett Publishing.

Sextus, Empiricus (1996): *Outlines of Pyrrhonism*. Ed. and transl. by Benson Mates. Oxford/New York: Oxford University Press.

Shafer-Landau, Ross (2003): *Moral Realism*. Oxford: Clarendon Press.

Smith, Michael (2015): "The Magic of Constitutivism". In: *American Philosophical Quarterly* 52. No. 2, pp. 187 – 200.

Steinberger, Peter J. (1999): "The Standard View of the Categorical Imperative". In: *Kant-Studien* 90. No. 1, pp. 91–9.

Stern, Robert (2015): "Transcendental Arguments". In: Edward N. Zalta (Ed.): *The Stanford Encyclopedia of Philosophy*. http://plato.stanford.edu/archives/sum2015/entriesranscendental-arguments/, visited on July 11 2016.

Street, Sharon (2010): "What is Constructivism in Ethics and Metaethics?". In *Philosophy Compass*, 5. No. 2, pp. 363–384.

Timmons, Mark (2003): "The Limits of Moral Constructivism". In: *Ratio* 16. No. 4, pp. 391–423.

Velleman, James D. (2009): *How We Get Along*. Cambridge: Cambridge University Press.

Wiland, Eric (2012): *Reasons*. London: Continuum.

Deryck Beyleveld

Transcendental Arguments for a Categorical Imperative as Arguments from Agential Self-Understanding

Abstract: This chapter construes Kant's contention that a categorical imperative is a synthetic a priori principle as equivalent to Gewirth's claim that such an imperative is a dialectically necessary principle (a strict requirement of agential self-understanding). It is not concerned to defend either Kant's or Gewirth's argument for a categorical imperative, but to elucidate the "dialectically necessary method" (which rests on the dialectical necessity of a principle making it categorically binding) and to defend this method against David Enoch's critique of "constitutivism" (taken as trying to show that transcendental arguments for morality, construed as dialectically necessary ones, are futile, even if they can be successful, because normativity cannot be constituted in dialectical necessity). In the process, it relates the dialectically necessary method to internalism, naturalism, foundationalism, coherentism, and realism.

Introduction

According to Kant,[1] *if* a categorical imperative (CI) exists, "it must (completely a priori) already be bound up with the concept of the will of a rational being as such" *(GW* 4:427) without being contained within this concept *(GW* 4:420). So, proving that it exists requires a *"synthetic use of pure practical reason" (GW* 4:445), making it a synthetic a priori principle *(GW* 4:440; *C2* 5:31; 5:46).

It is generally presumed that Kant's synthetic a priori propositions require transcendental arguments for their justification. It is, however, debatable what Kant thinks a transcendental argument for a practical principle is. A very popular view is that, in *C2,* Kant reverses (and retreats from) his *GW* claim that agents are bound by the moral law (a CI for human agents, who are affected by heteronomous incentives) because they necessarily presuppose that they have freewill

---

1 I refer to Kant's works on the basis of the Academy edition of the *Gesammelte Schriften* (Kant 1990sqq), stating volume and page number. Translations are those of the *Cambridge Edition of the Works of Immanuel Kant* (Kant 1995sqq). I use the abbreviation *GW* for *Groundwork of the Metaphysics of Morals, C2* for *Critique of Practical Reason,* and *C3* for *Critique of the Power of Judgment.*

DOI 10.1515/9783110470215-008

(FW), by holding that the moral law is given to agents as the sole fact of pure reason, thus providing a different account of what makes it a synthetic a priori principle.[2] In my opinion, this is a mistake: Kant never abandons his *GW* view that a maxim M is constituted as a CI by its acceptance being a strict requirement of agential self-understanding (by the fact that a human agent, call her "Agnes", misunderstands what it is for her to be an agent, and denies implicitly that she is an agent, by denying that she unconditionally ought to comply with M). In Alan Gewirth's (1978) terms, the CI is justified by showing that M is dialectically necessary for Agnes.[3]

I will offer reasons for this opinion; but my primary aims are to elucidate the dialectically necessary method (DNM), by outlining Gewirth's argument for his Principle of Generic Consistency (PGC),[4] and by construing Kant's reasoning for the CI in the guise of the Formula of Humanity (FoH)[5] and the Formula of Universal Law (FUL) in its terms;[6] and then to defend the DNM against David Enoch's (2006) critique of "constitutivism", which he attributes primarily to Christine Korsgaard[7] and David Velleman,[8] but also to Gewirth.

---

2 Seminally, Dieter Henrich (1960). Pauline Kleingeld (2002, pp. 60–61) provides a brief overview of retreatist positions.

3 E.g., Onora O'Neill (2002) and Pauline Kleingeld (2010) also think that Kant does not retreat from his *GW* position. O'Neill, however, thinks that Kant's appeal to the fact of reason in *C2* offers no justification for the moral law, serving a different aim, which contrasts with my view that "the fact of reason" is just another way of stating his position in *GW*. Kleingeld's view is similar to mine on the issue of 'retreat' without using Gewirthian terminology, but is less expansive, and views the issue of "reversal" differently.

4 The PGC requires Agnes to grant all agents positive and negative rights (GR) to generic conditions of agency (GCAs). A GCA is something Agnes needs to be able to even try to act (something the absence of which has a negative effect, either immediately or if prolonged, on her ability to act at all) or to have any general chances of success in achieving her purposes, *regardless of what her purposes are or might be.* GR are rights under the will-conception (meaning that Agnes can release other agents from their duties to her under her GR). Further specification is unnecessary here.

5 *"So act that you use humanity, whether in your own person or in the person of any other, always at the same time as an end, never merely as a means"* (GW 4:429).

6 *"[A]ct only in accordance with that maxim through which you can at the same time will that it become a universal law"* (GW 4:421).

7 Specifically, claims made in Korsgaard (2002).

8 E.g., Velleman (2004). I will not consider Korsgaard's and Velleman's positions.

The DNM[9]

The DNM's Rationale and Criteria

The DNM presupposes that only agents—those able (because of their capacities for reason and understanding) to pursue means voluntarily for their chosen purposes and disposed to do so—are intelligibly addressors or addressees of practical precepts of any kind concerning the permissibility of their behaviour, and that simply by virtue of having capacities for reason and understanding, Agnes cannot evade the question of what, if anything, she may do/ought to do. Thus, the question necessarily arises for Agnes of the possibility of a CI (a maxim that reason requires her to comply with regardless of anything only contingently related to her), which is equivalent to the question of the possibility of purposes that reason requires Agnes to regard as ends in themselves.

In effect, the DNM construes Kant's assertion that a CI is connected completely a priori with the concept of the will of a rational being as such but not contained in it, as the view that a CI is a maxim M that is dialectically necessary for Agnes (A) to accept, an M of which it is true that $\{AM\}_{(A)}$.[10]

$\{AM\}_{(A)} \rightarrow$[11] "Agnes categorically ought to comply with M" because $\{AM\}_{(A)} \rightarrow$ "If Agnes denies that she ought to comply with M then she simultaneously implies that she is not an agent (by misunderstanding what it is for her to be an agent) and that she is an agent (because she presupposes that she is an agent in making *any* claim *about* what she may do/ought to do)". So, the only coherent attitude Agnes can have towards M is that she unconditionally ought to comply with it, and the DNM's criterion *for rationally permissible action* (CRA) is: "It is only rational for an agent to act in accord with a maxim if doing so complies with the agent's dialectically necessary commitments".

Correlatively, the DNM's criterion *to establish a CI* (CDNM) is: "Agnes must accept, and may only accept, her dialectically necessary commitments".

The DNM is conducted entirely within Agnes' first-person dialectically necessary viewpoint. This does not mean that Agnes may not refer to any other agent (say, Brian) or consider what he might think or do; merely that, in judging

---

9 My elucidation of the DNM builds on Beyleveld (1991), which received Gewirth's endorsement (Gewirth 1991), and Beyleveld (2013) and Beyleveld (2016) in particular.

10 "AM" = "Agnes ought to comply with M". Placing AM in face brackets signifies that AM is dialectically necessary, with the subscripted suffix (A) signifying that it is for Agnes that AM is dialectically necessary.

11 "$\rightarrow$" = "entails".

her dialectically necessary commitments, she may (and must) do so only if this is dialectically necessary for her.

The Gewirthian Argument for the PGC

The PGC is dialectically necessary for Agnes, = $\{PGC\}_{(A)}$, if

1   The Principle of Hypothetical Imperatives (PHI), "If having X (or doing X) is necessary for Agnes to pursue or achieve E, then Agnes ought to act to secure having X (or do X) or give up pursuit of E", is dialectically necessary for Agnes, = $\{PHI\}_{(A)}$.

2   There are GCAs.

3   Dialectically necessary commitments are (i) distributively universal (i.e., "It is dialectically necessary for Agnes to hold that she ought to do or have X" = $\{AoX\}_{(A)}$, → "It is dialectically necessary for Brian to hold that he ought to do or have X" = $\{BoX\}_{(B)}$), which is uncontroversial; and (ii) collectively universal (i.e., $\{AoX\}_{(A)}$ → $\{BoX\}_{(A)}$), which is highly contested.

1 coupled with 2 →

4   "It is dialectically necessary for Agnes to hold that she ought to defend having the GCAs (AoA), unless she is willing to accept generic damage to her ability to act (^{A})" = $\{AoA^A\}_{(A)}$.

4 coupled with 3 →

5a   (by distributive universalisation) "It is dialectically necessary for Brian to hold that he ought to defend having the GCAs, unless he is willing to accept generic damage to his ability to act" = $\{BoB^B\}_{(B)}$ and

5b   (by collective universalisation) "It is dialectically necessary for Agnes to consider that she ought to defend Brian's having the GCAs, unless he is willing to accept generic damage to his ability to act" = $\{AoB^B\}_{(A)}$, ≡

6    $\{$Brian has the GR$\}_{(A)}$ = $\{BGR\}_{(A)}$, which →

7    $\{AGR\}_{(A)}$, because $\{AoB^B ≡ BGR\}_{(A)}$ → $\{AoA^A ≡ AGR\}_{(A)}$.

6 coupled with 7 →

8    $\{PGC\}_{(A)}$, →

9      $\{PGC\}_{(A\&B)}$ (by distributive universalisation).

Gewirth's own argument for 3(ii), the "Argument from the Sufficiency of Agency" (Gewirth 1978, p. 110), is as follows: 7: $\{AGR\}_{(A)}$ → 7a: {"Agnes is an agent" → "AGR"}$_{(A)}$. This is because, if Agnes denies "Agnes is an agent" → "AGR", she holds "AGR" → "Agnes has a property D that she does not necessarily possess as *an* agent", so holds that if she does not have D then she may not hold "AGR". But then she violates the CDNM by holding something not permitted by 7. Ergo, she *must* deny that having D is necessary for AGR, and so accept 7a. But 7a → 7b: {"Brian is an agent" → "BGR"}$_{(A)}$. So, $\{AGR\}_{(A)}$ → $\{BGR\}_{(A)}$. Ergo, 3(ii): $\{AoX\}_{(A)}$ → $\{BoX\}_{(A)}$.[12]
    Alternatively:

i.   Suppose $\{AoX\}_{(A)}$.
ii.   To comply with AoX, Agnes needs Brian not to interfere with, and when she is unable to do so by her own unaided efforts, to defend her compliance. So,
iii. $\{AoX\}_{(A)}$ → {Brian ought to act in accord with AoX}$_{(A)}$, = $\{BocAoX\}_{(A)}$.
iv. $\{AoX\}_{(A)}$ → $\{BoX\}_{(B)}$. So $\{\{BoX\}_{(B)}\}_{(A)}$.
v.   By the CRA, iii is intelligible only if Brian can accept BocAoX without implying that he is not an agent ≡ only if BocAoX does not require him to act contrary to BoX. So,
vi $\{AoX\}_{(A)}$ → {" BocAoX" *iff* "BoX"}$_{(A)}$. Ergo,
3(ii) $\{AoX\}_{(A)}$ → $\{BoX\}_{(A)}$.

This has the advantage that nothing specific needs to be shown to be dialectically necessary to show that dialectically necessary commitments are collectively universal.[13]
    So, in essence, the Gewirthian argument is: As an agent, Agnes is necessarily confronted with the idea of a CI. If she fully understands this idea (and it is dialectically necessary for her to do so), she will accept that there is a CI: "Agnes ought to act only in accord with a maxim that does not conflict with her dialectically necessary commitments".

---

12 This argument makes dialectical necessity the *ratio cognoscendi* for the moral law and agency the *ratio essendi* for the PGC.
13 A third argument is presented in Beyleveld (2013, pp. 218–219). I consider that all three arguments entail each other.

Then, given (3), the CI is: "All agents ought to act only in accord with a maxim that does not require action contrary to any agent's dialectically necessary commitments".

This is not empty. Given also that there are GCAs, $\{PHI\}_{(A\&B)}$ renders it dialectically necessary for all agents to respect every agent's need for the GCAs..

Kant and the DNM

That Kant holds the moral law to be dialectically necessary in *GW* is plausible. Given his view that FW and the moral law are reciprocal *(GW 4:447; C2 5:29)* and that the CI is the form in which the moral law appears to human agents *(GW 4:454)*, his contention that agents necessarily suppose that they have FW (hence necessarily suppose that the moral law applies to them) as the only *idea* under which they can act (as the only condition under which they can understand themselves as acting) *(GW 4:448)* is readily construed in this way. This is supported by his view that a synthetic a priori proposition is one in which two cognitions are bound together by their connection with a third in which they are both to be found *(GW 4:447)*, because he identifies this third cognition with the positive concept of freedom *(GW 4:447)*, which is produced by agents recognising that they belong to the world of understanding *(GW 4:452)*.

My view, that Kant never departs from holding that the moral law is dialectically necessary, is that to say that the moral law is given as the fact of reason *(C2 5:31)* is to say that the moral law is dialectically necessary.[14]

As I see it, Kant's transcendental argument for the moral law, in both *GW* and *C2*, has two phases:

---

[14] If so, Pauline Kleingeld (2010, p. 65) is right that the fact of reason "is the *product* of reason's own activity".

Ph 1:   By virtue of being an agent, the question of the possibility of a CI/the moral law/pure reason being practical necessarily arises for Agnes. As such, she is necessarily presented with the reciprocal *concepts* of a CI/pure practical reason/the moral law (in consequence of which she is presented with the concept of FW).[15] However, if she understands these concepts, she must accept that there is a CI, "Comply with a CI!" and understanding the concept of a CI *also* requires her to accept that it takes the form of the FUL/FoH. Since she must have the concept of a CI in order to understand what it is to be an agent, it is dialectically necessary for her to accept the FUL/FoH.

Ph 2:   Nevertheless, the concept of a CI is a delusion if the idea that Agnes has FW is incompatible with the synthetic a priori proposition that every event has a cause. However, no incompatibility exists, and because the dialectical necessity of FW (in being the *ratio essendi* for the CI) gives content to an idea of freedom that even speculative reason must presuppose, the CI is not a mere idea of pure reason but has objective reality for practical purposes.

To the contrary, "retreatists" contend:

R1   In *GW* Kant holds that FW is the *ratio cognoscendi* of the moral law. But in *C2* he claims that the moral law is the *ratio cognoscendi* of FW, with FW being the *ratio essendi* of the moral law.

R2   Consequently, he abandons his *GW* claim that the moral law can be given a morally neutral foundation. It is only possible to show that those who accept that there is a CI must hold the CI to be the FUL/FoH. But, because it is generally accepted that there is a CI, the question of its existence does not arise in ordinary practical human discourse. To say that the moral law is given as the fact of reason is to say that the question of the existence of a CI does not arise in everyday practical dealings.

---

15 Due to this reciprocality, nothing hinges on the fact that, in *GW,* Kant reasons from the concept of pure reason to FW to the moral law, whereas in *C2* he reasons from the concept of pure reason to the moral law to FW. Compare Kleingeld (2010, p. 70).

Proving my construction is beyond the scope of this chapter:[16] although I will offer reasons for it, the point of doing so is to show how Kant might be construed as consistently employing the DNM, which will assist me to further elucidate the DNM.

What then are my reasons for my construction? For a start, R1 and R2 contradict Kant's statement that *C2* presupposes *GW* insofar as *GW* "provides and justifies a determinate formula" of the moral law *(C2 5:8)* in echo of *GW* being "nothing more that the identification and corroboration *of the supreme principle of morality*" *(GW 4:392)*. This places the burden of proof squarely on retreatists, requiring them to provide evidence for their view sufficient to convict Kant of amnesia, self-incomprehension, or disingenuousness, while non-retreatists need only show that it is not wholly implausible to attribute their view to him.

Regarding R1, there are least two reasons to think that Kant always held FW to be the *ratio essendi* of the moral law.

First, he says that the possibility of a CI is explained by the necessary presupposition of FW *(GW 4:461)*, which is to say that FW is the *ratio essendi* of the moral law.

Second, the *deduction* in *GW* is "of the concept of freedom from pure practical reason" *(GW 4:448)*, which echoes "Pure reason is practical of itself alone" and gives agents the moral law *(C2 5:31)*. The *GW* statement explains why, having apparently claimed that the moral law is dialectically necessary for Agnes because it is dialectically necessary for her to hold that she has FW, Kant thinks that there might be a circle in his justification of the moral law *(GW 449–450)*. It also explains why he thinks that the circle is not genuine. The dialectical necessity of the concept of FW for Agnes is established by the dialectical necessity of the *concept* of pure practical reason (inherent in her understanding that the question of the possibility of a CI is necessarily raised for her by her possession of reason and understanding), from which it follows that Agnes must accept that there is a CI. There is no circle because showing the dialectical necessity of the concept of a CI does not require the existence of a CI to be assumed.

Regarding R2:

(i)   To hold that the moral law is the *ratio cognoscendi* of FW *(C2 5:4)* does not preclude the moral law's justification being its dialectical necessity. Note then that Kant does not treat "moral consciousness", the "fact of reason" *(C2 5:31)*, as a given. It is rendered possible by a process of ab-

---

16 I intend to do so in a future paper.

straction and mental unification *(C2* 5:30) that can be linked to the processes cited in *GW* 4:452, 457 and, see below, *C3* 5:293 – 295.

(ii)   Taking the "common human understanding" to be what ordinary persons take for granted does not square with Kant's contempt for treating widespread acceptance as the yardstick for philosophical claims *(GW* 4:409 – 410), nor with his explicit repudiation of the fact of reason being an empirical fact *(C2* 5:31), nor with his insistence that "the moral law is given ... as a fact of pure reason of which we are a priori conscious and which is apodictically certain" and "stands of itself altogether a priori and independently of empirical principles" *(C2* 5:46). Instead, I think Kant's references to "the common human understanding" are to the *"sensus communis"*, an a priori faculty of judging "that in its reflection takes account (a priori) of everyone else's way of representing in thought" *(C3* 5:293), which has three maxims – yielded by exercising the cognitive powers that are "the least that can be expected from anyone who lays claim to the name of a human being" *(C3* 5:293) (those minimal capacities necessary to possess awareness of one's existence), which comprise "understanding", "power of judgment", and "reason" *(C3* 5:197 – 198). These maxims, which appear as early as Kant's *Logic* (9:57) are:

> To think for oneself; 2. To think in the position of everyone else; 3. Always to think in accord with oneself. *(C3* 5:294) ... [T]he first of these maxims is the maxim of the understanding, the second that of the power of judgment, the third that of reason ... [which can be achieved only] through the combination of the first two [maxims]. *(C3* 5:295)

I suggest that, applied to practical reason, the maxim of understanding directs Agnes to comply with any maxims she must adopt in order to think of herself as the particular agent she is (with any maxims that are dialectically necessary *for her*) (which, applied to *GW* 4:437 – 438, requires her to consider humanity in her person to be an end in itself). However, the power of reflective judgment requires Agnes to recognise that she cannot be the particular agent she is without being an agent *(C3* 20:211).[17] So, not only is *Brian* required to comply with any maxims

---

17 As against, the "determining" power of judgment, which requires her to recognise that *she* can only be an agent if she is the particular agent that she is.

that are dialectically necessary *for him* (thus, to consider his humanity to be an end in itself), but *Agnes* must also comply with any maxims that are dialectically necessary *for Brian* (hence *Agnes* must consider that Brian's humanity is also an end in itself). The power of reflective judgment generates the maxim of judgment, which requires Agnes to set herself apart from the subjective private conditions of her thinking (involved in exercising her power of understanding) by reflecting from a universal standpoint, which she can only do by adopting the standpoint of others *(C3* 5:295). Reason (requiring her cognitive faculties to operate coherently) then *permits* Agnes to adopt a maxim for herself only if this is consistent with maxims that are dialectically necessary for *any* agent (entailing that Agnes ought to comply with the maxim that every agent's humanity is an end in itself).

So interpreted, the maxim of reason amounts to the FUL/FoH justified as dialectically necessary for Agnes.

(iii)   Kant does say that "the objective reality of the moral law cannot be proved by any deduction"; but this is any deduction "by any efforts of theoretical reason" *(C2* 5:47). Also, while he does offer an argument for the moral law "fully sufficient to take the place of any a priori justification" *(C2* 5:48), if he is not to be contradicting himself, we must, again, read this as "any a priori justification *from the possibility of theoretical knowledge*", because it is that the moral law "is itself laid down as a principle of the *deduction* [my emphasis] of freedom as a causality of pure reason" that gives a positive determination to the idea of freedom that speculative reason needs to presuppose for itself *(C2* 5:48), which echoes his assertion that the presupposition of FW is not only compatible with "the principle of natural necessity", but necessary in idea for a being conscious of his causality through reason *(GW* 4:461).

(iv)   Kant says (consistently with the DNM) that understanding the idea of a CI commits agents to accept that there is a CI when he says that the apodictic nature of the moral law is contained in its problematic nature *(C2* 5:31), and when he draws an analogy between his argument for the moral law and the ontological argument for the existence of God *(C2* 5:105).

(v)   The retreatist idea of the fact of reason does not fit Kant's "three-term" depiction of a synthetic a priori principle in general in *C3* 5:197, which corresponds to that given in *GW*.

My construal implies that, in *GW*, phase 1 of Kant's argument is already completed before *GW III*, which carries out phase 2. Note that Kant only refers to a "deduction" in connection with phase 2, in both *GW* and C2. So, we might say that phase 2 is the deduction part of his transcendental argument and phase 1 the exposition part. The latter part involves not only specifying the CI on the assumption of it (which is analytic), but the claim that the CI is dialectically necessary as well. In line with this (and contrary to the explanatory note provided by the editor) I consider that when Kant says that *"rational nature exists as an end in itself"* is the ground of the CI *(GW* 4:428 – 429), he claims that to act rationally is an end in itself on the criterion of the DNM's CRA, and he is actually saying that pure reason (on the basis of the CDNM) produces the moral law, that the moral law is given as the fact of reason.

The central differences between Kant and Gewirth derive (see Beyleveld 2016) from Gewirth's claim that $\{PHI\}_{(A)}$, which implies that the moral law is grounded in dubiety about both FW and determinism, versus Kant's claim that the moral law and FW are reciprocal ideas. Consequently, Gewirthians (versus Kant) eschew the existence of perfect duties to self under the CI, and regard the essence of being an agent, not as possessing FW, but in being subject to existential anxiety (hope-fear) regarding all metaphysical matters. The Gewirthian argument does not require a phase 2 because the place of $\{PHI\}_{(A)}$ in it prevents the issue of the dialectic of reason that prompts Kant's phase 2 from arising.

The DNM and Enoch's Critique of "Constitutivism"

Enoch's Critique

David Enoch (2006) attacks "constitutivism", which holds that
(a) "normative standards relevant for actions ... fall out of an understanding of what is constitutive of action" (Enoch 2006, p. 170); or
(b) normativity is grounded "in what is constitutive of action" (Enoch 2006, p. 170)]; or
(c) there are specific aims, desires or motives that are constitutive of agency (Enoch 2006, p. 173, p. 175); or
(d) the dialectical necessity of a principle renders its "ought" categorically binding on agents (Enoch 2006, p. 189 n. 42).

Enoch treats (a)–(d) as equivalent, implying that constitutivists hold the thesis (CT): "Supposing that $\{AoX\}_{(A)}$, Agnes is an agent only if, per (c), she complies with AoX and, per (b), considers that she ought to, and this is why $\{AoX\}_{(A)}$ renders AoX categorically binding on her".

He attributes the following objectives to constitutivists:

> addressing the sceptic, accommodating externalist[18] intuitions consistently with internalism,[19] and coming up with a naturalist theory that is immune to the ... open question argument.[20] (Enoch 2006, p. 177)

Suppose $\{AoX\}_{(A)}$.[21] According to Enoch, CT is untenable because Agnes might not care whether she is an agent rather than a shmagent (someone unlike an agent only in not having AoX-compliant purposes/not accepting AoX). So, to show that AoX is categorically binding on Agnes, she must be given a reason (independent of the DNM) why she ought to be an agent rather than a shmagent/ why she ought to care whether or not she understands what it is for her to be an agent (Enoch 2006, p. 179). Consequently, constitutivism cannot cope with the anti-naturalist challenge (Enoch 2006, p. 193).

Enoch's objection is akin to the claim made by Millard Shumaker (1979) that $\{PGC\}_{(A)}$ does not give Agnes a categorical reason to comply with the PGC unless the "pain of contradiction" incurred by non-compliance will necessarily deter her from acting contrary to the PGC. Shumaker contends that Agnes' dialectically commitments cannot do the work the DNM assigns to them because they do not necessarily give her narrow internalist reasons to act. Since Enoch links the DNM to narrow internalism, he should agree that Shumaker's point is well taken, as this explains his claim that CT implies the false proposition that making Agnes understand what it is for her to be an agent will make her comply with AoX (Enoch 2006, p. 171).[22] But Enoch's intention is to show that the required independent reason must be a robust realist (externalist) one.

---

18 "[E]xternalists insist that one's normative reasons do not depend on one's desires, that such dependence is already objectionable unless the desires have something normative going for them" (Enoch 2006, p. 193).

19 "Internalism" involves the proposition "that it is necessary for one's having a [justificatory] reason to act in a certain way that one be motivated—perhaps under suitable conditions—to act in that way" (Enoch 2006, p. 173). I call this thesis (which derives from David Hume) "narrow internalism".

20 This alleges that "normative judgments cannot be reduced to descriptive ones because any such reduction will lose the very normativity it was supposed to capture" (Enoch 2006, p. 174).

21 Enoch is not concerned with whether or not $\{AoX\}_{(A)}$ is true, but only with what the significance of its truth would be.

22 Enoch links this criticism to David Lewis (2000, p. 60), who views "constitutivism" as implying that "philosophy can replace the hangman". Cf. Robert Nozick's lurid claim that Gewirth displays commitment to "philosophy as a coercive activity" guided by the objective of producing

Anyway, CT is ridiculous because it entails that it is impossible for Agnes to act irrationally,[23] which runs counter to the thesis that "'ought' implies both 'able to do' and 'able to not do'". But, happily, Enoch's critique is misdirected at the DNM, which does not implicate CT, and eschews narrow internalism without being committed to robust realism.

Refuting Enoch's Critique

None of Enoch's characterisations of "constitutivism" are equivalent to each other; but I am only concerned to show that the DNM does not involve CT.

Per the DNM, Agnes' *required acceptance* of AoX falls out of her *understanding* what *constitutes understanding her agency*, not as per Enoch's characterisation (a), that AoX falls out of her *understanding* what *constitutes action/agency*. This is not a distinction without a difference. First, $\{AoX\}_{(A)}$ does not ground AoX itself, but "Agnes ought to accept AoX". Secondly, that Agnes ought to accept AoX, is not revealed by appreciating what is contained in the concept of action/agency, but by Agnes appreciating what is required for her to understand what it is for her to be an agent. $\{AoX\}_{(A)}$ does not imply that AoX is a necessary truth (analytic) nor that AoX or its acceptance is contained in the concept of being an agent. What it shows to be analytically contained in the concept of being an agent is that Agnes only fully possesses agential self-understanding if she accepts AoX, not that she is an agent only if she accepts AoX. This contrast between analyticity and dialectical necessity accords with Kant's depiction of a synthetic a priori practical principle, in which agential self-understanding is the third term that links the idea of Agnes as the particular agent she is to the CI, as against an analytic principle that links the idea of Agnes as the particular agent she is directly to the CI.

Not grasping this distinction leads Enoch to attack a strawman. Worse, his attack is unintelligible if directed at the genuine DNM. Given $\{AoX\}_{(A)}$, his contention that Agnes may evade acceptance of AoX by claiming to be a shmagent *rather than* an agent is only intelligible on the premise that (as the result of the DNM) Agnes is an agent only if she accepts AoX/has AoX-compliant purposes, and a

---

"arguments so powerful they set up reverberations in the brain: if the person refuses to accept the conclusion, he dies" (Nozick 1981, p. 4), and Jeffrey Reiman, who says that an agent's dialectically necessary normative judgments are "a kind of compulsion that grabs hold of the reasoning faculties of a prospective agent" (Reiman 1990, p. 62).

23 Not merely, as Enoch (2006, p. 178 n. 22) suggests, difficult to see how she can act irrationally.

shmagent if she does not accept AoX/does not have AoX-compliant purposes. But, per the DNM, agents are those able and willing to pursue purposes voluntarily, *regardless of what those purposes are or might be.* Establishing $\{AoX\}_{(A)}$ does not miraculously alter this definition. It reveals that agents, as beings willing and able to pursue purposes voluntarily, *ought* to accept (= it is dialectically necessary for them to accept) only AoX-compliant purposes.

So, given $\{AoX\}_{(A)}$, it is incoherent to require a DNM-independent reason to be given to Agnes why she ought to be an agent *rather than* a shmagent before AoX may be held to be categorically binding on her. This is because Agnes cannot be a shmagent (who pursues purposes voluntarily that are not AoX-compliant) without being an agent (who pursues purposes voluntarily). By rejecting AoX, Agnes not only implies that she is not an agent, but also that she is not a *shmagent.* And, if she implies that *she is not a shmagent* by rejecting AoX, she cannot coherently claim that she may reject AoX because *she is a shmagent.* For this reason, given $\{AoX\}_{(A),}$ the question why Agnes ought to be an agent rather than a shmagent/ought to care whether or not she understands what it is for her to be an agent cannot arise coherently for her, whether the demand for a reason is a narrow internalist or a robust realist one, and this means that a categorical imperative just is a dialectically necessary maxim.

The DNM and Internalism

The DNM works with a broadly internalist view of reasons for action, in which a reason for Agnes to act must speak to *Agnes'* reasoning. This is why it is conducted from Agnes' internal viewpoint as an agent.

But proponents of the DNM are not narrow internalists, because they do not offer agential self-understanding as a *goal of action* that agents necessarily have, but (in line with Kant's maxims of the *sensus communis)* as a condition for Agnes to intelligibly attribute agent-individuating desires and choices to herself as reasons for her to act. They claim that Agnes can only *think of herself* as being subject to an hypothetical imperative (the only kind of imperative that narrow internalists recognise), on the basis of understanding what it is for her to be an agent, on which basis she ought to recognise that she ought to structure her practical thinking in accord with her dialectically necessary commitments.

I anticipate that some will object that this is not how Gewirth argues for the PGC, because a widely accepted view is that he holds that Agnes must consider that she has the GR because she needs the GCAs (irrespective of her purposes) in order to act, i.e., because her GCAs are categorical instrumental needs of her agency (e. g., Bond 1980, pp. 50 – 51; Williams 1985, Chapter 4; and, surprisingly,

Korsgaard 1996, pp. 133–34); on which basis the argument fails because Agnes does not have an instrumental need for Brian to have the GCAs regardless of *her* purposes.

But this is not how Gewirth argues. His argument does not proceed from the narrow internalist "ought" in AoA^A (an hypothetical imperative, requiring Agnes to defend her GCAs only if she is unwilling to accept generic damage to her ability to act) but from {AoA^A}$_{(A)}$, where the operative "ought" is that Agnes unconditionally ought to conform her practical reasoning to AoA^A because it is dialectically necessary for her to accept AoA^A, this "because" not being a reason in narrow internalist terms. As should be clear from my presentation of the argument, the hypothetical "ought" AoA^A plays no role in justifying the claim that dialectically necessary commitments are necessarily *collectively* universal. The fact that *it is the PHI* that is dialectically necessary for Agnes merely determines that her dialectically necessary commitments must be structured according to the will conception of rights, and her categorical instrumental need for the GCAs *then* requires these rights to be to the GCAs. It is the fact that Agnes's commitment to the PHI *is dialectically necessary* that does the work.

The DNM and Naturalism

When Gewirth (e.g., 1978, p. 102) says that his argument for the PGC derives "ought" from "is", he does not claim to derive the PGC from the fact of Agnes' agency, but that Agnes ought to accept the PGC from *the fact* that {PGC}$_A$ (Gewirth 1978, pp. 158–159). Indeed, he claims that this fact constitutes Agnes being categorically bound to accept the PGC. And, as I have interpreted Kant, when he says that the moral law is given to agents as the fact of reason (or the sole fact of pure reason), the fact referred to is nothing other than that the CI's categorical binding nature is constituted by the fact that {CI}$_A$.

Of course, if dialectically necessary commitments are necessarily collectively universal, then it is dialectically necessary for Agnes to hold that being an agent is the *ratio essendi* of the moral law/CI/PGC, i.e., that it is dialectally necessary for her to hold that it is because they are agents that agents are ends in themselves (whether in Kant's or Gewirth's interpretation of this), which is to say that it is *dialectically necessary* for Agnes to accept the naturalist thesis that "ought" can be derived from "is". But this does not make "Agnes is an end in itself because she is an agent" a truth about the nature of agency, for this statement is justified as a requirement of Agnes' agential self-understanding, not as a freestanding statement about the nature of agency (or her agency). If you like, Agnes must treat the statement "The fact that Z is an agent makes Z an end in itself" as a necessary truth only for the purpose of agential self-understanding. So, because the acceptance of normativity is constituted in agential self-understanding, it is a statement that is normatively required, not a normatively-neutral one. In this way, the naturalism the DNM supports is immune to the open-question argument.

The DNM and Foundationalism

Showing that, e. g., $\{M\}_{(A\&B)}$ is intended to provide a foundation for all practical, not only moral, deliberation by rendering rationally *impermissible* all action not compliant with M by rendering scepticism about the categorically binding nature of M's "ought" incoherent.

However, Enoch considers that showing that $\{M\}_{(A\&B)}$ is intended to "defeat the sceptic" (Enoch 2006, pp. 182–185) by rendering scepticism about M's "ought" logically *impossible*, which intention he claims is carried out on an adversarial model that requires the sceptic to operate on the constitutivist's terms not those of the sceptic.

However, to render scepticism rationally indefensible is distinct from rendering it logically impossible, because to deny that one is an agent is not to cease to be an agent.

I surmise that Enoch's characterisation of the anti-sceptical objectives of the DNM derives from his misattribution of narrow internalism to its proponents and/or to his failure to recognise the difference between analytic a priori and synthetic a priori (dialectically necessary) judgments.

I also do not see how Enoch's adversarial model applies to the DNM. This is because, *from Agnes' dialectically necessary perspective* as an agent, the question why *Brian* ought to accept *her* normative claims does not arise. The only proper question is why *Agnes* ought to accept *any* normative claims. In the DNM, Agnes is both the protagonist (qua being *an* agent) and the sceptic (qua being *the particular* agent that she is) about normative claims, because of the biconditional relationship that exists between her view of herself as *an* agent and her view of herself as the particular agent that she is that operates within the standpoint of agential self-understanding.

The DNM and Coherentism

Foundationalism is often contrasted with "coherentism". Foundationalists try to derive conclusions logically/conceptually from premises that cannot be denied rationally or are alleged to be self-evidently true, whereas coherentists (who appeal to considerations like reflective equilibrium) merely aim to defend conclusions as being supported by premises that are widely accepted/deeply entrenched: the idea being to find principles that are supported by a wide range of deep commitments, with better accounts being those that are supported by a wider range of deeper commitments.

However, the contrast between the DNM and "coherentism" is that the former operates only with dialectically necessary commitments, whereas the latter permits dialectically contingent inputs. Thus, the contrast between the DNM and "coherentism" is better portrayed as that between foundationalist-coherentism and non-foundationalist coherentism, or as that between coherentism that is not narrowly internalist and narrowly internalist coherentism.

The DNM and Realism

Per Enoch, the DNM is externalist because its broad internalism maintains that normative requirements, as strict requirements of agential self-understanding, do not rest on anything contingently connected to Agnes' agency. But the DNM does not support "narrow externalism" ("robust realism"), the view that "there are non-natural normative truths that have an ontological status independent of agency" (Enoch 2006, pp. 194–196) or the mere requirements of agential self-understanding (Enoch 2011, p. 229) (which may be considered to be foundational non-coherentism).

Conclusion

I have offered the DNM as an interpretation of what Kant considers to be a transcendental argument for a practical principle, and argued that if a practical precept can be shown to be dialectically necessary for agents then it is categorically binding on them. I have shown that David Enoch's critique of constitutivism does not apply to the DNM because he (a) confuses the thesis that normativity is grounded in what constitutes agential self-understanding with the "constitutivist" thesis that it is grounded in understanding what constitutes agency; (b) fails to distinguish dialectically necessary requirements from analytic ones (thereby presupposing that there is no distinction between denying being an agent and not being an agent); and (c) does not distinguish narrow from broad internalism, so falsely associates the DNM with narrow internalism because it is not narrowly externalist.

Objections against the DNM come from two main camps: narrow internalism and narrow externalism. Both raise the question, "Why should Agnes care whether or not she misunderstands what it is for her to be an agent?" But if Agnes has dialectically necessary commitments, this question does not arise coherently for her, because then for her to misunderstand what it is for her to be an agent is for her to imply that she is not an agent, on the basis of which she cannot coherently ask for *any* reason for her to act.

In a later paper, Enoch says that he is willing to consider the viability of the thesis that we ought to care about self-understanding because *"that's just what it is to have a reason"* (Enoch 2011, p. 229). This is ironic, because this is just what the thesis of the DNM is. Enoch has not shown, as he intends, that it is misguided to try to establish a CI on the basis of its dialectical necessity.

Bibliography

Beyleveld, Deryck (1991): *The Dialectical Necessity of Morality: An Analysis and Defense of Alan Gewirth's Argument to the Principle of Generic Consistency.* Chicago: University of Chicago Press.

Beyleveld, Deryck (2013): "Williams False Dilemma: How to Give Categorically Binding Impartial Reasons to Real Agents". In: *Journal of Moral Philosophy* 10. No. 2, pp. 204–226.

Beyleveld, Deryck (2016): "Gewirth versus Kant on Kant's Maxim of Reason: Towards a Gewirthian Philosophical Anthropology". In: Per Bauhn (Ed.): *Gewirthian Perspectives on Human Rights.* London: Routledge, pp. 13–29.

Bond, Edward J. (1980): "Gewirth on Reason and Morality". In: *Metaphilosophy* 11. No. 1, pp. 36–53.

Enoch, David (2006): "Agency, Shmagency: Why Normativity Won't Come from What is Constitutive of Action". In: *Philosophical Review* 115. No. 2, pp. 169–198.

Enoch, David (2011): "Shmagency Revisited". In: Michael Brady (Ed.): *New Waves in Metaethics.* London: Palgrave Macmillan, pp. 208–233.

Gewirth, Alan (1978): *Reason and Morality.* Chicago: University of Chicago Press.

Gewirth, Alan (1991): "Foreword". In: Deryck Beyleveld: *The Dialectical Necessity of Morality: An Analysis and Defense of Alan Gewirth's Argument to the Principle of Generic Consistency.* Chicago: University of Chicago Press, pp. vi–xvii.

Henrich, Dieter (1960): "Der Begriff der sittlichen Einsicht und Kants Lehre vom Factum der Vernunft". In: Dieter Henrich (Ed.): *Die Gegenwart der Griechen im neueren Denken: Festschrift für Hans-Georg Gadamer zum 60 Geburtstag.* Tübingen: JCB Mohr, pp. 77–115.

Kant, Immanuel (1990sqq): *Gesammmelte Schriften.* Berlin: Reimer/de Gruyter.

Kant, Immanuel (1995sqq): *Cambridge Edition of the Works of Immanuel Kant.* Paul Guyer/Allen W. Wood (Eds.): Cambridge: Cambridge University Press.

Kleingeld, Pauline (2010): "Moral Consciousness and the Fact of Reason". In: Andrews Reath/Jens Timmermann (Eds.): *Kant's Critique of Practical Reason: A Critical Guide.* Cambridge: Cambridge University Press.

Korsgaard, Christine M. (1996): *The Sources of Normativity.* Cambridge: Cambridge University Press.

Korsgaard, Christine M. (2002): "Self-Constitution: Agency, Identity, and Integrity". The Locke Lectures. Subsequently published (2009) as *Self Constitution: Agency, Identity and Integrity.* Oxford: Oxford University Press.

Lewis, David K. (2000): *Papers in Ethics and Social Philosophy*, pp. 55–67. Cambridge: Cambridge University Press.

Nozick, Robert (1981): *Philosophical Explanations.* Cambridge, Massachusetts: Harvard University Press.

O'Neill, Onora (2002): "Autonomy and the Fact of Reason in the *Kritik der praktischen Vernunft*, pp. 30–41". In: O. Höffe (Ed.): *Immanuel Kant, Kritik der praktischen Vernunft*, Berlin: Akademie Verlag, pp. 81–97.

Reiman, Jeffrey (1990): *Justice and Modern Philosophy.* New Haven: Yale University Press.

Shumaker, Millard (1979): "The Pain of Self-Contradiction". In: *Journal of Religion* 59. No 3, pp. 352–356.

Velleman, David (2004): "Precis of *The Possibility of Practical Reason.*' In: *Philosophical Studies* 121. No. 3, pp. 225–238.

Williams, Bernard (1985): *Ethics and the Limits of Philosophy.* London: Fontana.

Marcus Düwell

Transcendental Arguments and Practical Self-Understanding—Gewirthian Perspectives

Abstract: This chapter discusses some philosophical assumptions in the use of transcendental arguments in Alan Gewirth's method of dialectical necessity. With this method Gewirth aims to show that agents must hold some beliefs in order to understand themselves consistently. *Firstly*, it is argued that this method is not in the first place used to convince the sceptic, but rather that the aim is gain a reflective understanding of ourselves. Since the methodology investigates 'judgments' and their role for the subject, we should see it as part of a hermeneutical enterprise to gain a form of reflected practical self-understanding. *Secondly*, the paper questions the distinction between 'dialogical' and 'monological' forms of transcendental justification in ethics. It is argued that the investigation of dialectically necessary judgments of the subject has the aim of showing in which ways the subject must respect the other in order to understand himself consistently. Those normatively committed subjects must be presupposed by discourse ethicists as well, otherwise the dialogue will not reach its goal of generating normatively acceptable outcomes. *Finally*, the chapter sketches some consequences of seeing the role of transcendental arguments in gaining a reflected form of practical self-understanding. If moral commitments are based in 'judgment', the power of judgment is of crucial importance and we must consider how the institutional and individual conditions needed to protect and develop this basic capacity can be protected and increased.

0 Introduction

What could the goal of using a transcendental argument be? The most widespread answer would probably be: to convince the sceptic. This would mean that the place of a transcendental argument is in a specific agonistic situation where important (theoretical or practical) convictions are contested. It evokes the objection that it is perhaps neither necessary nor possible to respond to these contestations. Can human beings seriously contest (if they are *compos mentis*) that there is an outside world, that there are other human beings, or that the killing of babies for fun is morally wrong? Perhaps it is impossible to raise serious doubts regarding the outside world from a practical perspective,

DOI 10.1515/9783110470215-009

since such a perspective already presupposes this world, and perhaps we don't need a transcendental argument to come to this insight? And in the moral domain: Can a conviction such as that the killing babies for fun is morally acceptable not only be held by a cynic who will not be convinced by transcendental arguments because he will not care for such arguments in the first place? Many seem to see the reference to transcendental arguments as expressive of the search for a kind of certainty that is not necessary for human beings, and will not be achieved through the transcendental argument. Even if the transcendental argument does some work, how should we understand its function? Should we assume that the 'Cartesian Ego cogito', that the atomistic individual finds some certainty in his/her soul? Would we not necessarily be committed to a strange form of social ontology if we engage in such a form of transcendental philosophy? Even if the transcendental argument works, what would we have achieved? Perhaps we would know that we shouldn't kill babies for fun, but did we not already know this?

I have doubts that this is an appropriate understanding of a role of transcendental arguments. I propose that we should not see transcendental arguments as attempts to defend theoretical and practical convictions against the sceptic in the first place. I propose that we see the role of transcendental arguments rather as disclosing the way in which human beings can understand why they ought to subscribe to moral commitments. The primary aim is not to convince the sceptic of that he should have some moral commitments, but to understand why we should have such commitments in the first place. This view is inspired by Alan Gewirth's justification of his supreme principle of morality (first presented in Gewirth 1978). Gewirth justifies his principle by showing that all agents must believe that some judgments are dialectically necessary for them. For Gewirth, 'dialectical judgments' have a self-reflexive structure. While an assertoric judgment would be 'x is green', a dialectic judgment is 'A is of the opinion/believes/hopes/fears that x is green'. While the former is a judgment about the object in question, the latter is a judgment about a belief, conviction or attitude of A. The dialectical judgment 'x is green' is contingent, in the sense that it is correct to the extent that A really believes 'x is green'. But Gewirth claims that some of the beliefs we have are not contingent; if we do not have them we cannot consistently understand ourselves. The respective judgments are 'dialectically necessary'. Dialectically necessary judgments are those that all agents must accept because if they were to deny them, they would not be capable of consistent self-understanding. An example would be Gewirth's starting point: I as an agent must believe that the goal of my action is good. If we assume that this 'good' does not refer to a moral good but refers to a positive evaluation of the goal of my action, then—Gewirth would say—I cannot deny that for me the goal of my action is a good. If he calls this judgment 'dialectically necessary' he does not claim that the goal of action must be good from the perspective of others, he rather claims that it is dialectically necessary for the agent.

Gewirth uses this methodology to further show that some dialectically necessary judgments imply other dialectically necessary judgments. If I understand that I have to subscribe to judgment A, then I must also subscribe to judgment B that is implied in A because I cannot consistently understand myself as subscribing to A if I deny B. With this methodology Gewirth shows that there are fundamental beliefs which all agents must hold. Gewirth claims that moral judgments should not be understood as judgments about a morality that is valid independently from us as agents. We should rather assume that moral judgments are judgments about action-guiding beliefs which are valid because if we did not subscribe to them, then we would not be able to consistently understand ourselves. Morality is not grounded in an independent sphere of values, but morality rather has to do with an appropriate way of understanding what it means to be a human being. If morality has such a self-reflexive structure, then, methodologically considered, justifying morality can only proceed in a self-reflexive way as well. Therefore, transcendental arguments are appropriate ways for justification in ethics.

Below I will present some steps of the Gewirthian argument more in detail, but the aim of this paper is not to present an extensive defence of this theory.[1] Rather, I have the impression that there are some misperceptions of this approach which hinder an appropriate discussion and I want to critically discuss them. There is, *first of all*, the assumption that we should rely on transcendental arguments because we need to convince the sceptic. I argue, however, that the aim is rather to gain in self-understanding. *Secondly*, I will question the legitimacy of the criticism that this methodology is only monological, solely interested in individual self-reflection and ignoring the social dimension. *Finally*, I will outline some consequences that may follow for the application of this approach if we interpret it as a methodology for developing a consistent form of practical self-understanding.

---

1 For important discussions see Bauhn (2016), Beyleveld (1991), Boylan (1999), Regis (1984), Steigleder (1999).

1 Transcendental arguments—not for the sceptic

There is a longstanding tradition wherein transcendental arguments got their function within the attempt to be *certain* about our theoretical or practical commitments. Examples are discussions with the sceptic—some of them going back to ancient philosophy—about the possibility of truth in general, about the possibility of our gaining reliable knowledge, or about the existence of the outside world. Some discussions with sceptic are about the most fundamental levels of gaining knowledge and reliable beliefs in general, some focus more on questions about the extent to which we are able to determine such knowledge on a concrete and specific level.

With regard to theoretical doubt (regarding the existence of the external world and our possible to gain reliable knowledge), the dependence on transcendental arguments seems to impose on us an idealistic metaphysics or the burden of defending an objective or absolute idealism. Alternatively, a pragmatist could argue that it is pragmatically impossible to doubt the existence of the outside world because as acting beings we already pragmatically accept that there is an outside world (I do not want to discuss whether this is a convincing argument, but at least it is a possible strategy). The situation is somewhat different when it comes to moral convictions. It is prima facie not pragmatically impossible for an agent to hold the conviction that cheating, lying or killing are morally acceptable, or to assert that we cannot decide about the validity of morality at all; the moral sceptic is (at least prima facie) a possible figure. We need an argument to show that such positions are wrong or self-contradictory—and transcendental arguments are candidates for such precisely an argument.

At the same time, the threat of 'idealism' is not necessarily a problem for the defender of a transcendental argument. This would only form an inescapable problem if 'moral realism' were the only alternative to a relativistic or sceptical position. But this is not the case. It is not necessary to assume that a judgment like 'lying is wrong' can only be correct if this judgment articulates a subject-independent truth. We can, for example, understand it as equivalent to the judgment 'no agent should lie'—a proposition that does not necessarily rest on the assumption of realism. It is furthermore not evident that moral realism provides a more solid or robust basis for the validity of moral convictions, because there is the epistemological question of how we can gain knowledge of such subject-independent moral facts.

So, if moral scepticism is a possibility, and if in the moral domain the idealistic threat is not eo ipso a problem, we could discuss what role transcendental arguments could have here.[2] But why should the transcendental argument be directed towards the sceptic? Why should the transcendental argument should help us to convince a sceptic that moral considerations should guide his actions, or what kind of moral considerations are reliable? If the sceptic cannot see that inflicting useless pain on babies for fun is bad, will a transcendental argument help to convince him? And—to be honest—I myself have never really contemplated this as a possible moral conviction, so why do I need a transcendental argument to convince myself?

My proposal would be to remove—for heuristic reasons—the sceptic from the picture. It is not that I think that it is impossible or useless to convince the sceptic via transcendental arguments. Rather we should not rely in the first instance on transcendental arguments because we want to convince sceptical opponents in an agonistic battle. Likewise, we do not rely on them because we want to gain a level of intellectual certainty that may for practical purposes be superfluous. But it is crucial for understanding morality and for understanding myself as a practical being that I understand the reasons why I would be doing something wrong if I were to not subscribe to moral commitments. We should therefore see transcendental arguments as important for our reflected practical self-understanding as human beings. This means that we would not understand ourselves adequately as practical beings without such a transcendental reflection. In that sense, transcendental arguments should be seen as embedded within more comprehensive attempts to understand ourselves, to make sense of our lives. Understanding myself in a practical perspective has not only to do with reflections on my individual goals in life, my ambitions, my aspirations and values, but also with an understanding of more general dimensions of my existence as an agent. Gewirth's claim would be that some of the beliefs an agent must hold are necessary for the agent to hold simply in order to be able to understand him- or herself. Such practical self-understanding is fundamental because it is presupposed in each form of practical orientation. We may assume that there are limits to self-understanding, we can claim that we can never be fully transparent to ourselves, and we can even claim that this is necessarily the case for human beings. But even this insight in the limitation of our self-understanding will be a form of self-understanding.

---

2 Just for clarification: I assume that the use of transcendental arguments in the practical domain is not independent from their possible role in the theoretical domain. I assume, therefore, that my considerations would have some relevance for the theoretical domain as well. But this is clearly beyond the scope of what I can possible discuss in this paper.

Such an approach to practical self-understanding is in some regards embedding the understanding of morality in a *hermeneutical* perspective.[3] This means it starts with the assumption that understanding is fundamental for human beings, that understanding is always dependent on my perspective on beliefs, and that understanding is always dependent on specific forms of self-understanding. It could come as a surprise that I relate such an approach to the hermeneutical tradition, since the idea of dialectical necessity aims at the justification of moral universalism, whilst hermeneutics seems to be the discipline that emphasizes historical relativity *par excellence*. Methodologically, such a tension is not necessary.[4] A hermeneutic approach takes as a starting point the living human being and his/her interpretation of the world. It begins with the world as it is given to the human being. It focuses attention on the way the world appears to us, and it asks what aspects of the world our perspective ignores and what is invisible to the eye of the beholder. It tries to understand the way in which specific perspectives on the world are dependent on specific traditions, and what perspectives within these traditions have been omitted. A hermeneutic approach will perhaps confront old pathways of understanding with other possible perspectives on the world. Or it will convince us that we have no alternative to understanding the world along the lines that traditions have explored for us.

However, methodologically, such a hermeneutic approach does not preclude universalistic assumptions right from the beginning. We must, for example, assume that we understand what understanding entails, we must wonder what kind of capacities we must have in order to be able to understand something at all. 'Understanding understanding'—to borrow a term from Wayne Waxman —is a self-reflexive endeavour from the perspective of the living and acting being. This form of reflexive self-understanding requires at least some elements of a philosophical anthropology without which we would not be able to understand ourselves as understanding beings. It further requires that we develop an understanding of the capacity to form judgments—Kant's central project. In all these respects, a hermeneutical approach cannot be without some elements that transcend historicizing claims. What Gewirth calls "dialectical necessity" is perfectly compatible with such a hermeneutic starting point. It starts with the self-reflection of the agent, and asks which judgments agents must embrace regarding themselves, and Gewirth finds a principle that agents cannot deny from their perspective.

---

3 See also in this context Düring/Düwell (2015).
4 Just as a historical side-note, I want to remind the reader that the hermeneutical tradition should not be reduced to authors like Heidegger, Gadamer or Rorty. In the 19th Century, we find authors like Schleiermacher and Dilthey who are much closer to the Kantian tradition.

This is a general principle, open for new interpretations of its normative consequences under new and changing situations and circumstances; it does not require a fixed set of norms. This means that it is possible that in different historical contexts, it would have different consequences. But it is also possible that some normative convictions that people have embraced in the past have been wrong; many people failed to consistently understand themselves when they were treating others as slaves etc. I do not want to make this claim here, the relevant point is the methodological remark that it is not impossible from a hermeneutical starting point that some convictions are dialectically necessary. When a hermeneutical approach assumes that the self-interpretation of human beings is bound to historic circumstances and is informed by historically developed patterns of perceptions etc., it does not exclude the possibility that some forms of self-understandings are just inconsistent. It would be dogmatic if a hermeneutic perspective were to exclude this a priori.[5]

2 Monological vs. dialogical forms of transcendental justifications—a false dilemma

If we understand the function of transcendental arguments as being a methodology for getting a reflected form of practical self-understanding, we presuppose that the first-person perspective deserves some priority. This is criticized by discourse ethicists (Apel 1980, Habermas 1990) and more recently by Darwall's plea for a second-person-standpoint (Darwall 2006) as being impossible after the so-called 'linguistic turn'. Mental phenomena, moral convictions and rational activity in general are only possible on the basis of language, and language cannot be developed by the individual subject himself/herself, but is given to us on a col-

---

5 If I relate Gewirth to the hermeneutical tradition, it is perhaps helpful to mention that I think that Gewirth's self-interpretation that his theory is a form of ‚naturalism' is disputable. Of course, he is correct in the sense that he wants to provide an ethical justification that is made for human beings with natural desires, problems and goals like you and me. But the term 'naturalism' gives rise to the question of how to understand this term. If his theory were to be 'naturalistic' in the sense of presupposing a kind of objective, biological theory that describes the human being 'from the outside', it would confront us with an is-ought-problem and would not do right by the concept of dialectical necessity. The starting point of the idea of dialectical necessity must therefore strictly be hermeneutic in the sense that the justification has to be developed from the first-person perspective. But Gewirth is not committed to a form of transcendental idealism; in that sense a follow-up question could be what consequences the idea of dialectical necessity has for our understanding of the natural world.

lective level (as we know from Wittgenstein's 'private language argument'). The (rational) subject can only be understood as result of or in relation to others. This also means that the reliability of moral convictions cannot be saved by reference to rational considerations within the subject's perspective, since such a rational subject can only be adequately understood from a relational perspective. A justification of morality must, therefore, start on an intersubjective level, and cannot start with the individual self-reflection as Kant would have it when he proposed that the subject should try to universalize his/her maxims. Discourse ethics therefore started its programme as a transformation of idealistic philosophy and replaced the role of the subject in the justification of morality with the community of communicative partners (Apel 1980). This transformation entails a priority of *procedures* insofar as the idea of universalization has to be performed by the community and not by the individual subject. Within the Kantian project, the *subject* has not only to perform the *procedure* of universalizing maxims, but also has a specific *status* as a rational being, the status that deserves respect as an 'end in itself'. Therefore, Kant (1998/1785) thought that the first two formulations of the Categorical Imperative were identical; the *Formula of Universal Law* that prescribed the duty to ask yourself whether you can will your maxim as a universal law and the *Formula of Humanity* according to which you must respect humankind as an end in itself. For Kant, respect for the human being is grounded in his rational capacity and this rational capacity obliges him to be consistent in his actions by proving the possibility of universalizing his maxims. If discourse ethicists replace the idea of universalization to a collective level, this identification is no longer possible, and the role of the subject within this dialogically transformed philosophy has changed. Against this background, some propose that there is a division regarding the use of transcendental arguments between the tradition of Apel and Darwall's so-called 'dialogical strategies' as opposed to 'monological' forms of transcendental arguments in the line of Kant, Gewirth or Korsgaard. I have some doubts as to whether this opposition makes sense, and I want to briefly show that these doubts are justified.

To begin with, I agree with the discourse ethicists and their friends that the individual human being cannot understand itself as the source of normativity that yields normativity ex nihilo. Individuals are born to other human beings who have taken care for them, have taught them to walk, eat, speak, love etc. The individual cannot understand himself/herself if he/she has not been brought up in an intersubjective context. Not only are the basic faculties of speaking, thinking, judging, orienting oneself in the world developed with the help of others, but the patterns, the structures and shared contexts of thinking are also learned in intersubjective contexts. We cannot understand ourselves without such a social world; understanding is only possible on the basis of the social world. An appropriate understanding of the phenomenological perspective of the subject will already entail references to the other: we care for others, we fear others, we love and we hate them. I will not be able to describe the goals of my action, desires and interests without anticipation of the goals, desires and interests of others, without inspiration from others and without responsive attitudes towards a social world. It would be phenomenologically implausible to reconstruct the individual in an atomistic sense and to bring the other into the description only on a secondary level. The other and the life-world are present in my experience right from the beginning. But this does not give these socially shared structures of the life-world normative authority without my endorsement. It is still possible to relate reflectively to this social world, and we can understand which structures we see as important and valuable, and which we can or will not endorse.

The critical question to the discourse ethicists (and Darwall) is whether we can develop a basis for justified normative commitments simply on an intersubjective level. Of course, we develop our normative commitments in a shared social world. But the task of a transcendental justification would be to prove the reliability of those commitments. Is it possible to do this without relying on beliefs that the subject must hold? If the subject that engages in communication prides himself/herself on being a brute, behaviouristic and egocentric actor and interprets others in the same way, why should such a subject give priority to intersubjectively acceptable commitments? Does generating normative commitments on an intersubjective level not already presuppose that the subjects involved understand themselves as being obliged to take the perspective of others into account? Agreements between agents and socially shared norms must, in that sense, be based on the agents' insight that they ought to accept specific commitments. Intersubjectivity presupposes subjectivity.[6]

---

6 As a side remark: One can, of course, think about the possibility of anchoring the priority of the dialogical perspective in a phenomenology such as that of Emanuel Lévinas. This would, however, mean that the entire burden of justification rests on a specific ontology (and with this ontology a specific religious world view) which certainly would go beyond the ambitions of Habermas and even of Apel. But furthermore, this option comes with a high price. In Lévinas' view, the agent finds himself/herself in a position where normativity emerges directly from the authority that the other has over me, I am a hostage of the other. According to Lévinas, this authority is even fundamental for the possibility of developing language, worldviews and orientation in life. In that sense, the authority precedes the possibility of understanding and I cannot judge whether this authority is a good thing because it transcends this judgment. The extent to which it is possible for the subject to reflectively relate to this authority of the other in the first place, by rejecting or endorsing it, is dubious. The necessity is different from the Kantian line of

Whilst the discourse ethics-perspective is not possible simply as a solely 'dialogical' perspective, the Gewirthian (and likewise the Kantian) view is not solely a 'monological' one, and I want to explain that somewhat extensively.[7]

To begin with, Gewirth does not presuppose a solely egoistically driven, brutish agent that would suddenly see the light and understand that he should be morally committed when he has the insight that he ought to follow his dialectically necessary commitments. He likewise does not presuppose that the agent is already necessarily a well-intentioned, caring being whose moral commitments result from his good heart. He also does not presuppose an empty, abstract and atomistic being who does not have inclinations, desires, goals and aspirations or who has to abstract from all of these when he starts to reflect on his normative commitments. He rather presupposes agents who have inclinations, desires, values and aspirations, agents that love, hate, have appetites etc.— basically agents like us. Of course, these agents are bodily, linguistically and socially embedded. But the normative convictions to which we see ourselves as necessarily committed do not result from the specific desires, goals and convictions that we have. Rather, they result from the self-reflexive insight that we can only understand ourselves as agents consistently if we understand that some commitments are necessarily required for the possibility of understanding ourselves.

It is important to understand that this approach should not be read as a form of contractualism, according to which we all would agree that it is advantageous for each of us to make arrangements to protect our basic interests. Gewirth rather proposes that we must prove whether we can make sense of ourselves as agents without being committed to some beliefs. These necessary beliefs do not start with the content of our goals and desires, they start with an understanding of ourselves as having goals of action. Gewirth claims that as an agent I must be committed to the belief that the goal of my action is a good for me.[8]

---

thinking; it is rather that I understand that I must endorse specific commitments because I must want them rationally.

7 I assume that the considerations regarding Gewirth could in a similar way be applied to Kant but I cannot discuss this here. For a Kant-Interpretation which would go in this direction: see Steigleder (2002).

8 This holds only for goals that we have effectively endorsed and do not merely entertain in thought; this distinction is equivalent to Kants distinction between 'wanting something' and 'wishing something', 'Wille' vs. 'Wunsch'. I can wish to achieve something but there can be reasons that I do not see is as a good. Only for a real goal of action, something that determines my action, I cannot deny that I see it as good.

Gewirth further assumes methodologically that there are internal connections between dialectically necessary beliefs, in the sense that if I must hold a specific belief I also must hold other beliefs if they are necessarily implied by this belief. Therefore, he concludes: if I cannot understand myself as an agent if I do not assume that my goals of actions are good, then I must also believe that the necessary requirements for being able to realize those goods are a good for me as well. If I want something as a good I also have to want that what is necessary to realize it. Of course, I can decide to refrain from seeing a specific goal as my goal of action if for some reason I cannot endorse this requirement as a necessary requirement for my action (if I understand that killing someone is the only way to become rich, perhaps I decide to refrain from striving for richness). This is, however, not a reason to assume that seeing a goal of action as a good does not imply that I must consider the necessary requirement for reaching this goal to be a good as well, it is rather only a modification of my goal of action. Gewirth further claims that some requirements are not only necessary for specific actions, but are necessary for agents on a more generic level. We need some goods for maintaining and extending our agential capacities, which Gewirth calls the "generic conditions of agency". He distinguishes "freedom" (as the possibility to choose goals of actions at all) and "well-being" (as having the goods that are necessary to realize goals). Although Gewirth assumes that specific goods are to a greater or lesser extent necessary conditions of agency, he simultaneously stresses that these are not merely relevant for specific purposes but always also necessary for the functioning of agents on a generic level. We can discuss what these goods are, how we can determine these goods, and whether the hierarchy of goods that Gewirth introduces is plausible; but this is not the topic in this context. But whatever these generic goods are, the agent must assume that she has to want them, simply due to the fact that she is an agent who wants to realize specific goods.

It is important to remember that Gewirth reconstructs assumptions that agents must believe from their own perspective. That means that he presupposes the first-person-perspective here, and is reconstructing the necessary implications between judgments that agents must be committed to. So far no other agents have come into the picture. That does not mean that Gewirth assumes that the agent is an atomist, solipsist, egoist or otherwise socially dubious figure. As an agent, I care to different degrees for other people, I depend to different degrees on other people, I love others or I hate them, I have sympathy or I'm indifferent. Gewirth assumes that all these kind of attitudes that people happen to have are present. But if I do not love some person, I would not do something wrong to them (perhaps they are even relieved about this). So, the question is what kind of attitude I ought to have and ought not to have in a morally relevant sense, or in other words: which attitudes towards others are morally wrong, and which are morally required? The aim of the transcendental exercise is to understand the way in which the other must be built into the sequence of the agent's dialectically necessary judgments.

Steigleder introduces two premises in his reconstruction of Gewirth's argument that have to be made in order to understand the role of the moral, other-regarding dimension of the sequence (see for the following: Steigleder, 1999, 262 ff.). The first premise is that my access to the generic goods can be influenced from the outside. The extent to which I have access to the generic goods is not in my power, whether I am deprived of important good, or whether I need goods that are not accessible at the moment. If it is dialectically necessary that I ought to want the generic goods, it is dialectically necessary for me to defend myself against external interferences to my generic conditions of agency. Such interferences may be of different kinds: there are interferences where others are actively restricting my freedom illegitimately, but there are also cases where others deny me goods that they could provide, and that I need for my purposive agency. The importance and urgency with which I need those goods can differ, and so can the form of external interference and my dependency. If I must want the generic conditions of agency, I must, through dialectical necessity, judge that I cannot want those interferences.

Steigleder's second premise is that my generic conditions of agency are not only endangered externally, but are also endangered by others. Under conditions of this premise, I must want that others do not interfere with my liberty or that they provide me with the necessary support that they could give. So, only at this point do the dialectically necessary judgments concern a rational claim against others. If it is dialectically necessary for agents (if they only can understand themselves correctly) not to want interferences in the generic conditions of agency, then they also have to want that others refrain from damaging the generic goods or give support if needed and if they are in a position to do so. The other in this step is not the concrete other but a generalized other. This dialectically necessary judgment aims to understand, from the perspective of the agent, the attitude towards the other she must endorse, and to show that it would be practically inconsistent from the perspective of the agent to allow the other to interfere in her liberty and not to help her if she is in need. The sequence explains what kind of normative attitude towards the other a practical being who understands herself consistently ought to have.

This sequence of dialectically necessary judgments can now form the basis for the supreme moral principle if we understand that these judgments are not dialectically necessary for me because I am white, male, a philosopher, German, or because I am a fan of Pergolesi and Single Malt Whiskey, but they are only dialectically necessary on the basis that I have to understand myself as an agent. But if that is the reason for the last judgment, then I must believe that other agents also must subscribe in the same way to the sequence of dialectically necessary judgments, because there was nothing in the sequence that only holds for me as specific individual; rather, it holds for all agents. All agents can only understand themselves consistently if they subscribe to the idea that other agents should respect the generic conditions of agency for all agents, should refrain from endangering them and should support each other when the need of generic goods make this necessary, and that is precisely what Gewirth's 'Principle of Generic Consistency' (PGC) requires.[9] Because we must assume that all agents can only understand themselves well if they subscribe to this principle, it should therefore govern the relationships between agents.

To be clear about the status of this sequence and the premises that are introduced: it is not an attempt to reconstruct how a solipsistic figure suddenly comes to the insight that there are other people and that he wants something from them. The entire sequence does not rest on specific presuppositions concerning desires, concerns, goals, affiliations and aspirations that people may have. It only presupposes that people care about something, and that they have goals of action to strive for. If we did not have goals of action then we would have no goods, and the entire sequence would not get off the ground in the first place. The sequence does not give a specific status to those goals, desires and aspirations as such, but rather gives a normative status to ourselves as beings who are capable of wanting something, of caring for something and for others, of striving for something, and it explains what kind of rational commitments beings with these capacities ought to have in any case, independently from what they care and strive for. The approach does not propose that we should abstract from ourselves as practically embedded beings, but it proposes understanding what kind of commitments all practical beings share if they understand themselves.

This approach shares an important assumption with discourse ethics. At its core the Gewirthian approach is not monological. In a monologue I would not come to the point of understanding that I must see the other as someone with

---

9 It is important to realize that there is not an 'ought' (the normative requirements of the PGC) that follows from an 'is', but that the sequence shows that if I understand myself as an agent it is dialectically necessary to understand myself as rationally committed to the requirement to respect the generic good of agency for all agents, and because this practical self-understanding is dialectically necessary for all agents, it can and should form the basis of a *sensus communis*. In this sense, the PGC is not true but dialectically necessary.

the same capacities[10], as someone with whom I share a relevant perspective, a perspective as a being who is able to exercise his freedom, someone who is able to understand himself as an agent, a being that is able to care for other people and a being for whom it is fundamentally important to live under conditions that allow him to strive for self-fulfilment. But I will only understand that I ought to take the perspective of the other on all those things normatively seriously if I understand that the normative commitment to the evaluation of those capacities has its foundation in contingent elements of my individual self-understanding, in my tender heart, my heroic attitude or my smart personality. Because I can see that the normative commitment to respect the generic conditions of agency is not only obligatory for me but for all agents, this respect should govern our intersubjectively shared world. I cannot see how discourse ethics can generate normative commitments from a discourse if it does not presuppose that the subjects that engage in this discourse are already committed to respecting this normative status of agents.[11]

3 Morality and practical self-understanding—on the application of the PGC

I want to conclude by sketching some consequences that are relevant when we draw our attention to the fact that the PGC is grounded in the first-person perspective and is a methodology to prove the consistency of our moral self-understanding; basically, I want to shortly sketch some implications for the application of the PGC. Even if one agrees that such a form of transcendental justification is convincing, one may have doubts about to what extent such an approach can provide guidance in concrete moral questions. Gewirth himself discusses a variety of implications, particularly a methodology for determining a hierarchy of generic goods according to their 'needfulness for agency'; he distinguishes direct applications of the PGC (when determining individual rights) from indirect applications (regarding the role of institutions necessary to protect rights) and he proposes some procedural rules following from that (Gewirth 1978). In the meantime, a variety of scholars have discussed how one can work with this methodology in discussions about bioethics, environmental eth-

---

10 There is a parallel here between the Gewirthian approach and the so-called 'capabilities approach'. For a critical comparison between Gewirth' and Nussbaum's version of the capabilities approach see: Claassen/Düwell (2013).
11 Schönrich reconstructs discourse ethics in a similar direction, see Schönrich (1993).

ics, legal theory etc. But I estimate that it is necessary to further discuss the underlying philosophical assumptions and their relevance for concrete normative discussions.

To begin with, the important starting point is that Gewirth investigates normative commitments from an analysis of judgments agents cannot deny: it is about 'judgments'. That is important because sometimes this approach has been misunderstood as providing an analysis of implications of the *concept* of 'agency'. But if we were to understand this methodology as a kind of conceptual analysis, nothing that Gewirth claims is valid (but he obviously does not claim this). Gewirth does not analyse concepts but *judgments* in which agents are applying concepts to themselves. Therefore, the capacity to form judgments is fundamental for the entire argument (see Düring/Düwell 2015). If the argument is an investigation into the kind of beliefs we ought to hold, we cannot simply talk about values and goals that are independent from us, it is rather important that we are capable of understanding the role that these values do, can and should play for us. That means that human beings should be able to understand themselves as authors of their commitments, as beings that are able of endorsing and rejecting them. Even if Gewirth shows that some normative commitments are necessary and undeniable, he shows this by referring to us as beings that are capable of judging, and this approach therefore cannot bypass the judgment of individuals. This means that the capacity, the *power of judgment* is of central importance; it is presupposed in the entire sequence of necessary judgments. This means we must understand what conditions are relevant for developing and enhancing this capacity, and under which conditions it can likely be undermined and endangered.

This is relevant for the way we give shape to the political, social, economic and technological dimensions of our world. Human beings should be able to make judgements about the moral dimension, and there should be possibilities to steer the design of the relevant institutions in a morally acceptable way. It is neither necessary nor feasible that each of us is able to understand and judge the relevant practical dimensions, but when it comes to developments in economy and technology, a central moral criterion would be to ask to what extent our power of judgment is increased, diminished or endangered. If human beings are not able to orient themselves in the world in a way that they can themselves judge the relevant aspects of the conditions of their life, this would be problematic from this approach.

However, the power of judgment cannot be exercised only on the most abstract level of moral thinking. If my interpretation is right, and the Gewirthian framework starts in a sense with a form of hermeneutical form of self-reflection, then the moral reflection should be embedded in broader, more comprehensive forms of reflected self-understanding. This implies the ability of individuals to gain an understanding of their individual goals of actions as well as why and how these are important to them. This implies on a collective level that collectives are able to understand the normative dimensions of the conditions under which they live. If we can understand morality only by understanding ourselves, it is important that each of us has the ability to understand him- or herself as an individual, to understand ourselves as collectives and to understand ourselves in our normative commitments as human beings. It is not that we must exercise this ability extensively, but it is important to protect, maintain and develop the capacity to form judgments. For Kant it was important for the exercise of the power of judgment that we can develop it in the free play that the aesthetic experience allows, and perhaps the possibility of aesthetic experience is important for a developed moral life, for the possibility to discover possibilities of actions and to relate to them reflectively (Kant 2000/1790, see as well Düwell 2000). Perhaps we can understand our moral commitments only if they are embedded within human beings' broader perspectives on understanding themselves by asking what it means to be a being that is able to orient itself in the world.

Literature

Apel, Karl-Otto (1980): *Towards a Transformation of Philosophy*. Milwaukee: Marquette University Press.

Bauhn, Per (Ed.) (2016): *Gewirthian Perspectives on Human Rights*. New York, London: Routledge.

Beyleveld, Deryck (1991): *The Dialectical Necessity of Morality. An Analysis and Defense of Alan Gewirth's Argument to the Principle of Generic Consistency*. Chicago, London: The University of Chicago Press.

Boylan, Michael (Ed.) (1999): *Gewirth. Critical Essays on Action, Rationality, and Community*. Lanham, M.D.: Rowman and Littlefield.

Claassen, Rutger; Düwell, Marcus (2013): The Foundations of Capability Theory: Comparing Nussbaum and Gewirth. In: *Ethical Theory and Moral Practice* 16, No. 3, pp. 493–510.

Darwall, Stephen (2006): *The Second Person Standpoint: Morality, Respect and Accountability*. Cambridge, MA: Harvard University Press.

Düring, Dascha; Düwell, Marcus (2015): Towards A Kantian Theory of Judgment: The Power of Judgment in its Practical and Aesthetic Employment. In: *Ethical Theory and Moral Practice* 18, No. 3, pp. 943–956.

Düwell, Marcus (2000): *Ästhetische Erfahrung und Moral. Zur Bedeutung des Ästhetischen für die Handlungsspielräume des Menschen*, Freiburg, München: Alber.

Gewirth, Alan (1978): *Reason and Morality*. Chicago/London: The University of Chicago Press.

Habermas, Jürgen (1990): *Moral Consciousness and Communicative Action*. Cambridge, MA: MIT-Press (German Original 1983).

Kant, Immanuel (1998): *Groundwork of the metaphysics of morals*. Trans. by Mary J. Gregor. Cambridge/New York: Cambridge University Press. (German Original 1785)

Kant, Immanuel (2000): *Critique of the Power of Judgment*. Trans. by P. Guyer and E. Matthews. Cambridge: Cambridge University Press. (German Original 1790)

Regis, Eduard Jr. (Ed.) (1984): *Gewirth's Ethical Rationalism: Critical Essays with a Reply by Alan Gewirth*. Chicago: Chicago University Press.

Schönrich, Gerhard (1993): *Bei Gelegenheit Diskurs—Von den Grenzen der Diskursethik und dem Preis der Letztbegründung*. Frankfurt: Suhrkamp.

Steigleder, Klaus (1999): *Grundlegung der normativen Ethik. Der Ansatz von Gewirth*. Freiburg/München: Alber.

Steigleder, Klaus (2002): *Kants Moralphilosophie. Die Selbstbezüglichkeit reiner praktischer Vernunft*. Stuttgart: J.B. Metzler.

Gerhard Schönrich

Transcendental Arguments in Favour of Absolute Values

Abstract: Do values exist? Do absolute values exist? In connection with Kant, Korsgaard regards rational autonomy of human beings as an absolute value. In contrast to Kant she considers this value as a non-moral value. The draft of a transcendental argument, she gives, is incomplete. First: Why should we value ends? The pursuit of ends doesn't imply that these ends are valuable. We often aim at ends of any worth. A skeptic would challenge the claim that values exist. Second: It is not sufficient to regard ends as good. Perhaps we may be wrong not only in particular cases, we may be mistaken systematically, if there is no such thing as value at all. We are able to bridge the gaps by proving that there is at least one valuable end, and that this end is of a final goodness. Such a unique case is given, when we value our competence to put ends on our own which is in the same way a competence to value something. To meet the conditions of a transcendental argument, the proof has to be invulnerable by the skeptic. Here we benefit from considering the analogous case of token-reflexive utterings like "I am now here". Uttering a sentence denying a propositional content like this results in a performative inconsistency. Hence we can't be wrong in valuing our rational autonomy. But the claim that this autonomy is the final source of value, is not universally valid.

1 Korsgaard's Argument

Korsgaard believes that our humanity is an absolute value. In this context "humanity" is understood as an agent's ability to put ends on herself and to pursue them afterwards. To better differentiate between this notion of the term "humanity" and its more common understanding as "dignity of man", I am going to use the phrase "rational autonomy" instead of humanity. Korsgaard uses these terms synonymously. Rational autonomy is marked by two central traits:

(RA)   S is rationally autonomous iff S is able out of free will

   (i)   to choose ends,

   (ii) to impose onto herself principles and laws according to which these ends will be chosen and realized.

DOI 10.1515/9783110470215-010

Understood as a self-imposition out of free will, rational autonomy must not necessarily comply with the Moral Law. A subject S can meet the two conditions of rational autonomy, without imposing on herself any moral law. Gerold Prauss terms such neutral autocentrism as "rational self-love" (Prauss 1983, p. 144). In the following we will see that Korsgaard's argumentation relies on this non-moral understanding of rational autonomy.

Korsgaard's basic idea is that if we want to understand ourselves as rational agents, we have no choice but to regard our rational autonomy as an absolute value. She claims to be in possession of a transcendental argument in favour of this hypothesis. In fact she developed several variations on that argument, most of which have been thoroughly analysed and criticised by Robert Stern (see Stern 2011, pp. 82ff., 85). In this paper I will discuss the version which is, as I suppose, not only the clearest but also the simplest one:

> The argument is in a simple sense transcendental: we regard some of our ends as good, even though they are obviously conditional; there must be a condition of their goodness, a source of their value; we regard them as good whenever they are chosen with full rational autonomy; so full rational autonomy is the source of their value (Korsgaard 1986, p. 500; see also Korsgaard 1996, pp. 123f.).

The crucial point about this is: It is already sufficient for the argument, if we believe that our rational autonomy is valuable. Or rather it is not necessary for the argument that our rational autonomy is indeed valuable, as long as we do believe that it has value. This version of the argument is not strong enough as it is, as Korsgaard admits herself: "You might want to protest against that last step. How do we get from the fact that we find ourselves to be valuable to the conclusion that we are valuable?" (Korsgaard 1996, p.124). If Barry Stroud is right, then all transcendental arguments are afflicted with this structural weakness (see Stroud 1968). Yet Korsgaard's argument suffers from an even bigger informational gap: Korsgaard doesn't tell us the axiological background assumptions of her argument. But how we reconstruct her argument and therefore how we are going to solve its problems, depends heavily on the theory of value on which I build my analysis.

Korsgaard writes in reference to Kant about "conditional" and "unconditional" values. But using these terms, she is clearly speaking about something that is good in an instrumental or final way. She wants to settle the question whether or not some things are only of conditional value because they derive their entire value from the existence of something even more valuable, or from things valuable on their own. Replacing "conditional" with "instrumental" and "unconditional" with "final" we can reconstruct her argument in the following way:

(1) We believe that some of our ends are good/valuable, even if these ends are obviously instrumental.

(2) Every instrumental value must have a source, straight from which its value is derived.

(3) We believe that our ends are good/valuable whenever they are chosen with full rational autonomy.

(4) ...

(5) Therefore the rational autonomy is a final value and the source for all instrumental values.

This version of the argument can obviously not reach its goal since one step—premise 4—is still missing. This blank space is connected with the main problem: The axiological foundation of the argument has not been explained. But what kind of value theory could serve as a sound foundation for Korsgaard's argument?

Value realism is clearly not an option. A realist about values doesn't need a transcendental argument in the first place. She could only rely on a theory about the way values can be felt, experienced or conceived. Value realism is furthermore a highly problematic position. What queer entities must values be which exist beside the stones, trees, tables, atomic nuclei and electrons of our world? I'll presume without any further discussion that this position is philosophically unfeasible.

What could be the alternative? A value subjectivism? Is something already valuable just because we or a certain social group believe that it is valuable? This position is to weak to help Korsgaard's argument: It is already a sufficient explanation for a value subjectivist if we regard something as good. This is where a skeptic about values would start her argument: It is sufficient for our end directed actions and decisions to be meaningful if we believe them to be of value. There are no such things as values. As a consequence of this rational autonomy needs not to be valuable. It is sufficient that it seems valuable to us. Korsgaard on the other hand wants to explain how we get from "we find ourselves valuable" to "we are valuable". So, how do we get to the claim that we are valuable in terms of our rational autonomy?

2 The Axiological Foundation

What are values if we don't understand them in a realistic nor in a subjectivist manner? Those who deny realism towards values seem to share the following intuition:

> *Dependence-Intuition:* Values can only exist if there exists someone with a pro-attitude. Pro-attitudes are mental states of appreciating, approving, liking etc. directed to the appreciated, approved etc. content.

We also share the intuition that values are not contingent, even if they depend on pro-attitudes. It's not as if everything a social group finds to be good becomes valuable because of that. The Nazis' concept of a master race will surely not transform into a value even if many people start to find it valuable. In our everyday life we argue and disagree with other people about the question whether or not some things are values. Therefore we obviously share an intuition of the following sort:

> *Objectivity-Intuition:* We can always be mistaken in our acknowledgement of the contents of our pro-attitudes. Something doesn't become a value just because it is being valued by some subjects. Values equal an objective status.

Both intuitions are compatible as long as it is only required for the objective status that an appropriateness condition is met by the pro-attitudes. This permits to hold off a value subjectivism or skepticism on the one hand and naive realism on the other hand. So to be valuable or to be good can be defined in the following way (see Schönrich 2013, p. 334):

> *(V)* It is good/a value that p, iff there is a S, so that
>
> (i) S would have ψ with content p (under suitable circumstances);
>
> (ii) ψ is a pro-attitude;
>
> (iii) it is appropriate to have ψ with content p.

This analysis-tool enables us to deliver a sound axiological foundation for Korsgaard's argument and therefore provides the possibility to bridge its previous gaps. Introducing a contra-attitude ψ' in line (ii) the same scheme works *mutatis mutandis* for the *definiendum*: "It is bad/valueless that p". As a first approximation we can describe full rational autonomy as the capability to adopt pro-attitudes or contra-attitudes towards p at will.

For additional transparency: The phrase "It is a value/it is good that" respectively "It is bad/valueless" is understood as an operator that is applied on the content of a value proposition (the proposition "that p"). The definition excludes the dependency from just in fact pro-attitudes. According to (i) it is not necessary that S actually has the pro-attitude as long as it is possible for S to adopt the pro-attitude once suitable circumstances are met. After all, subjects who value something do sleep from time to time or sometimes don't adopt certain pro-attitudes because they are unaware of them or because they are mistaken.

If we want to fully understand Korsgaard's argument we must give a sketchy classification of pro-attitudes like appreciating, liking, admiring etc. and contra-attitudes like disapproving, hating, despising etc. These attitudes are either instrumental or final. The difference can be characterised in the following way: It is the case that someone values something instrumentally, if and only if S has a pro-attitude respectively contra-attitude with content p and believes that p only because of the existence of q. In case that someone values something finally, there is no q for the sake of which p could be valued. Something is an *instrumental value* if p can only be valued, because q makes it valuable and if S values p only because of q. So it is part of the appropriateness-condition of instrumental pro-attitudes that p is valuable only because of q. Whether or not S knows about this, can be ignored at this point. Something is a *final value* if it is being valued for its own sake. It is true for all non-relative final values that: p is being valued and there is no q, because of which p could be valued instrumentally. In a weaker definition we can state that p is a final value if there is a q which is an instrumental value because of p. In that case p would be a final value in relation to q.

Something is a *relative value*, if S values p only in certain respects; if S values p in every possible respect it is an *absolute value*. A value which holds only under certain circumstances (in a certain context) is a *conditional value*. A value which is true in every context is an *unconditional value*. For example we wouldn't understand prudence as a value if it is being attributed to a criminal, because it would make that person only more dangerous. So there is a conceptual difference between *absolute vs. relative* and *conditional vs. unconditional* pro-attitudes. This difference leads us to the following cross classification: Something that is valuable in every aspect must not be valuable under all circumstances. Something that is valuable under all circumstances i.e. something that is unconditionally valuable, might be only valuable in a certain respect, i.e. be only of relative value.

The analysis can be understood as a *fitting-attitude*-approach. It requires that the pro- attitude is appropriate to the object it is directed to. The attitude ψ is appropriate if S has the "right" reasons" to adopt ψ with content p. *Reasons* point to the independent and objective properties of the object to which the pro-attitude is directed. These reasons justify S in adopting the pro-attitude ψ. The reference to such properties explains why the pro-attitude ψ is appropriate.

What we term "value" supervenes upon the relation of the properties to the corresponding attitudes, if and only if these attitudes fulfil the appropriateness-condition, i.e. if there are "right" reasons for adopting this attitude. The properties of the object of the attitude as naturalists conceive of them, are not the subvenient value creating basis. Only the properties insofar they are reasons to adopt a certain attitude constitute the value creating basis. A value consists in the fact, that S has such reasons to adopt a certain pro-attitude. It doesn't matter whether or not she in fact adopts that attitude. If two objects are identical in all their non-axiological subvenient properties and both give a subject reasons to adopt an appropriate pro-attitude, then they are also identical in their supervenient axiological property, i.e. to be of value.

Only appropriate attitudes are value-conducive ones. This requirement distinguishes the *fitting-attitude* approach from subjectivism and subsequent skepticism. What is an appropriate pro-attitude? "Appropriateness" means that the object the attitude is directed at must be worth of adopting the attitude in question. There must be properties of that object delivering reasons which justify S in adopting the attitude. But how can we exclude the wrong kind of reasons? Sometimes we have reasons to adopt a pro-attitude to something of any worth at all (*mutatis mutandis* for adopting a contra-attitude).[1] For example if I can avoid heavy pain only by adopting a pro-attitude towards an evil demon who will punish me if I don't admire him, then I have indeed a good reason for doing so, even though the demon is bad and the appropriate attitude towards him would be hating him. The reason I have for adopting a pro-attitude towards the demon is not content- or object-related, but attitude-related.[2] It is the pro-attitude which is saving me from suffering. We have to differentiate between content-reasons for adopting an attitude ψ and holding reasons for having ψ. Only content-reasons count for the appropriateness of an attitude and support the assumption that p is a value respectively that p is valueless. Confusing content-reasons with reasons for bringing about an attitude is a case of value error. The desirability of an attitude does not determine a value. As a first approximation:

---

1 The "wrong kind of reasons" problem and the evil demon case is debated largely by Rabinowicz/Rønnow-Rasmussen (2004); Olson (2004); Stratton-Lake (2005), Danielsson/Olson (2007) and others.

2 This differentiation goes back to Parfit's well known difference between *object-given* and *state-given reasons* (see Parfit 2001).

(*App*)   It is appropriate to adopt a pro-attitude ψ towards p, iff there is a S so that

(i)   S has sufficient reasons for adopting ψ and

(ii)   these reasons are grounded in p and not in ψ or

(iii)   these reasons are grounded in q and q is the final source of p's instrumental value.

There are three ways S can be mistaken: (i) Confusion about the supporting role of the reasons. There may be defeaters like undermining and overtrumping reasons. (ii) Confusion about content- or attitude-relatedness of reasons and (iii) Confusion about instrumental or final reasons. Sometimes S regards p as of final value, even though the value of p is derived from the value of q. This confusion explains why S sometimes makes a fetish of p: Imagine S loving his car for its own sake, instead of regarding it as a means for mobility. Whereas confusions of type (i) seem to be rather trivial, confusions of type (ii) and (iii) are more difficult to disentangle.

3 Scrutinizing the Premises

Premise (1) seems to be unproblematic. Even a skeptic wouldn't deny that there are some subjects who think that some of their ends are valuable. And even a skeptic admits the fact that people sometimes are confused about what to regard as valuable.

Premise (2) can now be explained on basis of my axiological assumptions: An instrumental value p exists, because there exists something else that is valuable, namely q and the value of p is derived from q. In this case q is the source of p's value. Now it could be the case that even q is only valuable as long as there exists an r which is valuable. The entailed regress can only be stopped if there is an actual ending s, so that there is no other value t, for which s could be instrumentally valued. The last value in such a sequence cannot be a relative final value, like for example r in relation to q. It must be a value for its own sake.

Premise (3) is less obvious. For the defence of premise (3) we need a principle that allows to connect the competence to choose ends autonomously with the competence to value something. To choose an end out of free will and to value something isn't the same.

(*VE**) It is true for at least one end p: If S chooses p autonomously as an end, then S believes that p is valuable [then S would adopt a pro-attitude with content p].

While that version of the principle is plausible, it is still too weak. Even a skeptic towards values could accept this principle, because (*VE**) does not warrant that ends are in fact values, even though they are chosen autonomously. S might be systematically mistaken in thinking that something is valuable: We might therefore live in a world devoid of values. Regarding something as valuable, i.e. adopting a pro-attitude with content p does not imply that p is in fact valuable. So if we want the argument to hold at least one of the ends S regards as good must be good. We need an argument to support the stronger hypothesis:

(*VE*) It is true for at least one end p: If S chooses p autonomously as an end, then p is a value [then S would adopt an appropriate pro-attitude with content p].

How can we justify (*VE*)? Following the Kantian-Korsgaardian argumentation there is one special case in which an end proofs to be a value at the same time it is chosen. In regarding its rational autonomy as an end, the subject is directing a pro-attitude on itself. This pro-attitude is rational self-love. What I have to show now is, that it is not enough for that subject to think of its rational autonomy as a value, but that this autonomy is really valuable, i.e. that the corresponding pro-attitude is appropriate.

Premise (5) states that rational autonomy is a final value, and as source of all instrumental values an absolute value. But to conclude to (5) I have to supplement the missing premise (4) now:

(4) To choose rational autonomy as an end (to believe that rational autonomy is valuable) is a manifestation of rational autonomy.

Believing that something is valuable means *adopting a pro-attitude.* So let us adopt a pro attitude—the attitude termed self-love—to rational autonomy. Following the axiological scheme (*V*) something *is an absolute value*, if and only if S would *adopt an appropriate pro-attitude for its own sake to p.* Hence the question is: What does it mean to adopt an appropriate pro-attitude to rational autonomy? Under which conditions is self-love—loving oneself for its own sake—appropriate? So what is the story fleshing out the previous scheme of analysis?

Korsgaard starts her story with a self-referential spin that is necessary to make her transcendental argument possible. According to Korsgaard we don't value rational autonomy in the same way we value justice or democracy.

When we value our rational autonomy we value ourselves at the same time. We are valuable to ourselves. But how is this spin compatible with the objectivity-condition that defends us against value subjectivism and value skepticism?

Since rational autonomy could be a final value under all possible circumstances, we have no problem to show that it is an unconditional value. On the other hand it is kind of difficult to proof that rational autonomy is also an absolute value. Rational autonomy is a value to me. So in a certain perspective I am a value, namely in the personal perspective of the person that I am. Apparently a relative value like this cannot be an objective value at the same time. Even worse: In a later paper Korsgaard appealing to Kant identifies "self-love" as the entry point to the final source of value (Korsgaard 1998, p. 54).

Let's summarize the discussion so far:

Rational autonomy is a value-for-S, iff

(1) S would adopt the pro-attitude of self-love;

(2) the object of self-love would be loved for its own sake (final);

(3) this pro-attitude is appropriate in every respect (absolute) and under all possible circumstances (unconditional).

4 Is rational autonomy a value for myself?

First of all the generalising phrase "value-for-S" is ambiguous:

(1) The relativisation can be understood *extensionally* as a value for a certain S. In that case the question is what instances can be inserted for the placeholder "S". If we insert a referential term that picks out only myself, then the value we've been looking for will only be a value for myself and nobody else.

(2) The relativisation can also be understood *intensionally* as a perspective or as a general respect. Something can be valuable in a certain perspective or respect but not in a different one. We sometimes express such respects in very general terms: Some values are only valuable in an epistemic, economic, moral, etc. respect. On the other hand I can define respects very specifically, so that they describe only one view. Namely my own view. The view of the unique person that I am.

So why not choose the extensional reading (1)? We cannot control the degenerative variations of self-love, if we interpret the argument according to the extensional reading. Such an interpretation produces the wrong reasons for the appro-priateness-condition of the pro-attitudes.

Rational self-love has to meet some additional requirements to the appropri-ateness-condition. The emotional attitude of self-love can easily be deceived and can easily degenerate to an attitude that is not compatible with the rationality-condition. Kant calls the degenerative variations of self-love "egoism (Eigen-liebe/philautia)" and "self-conceit (Eigendünkel/arrogantia)" (KpV, AA 05, p. 73). If we leave the subtle differences aside, both terms mark an egoist as someone who "directs all ends to herself" ("welcher alle Zwecke auf sich selbst einschränkt") (Anthr., AA 07, p. 130). The attitude of rational self-love is about choosing one self as an end. Therefore any subject that adopts that attitude will restrict all ends to itself. So what distinguishes rational self-love from its de-generate variations like egoism and self-conceit?

If I adopt the attitude of self-conceit, I value myself because of being a unique and irreplaceable person, with a unique history. So I value what makes me identifiable. What is good if I direct my love to another person becomes wrong in case of self-love, namely to understand the properties of a person as *identifiers*. Self-love will degenerate to the irrational attitude of self-conceit if the properties of the "beloved self" are given the role of *identifying* reasons.

Rational self-love is not about my unique personality: It is about loving all of humanity in my own person (see Korsgaard 1996, p. 249 ff. and 1998, p. 54). Whatever the properties are, that make myself worth to be loved, they must not function as *identifiers* but as *justifiers*. While the love to a women for example must not be justified by reasons that derive from her properties. I love her on the basis of *identifiers* for being the unique person she is. Rational self-love on the other hand needs to be justified.

If we use the relativizing term "value for..." following the extensional read-ing, we pick out with the subject also its properties and history, that allow us to identify that subject as unique. The properties become *identifiers*. In that case we can't prevent the possible degeneration of self-love to self-conceit any more. The intensional reading can be an alternative to that: In this case we do not ask for whom something is a value but in which respect or perspective something is a value. If we narrow down the respect really specifically then we are able to pick out S. We arrive at the following scheme of analysis:

(V_{in})   It is good/a value, that p, in respect R, iff there is a S, so that:

    (i)   S would have ψ with content p (under suitable circumstan-ces);

    (ii) ψ is a pro-attitude;

(iii)   it is appropriate in respect R to have a pro-attitude ψ with
content p.

In this case we got to specify the appropriateness-condition:

(iii*)   it is appropriate in respect R to have the pro-attitude ψ with content p, iff there are reasons of the type R.

The appropriateness-condition of self-love towards rational autonomy must be
tightened in one further aspect. The reason for adopting self-love must be universalisable. So every person swapping places with me should be able to accept my
reasons and therefore be able to use these reasons to justify why she adopts the
pro-attitude of self-love. While a reason to adopt rational self-love is connected
with the subject, it is not restricted to it. This reason can still be acceptable to
everyone else. My suggestion for a definition:

(RSL)   Pro-attitude ψ is *rational self-love* iff

(i)   the reasons are grounded in the self the pro-attitude ψ is directed at

(ii)   these reasons fulfil the role of *justifiers* and

(iii)   these reasons are universalisable.

Condition (iii) is based on an universalisation-principle:

(UP)   If x is a value-for S, then y is a value-for-S*, if x and y share the
same relevant subvenient properties.

Because of that we can assume that the subvenient properties which define S as
rational and autonomous, are the same for all S. According to the principle of
supervenience the supervenient properties (in this case the value) are the
same. So (UP) allows that if I am a value for myself everyone can appreciate
the value I am for myself. Rønnow-Rasmussen does not accept this consequence
(see Rønnow-Rasmussen 2011, pp. 93f.). He insists that the properties in question
are reasons which pick out a unique individual. This is right for personal values,
but is misleading in the case of rational self-love, because it lends support to
egoism and self-conceit. In this case rational autonomy would exist only as a
value-for-myself and nobody else.

Only universally applicable reasons can be relevant. They are relevant in the
sense that everyone virtually changing places with me is able to accept my reasons and use them as justification for adopting the pro-attitude of self-love.
Therefore, the reasons for self-love are not private in a strict sense. They are
not bound to a single person and her unique history and experiences. Let's as-

sume for a moment that I love myself out of self-conceit. Then I would love myself as the unique person that I am with all my preferences and ends, just because I am that unique person. So all my ends are egoistically directed toward myself. If I were to swap places with other persons most of them wouldn't be able to adopt my reasons. While another person might understand my reasons, she can't share them. My reasons to love myself out of self-conceit as a unique person, cannot be shared by another person even if she took my place. There are no reasons for her to fulfil my preferences and support ends that are directed towards myself; but she has good reasons to value rationality and autonomy even if these reason are directed to me.

5 What makes Korsgaard's argument a transcendental argument?

Transcendental arguments are anti-skeptical arguments. They try to show that in order to be meaningful the skeptic's challenge must presuppose what he is denying. Kant's "refutation of idealism" may serve as a paradigm: To express her doubts on the existence of an outer world the skeptic has to assume that we have experiences of a certain sort. The transcendental argument then aims at demonstrating that a necessary condition for the possibility of having such experiences is just the existence of outer objects questioned by the skeptic.

Stroud disputes the scope of arguments of this kind. In order to make skeptical claims meaningful it is enough that we believe, that they are true, they must not actually be true. Our having this belief enables us to give sense to what we say (Stroud 1968, p. 255). So transcendental arguments fail. Anyway, in a later paper (Stroud 1999) Stroud defends a weaker sense of transcendental arguments: they have to demonstrate the invulnerability and indispensability of certain claims. Following these lines of analysis my strategy must be a twofold one:

1) Contrary to Stroud (1968) I have to demonstrate that it is not enough to regard something as valuable, i.e. acknowledging only pro-attitudes with content p, but denying appropriateness, because in doing so, the skeptic presupposes what she is denying. So it is possible that there are values.

2) In compliance with Stroud (1999) I restrict the scope of the argument. An appropriate pro-attitude towards rational autonomy like rational self-love is invulnerable by the strikes of the skeptic. Denying rational autonomy is self-refuting, because adopting a contra-attitude towards rational autonomy is equivalent to instantiating rational autonomy. So there exists at least one final and absolute value for subjects like us.

Ad 1) Is it enough to regard something as valuable? What does the skeptic deny and what does she take for granted? Endorsing Premise (1) and (*VE**) she takes our every day life of valuing as given. There are subjects adopting pro-attitudes ψ with a content p. Obviously she denies that there are values at all, i. e. something corresponding to pro-attitudes or something supervening on those attitudes. According to the skeptic our value-driven talk is satisfactorily explained by showing that S regards a certain content p as valuable. So there is no objective meaning in value talk. The denial of objectivity is compatible with social constraints on the arbitrariness of pro-attitudes. Some groups or societies may sanction certain attitudes and promote others.

Taking our everyday life at face value the skeptic has to deal with confusions too. Sometimes we criticise people for regarding something as valuable that seems to be of no value at all. Confronted with this problem the skeptic can refer to undermining or overtrumping defeaters of the reasons supporting the attitude in question just like we do in my frame of analysis.

But there is a sort of non-trivial confusion that can't be easily cleared away in this manner. A merchant refraining from shortchanging not because he regards shortchanging as bad, but because he believes that his behaviour is better for drawing profit in the long run, appreciates a good thing for wrong reasons (see Kant, AA 04, p. 397). For example in the evaluative talk of every day we regard greed of gain, ambition, imperiousness as bad, knowing that the correspondent pro-attitudes are of value, because they promote economic and social competition we all benefit from (see Kant, AA 07, p. 274). Kant is aware of this deep-rooted asymmetry between reasons for adopting a certain attitude towards p and second-level attitudes towards attitudes like this. The principle: "If we adopt a pro-attitude ψ as good (i. e. we regard something as good), then we ought to regard instances of ψ to be of the same value" is obviously not universally valid (see Schönrich, pp. 23 ff.)

Lacking a condition of appropriateness to be met by ψ, the skeptic must do without the concept of appropriateness. Any case of regarding something as good respectively as bad is of equal value. The skeptic doesn't possess the conceptual means to differentiate between adopting an attitude on the basis of wrong content-reasons and an attitude on the basis of right content-reasons and subsequently she is unable to differentiate between attitudes which are valuable even though S is mistaken in adopting them, and attitudes which are of no value at all even though S is not mistaken in adopting them.

To bring the point home, imagine a skeptic encountering the evil demon. In view of the pain she will suffer if she is not adopting the right attitude, she can choose between a pro-attitude like admiring or appreciating or a contra-attitude like despising or hating the demon. So her regarding the demon as bad and at the same time regarding him as good results in an inconsistency; the skeptic runs the risk of becoming schizophrenic. Suppose she regards the demon of no value at all. So she should adopt a contra-attitude like despising the demon. But she knows that adopting a pro-attitude like admiring the demon would save her from suffering heavy pain. Why should she prefer the one attitude to the other? How is she able to admire someone she despises?

In the terms of my analysis we easily are capable to disentangle these confusions, because we keep up the independence of the content p of the attitudes. Strengthening the *Objectivity Intuition* some philosophers prefer a more realistic vocabulary: "independence of content" means "objective valuable". We distinguish between the *objective value of p* on the basis of content-reasons for adopting an appropriate attitude towards p and the *value of ψ* on the basis of attitude-related reasons for having or entertaining ψ. Obviously there is no content-reason to admire the demon, which would make such an attitude an appropriate one. But there is a state-related reason making this attitude ψ instrumentally valuable, because avoidance of pain is a final value handed down to ψ by this source. If the skeptic wants to completely describe our evaluative talk of every day she must presuppose what he is denying. She has to acknowledge the *Objectivity-Intuition* or to put it in our terms: the concept of appropriateness.

It is of no avail to insist on a distinction the skeptic is in fact able to draw on the basis of her assumptions: first-order attitudes with content p and second-order attitudes directed at first-order attitudes. Can she transform the role of the appropriateness-condition into the role of second-order attitudes? Nota bene: The skeptic cannot accept full-blooded content-reasons understood as attitude-independent reasons to value something. According to the skeptic reasons pertain to properties of attitudes like their desirability. Assuming higher-level attitudes the skeptic now has a reason to hate the demon on the first level, whereas on the second level she has a reason to admire him. The question remains: If it is desirable to hate the demon, how can it be desirable to admire him, even if admiring him is only of instrumental value? The skeptic is not allowed to say as we do that one of these attitudes must be inappropriate in regard to the demon.

Ad 2) Is it possible to deny rational autonomy? Due to the self-reflexive structure of self-love, we are very well able to defend the argument against skepticism.

Rational autonomy is just the capability to adopt pro- or contra-attitudes at will. It is the condition which makes possible such attitudes. What does it mean to deny rational autonomy? Put in the terms of attitude a denial of rational autonomy means to adopt a contra-attitude, i.e to dispraise or hate rational autonomy instead of loving it. But in adopting such an attitude even the strongest dispraiser of rational autonomy has to instantiate just this competence. So the attempt to deny it leads to an inconsistency.

Considered from the other side: Adopting the attitude of self-love S is directed to a property of S, namely the competence to choose her own ends and to value something autonomously. So if S uses her competence to value something she is performing just that which is being valued. Or to put it differently: Rational self-love is a manifestation of what self-love is directed to. In difference to values like justice or democracy the appropriate pro-attitude for rational autonomy is an instance of that value. That's not true for a value like justice. The pro-attitude directed to justice isn't a manifestation of justice itself.

We can use sentences like "I am now here" as an analogy to this particular case of self-love. If that sentence is uttered at a certain point in space and time, by a certain subject like myself this sentence is pragmatically and necessarily true. If this sentence is uttered according to the previous description it can't be wrong. Yet the sentence is not universally true. We can think of possible worlds where it is wrong, for example if the sentence is being uttered by an answering machine while I am gone. Hence it isn't true for all possible worlds, i. e. the sentence is not universally true.

In case of the pro-attitude directed to our own competence to value something we can cautiously attempt the following generalisation: Wherever something is being valued, there will also be a manifestation of the competence to value that thing. Every case of self-love (that fulfils the rationality-condition) warrants that rational autonomy is truly a value. The success of this anti-skeptical manoeuvre lies in the fact that we never left the control zone of the subject: We don't deal with the external world and we speak only about the competences and attitudes i. e. about the internal sphere of a subject or agent (see Skidmore 2002, p. 127).

If I value myself (fulfilling the rationality conditions) and claim to be a value in terms of my rational autonomy, then my claim is invulnerable to skeptical objections. My statement about value at that point in space and time can actually not be wrong. An entirely different question is whether or not it is also indispensable to value oneself (see Stroud 1999, p. 166). Perhaps it is possible to stop valuing oneself without dispensing of one's rational self at the same time. This question has to remain unanswered at this point.

Bibliography

Danielsson, Sven; Olson, Jonas (2007): "Brentano and the Buck-Passers." In: *Mind* 116, pp. 511–522.

Kant, Immanuel (1900 ff): *Werke. Akademie-Ausgabe* (= AA), Vol. 5 (= KpV) and Vol. 7 (= Anthr.), Preussische Akademie der Wissenschaften. Berlin: Reimer.

Korsgaard, Christine M. (1986): "Aristotle and Kant on the Source of Value." In: *Ethics* 96, pp. 486–505.

Koorsgaard, Christine M. (1996): *The Sources of Normativity*. Cambridge: Cambridge University Press.

Korsgaard, Christine M. (1998): "Motivation, Metaphysics, and the Value of the Self: A Reply to Ginsborg, Guyer, and Schneewind." In: *Ethics* 109, pp. 49–66.

Olson, Jonas (2004): "Buck Passing and the Wrong Kind of Reasons." In: *The Philosophical Quarterly* 54, pp. 295–300.

Parfit, Derek (2001): "Rationality and Reasons." In: D. Egonsson/J. Josefsson/B. Petersson/ T. Rønnow-Rasmussen (Eds.): *Exploring Practical Philosophy*. Aldershot: Ashgate, pp. 17–39.

Prauss, Gerold (1983): *Kant über Freiheit als Autonomie*. Frankfurt a.M.: Klostermann.

Rabinowicz, Wlodek; Rønnow-Rasmussen, Toni (2004): "The Strike of the Demon. On Fitting Pro-attitudes and Value." In: *Ethics* 114, pp. 391–423.

Rønnow-Rasmussen, Toni (2011): *Personal Value*. Oxford: Oxford University Press.

Schönrich, Gerhard (2013): "Kants Werttheorie? Versuch einer Rekonstruktion." In: *Kant-Studien* 104, pp. 321–345.

Schönrich, Gerhard (2015): "Würde, Wert und rationale Selbstliebe." In: *Zeitschrift für philosophische Forschung* 69, pp. 127–158.

Skidmore, James (2002): "Skepticism about Practical Reason: Transcendental Arguments and their Limits." In: *Philosophical Studies* 109, pp. 121–141.

Stern, Robert (2011): "The Value of Humanity: Reflections on Korsgaard's Transcendental Argument." In: Joel Smith/Peter Sullivan (Eds.): *Transcendental Philosophy and Naturalism*. Oxford: Oxford University Press, pp. 74–95.

Stratton-Lake, Philip (2005), "How to Deal with Evil Demons." In: *Ethics* 115, pp. 788–798.

Stroud, Barry (1968): "Transcendental Arguments." In: *Journal of Philosophy* 65, pp. 241–256.

Stroud, Barry (1999): "The Goal of Transcendental Arguments." In: Robert Stern (Ed.): *Transcendental Arguments. Problems and Prospects*. Oxford: Oxford University Press, pp. 155–172.

Christian Illies

Neither for Beasts nor for Gods: Why only morally-committed Human Beings can accept Transcendental Arguments

> "Theory and teaching are not, I fear, equally efficacious in all cases: the soil must have been previously tilled if it is to foster the seed, the mind of the pupil must have been prepared by the cultivation of habits, so as to like and dislike aright. For he that lives at the dictates of passion will not hear nor understand the reasoning of one who tries to dissuade him; but if so, how can you change his mind by argument?"
>
> *Aristotle, Nicomachean Ethics, 1179*[b-]

Abstract: Transcendental arguments are arguments which aim to provide justification (possibly even ultimate justification) for some ethical and other judgments. In their most complex form they are indirect arguments: they claim to demonstrate that a proposition is true by showing that it cannot be false. This kind of reasoning is not trivial. But what are we doing when we argue transcendentally? We can ask this question from an epistemological perspective but also from the point of view of moral psychology. The thesis of this paper is that understanding and accepting of indirect transcendental arguments require some form of moral commitment on the part of the reasoner, over and above that reasoner's purely rational capacities. Such a reasoner can be neither a non-human animal (as these lack any rational understanding of morality) nor a god (as gods, being morally perfect, need no moral commitment), but must have exactly those capacities which we, human beings, happen to have. This supports the observations of Aristotle, Confucius, and others: that only the good person can find the truth.

I Transcendental arguments in ethics: the debate.

Why is there ongoing disagreement concerning transcendental arguments in ethics? The cynic might opine that philosophers quarrel over almost everything, and that transcendental arguments simply provide another arena for such a debate. In an age, however, when many have scant trust in reason or in reasoning, all

DOI 10.1515/9783110470215-011

kinds of argument are under attack, simply by virtue of being reasoned arguments. Transcendental arguments in ethics would seem to be particularly suspect because they are not in tune with the (seemingly dominant) relativist convictions of most contemporary philosophers. Philosophical projects, such as that of Alan Gewirth, which aspire to provide secure foundations for practical ethical reasoning, seem for many simply outdated and irrelevant. Others suspect that transcendental reasoning reintroduces atavistic metaphysical (or even theological) ideas back into philosophy (Albert 1980, p. 14).

It is perhaps more productive to look at the unique features of transcendental arguments and ask what makes rational people disagree with respect to their force and authority. Why should anyone accept a sound transcendental argument as decisive? We can pursue this question (i) with regard to the rationality of the argument and/or (ii) with regard to the rationality of the person attending to the argument.

(i) We can explore the specific *rules of inference* employed by transcendental arguments, try to understand them better, and compare them with other rules. We can ask whether these rules of transcendental inference are convincing. This is a formal epistemological project.

(ii) We can look at the *particular reasoner* and ask why s/he might regard specific arguments as more (or less) decisive. This project raises questions that more properly fall within the remit of moral psychology and in what follows I will treat them in this way.

In the moral-psychological manner we can ask generally about any argument, 'Why should I accept it?' It is worth looking more specifically at indirect transcendental arguments in ethics and at their authority. Who is likely to accept them? I will argue that their authority for an individual depends partly on his or her moral personality; agents must be *morally committed*—and the more they are, the more likely will they accept the argument as powerful. An amoral sceptic, even if otherwise highly rational, could not possibly grasp such arguments.

In order to defend this thesis, I will firstly give an account of transcendental arguments in general and of indirect transcendental arguments, and their specific features, in particular (II). It will then be asked why a rational person might not accept a sound argument couched within the logic of practical reason (III). In the next section we will ask the same in the case of indirect transcendental arguments. What are the specific circumstances under which it is difficult for a reasoner to accept a sound indirect transcendental argument? The answer to this question is the central thesis of this paper. Moral commitment is the crucial factor (IV). Finally it will be shown that this thesis can be related to traditional insights in moral philosophy as articulated by Confucius, Aristotle, Kant, and others (V).

II Indirect transcendental arguments

a: structure

A transcendental argument is designed to show that some judgment is true because it cannot be rationally rejected. Transcendental arguments follow a procedure Kant first explored in his *Critique of Pure Reason*. Their basic structure is this: a proposition p must be the case for q to be possible because the former is the necessary condition for the possibility of the latter: q only if p.

To indicate the specific type of the material implication ("only if ... then"), we might introduce the symbol ▸▸ for this transcendental conditional: q ▸▸ p. The transcendental conditional is also a material implication (i. e. p is a necessary condition of q) but it is more than that. What more is involved varies according to different interpretations, but in my view, as I have suggested elsewhere, the more amounts to: "One cannot reject p if one accepts q". But how do we discover whether p is the transcendental condition for q? The general answer given by Kant and others is that p cannot intelligibly be thought away without losing q. The condition is therefore a priori. In his theoretical philosophy, Kant examined the *conceptual* conditions (the categories of understanding) for the possibility of experience. The type of argument Kant used can be expressed formally in a way similar to *modus ponens (with* q and p as facts or states of affairs etc.) and the second premise as the transcendental conditional.

> Premise 1: q
> Premise 2: q ▸▸ p
> Conclusion: p

Thus an agent who accepts q as a starting point will be rationally committed also to accept p. In order for the argument to work, q must be a minimal notion which no rational agent can deny; because a sceptic who doubts q in the first place will not accept p. But this is exactly the quandary of this type of transcendental argument. If the starting point is too minimal, it will hardly lead to interesting conclusions. But a more substantial q will not be regarded as self-evident.ˉ This problem is particularly difficult in the realm of practical reason. Where might we find a substantial q to start our argument with? It gets worse, though. In order to avoid the naturalistic fallacy, this substantial q would also have to be *normative.ˉ* What, then, might that q be? It seems difficult to think of a fact or state of affairs that is un-debatable and *necessarily* normative; that is, a fact or state of affairs which cannot be thought of as being other than valuable. This is exactly what the sceptic is likely to question.

There is, however, a different type of transcendental argument: one which seems more promising for ethics. This type, essentially, is designed to show that something cannot be rejected rationally because even the sceptic must presuppose it. The crux is that any sceptical objection against an assumption is only intelligible, and thus can only be taken seriously, if the rejected assumption were true. That, in turn, means that all sceptical objections against it are self-defeating and therefore false. No one can, for example, rationally deny that we can reason or freely argue that we are not free, without some such "pain of self-contradiction", to use Gewirth's classic expression.

Arguments of this type were called 'retorsive' by the philosophical tradition because they turn the objection of the sceptic back against his or her own claim – and transform it into support of exactly the thesis the sceptic claims to deny. The impossibility of any consistent scepticism provides the rational ground for the starting point: the argument rests on the demonstration of it being irrational (since self-defeating) to refute the judgement in question. Descartes' quest for an Archimedean Point of knowledge can be read in this way. He argues that we know with certainty that we exist because an (existing) "I" is the necessary condition even for the possibility of doubting one's own existence. Doubt is not simply 'there' but must always be entertained by some reasoning (in this case, doubting) subject. Without existing, I could not perform the act of doubting. An even older example is found in Aristotle, in his refutation of the 'anti-rational' scepticism surrounding the Principle of Non-Contradiction. In Book *Gamma* of the *Metaphysics* (1005b35 – 1006a28), he points out that *any* sceptical attack on this principle requires that it itself be taken meaningfully, and is therefore self-defeating. Thus the validity of the very Principle of Non-Contradiction must be presupposed for any rational doubt or argument.

According to the transcendental conditional that is employed in these arguments, any scepticism about r implies the very same r as its necessary condition; where r refers to reason or some necessary aspect of reasoning (for example that there is a subject who/which reasons, or that the Principle of Non-Contradiction must be followed), and ¬r amounts to the sceptical objection that there is no r (or that r is wrong).

This scepticism is therefore self-defeating. Given that no self-defeating objection can be put forward rationally, the claim '¬r' cannot be true, because it claims the impossibility of what it presupposes. Even though the argument has a starting point that is similar to its conclusion, it is not circular (it does not reach a sceptical stance with respect to r *from* a sceptical stance with respect to r)." We can formalize this in a way parallel to the first kind of transcendental argument:

Premise 1: ¬r
Premise 2: ¬r ▸▸ r
1ˢᵗ Conclusion: ¬r is self-contradictory (thus wrong)

(▸▸ signifies the transcendental conditional.)

But the argument does not end here. Since we *cannot* judge r to be wrong without falling into self-contradiction, and since the Principle of Non-Contradiction holds (r and ¬r cannot both be true or both false at the same time, thus either r or ¬r), we conclude r:[1]

2ⁿᵈ Conclusion: r

There are three particular features of this indirect type of transcendental argument which are worth highlighting: the kind of transcendental conditional which it investigates (i), its apagogic nature (ii), and the type of self-defeat the sceptic faces.

(i)   The argument begins with the performative dimension of reasoning, i.e. reasoning understood as an utterance constituting an act. It asks for the transcendental conditions of this act, what might be called its "performative conditions" or "pragmatic implications". These are rather different from Kant's conceptual conditions. In the indirect case, the claim is that without these performative conditions being fulfilled, there would not be an intelligible *act* of reasoning. There is no doubt raised if there is no subject to entertain it: the subject is therefore the necessary performative condition of any reasoning (in this case, doubting) being possible.

(ii)   The argument demonstrates the truth of some judgement (or premise) in an indirect manner by showing that even the sceptic must accept what he denies. This justification is apagogic: it does not have a necessity deduced from any presupposed axioms, but it is seen to be true because it cannot reasonably be questioned and thus cannot be false.

---

1 K.-O. Apel argues that the self-defeat of the sceptical judgement '¬r' is only the first criterion for the truth of r. He adds a second criterion: such an r cannot be deduced through any rational argument without already presupposing its validity (1976b, p. 71). But this second criterion is given by the first: if the sceptical denial is self-defeating because *qua* being rational, it presupposes the denied r, then any reasoning will obviously presuppose it.

(iii) An agent who does not accept r is not merely logically inconsistent but is in a wider sense self-defeating; his or her thoughts (claims) and deeds (and their performative implications) are not in harmony. This specific form of inconsistency (or the consistency obtained in making the correct claim 'r') might more adequately be called "incoherence" because it goes beyond mere logical requirements. "Coherence" is about a harmonious integration of diverse elements which even include normative elements (some performative implications of actions are normative). Derek Beyleveld's expression of "foundational coherentism" is a good way to grasp this third feature of indirect transcendental arguments.

b: force and cogency

Arguments of this kind have been employed quite extensively in ethics, using concepts such as human autonomy, freedom, reason, or discourse. Karl-Otto Apel, for example, argues for a general and categorical ethics which can be transcendentally grounded on the concept of reason as a discourse. His argument runs as follows. We cannot escape being participants in a discursive community: even the sceptic affirms participation by making a rational contribution. Since we necessarily argue as a member of, and with regard to, this community, we have thereby already implicitly accepted those rules which govern the public language and the rational co-operation of human beings. The most important of these rules is that everyone engaged in the discourse must recognize and respect all participants as persons. This is the crucial point of the 'humanitas', as Apel puts it, which is presupposed in any act of understanding and reasoning (see Apel 1976a ii, p. 385).

What makes these starting points for indirect transcendental arguments so powerful is that they claim to be immune from sceptical doubt: any attempt to question them fails and serves as an affirmation of what was being denied. This is how these transcendental arguments most strikingly differ from deduction. Deduction will always face the problem of the soundness of its premises; that is why deduction can never provide the ultimate foundation we seek in this context. (See chapter 1 of Illies 2003)

Most importantly for ethical foundationalism, indirect transcendental arguments allow us to bypass the Naturalistic Fallacy. By looking at our actions or at reasons as forms of action, they focus on something regarded as normative, because goal-directed from the beginning. The performative conditions are partly normative. Discourse ethics sees reasoning as implicitly aiming at consent and agreement, and a discursive community as an ideal. In Gewirth's argument we find a similar analysis of action, understood as freely chosen, intentional behaviour enacted to achieve a purpose voluntarily selected by the agent. (Gewirth 1981, pp. 22, 26 – 27) By being intentional, actions are *always* affirmations of the very act of performing them and of all necessary aspects of the act (for example, the underlying freedom necessary for behaviour to be counted as action): when I 'do' something I inherently grant at least that it was worth being chosen by me. Gewirth analyses this in some more detail. Firstly, every action reveals a *selective attention* towards an end. Secondly, it shows the *directedness of an agent* towards an end. And, thirdly, it expresses the agent's *active interest* in achieving the end. (Gewirth 1981, p. 40) These essential aspects of actions demonstrate that it is appropriate to talk about an implicitly given value-judgement as a necessary performative condition of any action. Whether this is sufficient to build up full universal norms such as Categorical Imperatives is a different question; it is enough to see how the Naturalistic Fallacy can be avoided if the argument works. By beginning with actions, either ordinary actions or reasoning understood as act, indirect transcendental arguments uncover something that is already normatively loaded and whose normativity cannot be denied without self-contradiction. If the argument works, it is normative from the very beginning.

III Rational openness as a precondition for accepting practical reasoning

Let us first ask of the practical syllogism: Why would someone not accept this argument in general? If an argument is invalid, or based upon wrong premises, rational people do not accept it and are not moved by it; or at least they *should* not. It is interesting to ask why a rational agent might not be moved by *sound* practical reasoning. Let us assume that we have a sound practical syllogism relating to what we should do. Why would someone not accept it?

A common phenomenon is that a reasoner refuses in practice to follow the conclusion. Someone might have good reasons to do *f* rather than *e*, all things being considered, yet still do *e*. We all know that the environmental crisis demands a change of our consumption and energy use, but most of us do not do it. It is simply more comfortable to drive a car rather than to go by bus and it is convenient to use air-conditioning. When judgments and action are seen to have diverged in this way we traditionally talk about the problem of *akrasia* or weakness of the will. (At least, in this example, if we assume that people actually *know* what the environmental crisis demands of them. The climate sceptic questions one premise of the argument, namely that human action causes climate change.) Whatever the cause, there are cases where the agent is not sufficiently motivated to do *f* although s/he fully knows that s/he should do *f*; and this means that in some way s/he fails to overcome a situation in which their action contradicts their insights. As Robert Nozick remarks: "The motivational force of the argument ... can be no stronger than the motivation to avoid the particular inconsistency specified by the argument." (Nozick 1981, p. 407) In the case of *akrasia* the reasoner understands the conclusion and accepts it to the extent that s/he knows that it is true, and even forms an intention based upon it— but then simply fails to act on it. (Often it is accompanied with suffering arising from this weakness.) This is not a case of not accepting an argument. For our moral-psychological question it is of more interest to examine agents who are unwilling to accept a sound argument. Here I see three possibilities.

(i)   An agent might not accept the rule of logic according to which the inference operates. In the case of syllogism, this would be a fundamental form of anti-rationalism placing this person outside reasoning altogether. Of course, for the agent, this conclusion would not follow—but nothing would follow from anything for such an agent.

(ii) An agent might simply not draw a conclusion even though all the premises are provided. This is one analysis of negligence. For example: I knew that the ink-bottle was open and I also knew that the book was at the very edge of my table, but I did not draw the right conclusion that I should *not* place the inkle-bottle on the book. The book, with the bottle on it, dropped from the table and now ink is spilt on the floor and on the carpet. The more puzzling case is that wherein an agent clearly understands the premises and their relevance but simply *refuses* to draw the obvious conclusion, perhaps because s/he does not like it. Fanatics are good examples of this. If reality threatens to disprove their beliefs, they are likely to stop reasoning at a certain point. They refuse to draw obvious conclusions from evident facts. (As Freud reminded us, not even our reasoning is immune from being distorted by our wishes, attachments, and fixations.) More commonly, however, the fanatic will question the empirical evidence (at least one premise of the argument) and will re-read reality so that the ideologically desired conclusion might follow.

(iii) This brings us to the third way of refusing to accept, or being unmoved by an instance of practical reasoning. We may question the starting points or premises. In many cases this is the right thing to do, but in other cases we may end up refusing to accept a *correct* starting point. According to a popular (but untrue) legend, some cardinals refused to look through the telescope that was presented to them by Galileo. If these cardinals had looked through it (such is the implication of the legend) they would have had to accept empirical evidence (the premise of Galileo's argument) which spoke against *Ptolemy's* geocentric model of the universe. But they did not wish to be moved by argument.

What kind of agent, then, is it that is likely to accept practical reasoning in general? Clearly not an anti-rational sceptic as outlined above. Such a radical sceptic we would not have to be taken seriously anyway. Anyone who holds such an extreme position cannot claim to be making any serious points at all. Since all meaningful utterances must be framed within reason and its fundamental structures, the anti-rational sceptic cannot contribute anything meaningful or of interest. Aristotle remarks rather sharply that such a sceptic's contribution might be compared with that of a vegetable. (*Met.* 1008ª) The sceptic does not properly act *as a person* because s/he does not exercise that rational part of the soul which distinguishes the person from plants and non-human animals. While this remark is morally problematic, it is a useful analysis: the sceptic fails to realise an essential human capacity.

Let us examine the corollary. What kind of person might *not* refuse to draw a conclusion or might *not* question premises? From what has been said above we can conclude that the person, in order not to be negligent, must be willing to draw conclusions. S/he must, moreover, be open to new insights. The fanatic, as pointed out above, is likely to have a closed mind, not wanting his or her own ideas to be proved wrong. By contrast, an open rational agent is one who is unprejudiced and willing to gain new insight, even if such insight overturns his previous convictions. That is why it is not only ideologies which make people blind to rational arguments. *Passion* does the same. A person driven by very passionate desires or wishes will not listen to reason, as every parent of an adolescent knows. The person who is open to arguments must therefore be even-tempered and mature. Plato and Aristotle both observed this, and suggested that people reach a certain age before joining the academy to study philosophy.

IV Moral commitment as a precondition for accepting indirect transcendental arguments

Let us now ask more specifically why someone might not accept the conclusion of an indirect transcendental argument.

As in the case of a practical syllogism, a person might not accept the transcendental rule of inference *tout court*. Doing so would not amount to the radical anti-rationalism of someone who rejects even deductive logic. If a person is sceptical merely about the *method* of transcendental arguments s/he is not placed be-yond meaningful communication and can still take part in rational debate. The most obvious form of this limited rational disapproval of transcendental argu-ment is the rejection of the method. Someone who is not rationally convinced by an argument will not accept it: meta-ethical scepticism touches problems of moral psychology. But our issues are not with such meta-ethical scepticism. We are asking whether a person who has no rational objection to the method of indirect transcendental arguments in principle might still not be willing to ac-cept them (even if they seem sound). There are two possible causes of such un-willingness: the rejection of either the conclusion or the premise(s) of the indi-rect transcendental argument.

As with the case of the syllogism, a person might be unwilling to draw and accept the conclusion, in particular the second conclusion (above: that r). S/he might accept the starting point and the transcendental conditional but still be unsatisfied with the indirect method of reaching the conclusion. S/he might want a more obvious, emphatic argument to justify the conclusion, perhaps a *di-rect* argument. The transcendental argument shows 'merely' that something can-not be denied, s/he might say, but that is not enough. In one form or another, this point has been raised by many philosophers.

(It should be noted here that Aristotle did not see this as critical to his rea-soning but rather as a demonstration of the thesis that first principles *cannot be proved.* (*Met* (1006ᵃ5) Does this mean that he did not accept the necessity of drawing the second conclusion? No: because Aristotle makes it clear that the transcendental argument shows that there is no need for "proof". He makes a crucial terminological point, limiting the expression 'justification' to syllogisms. That is why he argues that it would show a lack of philosophical understanding if one were to demand "justification" in the case of these first principles. For Ar-istotle, the self-evidence is all that we can achieve—and it is the highest form of acceptance possible.)

Unwillingness to accept a syllogism by questioning its premises can also be found in the case of indirect transcendental arguments. Obviously there are many epistemic questions which can rightly be posed concerning the transcen-dental conditions of an action and how they can be identified. (How convincing is it to ask for necessary performative conditions of an action? How do we know that my (deliberate) action implies any proposition, especially a normative prop-osition? And what sort of normativity or value might it imply?) We are, however, interested in the problem of *acceptance* and should therefore ask what might make someone unwilling or unable to accept such premises in the first place? There seem to be (at least) two preconditions for not accepting the second prem-ise, the conditional. First: a person might be unable to reach the quality of detachment necessary for the self-examination of his or her actions. This disability results from committing acts without reflecting upon them. Such a person is described by Harry Frankfurt as a 'wanton': someone who is blindly driven by his or her impulses, wishes, or desires (Frankfurt 1971). A wanton could not possibly accept, or even understand, the transcendental conditional at all.

The second precondition for not being able to accept the premise comes from a lack of sensitivity. A person must regard his or her reasoning as a form of acting, and must look at such agency with sensitivity towards its implied goals (its normative dimension) in order to understand the necessary conditional. If the person cannot see his or her actions as freely chosen intentional and goal-directed phenomena, the person cannot possibly accept the conditional. For example someone who perceives himself or herself as a deterministic mechanism (rather than a free agent) could not identify performative conditions of the desired kind. His or her own actions, like the movements of a branch in the wind, would be aimless events (at least they would appear so to that person).

Who, then, might accept an indirect transcendental argument in ethics? From what has been said about the limits of accepting transcendental reasoning in ethics we can (inversely) arrive at the characteristics of someone *who is likely to accept these arguments.*

For a start, such a person would have to care about coherence. As we have seen, the acceptance of the conclusion of the indirect transcendental argument depends on the importance we give to the coherence between what we could possibly claim (or deny) on the one side and the implications of our claiming or arguing anything on the other side. When is the threat of incoherence, the "pain of self-contradiction", forceful enough to accept the conclusion, that is the correctness of its counterclaim? At this point we might rephrase Nozick's observation: *The motivational force of an indirect transcendental argument can be no stronger than the motivation to avoid the particular incoherence between my claim and the implications of my arguing at all.* It would be a profound incoherence to have some necessary belief (necessary because it cannot rationally be denied) and still question whether it is rationally right. Someone who deeply cares about this coherence will affirm the conclusion as the only way to bring all these aspect into harmony. (And coherence can come in degrees; we can be more or less coherent depending on how many elements (beliefs, experiences, etc.) we bring into some overall unity. Consistency, in contrast, seems clearer; something simply is or is not consistent.)

Secondly, we have said that the agent must possess a certain form of self-reflection. For two reasons the person must have a basic understanding of what normativity is. (i) S/he needs this because s/he must understand the normative dimension of his or her actions, the *affirmed evaluation* that is implicitly given with them as their necessary condition. If we follow Gewirth's detailed analysis, we find that all aspects presuppose a normative sensitivity, namely the notion of an end, directedness towards some aim or *telos*, and the agent's active interest in achieving this aim. (ii) This normative understanding is necessary because the agent must feel the pain of self-contradiction between a claim ($\neg$r) and the normative implications of his or her action, and must feel obliged to strive for overall coherence as an ideal. Thus only someone who knows that coherence is a kind of inner obligation (something that demands realization) will accept the argument.

What, then, are the human preconditions for accepting an indirect transcendental argument? Obviously, an agent must be rational in order to accept this (or any) reasoning. But that is not enough. An a-moral (or anti-moral) sceptic, even if otherwise highly rational, would not see himself as a responsible agent, for whom agency actually matters. Therefore, the argument is only accepted by a rational agent who adopts a critical reflexive attitude to his or her actions, who regards himself or herself as free and responsible in choosing actions, and who identifies the value implicitly given by these actions (acknowledging that even reasoning is itself an action). And most importantly, the agent must strive for an overall coherence in the sense outlined above; that is, he must feel obliged to be a (normatively) coherent agent. And it is exactly this coherence between actions and thoughts that is also the ideal of moral acting. We can therefore characterize him or her as a *morally committed rational person* (someone who seriously wants to follow some coherent ideal in what s/he does and says).

Does the morally committed person have to be fully moral in order to accept indirect transcendental arguments? It seems sufficient that s/he strive for coherence and be consciously directed towards a notion of the good. S/he does not have to have moral potential *fully realized*, but must be sufficiently motivated to act as a moral person, *viz.* caring about (necessary) coherence. And the *more* s/he is morally committed, the *more* likely will s/he accept the argument as powerful.

It is worth adding that a *perfect* moral being should be incapable of grasping an indirect transcendental argument—but for a different reason. A god, *qua* being rational, can fully understand deductive arguments. But because he is perfectly committed to what is good and true he cannot entertain any sceptical doubt about it ($\neg$r); and that is why he could not understand the indirect argument. He would not realize that it is self-contradictory to raise the sceptical claim seriously because he cannot do so. In other words, for a god, the argument would have no starting point. Luckily, though, a god does not seem to need this kind of argument: for a god the good is self-evident; he apprehends it directly. Otherwise he would not be god.

We can conclude that indirect transcendental arguments are suited to human beings who can be serious about their moral potential, sensitive to directedness towards the good, and who aim to be or become a coherent moral agent. We would not accept such reasoning if we were wantons or passion-driven animals lacking the required self-reflexive distance and control of our own actions. Nor could we accept such reasoning if we were gods, who apprehend truth and goodness directly. Indirect transcendental arguments are suited to free beings who are neither beasts nor gods. They are arguments for the imperfect being, for "the crooked wood of humankind", to use Kant's famous phrase, for whom nature has imposed "only the approximation of this idea" of morality. (Kant *KGS* VIII, 24)

V Conclusion

The central thesis of this paper is by no means new. Many philosophers have pointed out that there are preconditions for understanding the good and that being moral, or at least striving to be, is in some way the condition of the proper understanding of the good. Let us finish by looking briefly at two rather different authors who, like Aristotle, have emphasized some such deep connection: Confucius and Kant.

In the *Analects*, Confucius argues for a supreme virtue (*ren*) embracing all others, which is arguably one of his most important contributions to Chinese philosophy. (Fung Yu-lan 1952, p. 5) All human beings are in principle capable of realizing *ren*, he argues, because we all have moral potential. (See Chan 2011, p. 5) A gentleman (*Junzi*), which anyone can become, is one who has attained the virtues which together constitute *ren:* he is not born with them. [Confucius claimed that even barbarians can become gentlemen. (*Analects* 9: 14) "Is humanity really so far away? If I simply desire humanity, I will find that it is already here." (*Analects* 7: 30)] Realizing *ren*, however, is a kind of self-cultivation which requires learning, taking a critical stance against established social orders, and refining its own role therein: self-cultivation and self-reflection are inextricably interdependent. Self-cultivation is thus seen as an ongoing personal endeavour wherein people strive to realize their moral qualities. And only then is one able to *reason* properly. "If you learn without thinking what you have learned, you will be lost. If you think without learning, however, you will fall into danger." (*Analects* 2: 15) This "thinking what you have learned" for Confucius does not mean "abstract, theoretical cogitation", but means primarily "to keep one's attention focused on something, often a goal or ideal which one intends to achieve." (Ivanhoe 1993, 12–13) We might express this in other words:

one must be oriented towards the good, and committed to strive for it, for the very idea of moral reasoning to have a footing. Without this we could neither present nor absorb arguments concerning right and wrong in the first place (cf. Menke and Pollmann 2007, p. 63).

Even without explicitly addressing the methodology of transcendental arguments, Confucius makes a point similar to that which I have argued for in this essay: namely that moral reasoning presupposes moral commitment. But there is a further aspect of this fundamental moral commitment which he mentions and which we have not touched upon: *ren*, he argues, always implies some *regard for others*. By being oriented towards the good we must be willing to regard ourselves and others as persons. Confucius provides a variety of definitions of *ren* to his disciples, one such definition being simply 'love for others'. Similarly Mencius (391–308 BC), Confucius' greatest interpreter, characterizes *ren* as empathy with the suffering of others. (1 A: 7; 7B: 31; quoted from Lau 1970) He adds that, therefore, the central concern is having a "a heart sensitive to the suffering of others." (2 A: 6; 6 A: 6)

Even Kant, an author from a very different tradition, seems to combine the psychological-motivational aspect with the epistemic questions. In the *Introduction* to the *Theory of Virtues*, Kant writes rather surprisingly that love is a necessary predisposition for any moral reasoning. Love, in Kant's understanding, unites exactly those two aspects Confucius had presented more than 2000 years earlier. It is to be understood in the sense of a "delight for moral striving for perfection" and also as a directedness towards the (beloved) other. Kant argues in a similar spirit in § 32 of *Metaphysics of Morals* that gratitude towards others is a "holy" (i.e. every-lasting, not time-bound) duty (*Analects* 12: 22) because its absence would destroy the fundamental principles of all morality. And gratitude is also a moral state of the mind whereby we are directed affirmatively to the other.

Some contemporary philosophers who developed transcendental arguments in ethics have touched a similar point. They have argued that the transcendental conditional includes regarding others as autonomous beings (free agents) and respecting them as such. Gewirth's argument presupposes that we do, in fact, acknowledge others as free agents: that we begin with a certain moral sensitivity towards them. Without such presupposition Gewirth's reasoning would not reach further than an individual agent's claims to rights. Karl-Otto Apel, Wolfgang Kuhlmann, and Jürgen Habermas argue similarly in this direction: namely that inter-personal respect is a precondition of the discursive community. If they are right, then someone who does not possess this other-directedness in the first place would not be able to discover it as a transcendental condition upon self-reflection. The atomic individual would be blind to at least some versions of the indirect transcendental argument.

Transcendental arguments of the indirect type, we conclude, help us to understand a very old philosophical insight, namely that "the soil must have been previously tilled if it is to foster the seed, the mind of the pupil must have been prepared by the cultivation of habits, so as to like and dislike aright." In this essay I have argued for what I consider the key condition of "tilled soil", namely that the reasoner must be morally committed; for without moral commitment there can be no understanding of these foundational arguments in ethics at all.

Bibliography

Aristotle (1982): *Nicomachean Ethics*. Trans. by H. Rackham. Loeb Classical Library: Harvard University Press.

Albert, Hans (1980): *Traktat über kritische Vernunft*. Tübingen: Mohr Siebeck.

Apel, Karl-Otto (1976a): *Transformation der Philosophie*. 2 Vols. Frankfurt a. M.: Suhrkamp.

Apel, Karl-Otto (1976b): "Das Problem der philosophischen Letztbegründung im Lichte einer transzendentalen Sprachpragmatik." In: B. Kanitschneider (Ed.): *Sprache und Erkenntnis. Festschrift für G. Frey*. Innsbruck: Inst. f. Sprachwissenschaft d. Univ. Innsbruck., pp. 55–82.

Aristoteles (1982): *Nicomachean Ethics*. Trans. by H. Rackham. Loeb Classical Library. Harvard University Press.

Brink, David O. (1989): *Moral Realism and the Foundations of Ethics*. Cambridge: Cambridge University Press.

Chan, Wing-tsit (2011): "The Evolution of the Confucian Concept of Jen." In: *Confucian Studies. Critical Concepts in Asian Philosophy*. London/New York: Routledge, pp. 3–26.

Finnis, John (1977): "Scepticism, Self-Refutation, and the Good of Truth." In P. S.M. Hacker/J. Raz, (Eds.): *Law, Morality, and Society: Essays in Honour of H. L. A. Hart*. Oxford: Oxford University Press, pp. 247–267.

Frankfurt, Harry (1971): "Freedom of the Will and the Concept of a Person." In: *Journal of Philosophy* 68. No. 1, pp. 5–20.

Yu-Lan, Fung (1952): *A History of Chinese Philosophy*. Trans. by Derk Bedde. London: George Allen.

Gadamer, Hans-Georg (1960): *Wahrheit und Methode*. Tübingen: Mohr.

Gewirth, Alan (1981): *Reason and Morality*. Chicago/London: The University of Chicago Press.

Illies, Christian (2003): *The Grounds of Ethical Judgment. New Transcendental Arguments in Ethics*. Oxford: Oxford University Press.

Illies, Christian; Na, JongSeok (in print): "The Justification of Human Dignity". In: Marcus Düwell et al. (Eds.): *Human Dignity in the Context of Bioethics—China and the West*.

Ivanhoe, P. J. (2013): "Virtue Ethics and the Chinese Confucian Tradition." In: Stephen C. Angle/Michael Slote (Eds.): *Virtue Ethics and Confucianism*, New York/London: Routledge, pp. 28–46.

Kant, Immanuel (1902): *Kants Gesammelte Schriften (KGS)*. Ed. by Königlich Preussische Akademie der Wissenschaften. Berlin: Walter de Gruyter.

Lau, D. C. (1970): *Mencius*. Trans. with an Introduction by D. C. Lau. London: Penguin Books.

Menke, Christoph; Pollmann, Arndt (2007): Philosophie der Menschenrechte zur Einführung. Hamburg: Junius.

Nozick, Robert (1981): *Philosophical Explanation.* Oxford: Oxford University Press.

Peirce, Charles Sanders (1931–58) *Collected Papers.* Vol 1–6. Ed. by Charles Hartshorne and Paul Weiss. Vol. 7–8. Ed. by A. W. Burks. Cambridge/Mass.: Harvard University Press.

Stern, Robert (1998) (Ed.): *Transcendental Arguments. Problems and Prospects*, Oxford: Clarendon.

Walker, Ralph C.S. (1982): *Kant.* London: Routledge.

Walker, Ralph C.S. (1989): "Transcendental Arguments and Scepticism." In: E. Schaper/W. Vossenkuhl (Eds.): *Reading Kant: New Perspectives on Transcendental Arguments and Critical Philosophy.* Oxford: Oxford University Press, pp. 55–76.

Schönecker, Dieter (2010), "Kant über Menschenliebe als moralische Gemütsanlage", *Archiv für Geschichte der Philosophie* 92, pp. 133–175.

C Transcendental reasoning inspired by pragmatism, linguistics, and theories of intersubjectivity

Konrad Ott

Normative Pragmatics: Approach, Promise, Outlook

Abstract: The article presents the foundation of a normative pragmatics seen as philosophical approach with ethical implications. It outlines the concept of social practice in a Hegelian fashion and makes explicit the idea that practices as being performed by persons refer (*ipso facto*) to their intrinsic goodness. The article also clarifies the "grounding" role of so-called transcendental arguments within normative pragmatics. Such types of arguments are conceived as "pragmatic retorsive arguments" (PRA). The inferential structure and the ethical significance of such arguments are outlined in some detail. Lingual practices, as discourse, are paradigm examples of pragmatic retorsive arguments since they make explicit the commitments of being an arguing participant in discourse. Finally, an outlook is given on how pragmatic retorsive arguments may, perhaps, work with reference to non-lingual practices.

1 Introduction

Normative pragmatics (NP) is part of both deontology and social practice theory since it makes explicit specific *commitments* being involved (implied, presupposed) in human activities being qualified as practices ("Praxis"). The constitutive idea of NP is about deontic forces underlying specific patterns of interpersonal agency. This initial idea of NP follows Brandom's approach of norms and commitments being *"implicit in practices"* (1998, p. 25). This approach might be appealing to common-sense intuitions about "implicitness" but it raises deeper questions of how to understand this "in"-ness philosophically. The usual answer is: as a kind of presupposition. NP supposes that acting in a specific manner includes specific suppositions (Tetens 2006, p. 68). The scheme of inference that refers to this idea has been analyzed by many scholars since Stroud (1968):

(1) p
(2) p $\rightarrow$ q
(3) Ergo: q.

The arrow $\rightarrow$ in this scheme of inference represents a relationship of necessitation between p and q. One can't get (have, do) p without q. Whoever asserts or

DOI 10.1515/9783110470215-012

performs p can't deny q without committing some kind of contradiction or self-refutation. Thus, a commitment to p implies a commitment to q. The signs "p" and "q" can, in principle, refer to lingual and to non-lingual entities and also to activities ("doings"). Premise (1) might mean that p "exists" or that p is "performed" by an agent. Within NP, human performances are more decisive. Transcendental arguments are (often refined) instances of this inferential scheme. Once upon a time, I argued that transcendental arguments rely on the concept of *pragmatic implication* (Ott 1997, ch. 2). Pragmatic implications are different from logical entailments since they rest on a complex interplay in between requirements, entitlements, expectations, and commitments of specific modes of human interaction. Within NP, "p" in premise (1) will primarily refer to human activities while q refers to some, say, *normative commitments* being involved in performing (doing) p as a kind of human interaction. By way of example: If I order a meal in a restaurant, the servant is entitled to expect that I will pay the bill. Even if a person in a restaurant only says: "*I wish to have a pizza and a beer*" the context of a restaurant pragmatically implies that this sentence is not a wish but an order. An order within the context of a restaurant pragmatically implies a commitment to pay the bill. Who orders can't claim that the proposition "*I wish to have a pizza and a beer*" (or: "Please, bring me a pizza and a beer") does not imply semantically/logically the proposition "*I am willing to pay for both*". The servant, however, is normatively entitled to expect such willingness. There is much of such normative *know how* in our moral, political and legal culture, in our customs, and even in the lifeworld. NP must take such common sense about commitments being implicit in practices ("role obligations") into account. Thus, NP supposes far more than monological mean-end-agency. It supposes the difference between single actions and commonly shared practices (Kaulbach 1982).

NP constitutes a *pragmatic* framing within which all basic concepts as presupposition, implication, (self)-contradiction, (self)-refutation, necessitation, requirement, entitlement, participant etc. have their meaning. The specific function of *transcendental (= retorsive)* arguments is to be determined by and embedded within the overall framing of NP. Thus, they are transcendental-pragmatic with some emphasis on "*pragmatic*". Such arguments are about "what it requires" or "what it brings all about" to participate in a commonly shared practice. Clearly, NP rests on some non-trivial assumptions about the commonality of practices which must be made explicit. Within NP it must be possible to answer Brandom's (1998, p. 25) crucial question: "What is it for an act to be correct-according-to-a-practice?" This question supposes the concepts of a) practice, b) single acts, c) correctness (rightness, appropriateness), and d) accordance.

NP may start with statements like: "This is what we do and how we do it!" There might be a reading of Kant's transcendental philosophy which supports NP. According to this reading, Kant supposes that humans *do* (perform) science, as physics, mathematics, and even biology. "Doing science" is presupposed in Kant's transcendental reasoning.[1] If so, the question occurs: Under which enabling conditions does the enterprise called "science" become possible? Or: Which requirements must be fulfilled if science is to be performed. This reading supposes that doing science is a genuine practice which entails an epistemic ethos (Ott 1997) as well as transcendental concepts as space, time, and causality.

Brandom: "One cannot address the question of what implicit norms are, independently of the question of what it is to *acknowledge* them in practice" (Brandom 1998, p. 25, emphasis added, KO). To Brandom, the "being" of such norms is related to the "grammar" (Wittgenstein) of practices and to some kind of acknowledgement which refers to this very grammar. The "authority" of such norms would be nothing but the "grammatical idea" of a practice at stake. Such practical acknowledgement goes *beyond* pure logic but it can be supported *by* means of logical (see section 4). The interest of knowledge within NP, however, is ultimately ethical, not logical. Within NP, logic is a useful device in order to make implicit norms of practices explicit. Logic is taken pragmatically as a mean, not as an end.

The usual way of how we, as participants of social practices, acknowledge such implicit norms is *endorsement*. We feel ourselves being committed by the meaning of what we are doing. By belief and attitude, we take something to be correct according to a practice (Brandom 1998, p. 25). In this sense, many commitments are endorsed in saying: "But she is my wife!" Such statements are not merely factual ones. They refer to the institution of marriage. We suppose that being married pragmatically implies some kind of caring for each other. Skeptics may deny that there is such meaning in human life. Skeptics might argue that propositions as "She is my sister" or even "X is a human being" are merely about matters of facts. As we know since ancient times, any particular skepticism might be radicalized to the entirety of theoretical and practical knowledge. Within NP, the problem of radicalized skepticism is also to be seen from a pragmatic lens (section 3). What role should doubtfulness play in our life? Given this question, radical(ized) skepticism is far less troublesome than many proponents and opponents of PRA believe. Within NP, casting doubt on assumptions and reasons is a move within discourse. Radicalizing skepticism is a

---

1 If one wishes to avoid the Kantian term "*transcendental*" within NP one can replace it by the term "*retorsive*".

way of abstract reasoning which is either trapped in self-contradiction or comes at some price (section 3).

A disclaimer seems appropriate at the end of this introduction. Human activities can be regulated by rules in many different ways that do not touch the problem of implicit norms. By way of example: If smoking on the beach should be prohibited, no PRA seems at place because there is no conceptual relation between "tobacco", "smoking" and "being on the beach". Enjoying the fresh air on the beach is not incompatible with smoking and smoking on the beach is not a self-refuting activity. To substantiate the validity claim *"Smoking on the beach should be forbidden!"* one must refer to non-conceptual reasons. Thus, it can be misleading to present presumptive PRA in the many "ordinary" cases of establishing rules (norms of action) by way of argument. Thus, NP is a limited ethical enterprise within our normative orders. It can't replace practical discourse about obligations, permissions, and rights. On the contrary, PRA are specific arguments which must be defended within such discourse. There is the danger of overstating the idea of implicit norms.

2 The Concept of Practice: A Hegelian Approach

To design the NP-framework conceptually requires far more than any single PRA, seen in isolation, allows for. In any case, the concept of *practice* ("Praxis") is constitutive to the NP-framing (Ott 1997, ch. 2). NP requires some understanding of what it means to join in a human activity *being qualified* as practice. "Social practices are implicitly normative in a way that mere behavioral regularities are not" (Brandom 1998, p. 625). If I get up at 6 a.m. every morning with my right leg first, this is regular behavior but not a practice. Thus, we face the problem to qualify some kinds of regular activities or agencies as being a real practice. Moreover, the concept of practice purports some ideas about "rightness" and "goodness" on the one hand, ideas of "bad" and "evil" on the other hand within the ways practices are to be performed.[2] This assumption refers to the Aristotelian idea of *"eupraxia"*. The *"eu"* indicates a second qualification-problem.

Therefore, NP faces *two* crucial qualification-problems with respect to the concept of practice ("Praxis"). *First:* Which human activities qualify as practice—and which do not? *Second:* What qualifies a practice as being performed "good"- and why? What are "good"-making conditions for practices? To address

---

2 I leave the question aside whether animals can perform practices. Breeding and migration may come close to it.

both questions we must presuppose some common sense moral knowledge of participants. NP can't start from "tabula rasa" but must start from our practical everyday life we are familiar with before doing conceptual analysis, (meta-)ethics and logic. Both qualification problems are addressed in turn. To address one problem properly one has to keep them both in mind.

The first qualification-problem can't be resolved by arbitrary extensional definitions. Any definition of practice seems to be either too broad or too narrow. If we are aware about the second qualification problem (*"eupraxia"*) we might shy away from defining "practice" in a way that the second problem can find solutions which run counter to our common-sense intuitions. By such intuitions, we would like *prima facie* to exclude organized criminal deeds ("Mafia"), terrorism, torture, slavery, genocide and similar activities from our conception of practice. We would like to include medicine and education even if such practices have external objectives, as healing from diseases and qualifying for professions. Thus, practices are not, as Aristotle says, only those interactions which are performed for the sake of the interaction itself. This would be too narrow a definition. Quite often, one faces a kind of "open question" in defining practice: Are dancing, cooking, diving, hunting, nursing, gardening etc. to be regarded as "real" practices? Do warfare and the secret services qualify as practices? What about prostitution and gambling? What about strikes, civil disobedience and resistance? Given such activities, NP might be trapped in moral and political controversies right from the scratch. Definitional questions are haunted by moral ones. NP, however, affirms such questioning since it may deepen our common reflexive understanding about agency, interaction, practices, goodness, normative orders etc. In any case, the first qualification problem can only find a reasonable moral solution by discourse about human interactions. If so, a principle of practical discourse *and* a full-fledged vocabulary of social and political philosophy must be presupposed in any attempt to solve the first qualification problem.

Such problems apply, *mutatis mutandis*, to the second qualification problem as well. An underlying conviction says that the *"eu"* in *"eupraxia"* should not terminate in personal or technical success only. By intuition, the *"eu"* refers to concepts as adequacy, flourishing, propriety, and felicity of the pattern of interaction. In such propriety (axiological) goodness and (deontic) rightness are blending into each other. *"Eupraxia"* means that something good has been achieved in a proper and rightful way. Thus, *eupraxia* has both an axiological and a deontic dimension. If so, criminal deeds do not qualify as practice (as one can't acquire property by stealing). In line of this concept formation, concepts of instrumental rationality, of individual utility-maximization, and of private intentionality can't serve as philosophical grounding for NP. The norms being implicit in practices go beyond prudential advice and functional imperatives (Ott 1997, ch. 2). One can't understand the second qualification problem properly without assuming the very possibility of any practice to fall prey to different kind of moral corruption and degeneration (as medicine under National Socialism). The goodness and rightness of practices is always fragile. If so, the concept of *eupraxia* supposes a comprehensive and commonly shared agential self-understanding of participants ("*ethos*").

Thus, *both* qualification problems rest on shaky grounds and, most philosophers would say, on far too many premises. NP rests on many assumptions and might be trapped right from the scratch in a muddle of commitments, attitudes, institutions, traditions, historical narratives of corruption and the like. NP might be a non-starter since its basic concepts might be essentially contested right from the scratch. But can a philosophical approach rest on essentially contested concepts? If not, retorsive arguments shouldn't be embedded in such fragile NP approach. They better should be freestanding instead, relying only on very modest and parsimonious premises. Tetens (2006, p. 74) argues that one should restrict transcendental arguments to suppositions being necessary for any reference to objects: Brains are necessary conditions for experiences. Humans have/make experiences. Therefore, there must be (functioning) brains. Tetens warns against an inflationary use of transcendental and retorsive arguments (2006, p. 94). On the other hand, we might drop NP as a philosophical approach too quickly just because we adopt ideals of purity and parsimony uncritically. There are reasons to discard the ideal of parsimony in practical philosophy because practical philosophy must be ontologically and semantically as rich as our practical life itself. Even in theoretical philosophy, the ideal of parsimony should not be overrated. It is not a criterion of truth and not decisive for theoretical choice. Tetens' warning in mind, I plea for some initial credit for NP. This is the pragmatic sense of "*petitio principii*": a plea for an allowance to start.

The starting point of NP is not a God's eyes view. In the origins of NP, there is nothing but *intuitions and convictions of participants*. Usually, participants of well-established practices (= "practicians") as science, education, and medicine are interested in the second qualification problem. Usually, they are not primarily interested in trying to escape their own "ethos" and its commitments via radical skepticism. To them, it is rather a point of decency and honesty, if not pride, to follow such traditional rules as "*salus aegroti suprema lex*" in medicine. According to their established ethos, necessitation of commitments being made transparent by PRA is not coercive at all to practicians. PRA are grounding and making explicit what has been endorsed already. The conclusions of PRA don't come as a surprise. Practicians usually require far less from PRA than logicians or ethicists who want to refute imaginary radical skeptics. The anti-skeptical force of PRA, to which we turn in the next section, serves for an ethically grounded moral self-understanding of practicians. Within NP, PRA are devices of assurance of how a given practice should be performed.

Both puzzling qualification problems can't be resolved by pure analytical philosophy. One has to take a look into the tradition of *"Praxisphilosophie"* as well. Aristoteles, Hegel, and Marx have reflected on practice in ways we should not ignore. Aristoteles draws a distinction between *"praxis"* and *"poiesis"* (NE, 1140). Praxis refers to goods and evils as well as to prudence. The Aristotelian concept of practice refers to types of agency within a polis whose actual propriety (*"Gelingen"*) aims at some common good which is never granted by God, nature or authorities, but comes only about by proper agency itself. Hegel does not reject the idea of *eupraxia* as being embedded in a comprehensive ethics of *eudaimonia, polis, mesothes, dikaosyne*, and *phronesis* (Kamp 1985, pp. 307–328). Hegel supposed this idea. Hegel, however, wished to integrate the productive ("energetic") forces of human labor and technology which *originate* in vital human energies into his concept of practice (Riedel 1976).

In his later work on the spheres of rightfulness, Hegel seems to imply that practices must operate within a comprehensive ethical system which gives substance to the idea of freedom (Hegel 1986, § 33). Outside of such system of rightfulness, there would be many activities but no "actual" practice. In performing practices, humans serve (favor, promote, support) each other within a comprehensive system of rightfulness. Practices constitute trust among humans. There must be an intrinsic relationship to mutual acknowledgement of agents being involved in practices even if there might be asymmetrical interpersonal relations in *some* practices, as in education, in economics, and in medicine.[3] Practices must entail respect for clients. To Hegelians, *economic* activities are genuine practices also, even if they rest on prudent self-interest and serve private welfare. If so, they are to be regarded as moments within a comprehensive system of rightfulness. Hiring labor, contracting, crediting, trading and exchanging economic goods are paradigm examples for such practices.[4] Economy and sports are, so to say, paradigm cases of competitive practices which suppose some ideas

---

[3] Teachers acknowledge pupils *as such* and physicians acknowledge patients *as such* different than citizens acknowledge each other *as such* or scientists acknowledge each other *as such*. How should workers acknowledge entrepreneurs (and vice versa)? The roles of participants may vary; decisive are expectations with respect to roles being taken within practices.

[4] To see economic activities as real practice, then, is to honor (or even appreciate) them only if they conform to such system of rightness. If so, an ethics of economics can't rest on the assumptions of rational egoistic welfare maximization. Given scope and purpose of this article, I leave this point aside which is constitutive for an ethics of economics that goes beyond business ethics.

about fairness.[5] Competitive practices can (dialectically) promote common goods even if they do so via antagonistic patterns of interactions. Since some types of competition look repugnant to sensitive moral persons, competitive practices are contested in detail. Can we substitute competitive practices by non-competitive ones based on solidarity and needs or shall we tame but not abolish competition?

This highly sketchy Hegelian concept of practice would rule out all activities which can't conform to the Hegelian spheres of rightfulness: formal law, subjective morals (the moral point of view), legal administration (Hegel: "Polizei"), institutional checks and balances, and constitutional law. Such non-conforming activities, then, do not qualify for practices. Given this conceptual outline, NP requires specification of concepts as *"actual propriety"* and *"felicity conditions"* with respect to specific practices which can conform to such spheres. PRA might be helpful precisely in this respect.

Marx focused the concept of practice on productive labor and class struggle. In his famous *"Thesen über Feuerbach"* (1969), he states that the human way of life is essentially practical and that all problems can and should be resolved by ways of practice. Facing the problem of proletarians' misery and exploitation he proposed the idea that revolutionary activity should be seen as actual practice.[6] This was a fatal reductionist move. Marx' reductionist focus of practice to productive labor, class struggle, and revolution has deeply affected the political ethics of Marxism, including critical theory and Castoriadis (1975). Contemporary Marxists should take a turn against such conceptual reduction of practice. Even to them, a step backward to Hegel might be a step forward. Revolutions might or might be not be legitimate on moral and political grounds, but as exceptional events within history, they do not qualify as practice. It seems questionable whether they are "locomotive engines of history" (Marx 1972). Revolutions are extraordinary, while practices are part of our ordinary life. Practices must be both established *and* performed in everyday life in order to become "actual" (Hegel: "wirklich").

---

5 I leave the problem aside whether warfare counts as practice.

6 "Kann Deutschland zu einer Praxis à la hauteur des principes gelangen, d.h. zu einer Revolution, die es nicht nur auf das offizielle Niveau der modernen Völker erhebt, sondern auf die menschliche Höhe, welche die nächste Zukunft dieser Völker sein wird?" (MEW, Vol. 1, p. 385).

3 Pragmatic Retorsive Arguments

Pragmatic retorsive arguments (PRA) raise specific validity claims within a practical discourse about basic rules and commitments being implicit in practices. PRA can also directly refer to discourse, seen as linguistic practice in its own right. Discourse ethics presents PRA in order to make explicit the role of a credible participant in discourse (Böhler 2014). To understand the deontic status and force of PRA one has to take the role of a *participant* in a given practice. The pragmatic concept of a participant is about taking (not: "playing") a role which is to be qualified as being "serious", "credible", or "engaged". Such qualifications are intrinsic to the concept of a participant. Strictly speaking, they are pleonastic. Even if PRA are given a logical structure, we understand them fully only from within.

PRA are arguments by which implicit norms of practices are to be made explicit. Generally, PRA propose the following claim: Whoever performs a given practice P (in a credible and serious way) has committed herself *ipso facto* to commitments C-1, C-2...C-n. These commitments are not imposed on the agent by any authority but are pragmatically implied in what the agent herself does. Any successful PRA constitutes a valid commitment (obligation) or an entitlement (right). PRA argue that all participants are committed or entitled to do x if the overall performance of a common practice should qualify as being "good" or "right". Such commitments are the deontological dimension of "*eu*"-practices. Valid PRA demonstrate that it is (in some sense) *self-refuting* (contradictory, idiosyncratic, strange, idle) to perform P and to deny C. PRA are a large family of arguments. It is clearly beyond the scope of this paper to propose a classification for PRA. I offer the following general PRA-scheme instead:

(1) Humans perform a practice P.

(2) P should be performed properly/"good"/"rightfully".

(3) Commitment C is a requirement of proper P.

(4) Rule R is a sound explication of C.

(5) Ergo: Any participant in P should prima facie follow R.

Conclusion (5), as a general imperative, can be easily specified to singular imperatives.

PRA are arguments which have to be made. Here, a peculiar dialectic occurs. On the one hand, PRA already presuppose general commitments of arguing as such (= taking seriously part in discourse). This is why Apel (1973) believes that presuppositions and commitments of arguing with others are *strictly* transcendental because they are supposed in the Popperian epistemic principle of refutation. Any PRA as such supposes rules of discourse. On the other hand, PRA as such must be open for refutation if the concept of argument requires the possibility of corroboration *and* refutation. Thus, PRA may fail. It seems prudent for NP to avoid coming into trouble with the epistemic principle of falsification. We take single PRA as being open for refutation.

Commitments C being presented via PRA presume to be, in some sense, *inescapable* for all persons who perform a specific practice. PRA, if sound, substantiate some C which is in some sense *non-optional* within a specific field of practice. The term "inescapable" indicates *at least* the necessity of fundamental belief revision about a given practice at hand in the case of rejection. Denial of such commitments would deeply affect the "grammar" (Wittgenstein) and the ethos of a practice. Such rejection always clashes with convictions about legitimate entitlements within practices. The term "inescapable" might have even stronger meanings. Via PRA it becomes clear to proponents, opponents, and bystanders ("neuter") that a specific commitment C can't be rejected without some kind of self-contradiction, be it a contradiction in terms ("*contradiction in terminis*") or a genuine contradiction between a proposition being stated and the act of stating it ("*contradiction exerciter*") (Siegwart 2010). At least, denial of C comes at a price, as expelling oneself out of discourse or the loss of any entitlement to complain about something. One may lose credibility and trustworthiness among practicians. Skeptics, of course, may be willing to pay such price. What to do about it?

PRA are clearly anti-skeptical in nature. Thus, they have been often designed as to refute imaginary radical skeptics *definitely*. In such design, PRA are about commitments which any skeptic must accept because they are implicit in (reasonable) doubtfulness. Arno Ros has argued (1989, Vol. 1, p. 197) that PRA are successful only if four conditions are met: 1) a statement being made by an skeptic, 2) the description of this statement as given by the proponent of PRA, 3) an enlarged interpretation of what the statement "means" (implies, presupposes) as given by the proponent, 4) an agreement of 2) and 3) as given by the skeptic.[7] To Ros, the basic structure of PRA can't grant condition 4) definitely. If so, rejection of PRA may come at the price of some idiosyncrasy, oddity, and idleness, but not at the price of logical self-contradiction. Sceptics may simply hold unusual inter-

---

7 "Rückbezügliche Argumente erreichen ihr Ziel nur dann, wenn der jeweilige Opponent eines Streitgesprächs die ihm vom Proponenten vorgehaltene Beschreibung seines eigenen Tuns als Opponent sowie die Deutung dieser Beschreibung rückhaltlos akzeptiert" (Ros 1989, Vol 1, p. 197).

pretations of what it means to assert, to promise, to belief, to warn, and the like. To Ros, the skeptic could say: "Yes, I am stating something, but this does not mean/imply/suppose that I am willing to argue for my statement." This fourth condition leaves, indeed, escape routes against the presumptive coerciveness of PRA. *Within* NP, however, oddity and idleness are prices to be paid even if logicians may shrug their shoulders about them.

Much intellectual rigor has been devoted by proponents of PRA of how to preclude remaining *escape routes* to imaginary radical skeptics. This is very tiresome and even boring a business. Even if there might some remaining escape routes to skeptics (idiosyncratic definitions, joy in paradoxes, solipsism, heroic nihilism, possible worlds), PRA can be successful in grounding implicit commitments of practices. I concede that some escape routes always remain open to skeptics. If skeptics like to take them, fine! *Let them slip away into their nowhere lands.* If they say farewell to common practical life we say farewell to them without regret. They have made themselves outcasts. This position is in line with Schopenhauer who argued that one should not devote much philosophical effort trying to conquer the citadel of solipsism but should pass by following more promising philosophical routes.

Proponents of NP must also concede that PRA are full of assumptions (Niquet 1991). Habermas' argument (1981) that communicative use of language is *prior* to a strategic use is an instance of PRA being full of assumptions. The argument says: Whoever wishes to make use of the strategic and persuasive power of speech successfully must suppose that others expect truth-oriented communication. Within the pragmatic of speech, success of persuasive strategies is conditional to implicit honesty expectations. The hydra-problem applies to PRA: If one has given a PRA a rough inferential structure, one sees the necessity to fine-grain them. The more they are fine-grained, the more remaining "*non sequitur*" may pop up. The intrinsic necessity of fine-graining PRA's may constitute even new escape routes for real or virtual skeptics. No PRA is "airtight".

With respects to success or failure of PRA within NP, one should distinguish "*perfectionist*" and "*satisfying*" approaches. While perfectionists go for a proof or wish to reach certainty (something beyond any reasonable doubt), satisfiers are glad with results which give solid grounding to our practices and orientation for practicians. How to refute radical skepticism *definitely* should not be at the core of NP. Remember that NP is a pragmatic approach which allows for pragmatic solutions. NP allows for satisfying solutions. Satisfying approaches can come in terms of "price tags". A satisfier can tell the skeptics: "Your position is idle and it comes at a high price to you". Generally, it can be said with confidence that radical skepticism is no low-cost position. Within NP, the problem of self-contradiction shifts, at least in part, from refutation to pricing. Such "pricing" might and should help to "open our eyes" with respect to the many commitments which form our practical life. This anti-skeptical pricing-strategy brings some intellectual fun into the rigorous (and sometimes boring) debates between transcendentalists and skepticism. It brings a grain of *"gaya scienza"* into NP.

To me, it would suffice to argue that skeptics have exiled themselves from our mundane practices. A person who denies reasonable PRA just by insisting on Ros' fourth condition ("To me it all means something different!") can't expect to be acknowledged as *fellow* within a practice. If fellowship pragmatically implies trustworthiness, skeptics are not trustworthy. If skeptics have exiled themselves, one may feel some regret about them but no guilt. Escaping skeptics can hardly argue that we *should* miss them. Outsiders as such are no heroic figures. If a skeptic would claim that outsiders are in a somewhat superior (intellectual or moral) position they would have to present some arguments. Otherwise, they can only state that outsiders are outsiders—period.

PRA have always referred to mundane human practices as their starting points. Of course, any argument must start from somewhere. This is not a severe problem for NP. It only becomes a problem if PRA are decontextualized from fields of human practices. Starting points are not strictly necessary but are contingent upon human life. If such contingencies belong to the grammar of the human condition we shouldn't try to overcome them. PRA within NP have no ambition to be valid in any possible world. We can start by modest assumptions about beings and doings in mundane everyday life. The problem of "all possible worlds" is irrelevant within NP. Such mundane practices are, for instance: attributing features to entities (Strawson), believing (Hintikka),[8] proposing (Brandom), promising (Austin, Searle), playing games (Wittgenstein), doing science (Kant, Rickert), arguing (Habermas, Apel) and the like.

Paradigm cases of such arguments refer to *lingual practices*. There are, for instance, many norms being implied in speech acts. Speech act theory is clearly a sub-discipline of NP (Levinson 1983). The paradigm cases of promising, warning, and confessing are well known. "Claiming" is a speech act, too. A mere utterance is not a claim yet. Within dialogue, one may ask whether an utterance U (as mourning) is meant as being a claim C. Commitments are implied in claiming as such. If P claims x, she implicitly claims its validity. Any serious claim, then, is a validity claim (Habermas 1981). Claiming *pragmatically* implies the readiness

---

8 Hintikka (1962) pointed at "doxastic implication". If a person P believes a, and if it is true that "a → b" then P is committed either to believe "b" or to revise her belief about "a". If we share beliefs, then belief revision is not just about the coherence of mental belief-states but there are expectations with respect to belief revision which constitute an "ethics of belief". In NP, one is not simply free to believe whatever one wishes.

and willingness to give and take reasons for one's own claim. Any claim has some inferential reference to other claims. A specific statement implies more generic statements. If I claim "This flower is red" I must hold *conceptually* that the flower is colorful even if it turns out *empirically* that the flower is yellow. If she can dance, she can move. Brandom's *"Making It Explicit"* is mainly a study in NP on the lingual level. Brandom distinguishes three layers of NP: a) inferential "normative reconstrual of the discursive in terms of deontic status", b) treatment of interlocuters "in practice, as committed or entitled, as exhibiting deontic statuses", 3) "practices of attributing deontic attitudes" (Brandom 1998, p. 637). Claiming pragmatically implies entitlements and commitments. Within the practice of discourse, we acknowledge each other as being claimants. We suppose that claims are not just jokes or plain noise. Claims as being claimed by claimants are constitutive for communities of interlocutors in discourse. We concede to Ros that skeptics may hold completely different views about claiming. If claiming is just "saying something meaningless" no implication holds. But this is simply not the meaning of claiming. NP essentially holds that there is common meaning of speech act verbs, as teaching, counselling, promising, claiming, warning etc. If there is not, NP loses grounding.

PRA have also been used in order to substantiate *supreme moral principles* (Apel, Kuhlmann, Habermas, Gewirth). There is a non-trivial premises in such ethical approaches: *If* the search for supreme moral principles makes good ethical sense, and *if* neither axiomatic statements nor naturalistic fallacies are viable options in modern ethics, and if one should avoid a *"regressus ad infinitum"* then there might be no "real" alternative to PRA in grounding ethics. Any Kantian project in ethics rests on such non-trivial meta-ethical premises. Apel's (1973) and Kuhlmann's (1985) *"Letztbegründung"* is a special Cartesian variant of such ethical argument. This approach supposes the Kantian idea that morality must find solid ground in supreme principles and that justification of supreme principles can't be derivative and must escape the so-called Münchhausen-trilemma (circular reasoning, infinite regress, ultimate axioms). PRA are the best-available devices for such ethical enterprise. Such ethical PRA rely on activities which are supposed in any more specific practice: *claiming* and *arguing* (Habermas, Apel) and *acting intentional and purposive* (Gewirth 1978*)*. In some sense, claiming/arguing and agency are *meta*-practices (Ott 1997). Such PRA address all persons who know how to argue (discourse ethics) or how to act (Gewirth 1978). If so, any moral principle based on such meta-practices via PRA can presume to hold within any more specific practice. To discourse ethicists, arguing *means* arguing to each other by giving and taking reasons with respect to contested validity claims. Some inferential sequences have been presented claiming to reach inferentially a conclusion of supreme ethical relevance, as "D" and "U" (Habermas) or "Principle of Generic Consistency (PGC)" (Gewirth). Gottschalk-Mazouz, Steigleder, Düwell, Illies and others, including myself, have modified and varied such inferential sequences which have moral principles in their conclusion. Within such sequences there must be a locus for retorsive reasoning. There is no other way to reach a conclusion without falling prey to the Münchhausen-tri-lemma. Still, I would be willing to defend my sequence which has a discourse principle "D" in its conclusion (Ott 2008).

Discourse ethical PRA constitute a (meta)ethical framework for practical discourse. Such PRA establishes rules of discourse as being supposed in claiming, refuting, criticizing, conceding, denying, supporting, and distinguishing. There are many lingual practices which contribute to the overall practice of arguing. If we, for instance, remove conceptual ambiguities in order to avoid fallacies out of ambiguity we contribute to discourse. Such PRA clarifies the complex role of being a participant in practical discourse and what it means to contribute to discourse. By such discourse-analytical PRA, we can, at least, recognize that there is no moral validity to be found somewhere outside of practical discourse.[9]

Can Gewirthians endorse this result? One critical point in Gewirth's concept (1978) was to analyze agency in terms of intentionality and purposiveness. To critics (Ott 2005), the original concept of agency remained too monological from the outset to ground ethics. Entitlements being supposed in monological reflection about one's own agency are not sufficient for ethical grounding. Results of such reflection must be stated as universal principle and must be acknowledged by all other agents. If agency, however, would be conceived right from the scratch as interaction among each other that shapes the self-understanding of all agents collectively (and not just distributively), thinks would look different. If Gewirthians would suppose a collective concept of common inter-agency, then they present a promising validity claim in favor of a set of human rights via an agency-based retorsive argument. Such argument may ground the moral practice of right-claiming. Discourse ethics and Gewirthians could form a "great coalition" held together by meta-practices: arguing and interaction.

---

9 I wish to add rules of discourse which refer to experiences being made within speech, as the experience of being "silenced" or "deceived".

4 Logical Reconstruction

NP, being a field of ethical inquiry, needs both a topology *and* a logic (Illies 2003). It both needs heuristic exploration *and* logical refinement. By means of formal logic, PRA can be refined. Logic is a helpful device to make retorsive arguments transparent. Habermas writes (Studienausgabe, Vol. 3, p. 356) with reference to Niquet's book that the idea to derive ethical principles as "D" (and, perhaps, "U") from presuppositions of discourse is clear by intuition, but its formal substantiation would require sophisticated (Habermas: "umständliche") debates about transcendental/retorsive arguments. The many reflections, comments and distinctions to be found in Niquet (1991) are, indeed, sophisticated, puzzling, and sometimes confusing. Habermas seems to fear that a meta-debate on transcendental arguments may rather obscure our solid intuitive knowledge about commitments of arguing. There might be, however, more promising and elegant logical ways to present retorsive arguments than Niquet has presented.

Geo Siegwart has presented such pathways in his "*Exerciter*" (2010). Siegwart's approach takes PRA as they are presented in ordinary language. In a first step of logical reconstruction such arguments are transposed in a semi-formal structure. This first step of logical reconstruction is governed by maxims of hermeneutical benevolence. In a second step, such raw arguments (Siegwart: "*Argumentationsrohlinge*") are given a logical structure. As paradigm example, the self-contradiction of skeptical denials of truth, as to be found in Thomas Aquinas, becomes evident. The intuitive grammatical understanding of "whoever denies that there is truth, concedes that there is truth" ("qui negat, concedit") takes a formal logical form. I deeply appreciate such logical fine tuning of PRA. "Exerciter" is a must for all friends of retorsive arguments. We can argue with Siegwart that there is, indeed, a logical sequence (Siegwart 2010, p. 70) which is both vertically and horizontally intact and which demonstrates that the denial of truth constitutes a scenario of self-contradiction by which the existence of truth can be inferred ("derived"). This logical scheme can be used to reconstruct other PRA. Following Illies (2003), one has to distinguish between the logical force and the "authority" of PRA. To NP-approach, the ultimate authority stems from the practices we wish to perform continuously. Logic is a helpful device for making it explicit.

5 Outlook

But what about Illies' (2003) proposed enterprise of further heuristic explorations? For the time being, NP is explorative. It has some foothold in lingual practices and, perhaps, in a general notion of common agency. We should rely on lingual PRA as being a paradigm example and move forward to non-lingual practices. The Hegelian concept of practice (section 2) can be enlarged. NP might be *hypothetically* enlarged to common *non-lingual practices*, as cooking, nursing, hosting, healing, serving, ordering, playing games and the like. If I cook for you, you are entitled to expect that the meal I serve you is not poisoned. If I host you, you are entitled that I don't rob or rape you at night. Moving to my field of expertise in environmental ethics, I like to apply this practical turn of NP to human modes to interfere and even interact within nature. Are there basic "sustainability"-commitments presupposed in doing agriculture ("cultura"), fisheries and forestry? Is deforestation a kind of forestry or is it opposed to forestry? Is long-term responsibility with respect to soils intrinsic to the practice of agriculture? Are there any commitments within the practice of domesticating sentient animals? Might there be a moral moment in the very meaning of "domestication" (belonging to a human "house")? Economic practices might be another aspect of this practical move: What are the commitments being implied in taking credits? Can there be trade without commitments to property rights? Is efficiency a basic commitment against wastefulness? What about commitments of investing, even of foreign direct investments? Is there an enlargement of NP to the realm of political economy being possible? The practical turn of NP opens large unexplored fields of inquiry: environment and economy.

References

Apel, Karl-Otto (1973): *Transformation der Philosophie*. Frankfurt a.M.: Suhrkamp.
Aristoteles: *Nikomachische Ethik*. Philosophische Schriften Bd. 3, Hamburg: Meiner.
Böhler, Dietrich (2014): *Verbindlichkeit aus dem Diskurs*. München/Freiburg: Alber.
Brandom, Robert B. (1998): *Making it Explicit*. Harvard: Harvard University Press.
Castoriadis, Cornelius (1975): *L'institution imaginaire de la société*. Paris: Èditions du Seuil.
Gewirth, Alan (1978): *Reason and Morality*. Chicago: Chicago University Press.
Habermas, Jürgen (1981): *Theorie des kommunikativen Handelns*. Frankfurt a.M.: Suhrkamp.
Hegel, G.F.W. (1986): *Grundlinien der Philosophie des Rechts* (1st ed. 1820). In: Werke in 20 Bänden, ed. by Eva Moldenhauer/Karl Markus Michel, Vol. 7, Frankfurt a.M.: Suhrkamp.
Hintikka, Jaako (1962): *Knowledge and Belief*. Ithaca: Cornell University Press.
Illies, Christian (2003): *The Grounds of Ethical Judgment*. Oxford: Oxford University Press.

Kamp, Andreas (1985): *Die politische Philosophie des Aristoteles und ihre metaphysischen Grundlagen.* Freiburg/München: Alber.

Kaulbach, Friedrich (1982): *Einführung in die Philosophie des Handelns.* Darmstadt: Wissenschaftliche Buchgesellschaft.

Kuhlmann, Wolfgang (1985): *Reflexive Letztbegründung.* Freiburg/München: Alber.

Levinson, Stephen C. (1983): *Pragmatics.* Cambridge: Cambridge University Press.

Marx, Karl (1978): *"Zur Kritik der Hegelschen Rechtsphilosophie"* (1st ed. 1844). Einleitung. *Marx-Engels Werke* 1956 ff. Vol. 1, Berlin: Dietz, pp. 378–391.

Marx, Karl (1969): "Thesen über Feuerbach" (1st ed. 1845). *Marx-Engels Werke* 1956 ff. Vol. 3, Berlin: Dietz, pp. 5–7.

Marx, Karl (1972): "Manifest der Kommunistischen Partei" (1st ed. 1848). *Marx-Engels Werke* 1956 ff. Vol. 4, Berlin: Dietz, pp. 459–493.

Niquet, Marcel (1991): *Transzendentale Argumente.* Frankfurt a.M: Suhrkamp.

Ott, Konrad (1997): *Ipso Facto.* Frankfurt a.M.: Suhrkamp.

Ott, Konrad (2005): *Moralbegründung zur Einführung.* Hamburg: Junius.

Ott, Konrad (2008): "Diskurs und Ethik". In: F. J. Wetz/V. Steenblock/J. Siebert (Eds.): *Kolleg Praktische Philosophie*, Vol. 2. Stuttgart: Reclam, pp. 111–152

Riedel, Manfred (1976): *Theorie und Praxis im Denken Hegels.* Berlin: Ullstein.

Ros, Arno (1989): *Begründung und Begriff.* 3 Volumes. Hamburg: Meiner.

Siegwart, Geo (2010): "Exerticer". In: Winfried Löffler (Ed.): *Metaphysische Integration. Essays zur Philosophie von Otto Muck.* Heusenstamm: Ontos, pp. 65–90.

Strout, Barry (1968): "Transcendental Arguments". In: *Journal of Philosophy* 65. No. 9, pp. 241–256.

Tetens, Holmes (2006): *Philosophisches Argumentieren.* München: C.H. Beck.

Walzer, Michael (1983): *Spheres of Justice.* New York: Basic Books.

Micha H. Werner

Social Constitutivism and the Role of Retorsive Arguments

Abstract: This paper argues that certain transcendental arguments can play a valuable role in moral reasoning: They can make explicit constitutive elements of our common practice of justifying our actions to one another, of addressing practical criticism, of deliberating together, or of constructing a sharable standpoint of practical judgment. Thereby, they can serve to reaffirm basic normative commitments that no one who makes practical claims or who complains against another person's conduct can avoid making. This amounts to a more modest interpretation of the potential of transcendental arguments than can be usually found in more traditional ("first personal") versions of Kantian constitutivism. However, the modest use of transcendental reasoning may suffice for all practical purposes, even though it is not designed to force a moral sceptic into endorsing moral principles.

I Introduction

Some philosophers, among them Karl-Otto Apel, try to develop arguments that would force any moral sceptic to subscribe to certain moral principles. According to these philosophers, vindicating morality means proving that its binding force is inevitable for everyone; and from this premise they infer that morality would loose its point if we could not provide all sceptics with compelling reasons to make moral commitments. Since we need a short label for these philosophers, and because I do not know of a less misleading one, let us call these philosophers *foundationalists*. Other philosophers claim that it is not only impossible but also unnecessary to convince all kinds of sceptics. In their view, practical philosophers should rather refer to the more or less contingent forms of normativity that are built into our social practices, traditions, and institutions. According to them, we need to argue from inside our moral practices, mainly using hermeneutical and reconstructive methods, and tapping into the critical potential already built into our existing ethos. Let us call the latter group *reconstructivists*.

This chapter is a revised and shortened version of a paper presented at the XXIII. *Kongress der Deutschen Gesellschaft für Philosophie* the original version of which will appear in its proceedings under the title *The Morality Club and the Moral Sceptic*.

DOI 10.1515/9783110470215-013

How should the debate between foundationalists and reconstructivists be resolved? In some way, reconstructivists are right. At least of a certain type of moral sceptics it is true that we neither can nor need to convince them. We just need to point out to them that there is something that they have to subscribe to *as soon as they make moral claims on others*.[1] Hence, reconstructivists are also right in stating that we should argue from inside, not from outside, our moral practices—or rather, we should say, from inside our common practice of moral reasoning. However, the so-called foundationalists are also right in some way. They are right in claiming that vindicating morality means showing that its prescriptions are binding for all moral agents.

These statements seem puzzling at first, at least in combination. Trying to clarify and reconcile them shall pave the way for a position we may call *social constitutivism*. The first move can be made together with the reconstructivists. It aims at showing that we neither can nor need to convert certain moral sceptics. It only seems to us that we have to, if we ask the basic question of moral justification from the monological perspective of a deliberating first person. However, the crucial question is not whether some agent, from her pre-moral and egocentric point of view, has good reasons to engage in the game of moral reasoning. The crucial question is whether, as long as she does not, she could defend her position against those who do, or whether they have good reasons to criticise her, and maybe even to sanction her, for some behaviour they deem immoral. Hence it suffices to ask what a moral sceptic—like any other agent—needs to accept *if* she addresses moral claims to others. The second move will bring us closer to the foundationalists again. To articulate the basic question of ethics in the way just described allows for a certain kind of constitutivism. This kind of constitutivism, which we may call *social* constitutivism, does not start from the pre-moral perspective of a solitary agent. Rather, it starts from the perspective of someone who already tries to construct a deliberative standpoint that she could *share* with others. Finally, we will briefly consider some implications for the project of normative ethics.

---

1 The relevant characteristic of a "moral" claim, in this context, is that it asks for recognition even where such recognition is not in the addressee's pre-moral interest. Hence, the presumed authority of a moral claim goes beyond that of a mere counsel of prudence; cf. Darwall's use of Hobbes' distinction between command and counsel in (Darwall 2006; 2013a/b).

II Practical moral scepticism and the basic question of ethics

Why should we stop trying to convince certain moral sceptics? Firstly, because we cannot convince them anyway. Secondly, because we do not need to. To begin with, it seems uncertain whether it is possible for any person to be a moral sceptic, at least over a longer period of time. However, if members of a certain species of moral scepticism—Sinnott-Armstrong (2006, p. 13) calls them *practical* moral sceptics—would actually exist, it would be impossible to provide them with reasons for morality. This is because these sceptics are not just unaware of a certain dimension of normativity—in this case, it would suffice to open their eyes, or make them look into the right direction. Rather, practical moral sceptics are agents who are able to capture the meaning of moral claims, but fail to see why these claims should have any binding force for them, why they should be moved by them. Of course, we could try to convince a practical moral sceptic that it would be advantageous for her to follow, or to publicly avow commitment to, certain rules which, due to their content, we might call "moral". In many cases, this might indeed be an advisable strategy. However, as Kant or Prichard may remind us, even if we would succeed, the moral sceptic would still be a moral sceptic, since the respective rules would have no *moral* meaning for her. Her reasons for following them would be egoistic and instrumental, not moral.

If this is true, we cannot convince practical moral sceptics. However, why do some philosophers think we should? Probably, it is because they look at morality from the monological perspective of a deliberating first person. Hence they ask: "Assume that I do not yet care about the concerns, the well-being, the interests, practical claims, moral arguments or evaluations of others. Which argument could then convince me to take moral reasons seriously?"

However, this way of putting the basic question leads to an insolvable problem: Reasons for morality must be reasons of the right kind, but the reasons of a true practical moral sceptic—of someone completely unmoved by the concerns other beings—can never be reasons of the right kind. If we approach moral bindingness from the perspective of a solitary individual who is not yet responsive to moral reasons, the resulting moral theory will be either scepticism, or a moral theory that gives the wrong kind of reasons for morality, or that includes an unwarranted step from non-moral to moral claims, or that includes a combination of such flaws. If we ask: "If I would not already subscribe to morality, what could give me a reason to do so?" the only possible answer will probably be: "Well, nothing". However, this might just show that we should put the question differently. We should rather ask: "What do I have to acknowledge, *if* I complain against how others treat me, *if* I criticise or justify some agent's behaviour, *if* I endorse feelings like guilt or resentment, etc.?" At first glance, this reformulation of the basic question of moral philosophy seems odd. Since why do philosophers try to defend morality against sceptical doubts? Probably because it is questionable whether we can ever be warranted *at all* in criticising or justifying actions, or in responding to them with feelings like guilt or resentment, etc. The desire for justification arises because we are sometimes uncertain whether we should continue to engage in these practices at all. It is the sceptic in ourselves we want to silence. However, if the point is just that we are uncertain whether φ-ing is legitimate and whether we should continue to φ, it does not seem helpful to ask "what do I need to accept *if* I φ?" If a convicted member of Cosa Nostra wonders whether he should break the rules of *omertà* and cooperate with the investigators, it may not help to say: "Well, if you are a member of Cosa Nostra, you must respect the *omertà*". Chances are that the convict already knows that breaking the *omertà* also means breaking with Cosa Nostra. He may be prepared to do both.

Still, I think that the suggested reformulation of the basic question is actually sound. Let us first consider two preliminary points.

First, it seems sound to assume that it is at least *possible* to look at practical issues from a shared deliberative perspective. It is certainly possible for us to strive for impartiality in our practical judgements (Nagel 1970). We can at least try to take the concerns of others equally important as our own. We are able to assign to others the same deliberative authority that we claim for ourselves. We do sometimes say to someone else: "I am about to do this or that, but you would be affected by my decision, so let us deliberate together about the best thing to do!" Deliberating together, we are able to take the practical concerns of others just as serious as our own—at least we are able to try to do so.

Second, it is plausible for us to assume that someone who does not at least try to take a shared deliberative standpoint *cannot justify her actions to others*. A moral sceptic cannot justify her actions to anyone else, at least not in a full sense. Obviously, this is not yet to say that the sceptic *ought* to justify her actions to us. It just means that she does not play the language game wherein it is possible to justify her conduct to others, and that she therefore cannot justify it, just as someone who does not participate in a game of chess cannot check an opponent's king. At least, she cannot justify her conduct in the full and unrestricted sense that is accessible to those who participate in the moral language game. Of course, the sceptic may convince us that her behaviour was instrumentally rational with regard to certain arbitrary goals she happened to have. She may also convince us that it was in some sense advantageous for herself or even prudent in some restricted, pre-moral sense. However, in itself this would not be a sufficient reason for us to *fully endorse* her behaviour from *our* point of view—regardless of whether we are also sceptics or not. As long as we do not, for some contingent reason, happen to identify with all of her concerns, nothing she could say could reasonably invite us to share her perspective. Of course, she could try to appeal to our egoism, by providing some sort of incentive. However, this would not serve to constitute a *shared* standpoint from which to consider practical matters. The sceptic cannot unite with us on one common practical standpoint, she cannot share with us a perspective in which we could endorse one another's conduct as a whole, and not only with respect to certain aspects, like the instrumental rationality it incorporates.

This is an important point, so let me try to express it in a different way once again: It is a conceptual truth about human action that human action can fail or succeed or be right or wrong in different regards and hence is open to critical judgement. This holds true for the actions of moral sceptics as well. Sometimes a sceptic will have to acknowledge that she misinterpreted a situation or that she did not choose the right means to her ends. Regarding such aspects of her action, even the moral sceptic will probably acknowledge the authority of others to make critical judgements about her own actions. However, as a moral sceptic, she will have to claim that the authority of others to criticise her actions is limited to empirical assumptions and matters of efficiency only. Her final goals, she will claim, cannot be the subject of other people's criticism, either because final goals cannot be rationally criticised at all, or because, concerning her own final goals, her own authority is the only authority that counts. Now, putting aside the question whether one can consistently defend (at least one of) these positions, it is clear that in both cases the moral sceptic could neither *justify* her ultimate choices to others nor *learn* something about these choices from them. For example, would she seriously ask others for advice about which of Kant's two alternative basic maxims she should adopt, the maxim of self-love or the maxim of morality (Kant 1968), she would have to assume that the judgements of her addressees about her own ultimate choices, ends, or maxims do actually count. She would thereby implicitly acknowledge their moral authority. This, however, would mean that she would not be a moral sceptic any more. In fact, she would have already made a decision against self-love as her maxim, that is, as the *ultimate* principle of her conduct. Since insofar as she gives others a stake in her choice of her allegedly ultimate principle, her *actual* ultimate principle is in fact *to act in accordance with principles that withstand intersubjective criticism*. This principle is different from and inconsistent with the maxim of self-love; it is rather, I think, another formulation of the maxim of morality. Hence, the sceptic cannot fully justify her conduct to others as long as she remains a sceptic. However, whether a moral sceptic can fully justify her actions or not does not seem very important to those who (like probably most moral philosophers) do not consider themselves moral sceptics but rather try to defend some version of normative ethics. They are rather interested in the following question: Does the moral sceptic somehow challenge the authority of morality?

There are two aspects to consider here. First, can the sceptic challenge the authority of morality for those who are not moral sceptics? To me it seems obvious that she cannot. In fact, she cannot even address us with provocative recommendations such as "stop your silly morality game, it is irrational!", since by doing so she would have to presuppose that there is a moral duty to be rational. One might reply that it is unjustified to call the duty to act rationally a *moral* duty. But however we may choose to call it, it needs to be an overriding and categorical duty, if the sceptic's intervention is to threaten morality; and this kind of duty is precisely the kind of duty the possibility of which a sceptic needs to deny in order to challenge morality. If sceptics could not even challenge moral obligations by claiming that they are irrational or that there is no reason to act on them, sceptics will certainly not succeed with any other, more substantial objections, since all such objections will already depend on an obligation to act rationally. Yet before we conclude that the sceptic does not seriously threaten morality we will have to consider a second question: Do moral norms apply to the sceptic? Let us think of the situation like this: There are two parties. One party we may call the "morality club". The other party is formed by the moral sceptics. Moral prescriptions can only be justified "from within" the morality club. So how could it be legitimate to apply them to the sceptics? Let us first consider what the "morality club" is. It is not a closed community with limited membership. Rather, we are all members *insofar as* we try to deliberate and judge from an impartial standpoint that could be shared by any agent. In fact, most of us are probably only temporary members, since, to put it in Kantian terms, most of us sometimes subordinate the maxim of morality to the maxim of self-love. Most of us are sometimes unmoved by impartial considerations and act in the way of practical moral sceptics. However, insofar as we are members of the "morality club", we will at least try to act only in ways we could fully justify to each other. We will ascribe to each other the same fundamental practical authority. We will all be committed to a principle *M* whose content we could express like this:

(*M*)   *Act only in ways that could be freely accepted by any agent who tries to justify her actions to any other agent alike.*

Principle *M*, which I think is a version of the principle of morality, is *a constitutive rule of the language game of moral justification*. As such, it cannot be rejected on pain of pragmatic inconsistency. Just by way of experiment, let us try to dismiss *M* and to defend a principle that includes *M*'s negation, namely: we shall not act in a way that could be universally accepted, but rather, we shall act according to some alternative principle *A*. Could we really *argue* in favour of *A?* Given our position, our arguments in favour of *A must not convince* others. Since if they did, others could freely accept the alternative principle *A*. In this case, however, the alternative principle *A* itself would fall, paradoxically, under *M*, i.e. under the principle of morality, that *A* was designed to replace. Of course, one might also try to challenge the proposed principle *M* by claiming that we should not act on any principle at all. However, it seems even more obvious that this position cannot be *argued for* in a non-self-defeating way.

Let us now suppose that a moral sceptic violates what members of the "morality club" consider a valid moral rule—for example, a student kills an ethics professor just because he used silly examples (like this one). Should we then just say: "Well, as members of the morality club, we would not have done that, but you are a moral sceptic, so we cannot object to what you did"? However, why should we not blame or even punish the student, as long as we can justify our blaming or punishing her to all those who do participate in the morality game? Of course, the moral sceptic, by definition, will not acknowledge the relevance of our justification for her own conduct. Would she take the moral stance, however, we should be able to justify even to her our blaming and punishing her—at least, this is what we have to presume if we regard our own action as legitimate. Perhaps she is tempted to complain that we treat her like a club member despite the fact that she is not (which is true but actually, I think, quite nice of us). Yet, if she would actually *complain*, she would certainly have to appeal to some sort of shared deliberative authority and would thereby become a club member, so that her complaint would be self-defeating. Of course, she might have other, reasonable objections, but whether this is the case or not can only be settled *within* the "morality club".

Still, one might still wonder whether to take moral principles as binding on someone who is not committed to morality does not somehow violate that person's autonomy. Implicitly, this question has already been answered. However, addressing it more explicitly allows us to shed some more light on the difference between social constitutivism and a more traditional Kantian view. Traditional Kantians would respond to the objection by claiming that the moral sceptic is not autonomous, or not rational, anyway. In some sense this Kantian response may be actually warranted. However, if there is something that the philosophical discussions since the publication of Kant's *Groundwork* make clear, it is that it not easy to spell this response out in a truly unambiguous and compelling way. Insofar, it would certainly be advantageous if we could just put aside the question whether a moral sceptic as such could be autonomous or practically rational. It would make things much easier if it would suffice o show that a moral sceptic would be unable to defend her actions to others, that is, would be unable to justify them in an unrestricted sense. And this is exactly what social constitutivism aims to show.

If we take the above points together, we can see why the alternative formulation of the basic question of moral philosophy, despite its "if—then" structure, is sound. The reason is *not* that the conditional is always true because it is somehow *impossible* to quit membership in the "morality club". The point is also not that it is impossible to quit membership in the morality club "autonomously" or "rationally". In contrast to traditional Kantians and monological constitutivists like Korsgaard or Gewirth, social constitutivism does not rely on any such claim. The reason is rather that the decision of an individual to quit membership does not affect the bindingness of morality *even for her*, since, whether or not one is a member of the "morality club", one cannot complain against being subjected to the rules of the morality game for the simple reason that "complaining" (in the sense that is relevant here) can only be understood as a move *within* the morality game.

III Why Social Constitutivism?

III.1 Constitutivism

If *foundationalists* are right in that morality should be shown to be binding for all agents, this does not imply that we must proselytise the sceptic. It may suffice to demonstrate what one needs to acknowledge *if* one tries to justify one's actions to other agents. Hence, within the plurality of our practices of practical justification, we need to find and make explicit the universal features of these practices that allow anyone to fully justify her actions. This means that we need to employ some sort of *constitutivist* strategy: We are looking for the constitutive elements of the language game wherein agents can fully justify their actions to each other. The considerations put forward in the preceding section about the impossibility of rejecting the principle of morality *M* already made use of a certain type of reasoning which is usually labelled "reflective" or "retorsive". This type of reasoning starts from the same assertion that it is meant to vindicate and aims at showing that the assertion in question cannot reasonably be dismissed since any attempt to do so already presupposes its validity. This seems to be what Aristotle tried to show with respect to the principle of non-contradiction (Aristotle 1999, 1005b ff.).

Why should we assume that retorsive arguments could play a crucial role in vindicating morality, as Apel (1988), Illies (2003) and others claim? I think that intuitionists like Prichard (1912), Kantians like Darwall (2006), and reconstructivists like Larmore (2008) are right in claiming that morality forms a genuine dimension of normativity and cannot be reduced to something else.[2] If this is true, however, any attempt to vindicate morality must actually start from *inside* our moral practices rather than from some pre-moral assumption. Moreover, unlike reconstructivists, I think that it does not suffice to point to the sheer existence of contingent moral practices when there are doubts about the bindingness of morality as such. The practice of moral justification certainly requires some critical principle, and we must be able to defend whatever this principle turns out to be against the strongest possible doubts and objections. Finally, given the first and second point, retorsive arguments appear to be exactly the kind of arguments we need. Unlike naturalist arguments or transcendental arguments of the "explorational" (Illies 2003, pp. 32 ff.) type, retorsive arguments definitely start from inside the challenged practices. They mainly make explicit certain practical commitments that we have already made and (a retorsive argument reminds us) that we continue making even in the very act of challenging them. Retorsive arguments can certainly be stronger arguments than just a hint to some contingent historical fact. Though they are not able to show that participating in certain practices (like the truth-game or the morality-game) is inevitable in itself, still they can establish that there is no standpoint outside certain practices from which one could challenge the constitutive rules of the respective practices.

However, retorsive arguments are usually seen as a kind of transcendental arguments, and do we not know from Stroud's famous paper (Stroud 1968) that transcendental arguments are not a promising kind of argument at all? I do not think so. As Robert Stern (2007) and James Skidmore (2002) rightly emphasised, Stroud's main concern is that transcendental arguments can only uncover necessary commitments *of our reason*. Hence, if we do not already presuppose a necessary relation between our reason and the world outside, these arguments cannot defeat something like external-world scepticism. This worry, however, does not apply to arguments that do not aim at establishing some truth about an external world, but just aim at vindicating some principle that is *internal* to our practices. Therefore, Skidmore argues, transcendental argu-

---

2 I should note that Larmore accuses Kant of not regarding morality as a genuine dimension. According to him, Kant did try to deduce morality from something else like freedom, autonomy, or practical reason (Larmore 2008, 43 ff., 105). I think that this criticism does not rest on the most plausible interpretation of Kant's project, according to which freedom, autonomy, and practical reason are not strictly pre-moral concepts.

ments may also be informative in the field of practical reason, if we use them (following Kant) just to uncover, make explicit or re-affirm normative commitments that are internal to, and constitutive of, practical reasoning, without adding any claims about the existence of moral facts outside our practical reasoning.

III.2 Social Constitutivism

Skidmore remains pessimistic about the prospects of transcendental arguments for morality, though. The reasons for his pessimism are not completely clear, as he refers mainly to a single example, Christine Korsgaard's attempt to vindicate the moral law in her book *Sources of Normativity* (1996). In my view, Skidmore is right in dismissing Korsgaard's argument, and he does so for a good reason. Interestingly though, his criticism does not refer at all to the transcendental step of Korsgaard's argument—a step that aims to show that humans must value their own humanity. Rather, like most of Kosgaard's critics, Skidmore takes issue with a subsequent step that purports to take us from (1) our commitment as rational persons to value our own humanity to (2) our commitment to value the humanity of all other rational agents likewise. This step is only necessary because the transcendental part of Korsgaard's argument starts from the monological perspective of a deliberating first person. Hence, Skidmore's reason to reject Korsgaard's argument is not grounded in the fact that Korsgaard's argument is transcendental, but in the fact that it starts from the standpoint of monological reasoning (this point remains true for Korsgaard's more recent version of her argument, cf. Korsgaard 2009). Yet we should note that the transcendental part of Korsgaard's argument—the part that is meant to show that we must to our own humanity if we value anything at all—is not convincing either: If it is the case that we value some x for the reason that we already are "human", then our valuing x cannot be the reason that commits us to assigning value to our humanity in the first place. It would only be necessary for us to value our humanity if it were necessary for us to value valuing—our ability to value anything at all. But it does not follow necessarily from our valuing x that we have to value our ability to value anything. In fact, it may not even be possible for us to appreciate the value of our ability to value anything, since it may be impossible to imagine, compare and evaluate both conditions: the condition of a being that cannot value anything at all and that of a being that can. Obviously, much more needs to be said about the different versions of traditional constitutivism than is possible in the given context.[3] However, my hunch is that Skidmore's pessimism about transcendental arguments in ethics is plausible as long as we share (with Korsgaard, Gewirth and other traditional constitutivists) the assumption that ethical reasoning needs to start from the monological perspective of a deliberating first person who asks herself why she should accept moral reasons. In my view, this assumption is unwarranted. The reason why the the the arguments of Korsgaard and Gewirth (1978) are so ambitious—probably overly ambitious—is that they try to conjure morality out of the hat after having put something else into the hat, like the instrumental rationality or the prudence of a solitary agent. Efforts to vindicate morality should rather take the form of an *internal self-reassurance* of a practice of shared deliberation, a practice that is already morally structured.

This is of course not a new idea. Rather, it is one of the core ideas of what Jürgen Habermas and others proposed under the name of "discourse ethics". It is also one of the main ideas in Stephen Darwall's book *The Second Person Standpoint* (2006). However, concerning this important point, some passages in the respective works of these authors remain somewhat ambiguous. In Habermas' case, this ambiguity emerges in the discussion on whether it is possible to refuse to participate in any practical discourse and whether this would endanger the normative force of discourse ethical principles. Presuming that some moral commitments can be justified by reconstructing the normativity internal to the practice of discourse itself, how can these commitments be valid for those who simply do not participate? Thomas Rentsch (1999, p. 59) and other critics of discourse ethics argued that we could get rid of obligations that are constitutive of practical discourse simply by refusing to participate. If the argument above (at the end of section II) is valid, it should be clear how this objection can be countered in the context of social constitutivism, but Habermas takes a different route. He argues that someone who refuses to participate in the practice of moral justification would probably be unable to maintain a stable personality (Habermas 1983, pp. 108 ff.). However, this response to Rentsch's objection does not seem convincing. Instead of vindicating the bindingness of moral obligations, it would turn them into a kind of virtue-ethical advice amounting to something like this: If you don't want to become crazy, you'd better join the morality club (cf. Apel 1989; Øfsti 1994; Werner 2003, pp. 78 ff.).

In Darwall's *The Second Person Standpoint*, there may be a similar ambiguity. It is one of Darwall's main points that as soon as we address a second-per-

---

3 For a more thorough critique of Gewirth see Werner (2002) and (2013) where the critique is defended against meta-critical remarks by Christoph Hübenthal (2006, 255 ff.).

sonal moral claim to another person we enter a mutual relation with an equal to whom we must ascribe second-personal competence, accountability, moral authority and, ultimately, human dignity. Moreover, Darwall thinks that the moral normativity which shows up in this relation is overriding and trumps all other practical considerations that would be accessible within a monological perspective (the perspective of the "naive practical reasoner", as Darwall calls it), including considerations of overall utility. However, can we not just avoid to address others second-personally? No, argues Darwall in a lengthy footnote against Fichte, because we can always be addressed by another person's "summons", and if this happens, we cannot simply break out of the second-personal relation which is thereby constituted (Darwall 2006, pp. 262ff., fn 26.). However, a few pages later he states that "even if we can't avoid [...] a summons, we can step back [...] and ask whether, on reflection, we should still accept [it]." This step back is a step back from an actual "second-personal" dialogue to philosophical reflection. Surprisingly, Darwall argues that this reflection does not need to "be second-personal itself" (Darwall 2006, p. 278). However, this statement seems inconsistent with Darwall's assumption that second-personal moral authority is the overriding form of normativity. For if the practical philosopher can—or even should—take a step back from the second-personal dialog, retreat into his shell, and, by way of traditional monological reasoning, think twice whether he should really take second-personal reasons seriously, it is the monological reasoning of the solitary philosopher that has overriding authority and not the actual dialog between accountable persons. Consequently, Darwall is unable to show subsequently why the solitary thinker, after his retreat, must necessarily leave his shell and enter the second-personal relation again. Hence, ironically, Korsgaard (2007) is right when she objects to Darwall that he cannot show that morality is unconditionally binding. This is ironic because the reason why Darwall's argument remains unsuccessful is not, like Korsgaard supposes, that he fails to approach morality from within the monological perspective of a deliberating first person, but rather that he lapses back into trying to do just that—that he still tries to convert the moral sceptic instead of showing why her perspective is irrelevant.

III.3 Enoch's objection

In this section I want to briefly discuss an objection that may be raised against the position of social constitutivism. It concerns a problem that at first glance seems to affect all versions of constitutivism, including social constitutivism: When a constitutivist tries to vindicate y by showing that y is among the constitutive elements of some x (e.g.: agency, practical reason, autonomy, or the ability to justify one's action to other agents), her argument will rely, at least implicitly, on some *definition* of x. However, can a constitutivist who wants to vindicate y not just *arbitrarily* choose a definition of x that allows her to prove that y is actually "constitutive" of x (e.g. simply *defines* x as "agency" rather than as "shmagency"; cf. Enoch 2006)? The challenge for traditional constitutivists is to defend a definition of x that is sufficiently "rich" to support their subsequent argument and to show, at the same time, that x, defined in such way, is still strictly "unavoidable" (e.g. that it is unavoidable "for us" to be an "agent" rather than a "shmagent"). Apparently, a similar worry concerns *social* constitutivism as well. We may wonder whether the notion of "justifying one's own conduct to others" cannot be interpreted in a less demanding way. In particular, why should we strive for "full" justification of our conduct? Why should one try to be able to justify one's conduct to *all* agents—why should one not rather address only one's own family, or one's own clan, or the citizens of one's own nation, or those with whom one wants to cooperate for mutual benefit?

The social constitutivist's reply starts by pointing out how difficult it is to maintain a particularist framework of moral justification for a long time: It will be hard to deflect critical questions about the exclusionary nature of the framework. In order to prevent the appearance of arbitrariness of that moral framework *even from within*, reasons for the exclusion of potential moral fellows need to be given, and sooner or later, these reasons will be scrutinized even by members of the restricted moral community. Note that the social constitutivist does not need to make the very strong claim that it would be *impossible* for an agent to be a particularist. Given the pervasiveness of partial moralities in human history, it would actually seem quite pointless to do so. All that the social constitutivist needs to claim is that as long as an agent does not try to justify her conduct to *all* others, there will be a standpoint from which her conduct can be criticised, maybe even sanctioned, and that she will not be able to complain without widening the scope of all those that she acknowledges as moral fellows (which may also contribute to an *explanation* of the tendency to more inclusive moral systems; cf. Kitcher 2011). While it is certainly easier (psychologically) to be a moral particularist than a moral sceptic, the fundamental challenges to particularism are basically the same as those faced by the sceptic. In both positions one lacks the means to defend oneself against moral criticism coming from an "outside" or a universalist standpoint.

The more general point with regard to Enoch's argument is that at least in the context of social constitutivism the choice of a definition of X (in this case: "justifying one's own conduct to others") cannot be completely arbitrary. Since in this context, the necessity to settle on a certain definition is not psychological or purely conceptual necessity ("I cannot understand myself other than as an agent, who..."). Rather, the definition of *X* has *practical* implications for those who endorse it and act on the basis of it. For example, the person who argues in favour of a "particularist definition" of practical justification (however such "definition" would look like) cannot immunise her own conduct against criticism from "outsiders" without at the same time squandering her opportunity to justify her own actions to "outsiders" (or universalists) or to object to the actions or judgments of all those who do not share her idiosyncratic concept of justification.

V Conclusion

Foundationalists and reconstructivists are both right in some way. Reconstructivists are right in stating that vindicating morality is essentially a kind of *internal self-reassurance* concerning the validity of principles that are built into deliberative or justificatory practices. Foundationalists are right in claiming that this self-reassurance can and ultimately needs to reflect on the constitutive principles of the most general practice of moral reasoning, a practice characterised only by the fact that we try to justify our respective conduct to each other, or that we try to construct a shared standpoint from which one's actions could be fully endorsed by anyone. Unlike traditional constitutivists assume, we do not need to show that someone who does not endorse moral principles can no longer understand herself as a rational or autonomous agent. We just need to show that the authority of the universalist moral standpoint cannot be challenged "from outside", e.g. by a practical moral sceptic or particularist. Social constitutivism gets on with the remaining task of making explicit and reaffirming the basic constitutive principles of our common practice of shared deliberation and practical justification. In this context, there is room for "modest" (Stern, 2007) uses of transcendental reasoning.

Bibliography

Apel, Karl-Otto (1988): *Diskurs und Verantwortung: Das Problem des Übergangs zur postkonventionellen Moral.* Frankfurt a. M.: Suhrkamp.

Apel, Karl-Otto (1989): "Normative Begründung der 'Kritischen Theorie' durch Rekurs auf lebensweltliche Sittlichkeit?" In: Axel Honneth et al. (Eds.): *Zwischenbetrachtungen: Im Prozeß der Aufklärung.* Frankfurt a. M.: Suhrkamp, pp. 15–65.

Aristotle (1999): *Aristotle's Metaphysics.* Santa Fe, N.M: Green Lion Press.

Darwall, Stephen L. (2006): *The Second-Person Standpoint: Morality, Respect, and Accountability.* Cambridge, Mass.; London: Harvard University Press.

Darwall, Stephen L. (2013a): *Morality, Authority, and Law: Essays in Second-Personal Ethics I.* Oxford: Oxford University Press.

Darwall, Stephen L. (2013b): *Honor, History, and Relationship: Essays in Second-Personal Ethics II.* Oxford: Oxford University Press.

Enoch, David (2006): "Agency, Shmagency: Why Normativity Won't Come from What Is Constitutive of Action." In: *The Philosophcal Review* 115. No. 2, pp. 169–198.

Gewirth, Alan (1978): *Reason and Morality.* Chicago: University of Chicago Press.

Habermas, Jürgen (1983): "Diskursethik—Notizen zu einem Begründungsprogramm." In: *Moralbewußtsein und kommunikatives Handeln.* Frankfurt a. M.: Suhrkamp, pp. 53–125.

Hübenthal, Christoph (2006): *Grundlegung der Christlichen Sozialethik: Versuch eines freiheitsanalytisch-handlungsreflexiven Ansatzes.* Münster: Aschendorff.

Illies, Christian (2003): *The Grounds of Ethical Judgement: New Transcendental Arguments in Moral Philosophy.* Oxford: Oxford University Press.

Kant, Immanuel (1968): "Die Religion innerhalb der Grenzen der bloßen Vernunft." In: *Werke: Akademie Textausgabe.* Berlin: De Gruyter, Vol. VI, pp. 1–202.

Kitcher, Philip (2011): *The Ethical Project.* Cambridge; London: Harvard University Press.

Korsgaard, Christine M. (2007): "Autonomy and the Second Person Within: A Commentary on Stephen Darwall's The Second-Person Standpoint." In: *Ethics* 118. No. 1, pp. 8–23.

Korsgaard, Christine M. (2009): *Self-Constitution: Agency, Identity, and Integrity.* Oxford: Oxford University Press.

Korsgaard, Christine M. (1996): *The Sources of Normativity.* Cambridge: Cambridge University Press.

Larmore, Charles E. (2008): *The Autonomy of Morality.* Cambridge: Cambridge University Press.

Nagel, Thomas (1970): *The Possibility of Altruism.* Oxford: Clarendon Press.

Øfsti, Audun (1994): "Ist diskursive Vernunft nur eine Sonderpraxis?" In: *Abwandlungen: Essays zur Sprachphilosophie und Wissenschaftstheorie.* Würzburg: Königshausen & Neumann, pp. 139–157.

Prichard, Harold A. (1912): "Does Moral Philosophy Rest on a Mistake?" In: *Mind* 21. No. 81, pp. 21–37.

Rentsch, Thomas (1999): *Die Konstitution der Moralität: Transzendentale Anthropologie und praktische Philosophie.* Frankfurt a. M.: Suhrkamp.

Sinnott-Armstrong, Walter (2006): *Moral Skepticisms.* Oxford: Oxford University Press.

Skidmore, James (2002): "Skepticism about Practical Reason: Transcendental Arguments and Their Limits." In: *Philosophical Studies* 109. No. 2, pp. 121–141.

Stern, Robert (2007): "Transcendental Arguments: a Plea for Modesty." In: *Grazer Philosophische Studien* 74. No. 1, pp. 143–161.

Stroud, Barry (1968): "Transcendental Arguments." In: *The Journal of Philosophy* 65. No. 9, pp. 241–256.

Werner, Micha H. (2002): "Minimalistische Handlungstheorie—gescheiterte Letztbegründung: Ein Blick auf Alan Gewirth." In: Holger Burckhart/Horst Gronke (Eds.): *Philosophieren aus dem Diskurs: Beiträge zur Diskurspragmatik.* Würzburg: Königshausen & Neumann, pp. 308–328.

Werner, Micha H. (2003): *Diskursethik als Maximenethik: Von der Prinzipienbegründung zur Handlungsorientierung.* Würzburg: Königshausen & Neumann.
Werner, Micha H. (2013): "Ist Wertenkönnen wertvoll?" In: Gerald Hartung et al. (Eds.): *Naturphilosophie als Grundlage der Naturethik.* Freiburg i. Br.; München: Karl Alber, pp. 187–214.

Wolfgang Kuhlmann

Transcendental-Pragmatic Foundation of Ethics. Transcendental Arguments and Ethics

Abstract: The transcendental-pragmatic version of discourse-ethics (Apel 1973, 1988, 2001; Böhler 1985, 2013; Kuhlmann 1985, 2007) is centered around its transcendental philosophical foundation, i. e. a transcendental argument. In the following paper this foundation is firstly presented cursory in contradistinction to the classical Kantian proceeding, it is then developed more precisely and in detail and finally it is defended against some objections especially concerning the relationship between transcendental philosophy and ethics.

I

Kant considers the philosophy of his time as entrapped in a desperate situation due to the predominant trends of dogmatism and scepticism and he understands his transcendental philosophy essentially as a means to establish by a radical critique of reason a secure foundation for his discipline, to make possible what he calls the "secure advancement of sciences" for philosophy. He asks: How is material philosophical knowledge, how are "synthetic apriori judgements" possible? And he shows in a very complex procedure, that without the so-called "synthetic apriori judgements", which themselves presuppose specific categories and forms of intuition, i. e. without the possibility of some philosophical knowledge, there will be no empirical knowledge in the sense of physics at all. The main point of his argument is: we can deny the possibility of synthetic apriori judgements only if we at the same time dispute the possibility of empirical cognition in the sense of physics, i. e. the possibility of a very important and central achievement of reason. The task of the sceptic is made difficult here by showing: If the sceptic attacks x then he must in the same time attack fundamental opinions, he don't want to attack at all, which normally are very important for him and which meaningfully to deny is not very easy.

The characteristics of transcendental argumentation most relevant for our context here are: (i) Reason (and together with it the faculty of cognition) is understood in the sense of *methodical solipsism*, that is as something, which can already be practiced and realized completely within one subject in isolation, within a subject, which is not dependent on communication in a communica-

DOI 10.1515/9783110470215-014

tion-community, that means which does not have from the beginning a social dimension. (ii) Transcendental philosophy in Kant is restricted to the realm of *theoretical philosophy*. Kant concentrates on the "conditions of the possibility" of theoretical reason only, of experience. (iii) Kant's main argument is a *weak transcendental argument* in the sense, that it is not excluded, that the basis of the argument, the thesis, that experience (in the sense of classical physics) is possible, could be contested by the sceptic. In any case it is not at all self-evident, that the sceptic will understand classical physics as something absolutely incontestable. (iv) Kant simply presumes that we can get reliable knowledge about the necessary presuppositions of valid experience by transcendental reflection. He provides expressly for a fundamental examination of our faculty of cognition which he executes in his "Critique of Pure Reason" ("critical" versus "precritical philosophy"), but that type of cognition he must make use of performing his "Critique" remains exempt from this examination. So its results in principle remain vulnerable as belonging to precritical philosophy. (v) Kant shows in his transcendental philosophy how because of our subjective preconditions of cognition we must think about the world. Since he shows this making use of the distinction between the phenomenal world and the thing in itself it is not totally excluded, that he is struck by the objections of Stroud (Stroud 1968) who maintains, that transcendental arguments can only show, that we must think so and so about the world, but not—what is actually intended—that what we must think is true, i.e., that the world in reality is so and so.

Transcendental-pragmatics starts with an assessment of the general situation of contemporary philosophy, which is very similar to that which provoked Kant to his great enterprise. It maintains that meaningful philosophical work capable of progress is no longer possible, if the currently dominating positions of radical fallibilism, historism and holism become completely accepted. [1] And it turns the so called "reflexive Letztbegründungsargumente" (arguments of non-circumventability) into the center of the conception, transcendental arguments with the function to provide that kind of knowledge, what we as reasonable i.e. non-radical fallibilists, historists and holists need in order to achieve meaningful work in philosophy capable of progress. "Reflexive Letztbegründungsargumente" (reflexive arguments for ultimate foundation) are arguments by which what we as participants in rational argumentation (discourse) must presuppose in

---

[1] They all agree in denying the possibility of material knowledge in a strong sense. But it is easy to see, that meaningful philosophical work capable of progress is possible only if one can know (in the strong sense of the word) how and in what direction one must endeavor in order to realize progress and not in the contrary regress. This means with respect to certain points real knowledge is indispensable.

order to be able to argue meaningfully and effectively is disclosed as knowledge which is for us uncircumventable and indisputable. The current formula of transcendental arguments: "If not x, then neither the (for us important) y," here gets the following form: If our convictions concerning the rules and presuppositions of meaningful argumentation (discourse) do not have the status of real knowledge, then rational decisions about the legitimacy of validity claims whichever are no longer possible at all and everything breaks down. We therefore have to characterize these convictions as knowledge in the strong sense.

Significant characteristics of the transcendental-pragmatic form of transcendental arguments are the following: (i) Reason, rationality, and with it discourse, the system of argumentation, are understood here as something inevitably bound to language, to communication, to interaction in a communication-community. Transcendental pragmatics mobilizes a reflexive argument to show this. By this idea the whole area, where one can look for a basis of transcendental arguments has fundamentally changed in comparison to Kant. Reason, rationality is no longer something which can belong to one subject alone and which could be thought of as being something extramundane, on the contrary it demands a multiplicity of real intramundane subjects speaking a real historical language and which as participants of a communication-community are always referring to this community. As such reason has from the beginning a social dimension. (ii) In the new frame the question is no longer the conditions of the possibility of experience but the conditions of the possibility of discourse, discourse understood here as the instance by which all validity claims which could be rational assessed i.e. at least the claims to truth and to rightness are judged. Thus the idea of transcendental philosophy becomes generalized. This generalization together with the fact—just mentioned -, that use of reason necessarily presupposes rules for the interaction of the participants of discourse, make it possible to make use of transcendental arguments not only in theoretical but also in practical philosophy. (iii) The conviction to which Kant essentially tries to reduce the validity of the synthetic apriori statements, the conviction, that experience is possible, is itself not readily to contest. But it is nevertheless possible to conceive of sceptics who will try this. The conviction however to which transcendental pragmatics essentially tries to reduce the validity of opinions about rules and presuppositions of meaningful argumentation, the conviction that meaningful argumentation is possible, cannot be meaningfully contested at all. We cannot meaningfully doubt or contest that opinion, for in order to do so, we evidently must in the same time rely on it. Meaningful doubts, meaningful objections are themselves moves in the game of discourse. In the place of a weak argument in Kants conception we here have a strong transcendental argument. And we maintain that this kind of argument can be called the real and the strongest possible form of transcendental arguments. (iv) In transcendental pragmatics transcendental reflection on reason, on discourse and on presuppositions of reason and discourse, i.e. the type of cognition, by which we know about the relevant "conditions of the possibility", is not used as in Kant simply and in a naive and dogmatic manner, which establishes for the sceptic the possibility to make his fallibilistic objections. Rather it is explicitly scrutinized and where it proves to be necessary replaced by a different and more appropriate kind of reflection ("strikte Reflexion"). (v) Finally it becomes possible within this radicalized version of transcendental philosophy (which by the way is able to dispense fully with the idea of a thing-in-itself) to cope with the objections of Stroud against transcendental philosophy.

II

We now try to give a more detailed reconstruction of the transcendental pragmatic foundation of ethics.

1. Firstly to the *motives* of this foundation. The most important seem to be the following three: (i) Ethics in general demands of us, that we do not simply we want to do, but that we firstly consider what we should do, especially what we—morally—are allowed to do at all. That means ethics imposes restrictions on our actions. But restrictions are only tolerable for reasonable beings, if there are good reasons for these restrictions. (ii) Evidently there are many different forms of ethics dependent on space and time, on history and culture. There are at least very different competing conceptions of what should count as the right ethics. A special form of ethics can demand recognition and observance only if it can mobilize better reasons as its competitors. (iii) There are forms of radical criticism of ethics a la Nietzsche, acting as critique of ideology or "genealogy". These forms do not contest that we have strong moral convictions and intuitions, but they provide an explanation of these intuitions which does not trace back them to a valid ethics, but rather to a powerful collective self-deception induced from outside. It is possible to come to terms with such a form of critique of ideology only for someone who is able to rely not only on strong moral intuitions but above all on strong arguments in favor of the legitimacy of theses intuitions.

Evidently the problem of foundation is an important and central problem of ethics. Such a foundation must provide answers to questions of the following kind: (i) Why should I respect this special restriction? Why I am not allowed to do this? (ii) Why should I respect and follow this ethics, this principle of morals and not that? (iii) Is there really something like a legitimate ethics at all? Why should I behave morally at all?

2. The problem resulting from this however turns out to be not trivial at all. The following factors make it especially difficult:

(i) The point here is not foundation of a moral claim going back to a principle already conceded. It is rather about the foundation of the principle itself, of a first or last sentence of ethics, from which anything else within ethics will be dependent.

(ii) This principle must itself be prescriptive, because it is prescriptive sentences, which should follow from it, which are to be derived from it. As such it could only be founded itself—in the usual manner—by deriving it from other prescriptive sentences.

(iii) This principle must hold categorically and without exception, i. e. its validity cannot be dependent on contingent circumstances, with respect to which it could be relativized. And there cannot be exceptions for its validity. Exceptions would be here falsifying counterexamples for the validity of the principle.

(iv) Very peculiar is the following condition: The foundation must establish here infallible knowledge: The principle of ethics to be founded here, will formulate what must be considered as the morally right, it will express the meaning of the concept of rightness. As such it has within the field of practical philosophy the same place value as the concept of truth within the field of theoretical philosophy. It follows: A foundation grounding the principle only as a fallible suggestion is pointless. For in founding it as such we must anticipate the possibility of a rational refusal or correction of this suggestion as a proposal missing the intended rightness, so as in theoretical investigations we—as fallibilists—always anticipate the possibility of convictions which miss the intended truth. But both is possible only if we count on valid standards with respect to which the respective proposals will be refused or corrected as not being right or true. Now evidently these standards themselves cannot be considered here as something fallible or corrigible[2], this means: The fallibilistic idea of a conviction, which is only a corrigible suggestion, presupposes the idea of a standard, which is itself not fallible or corrigible. Now the project of founding a principle of ethics is nothing else than the attempt to establish such an ultimate standard. Therefore fallibilistic modesty here is out of place.

---

2 If we would consider them as fallible we would get firstly an infinite regress and secondly the meaning of the expression "corrigible" would become immediately incomprehensible.

(v) After Nietzsche and his critique of ideology it is no longer possible to found ethics simply relying on current moral intuitions.

3. It follows: The normal, obvious types of founding, namely founding either by inferring (deriving) or by coherence considerations (reflective equilibrium) do not work here. Founding by deriving what is to be grounded from something what is envisaged as reason is not possible for we have to do with a prescriptive *principle*. Because of the prohibition of naturalistic fallacies a deductive foundation here could only be possible as derivation from another prescriptive sentence. But then this other sentence should be considered as the ultimate principle, i.e. foundation via derivation would only postpone not solve the problem. And evidently it is impossible to cope by this procedure with the problem of ascertaining the respective *last* premise. Therefore the procedure of linear derivation fails.—The second usual procedure, foundation via reflective equilibrium fails for two reasons. On the one hand the pretheoretical moral opinions and intuitions out of which one could try to establish a reflective equilibrium, are because of the Nietzschean critique of ideology no longer a legitimate base for this equilibrium. On the other hand the procedure of forming an reflective equilibrium amounts finally to a gradual approximation to an ultimate opinion, i.e. a fallibilistic solution of the problem. We just have seen, that this cannot work here.

4. If the usual procedures fail here, then we must use another approach and in order to do so we must widen our perspective. Our problem has for the time being the following general form: "We don't know, whether there is really something like a valid ethics and if so, how exactly does it look like? We are doubtful and want to have certainty." (P1) The foundation of ethics should establish this certainty.—Now it is important to bear in mind that foundations have only little—i.e. indirect—relation to the truth or rightness of what is to be grounded. A foundation cannot directly change the truth or rightness of a given sentence. It can change only the certainty we have with respect to the truth or rightness of a given sentence. And this certainty is sureness against doubts or objections.—What are the possibilities we have to establish such certainty, to secure a proposal from doubts or objections? Apparently there are two main strategies: On the one hand we can concentrate on the side of the attacked and try to sustain it. Here our problem gets the following more specific form: "Is it possible to found some fundamental moral norms, fundamental moral obligations?" (P2) And here we understand by "founding" that we transfer certainty, which is already existent in another place to the problematic attacked item. We have just seen that this procedure, the founding by *deriving* or *deducing* does not work here.—On the other hand we can concentrate on the side of the attacker. Here we could try—which is the most obvious—to weaken the factual doubt or objection, if possible to invalidate it completely by disclosing difficulties, contradictions within the factual objection. Since by this procedure evidently we can defend ourselves only from objections already established and known, but not against *every merely possible* objection, it does not help against doubts of the radical fallibilist.—But there is a variation of this procedure aiming at safeguarding against objections not only ad hoc and occasionally but basically and generally. Here we can exploit the fact, that doubts and objections qua complex achievements of reason have internal boundaries making inaccessible whole domains of convictions for them for structural reasons and so making them safe from doubts and objections. These internal boundaries result from the fact, that actions and achievements of reason are bound to preconditions and presuppositions on which it depends whether they are meaningful and effective or meaningless and ineffective. It is these presuppositions which cannot meaningfully be attacked i.e. be doubted or refused, for doubts and objections would invalidate and destroy themselves attacking the preconditions of their own effectiveness. Convictions belonging to the necessary presuppositions of meaningful achievements of reason ("conditions of the possibility") therefore can be regarded as convictions, for which a very high degree of certainty is attainable by foundation. At this point we arrive at what I think is the real fundamental idea of transcendental philosophy. The peculiarities of the problem—we have to do with *principles* and necessary are *infallible* solutions—suggest a special procedure namely that of transcendental philosophy. Moreover it is evident that *only* this procedure is able to provide infallible solutions. Only in this way we can protect ourselves against *every possible* doubt and objection, which with regards to their specific content we as yet cannot know.

After all we should give to our general problem (P1) another more specific form, e.g. this one: "Is it possible to disclose among the necessary presuppositions of meaningful achievements of reason even sentences (convictions), which a) are *morally relevant prescriptive sentences* and which b) could *be identified as infallible valid?*" (P3).[3]

5. Within the frame of Kantian transcendental philosophy—which Kant as is well known reserved for theoretical philosophy only—such sentences (convictions) of course cannot be disclosed. Making use of the means of Kantian transcendental philosophy it is neither possible to provide infallible results of transcendental

---

3 Disclosure of presuppositions of reason which are not refutable can be considered as founding only if foundation is regarded as something essentially centered on providing certainty.

arguments nor is Kant able to make plausible that "pure reason" contains as necessary presuppositions morally relevant prescriptive sentences. The first is impossible, because Kant mobilizes only a weak transcendental argument and in doing so relies on theoretical reflection, which remains unexamined (in the sense of critique of reason). The second is impossible, because it is not at all intelligible why his essentially methodical-solipsistic conception of reason should contain provisions for the solutions of possible conflicts between different subjects of reason.[4]—Within the frame of transcendental pragmatics where other presuppositions of reason are relevant and where the whole conception of reason is different from the Kantian the matter looks quite different. On the one hand transcendental pragmatics withdraws so to speak the front of transcendental philosophy. Instead of attempting to show that the conditions of the possibility of (a certain type of) experience are universally valid transcendental pragmatics limits itself to demonstrating that the conditions of the possibility of meaningful argumentation, of discourse, of rational assessing validity-claims (of what kind ever) are to be considered as universally valid. By this move transcendental pragmatics goes back to a more central part of the presuppositions of reason—a part unsurpassable with respect to centrality—and gains the possibility of disclosing opinions which are literally indisputable. They are indisputable, have guaranteed security against doubts and objections because doubts and objections which would attack them, would immediately destroy themselves and therefore must remain ineffective. Kantian arguments recurring to convictions which to contest is not easy, convictions, which to circumvent is more or less difficult, are replaced here by arguments recurring to such opinions, which to dispute or to circumvent is simply impossible. Weak transcendental arguments become here strong arguments of non-circumventability (Unhintergehbarkeitsargumente).—On the other hand transcendental pragmatics turns against the methodical solipsism characteristic for the mainstream of modern philosophy. It tries to bring forward a reflexive argument of noncircumventability in favor of the claim, that achievements of reason, to which inevitably belong claims to *intersubjective* validity (truth or rightness) are necessarily bound to communication within a communicative community (Kuhlmann 2009,

---

4 Kant's transcendental philosophy is conducted with respect to the cognitive relations between *one* subject of reason (*one* instantiation of pure reason) and the external reality. A plurality of subjects of reason (of instantiations of pure reason) and cognitive (perhaps even interactive) relations between them (including presuppositions for these relations) is in no way envisaged on the level of pure reason by the transcendental philosophy of Kant, nor is it considered as something necessary for carrying through the cognitive tasks which are analysed in the "Critique of pure Reason".

pp. 60 – 95). Thereby rational subjectivity, which is to be exploited by transcendental philosophy (transcendental arguments) gains an intrinsic social dimension. This means that to this subjectivity belong from the beginning rules for the coexistence and cooperation of the members of the communication community (this is now the real subject of transcendental philosophy), which communicate and interact in discourse, and these rules are in fact prescriptive and morally relevant.

As a particularly important *example* we single out the rule, according to which we as members of the discourse-community are obliged to try to *convince* (überzeugen) our addressees by our proposals , but not to *persuade* (überreden) them (a procedure which would be totally irrelevant for the purpose of common striving for truth in discourse). By having acknowledged this rule we have in effect accepted a rule ® which prescribes, that we have to take a position and attitude towards all other members of the discourse-community, from which we respect and treat the other members as reasonable, free and having equal rights.[5] Obviously this is a rule of great importance for ethics.—After all a solution seems to be possible which can cope with the conditions mentioned.

6. But there remains one important point. We said, that a fallibilistic solution would not meet the necessary demands.[6] Now the fallibilist can still object: "Indeed we cannot contest x meaningfully (i. e. without self-contradiction) *if* x is a necessary presupposition of meaningful argumentation. But that it *in fact is* such a presupposition must be recognized independently, for the contradiction in question can arise only if this is already conceded. So far we have no evidence in favor of this. But we can talk about noncircumventability ("Unhintergehbarkeit") in a strict sense only if we here can have infallible insights." This objection corresponds to the qualms mentioned that classical transcendental philosophy is relying in its enterprise only on a kind of cognition (transcendental reflection) which itself remains unexamined in the sense of critical philosophy.—Transcendental pragmatics answers to this objection by distinguishing between two different kinds of reflection and by bringing instead of the usually absolutized *theoretical reflection* now the so called *"strict" reflection* into the play, i. e. a kind of

---

5 Only if we respect and treat our addressee as reasonable, free and having equal right (if we expressly keep open all possibilities and chances for him to contradict and to refuse our proposal, our performance merits the designation of convincing (in contradistinction to persuading) (cf. Kuhlmann 1992, pp. 73 – 91).

6 Such a solution would be meaningless with respect to ultimate standards, which is just what is to be founded here.

reflection which is not in the same manner open for fallibilistic attacks as the theoretical reflection. –

Theoretical reflection is a cognitive endeavor which is realized by someone who contemplates an achievement of reason, e.g. a linguistic utterance, from the position and perspective of an external theoretical observer making it explicitly an object of his cognition. The result of this cognition, the cognitive representation of the utterance, is here something subsequently added to the utterance, which itself independently of the cognition already existed. And this result is fallible in every possible respect.

In contrast *strict reflection* is the cognitive conduct of an actor towards his action which he must bring into the play if he wants to perform his action, from which he must have knowledge in order to be the actor of his doing. In performing this cognitive conduct the actor remains in the position of an actor, he does not switch over to the position of an observer. And what he perceives from this position is for him his own action which he only concomitandly—so to speak: from inside—perceives and not an object perceived from outside and treated as a thematic object. It is essentially concomitant and not objectifying cognition.

As an example we consider a theoretician who on the one side refers via his theory to his object of inquiry in an explicit and objectifying manner, but who on the other side in the same time must in order to perform his main task refer too to his theory and to his referring to his object via his theory. The insights he gets by the latter concomitant activity from his own doings are not something subsequently added to objects which exist independently of their being perceived. In the contrary they are constitutive for his achievements as *his* achievements from which he must know in order to be able e.g. to decide in favor of them, to perform and to control them. The knowledge of his doings could be called *action-knowledge*, this is knowledge by which out of mere events in nature become actions of an actor, which intrinsically have a normative character, i.e. can succeed or fail. As something that is constitutive in this sense, action-knowledge is in a sense self-guaranteeing, and as such to a lesser extent exposed to the objections of a radical fallibilist as is theoretical reflection.

Now the main point is this: By strict reflection the following move becomes possible (we stick to the rule, we just introduced as example): We contest as an experiment the rules, according to which we must in discourse try to *convince* our addressees, whereupon we must respect them as reasonable, free and as having equal rights. We contest these rules experimentally in order to test, whether these rules are in fact noncircumventable (unhintergehbar) for us. In performing this test we inevitably make a move in the game of discourse ourselves: we maintain as true, as intersubjectively valid, that these rules are not valid.—If in our examination, whether this attempt can be successful, we could only rely on *theoretical reflection*, then the result of the examination would be: The attempt to dispute the rules in question fails,[7] *if* our pertinent beliefs about speech-acts in discourse are correct, namely that these speech-acts must be attempts to convince the addressees—and not to persuade—and that these attempts presuppose the rules in question. It fails, for then a contradiction would appear between that, what we at present maintain and that what we—in accordance with our theory of discourse which is essentially result of theoretical reflection—must belief about our speech-act and must presuppose in performing it. Certainly our theories about speech-acts in discourse and the resulting theoretical assumptions about specific actions in discourse are clearly fallible. Insofar it is not quite certain, that our attempt to dispute the rules really must fail. So we cannot consider these rules as something plainly noncircumventable (unhintergehbar).

If in contrast we can—making use of *strict reflection*—rely upon action-knowledge of our attempt to contest the rules, the argument looks differently: Again we experimentally dispute the validity of the rules prescribing us to try to convince our addressees in which we must respect the addressees as reasonable, free and as having equal rights. We check whether this attempt can be successful, but now we don't look for external evidences. Instead we confront our contention, that the rules in question are not valid, directly with our understanding of this contention which—as action-knowledge—we had to make use of (firstly as attacker secondly as examiner) in order that the examination could take place at all. (Here we did understand the contention in the following sense—this was the basis for our attempt to examine its validity: It is a move in the game of finding out the truth. A serious claim to truth belongs to it. This claim is raised in order to provoke assent or (well founded) denial on the side of the addressees. The claim aims at consensus in the sense, that finally everybody agrees with the (possibly altered or corrected) thesis and that nobody still will bring forward further justified objections. And here only such assent or dissent of the addressees count, which trace back to free insight and interest in finding the truth. Assent or dissent for other reasons would be totally irrelevant. All in all: Our contention is an attempt to *convince* the addressees and not to *persuade* them.[8])—We have to examine, whether the attempt to contest:

---

7 This means: the rule proves to be incontestable valid.

8 One could object here: "It would be sufficient, if we presuppose that there is raised a truth-claim to the contention. To consider the contention as an attempt to convince the addressees is not absolutely necessary and insofar not noncircumventable." This objection amounts to declare the pragmatic dimension of speech irrelevant. Against this we have to recall, that the idea of a validity claim can only be made explicit and comprehensible via the ideas of consensus and of

"I hereby contest (and by this try to convince my addressees, that my opponent is wrong, that is, I acknowledge rule ® as valid), that ® is valid", can be successful. We get the result: It must remain unsuccessful, if our understanding of the speech-act is correct. Can this understanding be wrong? The important point here is, that this latter question within the established frame of examination is no longer open, because our understanding is constituent part of problem to be solved. That our understanding is correct belongs to the presuppositions of the question, whether the attempt to contest can be successful. If in some way it would turn out, that our understanding is wrong, then nevertheless it would not result, that it is possible to meaningfully contest the validity of rule ® (and that ® insofar is circumventable as discourse presupposition). What would result is rather, that our problem disappears. In this case we would examine a contention with respect to the entitlement of its validity claim, to which a validity claim does not belong at all. It follows: If we really have the problem (have acknowledged the problem) than we have the solution and this solution is not fallible but infallible. It is impossible to successfully contest rule ®, it turns out to be noncircumventable for us.

In the foregoing we got an elucidation why a special—transcendental philosophical—procedure of foundation is necessary her, and what it consists in. The main points of our account were:

- As the center of transcendental arguments is considered here the idea of noncircumventability (Unhintergehbarkeit).
- Characteristic for transcendental pragmatics is the tightening of the idea of noncircumventability. Transcendental pragmatics does not rely on items which to circumvent is difficult (e.g. the possibility of experience in the sense of classical physics), but on such which cannot be circumvented at all (the possibility of argumentation, of discourse).
- In addition transcendental pragmatics tightens the idea of radical critique of cognition. Critically controlled is here not only empirical cognition (intentione recta) but also the cognition by which this critique of cognition is carried through, the transcendental reflection. As final level of critique of cognition a combination of strict and theoretical reflection is here brought into the play, which is capable to solve the special problems resulting from the task to really complete radical self-reflexive critique of cognition (Cf. Kuhlmann, W. (2013).

---

convincing. Without these ideas in the background the idea of a validity claim becomes meaningless.

- The overall result is a strictly reflexive argument of noncircumventability in the strong sense. And it is this, what is in my eyes the real (in an sense intended from the beginning) and strongest possible form of a transcendental argument.

7. We introduced our example (rule R) in order to elucidate the structure of the argument. In the same time the essential *ethical content* of the presuppositions of reason which can be mobilized in order to ground ethics has become visible. We are interested in the relations between transcendental philosophy and ethics in general and will not go into details of this content. Here only one short remark to the starting-point of discourse-ethics. It is—as we have seen—the dominating kind of interaction in discourse namely the efforts of the members of the discourse-community to mutual *convincing* (and not persuading) themselves. The attempt to convince the addressee is in a sense a very special, a paradoxical kind of activity, insofar as here with respect to the principal point of the action the otherwise most important feature of rational actions in general namely the control over the means of the action is suspended. If someone tries to convince his addressee of his proposal, he tries to bring about that the other accepts his proposal. But he does it in a way that he expressly does not ensure the success of his endeavors by control of the means of his action (e. g. threat and lures). In the contrary he wants the other to accept his proposal only by his free insight into the truth or rightness of it and he therefore runs expressly the greatest possible risk of failure, namely that the other refuses the proposal. This means, the main point here is not to treat the other as an instrument or as a means (to instrumentalize the other), on the contrary to treat and respect him as an autonomous subject. The assent of the other not going back to his free insight only would be worthless here. Thus it appears that the—what concerns theoretical reason—most central activity in discourse, the bringing forwards of validity claims, the attempt to convince the others, has a reverse, that makes it at the same time the center of practical reason. Tugendhat (1993, p. 80) rightly emphasizes the high accuracy of Kant in meeting exactly the moral point of view by his categorical imperative especially in the so called formula of means and ends.[9] Tugendhat translates this formula by the expression: "Instrumentalisiere niemanden!" ("Do not instrumentalize anybody!") and interprets it as the "principle of an ethics of universal (mutual) respect", ("Moral einer universellen Achtung").—Considering this it seems to be evident, that the structure of convincing, an activity

---

9 "Handle so, dass du die Menschheit, sowohl in deiner Person, als auch in der Person eines jeden anderen, jederzeit zugleich als Zweck, niemals bloß als Mittel brauchst."

whose gist is the not-instrumentalizing, is especially appropriate for founding a principle of ethics.—We must skip the difficulties resulting here from the relations between theoretical and practical discourse, from the relations between discourse and action, and from the idealizations we must make use of in discourse. The only thing we will do here is to underline the astonishing fact, that we demonstrably in every singular action, more precisely in every deliberation preceding our actions and accompanying them inevitably[10], raise validity claims and are so related to every possible subject of reason as to a subject, which to respect as reasonable, free and of equal rights we always already have accepted as obligatory. This means every move in the game of theoretical reason has as its reverse a correspondent move in the game of practical reason. Discourse-ethics is essentially memorization of these conditions easily overlooked.

III

We now have outlined that and how in our opinion ethics can be founded by means of transcendental philosophy (with the aid of transcendental arguments). In this final section we will shortly and only sketchily answer to objections maintaining that especially transcendental arguments are after all inappropriate for the aim of founding ethics. The most relevant are the following:

(i)   Transcendental arguments have the following general form: "If not x, then not y (which is something hardly circumventable, hardly to be abandoned). If we want y, we must want x too." Via this argumentation the principle of ethics to be founded inevitably gets the character of a hypothetical imperative.

(ii) A transcendental philosophical foundation of ethics necessarily results in justifying ethics as "condition of the possibility" of achievements of reason. But this means, that as the crucial reason for the acceptance of ethics a prudential or technical reason is acknowledged and not an ethical. We are obliged to treat and to respect the other members of the discourse-community not for sake of moral duty (Kant), but only *so far* or *if* we want the realization of discourses, of rationality. This means: our behavior towards the others—and indirectly the others themselves—figure here as means for the re-

---

10 Böhler: "Apriori des Begleitdiskurses" (apriori of dicourse necessarily accompanying actions), in:Böhler 2013, pp. 235ff.

alization of something outside morality, and this is a feature not fitting very well to the imperative just mentioned: "Do not instrumentalize anybody!"

(iii) If the result of transcendental pragmatical foundation of ethics is, that the moral principle of discourse-ethics is noncircumventable, than as rational beings we *must* acknowledge this principle, we *cannot not* acknowledge it. It follows, if we do not acknowledge the principle, than we cannot count as reasonable as certifiably sane subjects. But then neither our not-acknowledging is connected with guilt, nor our acknowledging it with merit. The "must in "we must acknowledge" it" cannot be an ethical or moral "must". And therefore the transcendental pragmatic attempt to found discourse-ethics must be considered as failing.

(iv) As B. Stroud points out transcendental philosophy can at best show that we *must believe* that something is so (in fact or rightly). But it cannot show that what we must believe is in reality so. Why should reality conform to our subjective equipment of reason?

Ad (i). If we consider results of weak transcendental arguments only resting upon such, which is hardly circumventable, then it is verisimilar to talk about hypothetical imperatives. But if as here it is about strong transcendental arguments resting upon such which is not circumventable at all, then we will not get hypothetical imperatives, whose antecedent (protasis) can be easily and legitimately negated. What we get here is instead an imperative, which is valid always and categorically if we have to do with an actor counting as reasonable.

Ad (ii). If we talk about someone who makes use of some means for the realization of his aims for technical or prudential reasons, then we normally imagine cases, where a competent and complete subject of reason in order to realize aims he has freely settled, chooses between different things lying outside and in front of him in order to use them as appropriate means. But here we deal with conditions where the expressions "prudential", "technical", "means", "instrumentalization" can be used only in a broader and metaphorical sense. We deal here—so to speak—with functional conditions *within* reason. "Achievements of reason" whose "conditions of the possibility" are relevant for us, is not an external, freely settled aim of reason, but rather a purpose tightly and internally connected to reason itself and presupposed in every special goal setting. In addition it is not an aim outside morality, for—as we have seen at the end—to every achievement of reason belongs in a sense the morally exemplary interaction between the members of the discourse-community.—And this interaction is not a means, which can be used or not used for prudential technical reasons, it is rather an integral part of reason itself. If we would take off this "means" there would remain nothing, which (as a complete subject of reason) could make use of whatever means. Therefore it is not true, that morality itself or that the other members of the discourse-community become instrumentalized here.

Ad (iii). We are not able to not-acknowledge the rules in question ("We must recognize and treat the other members of the discourse-community as reasonable, free and as having equal rights.") This arises in the performative selfcontradiction, which is expressly generated in transcendental pragmatics.—Now the result of such a contradiction can be interpreted in two different ways. On the one hand: We cannot not acknowledge the rule in question and accordingly refute it, because then we were not able to really establish an attempt to refute it which would be meaningful. The attempt to refute it would come down to the attempt to withdraw the necessary preconditions for refuting anything. On the other hand: The disputing thesis proves *false* in the confrontation with the presuppositions, we must presuppose in our attempt to refute the rule (and here the presuppositions are treated as true). These interpretations differ in locating the main result of the contradiction either in the annulment of the necessary presuppositions of the proceeding or in the annulment of the thesis itself.—The crucial point here is this: In the first case the attempt to refute the rule cannot count as a reasonable and imputable action at all. The not-acknowledging of the rule immediately results in the actors loss of his status as a reasonable person to be taken seriously. So he is always already excused morally.—In contrast the second interpretation admits of considering the opponent, who denies the principle of ethics nevertheless as a reasonable, free person of equal rights, who however admittedly does something (morally) wrong. This means here the possibility of an evil will is conceivable, of an actor who will the morally wrong but nevertheless can be taken seriously and is not ipso facto excused. And then it becomes possible to interpret our "must" (in "we must acknowledge...") as a moral "must".

Ad (iv). Stroud concedes: Transcendental philosophers can show, that we *must think* that things are so (in fact or rightly). He does not concede that they can show, that what we must think to be so, *is in reality* so. That is, he maintains: "We must indeed think: "This is true or right," however perhaps is what we must think, false." But maintaining this he contradicts his own concession that we must think that things are so by giving himself a counterexample. For by maintaining this he evidently does not think, what he conceded already he must think. This contradiction invalidates his objection. In my opinion his mistake traces back to the irreflexivity of theoretical reflection (cf. Kuhlmann 2009, pp. 118f.) which makes him ignore that he cedes to himself other possibilities as he concedes to his fellow- subjects he is speaking about, possibilities which are in strict sense open only for god.

After all it is perhaps no longer totally implausible, that a transcendental philosophical foundation of ethics is a meaningful and feasible enterprise.

Bibliography

Apel, K.-O. (1973): *Transformation der Philosophie*, 2 vols., Frankfurt a. M.: Suhrkamp.

Apel, K.-O. (1988): *Diskurs und Verantwortung*, Frankfurt a. M.: Suhrkamp.

Apel, K.-O. (2001): *The Response of Discourse Ethics*, Leuven: Peeters.

Böhler, D. (1985): *Rekonstruktive Pragmatik*, Frankfurt a. M.: Suhrkamp.

Böhler, D. (2013): *Verbindlichkeit aus dem Diskurs*. Freiburg/München: Alber.

Kuhlmann, W. (1985): *Reflexive Letztbegründung*. Freiburg/München: Alber.

Kuhlmann, W. (1992): *Sprachphilosophie, Hermeneutik, Ethik*. Würzburg: Königshausen & Neumann.

Kuhlmann, W. (2007): *Beiträge zur Diskursethik*. Würzburg: Königshausen & Neumann.

Kuhlmann, W. (2009): *Unhintergehbarkeit*. Würzburg: Königshausen & Neumann.

Kuhlmann, W. (2013): *Der Stufengang der Reflexion*, in: J. Beckers/F. Preußger/T. Rusche (Eds.): *Dialog, Reflexion, Verantwortung. Zur Diskussion der Diskurspragmatik*. Würzburg: Königshausen & Neumann, pp. 47 – 62.

Stroud, B. (1993): "*Transcendental Arguments.*" In: *Journal of Philosophy* 65, pp. 241 – 265.

Tugendhat, E. (1993): *Vorlesungen über Ethik*, Frankfurt a.M.: Suhrkamp.

Wulf Kellerwessel
Conceptual Pragmatism and Normativity: Clarence Irving Lewis

Abstract: Within the framework of his ethics, Clarence Irving Lewis has tried to justify fundamental, general norms through references on pragmatic (self-)contradictions. Focusing on "The Ground and Nature of Right" (1955) and "Our Social Inheritance" (1957) as well as further papers and published talks, this chapter introduces to Lewis' normative ethics. Further, Lewis' conception is confronted with some objections, resp. traditional challenges to a justified, universal, normative ethical theory, which is equally applicable to all human beings alike. The objective of the paper is to examine whether fundamental norms such as the prohibition of murder, of maiming, or arbitrary detention can be convincingly justified on the basis of Lewis' thoughts, especially against the background of the diverse challenges. I discuss those objections to finally assess Lewis' ethics.

Introduction

Clarence Irving Lewis (1883–1964) has tried to justify fundamental, general norms in the framework of his ethics through references on pragmatic (self-)contradictions. Since he started teaching philosophy, he considered ethics to be the most important branch of philosophy (cf. Lewis 1968a, p. 19; Lewis 1968b, p. 670). However, he did not finalize his moral philosophy: Lewis set the foundation, but (within his published works) has explored further details only rudimentarily.[1] Still, a number of Lewis' published writings are productive for normative ethics.[2] This is not so much the case in Lewis' most important work "An Analysis of Knowledge and Valuation" (Lewis (1946)), where he broadly develops his value theory, but his "The Ground and Nature of Right" (1955) and "Our Social Inheritance" (1957) as well as some of his essays are very rich in that respect, especially "Pragmatism and the Roots of the Moral" (1956/1969), "The Categorical Imperative" (1958/1969), and "Foundations of Ethics" (1959/1969). These titles

---

1 Cf. also Ewing's assessment on Lewis (1955) in Ewing (1957, p. 280).

2 In what follows, the unpublished items cannot be taken into account. According to Lange (1966), Lewis' inheritance covers around 9500 pages, predominantly of moral philosophical content. Murphey (2005), provides insights into the unpublished items.

DOI 10.1515/9783110470215-015

already suggest links Lewis' tries to establish in his theory of morals: to the moral philosophy of Immanuel Kant and to pragmatism.

In what follows, Lewis' conception of ethics is introduced, especially with regard to its foundation as well as the fundamental rules and norms. Subsequently, Lewis' conception is confronted with objections, resp. traditional challenges to a justified, universal normative ethical theory, which is equally applicable to all human beings alike. These objections are nihilistic resp. skeptical; the critics doubt the *possibility* of justified norms. Moreover, egoistic or group-egoistic positions question that norms can *equally* hold for every individual person within society. In addition, normative relativism rejects the *universality* of such norms. Last but not least, fallibilism questions that such norms can claim *timeless* validity or need to be considered revisable. The objective of the paper is to examine whether fundamental norms such as the prohibition of murder, of maiming, or arbitrary detention can be convincingly justified on the basis of Lewis' thoughts, especially against the background of the diverse challenges. I discuss the objections to formulate a final assessment of Lewis' ethics.

Lewis' moral philosophy and his attempt to justify a normative ethical theory

Lewis searches for rules of human behavior,[3] which are justified and can resist those objections. One of the terms central to Lewis' is 'rule', which already points to the non-empirical character of his conception of normative ethics. The assumption "No rule of action is right except one which is right in all instances, and therefore right for everyone" (Lewis 1946, p. 482) requires non-discrimination, which is not to be justified empirically. This is relevant in reference to the question of the justification of actions and practices, as Lewis elaborates in his early essay "The Meaning of Liberty" (Lewis 1948/1969). If a person considers a singular action as rationally justified, the same justification of that action must hold true for everyone else who acts under the same conditions (cf. Lewis 1948/1969, p. 148). Accordingly, Lewis in allusion to the "Golden Rule" formulates: "Thus it is a basic condition of human association that each recognize as right that only in his conduct toward his fellows which he is satisfied to recognize as similarly sanctioned in their conduct toward himself" (Lewis 1948/

---

3 Concerning the relation between rules and pragmatism in Lewis' work see also Rosenthal (2007, chapter 6).

1969, p. 148). Justifications, thus, involve the rule to treat similar cases equally, which Lewis' considers a "Law of Justice".[4]

In his later writings, Lewis is concerned with more extensive justifications. Most notably, he indents to prove that specific imperatives cannot reasonably be denied. Lewis' especially aims his criticism at moral skepticism. He wants to prove that representatives of skepticism cannot consistently hold their view; if they try to, they cannot avoid *pragmatic self-contradiction.*

Lewis already draws out the outline of his criticism in "Practical and Moral Imperatives" in 1949, where he argues that pragmatic contradictions occur if what is *predicated with a statement* is inconsistent with *making the statement* (the performance of the speech act). If a speaker, for example, denies that there are valid imperatives, and at the same time demands someone to accept this claim, this is a pragmatic contradiction: In the act of denying the existence of valid imperatives, the validity of an imperative is asserted (cf. Lewis 1949/1969, p. 132 f.). The argumentative mistake is, as Lewis argues, that "he who denies nevertheless assumes what he so denies in his denial of it, and otherwise makes no significant assertion" (Lewis 1953/1969, p. 168). In order to be able to make a meaningful statement, the speaker needs to utilize what he/she rejects and at that very moment, he/she contradicts himself/herself in the depicted way. The inherent contradiction could be resolved if the addresses of the statement do not consider what is said to be an attempt of meaningful communication; this assumption, however, reduces the pragmatic contradictory utterance to a joke or mere noise. Proceeding on the assumption that the speaker seeks meaningful communication, however, his/her claim constitutes a pragmatic contradiction (see also Lewis 1954/1970, p. 227).

By means of this mode of argumentation, Lewis aims to establish valid imperatives that cannot be reasonably contradicted; each attempt to dispute the imperative would be pragmatically contradictory. Lewis thus searches for a "foundation on which moral principles rest" (Lewis 1959/1969, p. 15) and, equally crucial, norms rest. Not only the content, but also the mode in which the norms in particular can be acknowledged and justified is still to be clarified (cf. Lewis

---

4 In "The Meaning of Liberty" Lewis deduces from the Law of Justice that no one can rightly claim liberties that he or she does not acknowledge for others (cf. Lewis 1948/1969, p. 149). This does not determine a specific social order, but some basic rights such as freedom of thought, freedom of expression, and freedom of assembly, as well as freedom from censorship. According to Lewis, these hold regardless of empirical facts (cf. Lewis 1948/1969, p. 155). Correlative norms therefore are to be observed as everyone has the right to claim these rights for oneself and, according to the principle of non-discrimination, has to acknowledge the same rights for everyone else.

1959/1969, pp. 18 f.). At a basic level, the "common rationality of men" is involved (cf. Lewis 1959/1969, p. 20). Lewis' in his approach, hence, searches for a rational foundation of norms, underpinned with insights from the philosophy of language, that all rational human beings have to accept. As rational actors, human beings can neither refrain from acknowledging moral imperatives, nor from accepting aims of prudence or cogent and consistent thinking. The attempt to deny the truth of moral imperatives (or commands of knowledge or cogent and consistent thinking) amounts to a *reductio ad absurdum* (cf. Lewis 1959/1969, pp. 63 f.). In practice, this thinking as well as the law of contradiction is indispensable (cf. Lewis 1959/1969, pp. 64 f.).

Lewis aims to work out what is right or wrong, resp. which imperatives (moral norms) one should pursue. He is especially concerned with drawing out what is objectively (and not only subjectively) right. Subjective rightness results from right intentions; objective rightness, by contrast, considers consequences of actions. More specifically, following Lewis, the action that is performed by an agent and has the highest probability to have good effects is the objectively right action (cf. Lewis 1955, pp. 51 ff.). Lewis' position is consequentialist but not utilitarian as utility maximization does not play a role in Lewis' thought. In other words: Someone who thinks he/she acts objectively right acts subjectively right; the objectively right action depends on the consequences of the respective action. The moral quality of the action in turn is determined on the basis of *fundamental* moral norms. (Cf. Lewis 1952/1970, pp. 190 ff.; 1953/1969, p. 163; 1959/1969, pp. 36 ff.) The assessment of the objective rightness thus draws from a non-empirical standard.

> It takes two things [...] to determine the rightness of action: a rule or directive of right doing, or something operative in the manner of a rule, and a judgment of goodness to be found in the consequences of the act in question (Lewis 1955, p. 75).

Evaluations of actions thus take the form of a syllogism: As major premise, a valid rule or principle (such as Lewis' categorical imperative drawn out below) is used that sanctions a specific action (or a group of actions) as well as specific consequences. The minor premise more directly determines the rightness of a specific action (the action is good if the consequences are; if they are not, it is not). The premise may include a maxim (such as "Do not lie"), a secondary principle of what is right or an empirical (generalized) value proposition (cf. Lewis 1956/1969, p. 113). The major premise can be formal, the minor premise is substantial resp. incorporates empirical evidence. Both premises together support a conclusion concerning the rightness or wrongness of a specific action. Wrong, resp. prohibited, are those actions that are contrary to one or even both premises: They either violate a valid moral rule or disregard the consequentialist element (transgressing the minor premise).[5]

It is evident that, according to Lewis, two elements are relevant when one evaluates specific actions: empirical knowledge concerning the consequences of action which is fallible as well as formal rules that should be consistent resp. cogent—and which, according to Lewis, can be justified in a way that they do not constitute fallible elements of the judgment. The *major* premise of what is right in Lewis' theory cannot be demonstrated, that is cannot be proven to be valid by means of (deductive) reasoning (cf. Lewis 1955, pp. 84 f.). The fundamental principles of ethics—in common with those of logic—to Lewis are conditional to for every deduction. The attempt to deduce these principles thus results in a *petitio principii*. The fact that fundamental principles cannot be demonstrated is grounded in the nature of things (cf. Lewis 1955, p. 85).[6]

Consequently, to Lewis, the validity of fundamental moral norms can only be proven in a different way. On that matter Lewis in "The Ground and Nature of Right" argues: "The ground of validity of imperatives must somehow lie in our human nature. Human nature calls for principles of right decisions" (Lewis 1955, pp. 85 f.). Accordingly, the justification cannot be entirely detached from human nature. Furthermore, it is beyond the sphere of a *single* subject. Equally, as argued earlier, it does not seem to concern empirical facts. 'Nature' logically cannot refer to facts about nature.[7] As in particular the following illustrates, it is not only the partial detachment of human beings from nature resp. the general

---

5 Cf. also Saydah (1969, pp. 84–89).

6 Still, the acceptance of logical principles for Lewis is not a result of an arbitrary decision. Admittedly, someone who argues in favor of logical rules of derivation already assumes those principles. A skeptic, who denies these rules, cannot consistently (logically) argue in favor of his denial. If he/she in defiance of this impossibility nonetheless argues that there are no logical rules of reasoning that need to be followed, he/she belies him/herself. The skeptic commits "an inconsistency between the content of assertion and the act of asserting it" (Lewis 1958/1969, p. 197; cf. Lewis 1957, p. 100). This constitutes a pragmatic contradiction: "As deliberate, and to be understood as deliberate, this act of assertion conveys the intent that what is said should be believed. But the content of the assertion made—the state of affairs it affirms to be actual—is one in which this assertor's assertions are not to be believed on the evidence of his making them. The act is self-frustrating of its own ostensive purpose" (Lewis 1958/1969, pp. 197 f.). The same holds true for the attempt to argumentatively deny the logical rules of reasoning. To argue against the rules of reasoning either makes the presentation of the argument irrelevant or one would not have to accept the reasoning as it would not be the result of a logic compelling reasoning (cf. Lewis 1958/1969, pp. 197 f.).

7 On the interpretation of this passage see also Collela (1992, p. 137)—who emphasizes the exceptional position of rational human beings within nature. See also Saydah (1969, p. 54), for whom ratio equally is central to the interpretation of Lewis' theory.

rationality of human beings, but the rational, in this context the regular, consistent and solid language usage, which assume the function of justification in Lewis' conception.

Central to Lewis' foundation of ethics is the *application* of the already portrayed *pragmatic contradiction*. Lewis uses this figure against a series of theses that deny the justification of moral imperatives or that are or a generally skeptical provenience. Lewis initially highlights that the assertion of something generally commits the author of the assertion to acknowledge *validity conditions:* If a skeptical thesis is formulated as an assertion, the speaker has to claim the rightness of that proposition or he/she does not argue anything at all. The first, however, implies that there is right and wrong or something like that. The denial of that implication leads to a pragmatic contradiction: Making this assertion, the skeptic claims the validity of his/her statement; to deny at the same moment the validity of this claim to Lewis is pragmatically inconsistent. By contrast, the negation of the skeptical assumption (which the skeptic based on his/her thesis cannot classify as "wrong") is consistent. Denying this finding, the skeptic would need to claim the rightness of a proposition, as otherwise, there would be no conflict or dispute. Conclusively, a skeptic cannot defend the given thesis without a pragmatic contradiction (cf. Lewis 1955, p. 7).

A similar argument can be put forward against a skeptic who denies the existence of "valid imperatives of right doing" (Lewis 1959/1969, p. 66) and who tries to substantiate that assertion by bringing forward arguments in its favor. Lewis elaborates:

> The skeptic's advancement of his own argument is a deliberate and governed activity on his part. It is a physical activity even, a piece of deliberate and overt doing. There are supposed to be rules about it, rules of valid inference. But the skeptical conclusion argued for is that there are *no* valid rules and *no* valid imperatives of the right government of action. And now we must ask the skeptic just why he expects us to feel constrained to accept this conclusion which his argument seeks to establish. He has, in the conclusion itself, repudiated all valid imperatives constraining anybody to do anything, and encouraged us to think that he himself rejects constraint by any rules of right upon his conduct. (Lewis 1959/1969, p. 66)

A skeptic, who denies the existence of *any* rules of the right government of action, cannot expect that others act in accordance with what he/she has stated. This would only be the case if he/she accepted at least one rule of right conduct, which relates to reactions to the argument brought forward and which implies that one should accept a valid argument and act accordingly. The general skeptical rule thematized above denies this fact resp. rules it out. Conclusively, Lewis argues that the skeptic is not able to take criticism concerning other reactions such as "Why should we not rather say to one another, 'I don't like this fellow's slant on things: let's ask him to stop interrupting our serious attempt to think straight on this matter'" (Lewis 1959/1969, p. 66); the skeptic, holding this view, rather bows out of the discussion (cf. Lewis 1959/1969, pp. 66 f.). In brief: "To argue for the conclusion 'There are no binding imperatives of conduct' commits a practical contradiction" (Lewis 1959/1969, p. 67). Consequently, Lewis takes as demonstrated that there are binding, mandatory imperatives of right doing. Contesting this insight constitutes "an incompatibility of the predictable consequences of *asserting* this proposition with the presumptive purpose of this act of assertion" (Lewis 1959/1969, p. 67).

For the same reasons that a skeptic cannot deny that there are binding imperatives of conduct, one cannot deny, following Lewis, the existence of valid normative judgements. Because

> one who asserts 'There are no normative judgments which are genuinely valid' falls into exactly that predicament, because any judgment of a statement made or conclusion drawn as being cogent and believable must necessarily be such a normative judgment. Such attempted repudiation of the normative at large can only be an adventure in intellectual self-frustration, denying in words what we cannot avoid assuming in practice, if we draw any distinction between the fallacious and the cogent. (Lewis 1959/1969, pp. 68 f.)

One cannot generally negate normative statements: "You shall not accept normative judgments to be genuinely valid" in fact is a normative statement and the speaker expects the addressee to accept it, which by implication is pragmatically self-contradictory. According to Lewis, such statements are presupposed for the evaluation of rational actions because these evaluating statements and conclusions concerning rational actions are normative statements.

If one agrees with Lewis that there are *general rules* that should be followed, the question whether there are moral norms that prohibit or demand a certain action and how those are justified is real and relevant. In "Pragmatism and the Roots of the Moral" Lewis formulates this fundamental norm (being an instruction) as follows: "You ought to act only in ways which conform to all rules of action which you recognize as valid in all instances and hence for everybody" (Lewis 1956/1969, p. 115 f.). One should only act in accordance with valid rules resp. norms one considers as being right and, furthermore, similar cases should be treated alike (cf. also Lewis 1957, p. 93). And this in turn implies that the rules equally apply to everyone. Lewis, however, presents additional formulations resp. variants on the fundamental norm, including—next to recourses to the "golden rule" (cf. Lewis 1957, p. 93)—the following elaborations:

> Remember your social situation, and remember that nothing can be a way of acting it is justified for you to adopt unless it is equally a justified way of acting for any other person

to adopt, fronting this problem which you face and in the same premises of action. (Lewis 1959/1969, p. 75)

The cited formulation seems to express the required generality, but—compared to the other variants—focuses more on the actual situation of making a decision. And yet other definitions emphasize the rule aspect ("Do no act which contravenes any rule which you would call upon other men to respect and to conform to"; Lewis 1959/1969, p. 75) resp. the recognition of equal rights of others –

recognizing our likeness to other men, on these fundamental points, we cannot fail to acknowledge that whatever will justify us in choosing what we do must be such as would, in identically the same premises of action, justify any other man in taking that same decision (Lewis 1959/1969, p. 79).

The command or principle of action that Lewis with reference to Kant calls "categorical imperative", demands compliance with generally valid rules considering and respecting the reality of others. Furthermore, Lewis claims that this imperative can be substantiated by means of verifying that a denial of the imperative constitutes a pragmatic contradiction.

The categorical imperative "dictates only adherence to ways of acting which do not contravene any rule recognized as thus universal, impersonal, and valid" (Lewis 1956/1969, p. 125). To deny this demand resp. its validity is to ignore valid rules in general, "to adopt as a rule the rule of disregarding rules of conduct" (Lewis 1956/1969, p. 125). This attitude to Lewis constitutes a further (particularly drastic) pragmatic contradiction: "That would be the ultimate in pragmatic self-contradiction" (Lewis 1956/1969, p. 125). As a consequence, the categorical imperative can only be denied at the cost of a contradiction. To Lewis that means: The imperative cannot (reasonably) be contested. With focus on the categorical imperative, this signifies: "It is *a priori* in the sense that, for any creature which is rational and must take his own decisions of conduct, it is nonrepudiable" (Lewis 1956/1969, p. 125).

As a consequence, Lewis assumes that in actual decision situations, taking the reality of others into account, one should act in accordance with those fundamental, general norms. This moreover includes the concept of universalizability—as rules are only rules if they equally apply to identical cases. Correspondingly, following Lewis, when deciding whether one accepts and consequently follows a rule, one needs to bear in mind whether one would equally accept the rule and desire its application if one was not the agent but rather the person affected by the action (under—apart from that—equal conditions). By implication, one ought "to respect other persons as the realities we representationally recognize them to be—as creatures whose gratifications and griefs have the same poignant factuality as our own" (Lewis 1955, p. 91). A "Law of Moral Equality" thus applies in relation to human beings.[8] One cannot deny that fact without contradiction. If one argues, for example: "This is right for me, but under identical circumstances and on the same identical premises, it would not be right for you, and I shall oppose you and prevent you from doing it", which amounts to a violation of that rule, the author of that statement commits "a contradiction in terms, because what he affirms as right is contradictory of the very meaning of 'right'" (Lewis 1958/1969, p. 186). A person who claims the moral right to a specific action under specific circumstances but who does not concede the same right to a different person under identical conditions commits a pragmatic contradiction (cf. Lewis 1958/1969, p. 200), which follows from the adjective "right". Therefore, to refuse equal rights with relation to equal actions under identical conditions is ultimately irrational (cf. Lewis 1959/1969, p. 82).

Several moral norms follow from the "Law of Moral Equality" such as the demand to grant others autonomy of decision (as long as this autonomy does not disregard the freedom of choice of others). Furthermore, it implies equality before the law (cf. Lewis 1955, p. 92). Moreover, it prohibits actions the general performance of which one would try to avoid (cf. Lewis 1955, p. 93) resp. which belong to a class of actions that are morally impermissible (Lewis names "exploitation" as an example). Nevertheless, this does not imply generalizations of fundamental norms such as "Do not steal" or "Do not lie". Actions such as lying may not belong to the class of actions that should be avoided (as, for example, the maxim to Lewis does not hold in a situation where speaking the truth might lead an insane murderer to his/her potential victims; cf. Lewis 1955, p. 94).[9] The consequences of actions resp. their (un)desirability thus, next to general rules, are criteria for judging actions. Still, subsidiary norms resp. fundamental norms such as the prohibition of lying arise—to Lewis they are fairly reliable criteria—resp. as empirical evidence shows, actions in accordance with those norms usually meet the requirements of the fundamental principles (cf. Lewis 1957, p. 102). However, such subsidiary norms, according to Lewis, are neither *a priori* nor analytical.[10] Within the framework of Lewis' theory, those norms are not strictly imperative and should not be followed in any

---

8 In relation to other beings capable of suffering, however, applies "merely" a "Law of Compassion"; cf. Lewis (1955, p. 91f.).
9 On Lewis' difficulties to deduce specific norms from general rules see also Rosenthal (2007, chapter 6).
10 On further consequentialist judgements about the rightness/wrongness of actions see also Lewis (1959/1969, pp. 25ff.).

case, due to the consequentialist element of his conception. Fundamental norms such as the prohibition of murder are amongst those subsidiary norms (at least according to Saydah's interpretation of Lewis' ethical theory; cf. Sayday 1969, pp. 91 and 101).

Discussing Lewis' Moral Philosophy

So far, the foundation of Lewis' normative ethics has been mapped out. In what follows, I explore whether and in how far one can argumentatively support the fundamental norms introduced earlier, such as the prohibition of murder, of the deprivation of liberty, of maiming or injuring (which reach beyond the categorical imperative). Furthermore, I discuss in how far those norms endure the challenges mentioned earlier.

Without question, Lewis takes the skeptical resp. nihilistic positions against which he argues seriously (see also Lewis 1959/1969, pp. 15 and 41). From a skeptic's viewpoint, one can challenge that Lewis actually managed to *rationally* justify the normative elements of his conception of ethics resp. his fundamental norms. The most important process of argumentation, which Lewis uses for his purpose, is the identification of pragmatic contradictions within the argumentation of opposing positions, considering the content of a statement as well as the statement altogether (including the performance as well as the conditions of an assertion). According to Lewis, representatives of nihilism or skepticism, who commit pragmatic contradictions, cannot rationally argue in favor of their positions. This is the case if they

- generally deny the validity of assertion by means of making an assertion
- altogether reject the acceptance of rules
- support the thesis that no argument is right or wrong (see also Saydah 1969, p. 59)
- demand to reject imperatives (in their statements) altogether
- advocate not to follow any instructions
- demand not to acknowledge normative judgments (see also Luizzi 1981, p. 49)
- announce that speech and action do not need consistency
- think one should be—on principle—unprincipled
- propagate that one should not consider other people and their interests.

To deny the categorical imperative to Lewis likewise is a serious mistake; to object the instruction to "Act according to rules which you would call upon others to respect and to conform to in any case" is to withdraw from rational argumentation as—due to the generality of the sentence—the imperative cannot be contested (cf.

Lewis 1958/1969, p. 200) resp. that amounts to acknowledging the rule not to accept any rules (cf. Lewis 1955, p. 125). As a result a (correspondingly radical) representative of nihilism or skepticism, who denies all this and commits the aforementioned pragmatic contradiction, might abandon any claim to validity, truth, or rightness and might rather only talk as he/she likes to hear himself/herself speak (cf. Lewis 1953/1969, p. 167). This finding still does not substantiate the justification of norms such as the prohibition of murder etc.—a nihilist or skeptic might concede to Lewis that imperatives and rules exist; however, this does not necessarily include the acceptation of the validity of norms such as the prohibition of murder. Lewis has not demonstrated that (or how) the commandment of compliance with those norms follows from his categorical imperative. Whether a justification of those norms, against nihilism and skepticism, is possible within the framework of Lewis' conception still needs to be investigated.

Lewis' engagement with egoism and group-egoism within his published writings is less elaborate. Nonetheless, there are references on the basis of which one can reconstruct Lewis' stance towards those positions. It follows from Lewis' categorical imperative that all forms of egoism and group-egoism that do not concede such preferences and corresponding actions to everyone in equal measure are unacceptable. In other respects, the categorical imperative does not rule out (group)egoistic positions (cf. Lewis 1949/1969, pp. 142 and 176; Lewis 1958/1969, p. 195). Still, there is need for further clarification. Inasmuch as Lewis' categorical imperative is crucial, it needs to be demonstrated what can be considered as "identical circumstance" and to whom the imperative applies. Lewis evidently assumes that only what makes a human being human is relevant—the human way of life—and nothing else (such as sex, skin color/complexion, or age; cf. Saydah 1969, p. 78). With that said, there seem to be at least specific versions of group-egoism that are incompatible with the categorical imperative. "Identical circumstances" to Lewis are determined with reference to the consequences of an action. What all this amounts to is that due to the fact that the imperative demands equal treatment of all human beings and that the perspectives of all the persons concerned need to be considered, only those forms of egoism and group-egoism may not to be ruled out that grant the same forms to others.

Lewis admittedly moreover believes that egoism is unwise and thus to be rejected for prudential reasons (cf. Lewis 1955, pp. 95f. and Lewis 1958/1969, p. 195).[11] Luizzi correctly establishes that egoism can formally last in Lewis' ethical theory but that it is unacceptable due to its consequences (cf. Luizzi 1981,

---

11 Concerning this complex topic in Lewis' thought see also Murphey (2005, chapter 10).

p. 60). This still does not constitute a categorical falsification of egoism resp. an irrefutable argument in favor of observing norms such as the prohibition of murder without exception, even in cases in which the adherence conflicts with egoism resp. egoistic claims (see also Ewing 1968, p. 613).

According to Lewis, group-egoism is as unwise due to the anticipated negative consequences of compliance (cf. Lewis 1958/1969, p. 199). The suggestion is neither sufficient to refute group-egoism nor to verify that norms such as the prohibition of murder need to be observed unconditionally, including situations in which the norm compliance conflicts with group-egoistic claims. Still, there are restrictions to group-egoism that follow from Lewis' categorical imperative (cf. Saydah 1969, p. 122).

Lewis' disposition towards normative relativism is just as little as towards skepticism (cf. Lewis 1959/1969, pp. 18 f.). And one could admit that norms, which can be justified by means of the argument of the pragmatic contradiction, due to the unlimited application of the same argument, are not relative. In how far additional fundamental, universal norms can be founded still needs to be examined, even though Lewis has demonstrated that diverse general imperatives, generally formulated norms and so forth cannot be explicitly called into question and thus must not be considered as relative.

Those general formulations of the categorical imperative also do not seem to be fallible as a denial is pragmatically contradictory. The demand for logical consistency, the concept of rule, and *general* requirements of communication are used in this argumentation in favor of Lewis' categorical imperative—all of which are timeless components. A fallibilism accordingly can only take effect in the range of applications (a fact Lewis admits; cf. Lewis 1952/1970, pp. 200 f.); it is thus "innocent" with reference to its justification.

But what are the difficulties of Lewis' conception of ethics in analysis of the challenges mentioned? Obviously, they are not located within the framework of a confrontation with fallibilism. Problems arise, above all, within the realm of nihilism and skepticism, namely if the binding character of fundamental norms is questioned. Lewis does not prove that such an obligation follows from the foundation of his ethics. Obviously, they do not immediately accrue from the *formal* basis Lewis established, even if the categorical imperative is considered to be indisputable. Within the framework of the concept, other elements are added to the formal part of the conception of ethics, as the practical syllogism depicted above, exemplarily shows: Here, empirical experiences become relevant (see also Lewis 1956/1969, p. 115)—and thus, an empirical element is integrated into the theory. As a consequence thereof (and in conformity with) Lewis' consequentialism brings in aspects that lead to ambiguities: Questions such as whether one may commit a theft if one accepts to become a victim of the same crime, or whether one may violate the physical integrity of others if one is willing to be treated in the same way, remains unanswered. Lewis' consequentialism apparently weakens the anti-skeptical thrust of his ethics: One cannot verify that such fundamental norms need to be observed rigorously on the basis of the formal part of his conception, since the formal element—Lewis' version of the categorical imperative—aims at equal treatment without a justification of such norms. The formal element of the theory is crucial to the assessment of consequences of actions but too vague in terms of content. Hence, no convincing reason for strict norm-compliance results from Lewis' elaborations.

This interferes with the controversy with egoism and group-egoism. Even if egoism overall does not constitute a prudent strategy (for instance in the situation of the prisoner's dilemma) one cannot reject that single egoistic actions might be prudent for an actor and thus rationally selectable. As long as formal equality, demanded by the categorical imperative, is not violated, isolated instances of egoistic actions that violate fundamental norms cannot be generally dismissed. In other words: According to this concept, violations of fundamental norms would not be prohibited if the respective actor concedes the same transgression to others (even if he/she is hit by it). He/she thus simply needs to consider actions that potentially have a negative impact on him/her to be rationally acceptable. Only if acting on egoistic principles threatens the existence of the social order which in turn is a precondition for egoistic action, egoism can be exterminated within the framework of Lewis' ethics: If the last-named event occurs, the rules of action conflict with the approved action, including its consequences (general norm-compliance—in a long-term perspective—would make compliance impossible). If that case can be excluded, an egoism that embraces formal equality remains an option (see also Saydah 1969, p. 125).

The engagement with group-egoism is assessed in a similar way: It cannot be generally rejected on the basis of the categorical imperative—as long as formal equality is acknowledged (conceding group-egoistic norms to others). Nevertheless, there are restrictions in relation to consequentialism and Lewis' posit of formal equality: One has to consider the action as acceptable from the perspective of all persons potentially affected by it. In fact, a rather large number of group-egoistic courses of action that violate fundamental norms are excluded, but not necessarily all. A final, exact judgement cannot be made on the basis of Lewis' statements on the matter.

The command of equal treatment comprised by the categorical imperative is general; in this respect, the fundament of Lewis' ethics is opposed to a normative relativism. Since the question whether or in how far fundamental norms can be deduced from Lewis' conception of ethics remains unanswered, the scope of the anti-relativism of the concept is equally disputable.

Assessing Lewis' Ethical Theory

How should Lewis' ethics be assessed? A positive characteristic is that Lewis' moral philosophy gets along with a few basic elements of the philosophy of language resp. the theory of rationality. It can be highlighted that Lewis' ethical theory does not presuppose a complete theory of rationality, but simply builds on specific elements of such a theory (prudence, consistency, soundness, rightness). Lewis moreover manages to pragmatically justify a number of general imperatives resp. norms in a way that they cannot be explicitly denied, without committing a pragmatic contradiction by means of the demand for consistency and validity resp. thanks to the scarce assumptions from the philosophy of language considering conditions of successful communication and discourse. These insights contribute to the refutation of nihilism and skepticism in their most general and radical forms. However, with reference to more specific, less comprehensive versions of those challenges, Lewis remains short on a respective justification of fundamental norms such as the prohibition of murder or of maiming. Equally, not all forms of egoism that negate basic norms can be rejected in total. Hence, Ewing is right when he ascertains—with reference to Lewis' a priori—that it "can only give the most general formal conditions of right ethical thought" (Ewing 1968, p. 618).[12]

On taking stock with reference to the central argument of the avoidance of the pragmatic contradictions we see that Lewis on the one hand can use the argument to verify the *general* existence of right and wrong imperatives resp. norms; on the other hand, the question which specific norm compliance one can claim with good reason remains open. Even if Lewis has convincingly argued that general, universal, and valid rules should be complied with, the central question, what norms are *valid* besides those most general rules, is unanswered.

Furthermore, Lewis inserts a moral element into his central justificatory formulations—and misses the target: a *justification of morals*. The fact that his categorical imperative cannot (reasonably) be rejected (without committing a pragmatic self-contradiction) is not grounded in a specific moral element but rather in the usage of the term "valid rule" within the formulation of the categorical imperative: "You ought to act only in ways which conform to all rules of action which you recognize as *valid* in all instances and hence for everybody" (Lewis 1956/1969, p. 115f.). And yet, what "valid" means in the context remains unanswered. The elements Lewis adds in further versions of his categorical imperative cannot close that gap; they are formal and can only imply demands of formal

---

12 Lewis only elaborates general criteria resp. principles (cf. Lewis 1957, p. 97f.).

non-discrimination. Differences with reference to the question what violations of which norms a person affected by the action is willing to accept if he/she can therefore equally transgress a norm cannot be rejected argumentatively. The deduction of generally binding norms is excluded due to possible divergences owed to consequentialism. Ultimately, the only achievements are a formal "equality before the rule" resp. the "Law of Equality". But those do not form a sufficient basis for the establishment of fundamental norms (see also Morris 1956/57, p. 203); a content-related element is missing. As a consequence, the norms fundamental to Lewis' ethics ultimately cannot be convincingly justified.[13]

The demonstration that there are principles of right action is not equivalent to the verification of the existence of binding fundamental norms of right action. Accordingly, Lewis has only illustrated that specific negations of general norms prove to be pragmatically contradictory if one tries to defend them. Furthermore, and going beyond, to integrate consequentialist considerations opens up a scope of action that does not suit the purpose of the command to comply with fundamental norms. Only those actions that conflict with the formal principle are prohibited within the framework of Lewis' theory, actions that disregard formal equal treatment. As a result, a number of violations of norms, but not all of them, are characterized as prohibited.

Still, Lewis' justification of ethics constitutes a step in the right direction, a step towards an argumentative validation of fundamental norms. At a decisive point within his argumentation, where he demonstrates pragmatic contradictions, Lewis applies logically *possible* uses of language (and not only actual or factual language uses). Therefore, not only actually advanced criticism can be invalidated but any possible criticism. Moreover, the basic idea of Lewis' ethical theory—to use the pragmatic contradiction as a strategy to justify fundamental norms—is capable for development. The method is suitable to justify—at least—some fundamental norms (cf. Kellerwessel 2003, chapter 3.2).*

---

13 Mothersill's points to similar evidence (cf. Mothersill 1968, p. 577), as it seems unclear how Lewis' basic assumption relates to moral norms such as "Keep promises you made", "Tell the truth", and so on. Lewis himself acknowledges corresponding difficulties in deducing individual norms; cf. Lewis (1957, p. 102f.).

* I would like to thank Dr. Annette Förster for translating this text. An earlier version appeared as Chapter 2.3.15 in Kellerwessel (2003); in german).

Bibliography

Baylis, Charles A. (1964): "C.I. Lewis's Theory of Values." In: *Journal of Philosophy* 61, pp. 559–567.

Ewing, Alfred Cyril (1957): "[Review of] The Ground and Nature of the Right, by C.I. Lewis." In: *Philosophy* 32, pp. 279–280.

Ewing, Alfred Cyril (1968): "C.I. Lewis on the Relation between the Good and the Right." In: Schilpp (Ed.) (1968), pp. 597–618.

Goheen, John D.; Mothershead, John L. (Eds.) (1970): *Collected Papers of Clarence Irving Lewis.* Stanford: Stanford University Press.

Kellerwessel, Wulf (2003): *Normenbegründung in der Analytischen Ethik.* Würzburg: Königshausen & Neumann.

Lange, John (1966): "The Late Papers of C.I. Lewis." In: *Journal of the History of Philosophy* 4, pp. 235–245.

Lewis, Clarence Irving (1946): *An Analysis of Knowledge and Valuation.* La Salle, Ill.: Open Court.

Lewis, Clarence Irving (1948/1969): "The Meaning of Liberty." In: Lewis (1969), pp. 145–155 (first published in: *Revue Internationale de Philosophie* 2, 1948).

Lewis, Clarence Irving (1949/1969): "Practical and Moral Imperatives". In: Lewis (1969), pp. 126–144 (talk delivered in 1949).

Lewis, Clarence Irving (1952/1970): "Subjective Right and Objective Right." In: Goheen/Mothershead (Eds.) (1970), pp. 190–202 (written in 1952).

Lewis, Clarence Irving (1953/1969): "The Rational Imperatives." In: Lewis (1969), pp. 156–177 (first published in: Ratner, S. (Ed.): *Vision and Action. Essays in Honor of Horace M. Kallen on his 70th Birthday.* New Brunswick, New Jersey 1953).

Lewis, Clarence Irving (1954/1970): "Turning Points of Ethical Theory." In: Goheen/Mothershead (Eds.) (1970), pp. 215–227 (talk delivered in 1954).

Lewis, Clarence Irving (1955): *The Ground and Nature of the Right.* Third printing 1965. New York: Columbia University Press.

Lewis, Clarence Irving (1956/1969): "Pragmatism and the Roots of the Moral." In: Lewis (1969), pp. 103–125 (talk delivered in 1956).

Lewis, Clarence Irving (1957): *Our Social Inheritance.* Bloomington, In.: Indiana University Press.

Lewis, Clarence Irving (1958/1969): "The Categorical Imperative." In: Lewis (1969), pp. 178–201 (talk delivered in 1958).

Lewis, Clarence Irving (1959/1969): "Foundations of Ethics." In: Lewis (1969), pp. 3–82 (talk delivered in 1959).

Lewis, Clarence Irving (1968a): "Autobiography." In: Schilpp (Ed.) (1968), pp. 1–21.

Lewis, Clarence Irving (1968b): "Replies to my Critics." In: Schilpp (Ed.) (1968), pp. 653–676.

Lewis, Clarence Irving (1969): *Values and Imperatives. Studies in Ethics.* Stanford: Stanford University Press.

Luizzi, Vincent (1981): *A Naturalistic Theory of Justice. Critical Commentary on, and Selected Readings from, C.I. Lewis' Ethics.* Washington D.C.: University Press of America.

Morris, Bertram (1956/57): "C.I. Lewis: Empiricist or Kantian?" In: *Ethics* 67, pp. 203–205.

Mothersill, Mary (1968): "Lewis as a Moral Philosopher." In: Schilpp (Ed.) (1968), pp. 571–596.

Murphey, Murray G. (2005): *C.I. Lewis. The Last Great Pragmatist.* New York: State University of New York Press.

Rosenthal, Sandra B. (2007): *C.I. Lewis in Focus. The Pulse of Pragmatism.* Bloomington, In.: Indiana University Press.

Sayday, J. Roger (1969): *The Ethical Theory of Clarence Irving Lewis.* Athens, Ohio: Ohio University Press.

Schilpp, Paul Arthur (Ed.) (1968): *The Philosophy of C.I. Lewis.* La Salle, Ill.: Open Court.

Jens Peter Brune
Transcending Value: Two Readings of Performative Inconsistency

Abstract: Kant's Humanity Formula of the Categorical Imperative has been frequently subjected to value-theoretical interpretations, which have served as a prelude to a complicated dispute between the protagonists of realistic and non-realistic interpretations of Kant. In this paper I wish to make a proposal on how Kant's writings about humanity as "an end in itself" can be reformulated in the context of a discourse-oriented approach. The broader goal is to gain a starting point for a discourse-ethical reconstruction of a principle of respected human dignity. On the way there, the first, rather explicative and transformatory step will be to illuminate the concept of the indispensability and irreplaceability of each discourse partner. Since an inferential reasoning does not seem adequate for defending this concept, the next two following steps will increasingly aim at a more self-referential, and finally reflexive (retorsive), thought process. I come to the conclusion that mutual respect of our discursive status transcends the question as to if and what kind of *value* we should confer upon each other.

Preliminary note

At the center of Kant's conception of human dignity lies the idea that humanity is "an end in itself." As such, the human being as rational being is "raised above all price and therefore admits of no equivalent." (GMS 4, 434) What constitutes the condition "under which alone something can be an end in itself has not merely a relative worth that is, a price, but an inner worth, that is *dignity*." (GMS 4, 435) The so-called Formula of Humanity as one version of the Categorical Imperative combines this idea with notions of deontological bindingness. The formula requires acting "in such a way that you treat humanity, whether in your own person or in the person of any other, always at the same time as an end, never merely as a means" (Kant, GMS 4, 429).

In the present discussion on the Formula of Humanity, the view represented by a number of renowned Kantian scholars is that Kant's notion of "humanity as an end in itself" as well as "[r]ational nature [...] as an end in itself" (Kant, GMS

DOI 10.1515/9783110470215-016

4, 429) refers to an absolute and unconditional *Wert* (value, worth)[1], which ultimately serves as the reason for the imperative that we should respect each other.
The various and, in fact, significantly divergent interpretations can be differen-
tiated by whether they value "humanity" or, respectively, the "rational nature" of
mankind as such (Hills 2008, p. 198), or whether they understand the "rational
nature" of mankind to be, more precisely, a "practical conception of identity"
(Korsgaard 1996a, pp. 122–23), a "power of rational choice" (Korsgaard 1996b,
p. 123), a "capacity to set ends and act according to reason" (Wood 1999,
p. 121; Wood 2008, p. 55; cf. Hill 1980, 86), or even whether they value the
"good will as an end in itself" (Dean 2006, Part I). With the exception of Richard
Dean[2], the above-mentioned authors share a value-theoretical interpretation of
Kant's concept of human dignity (if not of Kantian ethics as a whole). I will
henceforth refer to this as the 'value-theoretical line of interpretation' of the Humanity Formula. The differences here ensue with respect to the question as to
why "humanity" should be viewed as an objective, absolute value. This is the
point where opinion is divided: whereas Korsgaard sets "substantive moral realism" (Korsgaard 1996b, pp. 35–37, 44–48) against her version of a constructivist
reading of the Formula of Humanity (Korsgaard 1996a, Chap. 4), others, for both
exegetic as well as systematic reasons, adhere to a more or less weak realistic
interpretation of Kant's ethics, in particular, the Formula of Humanity (FitzPatrick 2005; Hills 2008[3]; Wood 2008, pp. 295–96, note 11) or regard this, at the
very least, as being on an equal footing with constructivism (Stern 2010, 2011,
2013). Finally, there are others who read Kant not as a value realist, as they do
not take him to be a value theoretician at all, but instead argue from a normative
primacy of the categorical imperative over absolute value. To this end, Oliver
Sensen has suggested a "transcendental-constitutive interpretation of Kant
(Sensen 2009a, 2009b, 2015).

My intention is not to establish my own position on issues of Kantian interpretation *within* the complex value-theoretical debate, nor on more general sys-

---

1 As Kant only employs the word 'Werth,' I use 'value' and 'worth' interchangeably; see Wood
(2008), Sensen (2009, p. 311, Fn. 8).
2 Dean maintains "that Kant's talk of the value of good will (or humanity) is 'a function of prior
and independent principles of right'." The good will is an end in itself and it "inspires a feeling
of respect or *Achtung*. It is fine to call this a feeling or respect or esteem for the value of humanity, as long as it is kept in mind that this idea of value is a way of capturing the more fundamental Kantian point that moral principles, and beings committed to moral principles, are what really inspire this feeling of 'esteem'." (Dean 2006, p. 148)
3 Alison Hills advocates a comparatively 'weak' version of realism in that she interprets "value
realism" as a position holding that "the correctness of our ethical judgments is not dependent on
our choices or our attitudes." (Hills 2008, p. 182)

tematic matters of substantial ethics and aspects of metaethics. Above all, I do not wish to take sides in the conflict over a realistic or non-realistic interpretation of Kant. My concern is rather to offer an alternative to the matter in dispute: a proposal on how Kant's writings about humanity as "an end in itself" can be reformulated in the context of a discourse-oriented approach—which comes very close to Stephen Darwall's "second-person standpoint." My aim is to gain a *starting point* for a discourse-ethical reconstruction of a principle of respected human dignity which is not directly caught up in the maelstrom of the value-realism and anti-realism debate. For this purpose, the *exposition of the thesis* in a *first*, rather explicative and transformatory step will focus on the concept of the *indispensability* and *irreplaceability* of each discourse partner. Since an inferential reasoning does not seem adequate for defending this concept, the next two following steps will increasingly aim at a more self-referential, and finally reflexive (retorsive) consideration. These steps follow from an *empirical reading* of the concept of pragmatic contradictoriness in a version that can be called a *'sense-critical'*—following Peter Strawson's use of the term "sense" in his famous "The Bounds of Sense."

1 Exposition and first discussion of the thesis: We all have mutually recognized each other as indispensable and irreplaceable subjects of our discourse contributions.

To gain a starting point for a discourse-ethical concept of human dignity, one could begin—with Kant in the background—by transforming the intelligible 'I' that accompanies and constitutes each act of cognition and volition into the *performative 'I'* of a non-misleading expression of intention or state of affairs, and with which I turn to myself and indeterminately many others in the 'role' of a current discourse partner (cf. Øfsti 1994). For an expression of intention to be attributable to me, the expression must be connected with a performative know-how in the form of "I intend to do x."

But what could it mean to say that, in statements such as "I intend to do x" or "I want x," the performative 'I' "is raised above all price and therefore admits of no equivalent" (Kant GMS 4, 434)? And how could one understand in this context Kant's saying that the "human being as person," i.e. viewed as an accountable being, possesses "a 'dignity' or an 'absolute inner worth'" (GMS 4, 433)? In our discourse-oriented context, I would interpret Kant's comments as follows:

when I say "I intend to do x" (e. g. hold a speech, close the window, go to sleep, etc.) the performative 'I' (that is, the 'I' which implicitly asserts that it know about itself that it has the intention to do x) is in a certain way just as indispensable as the "I think" of the transcendental synthesis of apperception or the "I want" of the synthesis of all objects of will in Kant's system.

The meaning of *'performative indispensability'* should be decoded with the "retorsive" or "self-referential" insight that I cannot delete or suspend myself from a discourse currently being carried out. To a certain extent, any attempt I would endeavor in that direction would always come too late. I cannot conceive any thoughts without connecting these thoughts with the concomitant knowledge of myself. [The validity status of this 'knowledge' is, of course, disputed.] Furthermore, my 'performative subjectivity' does not allow for any *substitute*, in the sense of relinquishing it—or leave it—to a second or third person so that I could let 'you,' 'her,' or 'him' think, speak, and act in my stead in the same act by means of that act—unlike an *advocatory* act that remains, of course, possible. And this applies to all who are capable of thinking, speaking, and acting. We can speak of a *performative irreplaceability* of each discourse partner *qua* performative subject.

If this perspective of a 'sublation' makes sense, the core idea of human dignity can be traced back to a moral right of all (potential) discourse-capable beings: to be able to take a discourse role without hindrance and to thereby be performatively indispensable and irreplaceable subjects of their discourse contributions. An attempt to contest this right of 'mine' or 'yours' in direct speech must lead to a kind of performative or pragmatic self-contradiction. What needs to be demonstrated, of course, is not just that each discourse participant presupposes *themselves* as performatively indispensable and irreplaceable subjects of their discourse contributions, but also that this presupposition of the argumentation is internally reciprocal. We can formulate this presupposition— before giving it its argumentative force—thus:

T: Each discourse partner presupposes themselves *and all other* discourse partners as performatively indispensable and irreplaceable subjects of all argumentation acts possible to them.

The question is:

Q: Do we already presuppose for our current discourse, to which I am now contributing, a reciprocity of *indispensability* and *irreplaceability* of all discourse partners—that is, of all those who could, as performative subjects of their argumentation acts, take a stand on my deliberations?

As a *first* attempt, it makes sense to base this reciprocity on a simple inference (deduction): *If* (a) each currently arguing party presupposes that she is an indispensable and irreplaceable subject of her argumentation acts ("that she ... acts" = p [for "that she" to "acts" say "p"]), and if (b) each of them must proceed on the assumption that each of the other arguing parties presupposes p, then (c) each of them as an arguing party presupposes each arguing party as an indispensable and irreplaceable subject of their argumentation acts. A comparable attempt to inferentially reconstruct Kant's thoughts on mutual recognition as an "end in itself" had already been put forward by Klaus Steigleder in his 2002 book *Kants Moralphilosophie*. Unfortunately, a closer look shows that the objection that I have raised elsewhere against Steigleder's attempt[4] is also relevant here: the inference which we may justifiably make on the basis of (a) and (b) is that each arguing party presupposes that p. This inference is nothing more than a generalization of the premise (a); and this generalization has already taken place in (b). As a (presumptively) valid conclusion, (c) does not exceed (b). A *mutual* recognition of the performatively indispensable and irreplaceable subjects of the argumentative discourse cannot be bindingly inferred. It remains to be shown that each, in carrying out their argumentation acts, 'necessarily' ('inevitably,' 'uncircumventably'[5]) presupposes not only themselves but all other parties as performatively indispensable and irreplaceable subjects of possible argumentation acts—that is, as potential co-subject in discourse.

For a *second* attempt, we should in fact take seriously the reflective reference, already addressed in the question (q), to the current discourse and the thereby already given constellation of perspectives. If in the first attempt, the inferential reasoning dominated a third-personal stance, that is a perspective in which 'I' (the author) speak about others from the 3rd person perspective ('I-they,' or more precisely, 'I—each arguing party'), we must now engage the inherently reciprocal subject—co-subject perspective, in which 'I' address 'myself' to 'you' (everybody who can hear what is spoken here or read what is written). In the constellation of the 1st/2nd person, which is 'always already' presupposed by us *hic et nunc*, the question presents itself:

> Can I, by addressing 'you' with this question, raise doubts about having always already recognized 'you' as a performatively indispensable and irreplaceable subject of 'your' discourse contributions?

---

4 See Brune (2010, chapter V, 2.3 (2)).

5 Apel (2001, p. 44) speaks of "non-circumventible and hence undouptable presuppositions."

As far as I can see, there are in principle only two plausible replies to this question:

> *Either* I expect no answer from 'you'—whoever you may be and regardless of when you may have entered this discourse with me. In this case, I didn't take my question seriously to begin with.

> *Or* I meant what I asked and await some sort of answer from 'you.' Yet, in this case, I already have—without knowing the content of 'your' reply—an answer to my own question: I have to presuppose that 'you' (whoever you may be) are a performatively indispensable and irreplaceable subject of 'your' reply to me.

Knowing *this* presupposition of my seriously meant question is completely independent from my inability, here and now, to know *Who* in the discourse will answer *When* and *How*;[6] I cannot even know if anyone at all will *actually* respond to my question. This proposition can be tested by anyone who hears this and asks herself the same question that I asked. Try it! You will, I contend, come to the same conclusion from your perspective.

To sum up: *If* this reflection on our current discourse would be convincing (and would be just as valid for all other types of discursive acts), then we could say in general: the *performative indispensability and irreplaceability of each subject* is evidently a necessary premise for all statements capable of meaning and validity made by all possible discourse partners—and thereby for any discursive accountability in general.[7] At the same time, the performatively pre-

---

6 It is important to see that I must be able to know this assumption regardless of *when* and *what* YOU as readers may think at this point—regardless, for instance, whether any of YOU may, while reading this text, find it incomprehensible ("I have no idea what he's talking about!" or "I don't understand what he wants from me!"). Any performatively initiated statement that refers to my argumentation is enough.

7 The concept of "indispensability" and "irreplaceability" of each performative subject presented here can be tied in to a debate in which Habermas wants to illustrate the linguistically inherent structure of mutual recognition to the early Luhmann: "The roles of asking questions and answering, of asserting and disputing, ordering and obeying are fundamentally interchangeable. However, this fundamental interchangeability is only valid under the condition of simultaneous recognition of the equally fundamental irreplaceability of individuals who assume each the dialog roles." (Habermas 1971, p. 194, transl. by the author) This would also be the discursive-pragmatic foundation for the concept, developed by Lutz Wingert (1993, pp. 90–92 et passim), of the "irreplaceable individual" in terms of the authorship of individually accountable actions that are situated in time and space. I myself have made use of the concept 'performative indispensability and irreplaceability' in order to complement Apel's emphasis on the *co-responsibility* in the argumentative discourse of *self-responsibility*; see Brune (2003).

supposed, reciprocal *recognition of all other possible discourse partner* as performatively indispensable and irreplaceable subjects of their discourse contributions forms the discourse's constitutive moment. As performatively indispensable and irreplaceable subjects, 'we'—i.e., all possible discourse partners—have the discursive status of a mutually recognized "end in itself" and offer a starting point for a post-Kantian, discourse-related reconstruction of the concept of human dignity.

2 Pragmatic contradictoriness: an empirical reading

However, upon observing the presupposition of performative indispensability and the irreplaceability of each performative subject, an objection immediately arises. Certainly it is the case that a statement needs a performative subject to be carried out. *Self-referential* statements make for a good illustration of this. For example, the statement

(p_s)   "The performative subject position of this assertion is indispensably and irreplaceably 'mine'!"

earns the predicate 'is true' only if the one to whom this statement refers also takes on its "performative subject position." Needless to say, any speaker is capable of fulfilling the truth condition of semantically self-referential statements of this type—as long as the speaker 'exists.'[8] A speaker that asserts (p_s) acts in principle like the 'I' in Kant's *Anthropology*, which tries, "as subject of thinking" or as "reflecting I," to ascertain the activity of its consciousness and—in doing so

---

[8] Two pertinent comments: (1) the statement p is only understandable as a semantically self-referential statement if a performative subject is already implicitly supplemented and thus understood in a pragmatic context [for example: "I am telling you / I am directing at you the assertion that (p)"]. The pragmatic context is more clearly recognizable in the statement "It's me." For the expression "*It* is me" to make sense as it comes through an intercom, the speaker must have the expectation (the situative preunderstanding) that the listener *supplements* certain pieces of information that the speaker could have made explicit: "It's me, Peter" or "It's me, the one you were expecting," or "It's me—we have a meeting now." (2) It no doubt makes sense to ascribe statements to speakers who had either never 'existed' in the flesh, do not yet or no longer 'exist.' "Hermogenes, son of Hipponicus, there is an ancient saying that knowledge of high things is hard to gain." When *I* quote this statement of Socrates (Cratylus 384 a-b), it is not excepted of me to take a position on the question of whether Socrates had really been a living person or not.

—does not encounter or come across a pure "consciousness of itself" in the sense of a pure apperception, but rather an "apprehension" or "empirical apperception."[9] The pragmatically remarkable feature here lies simply in the fact that any speaker, by asserting (p_s), *performatively* produces an individual reference for the possessive pronoun "mine" and thereby produces a verification evidence for (p_s). But this evidence is entirely empirical and thus of random nature. In other words: (p_s) is not an ordinary fallible hypothesis only because—due to the use of the pronoun—an empirical verification is structurally built in the assertion of (p_s).

It seems that with (p_s) we are looking at one of those "sentences" which, according to Karl-Otto Apel (1987, p. 185)[10], one "cannot understand without knowing that [they] are true." Our adversary would claim that the *pragmatic* (self-) contradiction that arises when somebody tries to negate (p_s) by saying

(α) "I assert that the performative subject position of this assertion is not taken on by me!"

traces back to a self-generated *falsification*. Understood this way, the inconsistency seems, in our context, similarly informative to declaring that "it's me" through an intercom, for instance.[11] The notion of *empirical*-pragmatic indispensability and irreplaceability, our adversary could continue, does not even allow the conclusion of an *intersubjective* identifiability of the concrete person who asserts (p_s). For it is certainly true that the following question remains open for others: *who* is it (or has it been), then, that performatively confirmed her empirical existence by means of the statement (p_s).[12] For example, if the police were to

---

9 Kant (1798, 7, 135 Fn.; BA 15).

10 Admittedly Apel would not have agreed that the point of such sentences is that by expressing them they become *empirically* verified.

11 A closer look tells us that the statement "it's me," spoken through an intercom, is by no means uninformative. These statements are only *meaningful* if the speaker expects from the listener a *prior understanding* that helps her to *complete* the speaker's statement into an understandable context. Such complimentary additions may be, for example, "It's me—the one that whose voice you recognize" or "it's me—the one you're expecting." And vice versa—the listener as well did not respond to the intercom without any expectation. I would argue the following: the assumption of *mutual* expectations is constitutive for any statement's context of meaning —whether these expectations are presently empirically confirmed, disappointed, or even abused. And this mutuality is built in all communicative relationships as an indispensable, i.e. argumentatively undeniable, moment.

12 And in this question there is, in principle, no knowledge advantage in the first person perspective regarding one's own statements, since it is fully possible for me—from the distance of retrospect—to doubt whether an utterance originated from me: "Did I say that?"

face the problem of investigating a concrete person who, in a kidnapping case, demanded a ransom through the telephone with their voice, they would not be aided by the kidnapper expressing a self-referential statement with the content (p_s). [13]

The decisive point of this objection is that the analysis of the self-referential statement (p_s), and thereby talking of a "performative indispensability and irreplaceability," only leads to presupposing the existence of a speaker as an *empirical* condition of an utterance. But presupposing the empirical existence of any speaker for the possibility of asserting (p_s) cannot be an argumentatively uncircumventable sense condition of the argumentative discourse, namely, for the simple reason that the speaker's individual existence—and therefore the empirical 'event' or occasion of asserting that (p_s)—is contingent. As empirically coincidental performative subjects of their discourse contribution, discourse partners hardly qualify for a transcendental or argumentatively uncircumventable status of being constitutive to the argumentation altogether.

This objection should be taken seriously. It could be raised to all such various versions of self-refutation that, according to John Finnis, are instanced by propositions which "cannot be coherently asserted, because they are inevitably falsified by *any* assertion of them" (Finnis 1977/2011, p. 66). The concept of performative self-contradiction, with which transcendental pragmatists like Apel and Kuhlmann want to demonstrate the argumentative uncircumventability of certain presuppositions of the argumentation, would be inapt for this task if it would turn out to be a concept of merely empirical-pragmatic contradictions. Marcel Niquet has demonstrated the empirical reading of pragmatic contradictions on statements that are usually used by transcendental pragmatists to exemplify their concept of self-refutation. Following examples from Apel's study of fallibilism (Apel 1987, pp. 159–60)[14], he investigates two phrases:

(β) "I assert that I do not exist (now)!"

and

(γ) "I assert that I am unconscious (now)!" (Niquet 1999, p. 87)[15]

---

13 A kidnapper who wishes to conceal his identity could therefore state (α) even without having any intentions to deceive.

14 Similar examples can be found in Kettner (1993, p. 196).

15 If Anton Leist is correct, a contradiction cannot be *directly* derived from such phrases—unless they are supported by the general premiss "no one can assert something if they do not exist" (Leist 2000, p. 124) or 'no one can assert something if they are unconscious.' Only then does an assumptive structure emerge that leads to a contradiction: (1) "I assert that I do not exist now," (2) "Nobody can assert something if they do not exist," (3) "I assert that I am assert-

According to Niquet it is indeed true that one cannot dispute one's own existence or consciousness without contradiction. This may be because of "the fact that the *empirical carrying out* of the speech act directly falsifies what is asserted." (Niquet 1999, p. 86)[16] I interpret this "direct falsification," which Niquet establishes with reference to Henry L. Ruf, to be in full accordance with our adversary. Whoever expresses (β) or (γ) produces performative evidence of their existence and consciousness that immediately refutes the propositional component of their statement.[17] For the sake of clarification, the corresponding assumptions can be added to the utterances (β) and (γ):

(β')   "I assert [and by doing so presuppose to have performatively *produced empirical evidence* that I contingently exist] that I do not exist (now)!"

and

(γ')   "I assert [and by doing so presuppose to have performatively *produced empirical evidence* that I am contingently not unconscious] that I am unconscious (now)!"

Following this pattern, we can also add an empirical presupposition to the utterance (α) so that the empirical-pragmatic contradiction seems obvious:

(α')   "I assert [and by doing so presuppose to have performatively *produced empirical evidence* that I am contingently the subject of this statement] that the performative subject position of this assertion is not taken on by me!"

But this understanding does not uncover any uncircumventably necessary presuppositions of the argumentation, because the following "robust intuition," shared already by Stroud (1968, p. 253), opposes it: "*another* speaker can assertingly-argumentatively dispute (deny) my existence, tell the truth with such an as-

---

ing something now"; ergo [by virtue of (2) and (3)]: (4) "I assert that I exist now," whereby (4) and (1) form a logical-semantical contradiction. Whoever treats (1) to (4) as propositions, as Leist does, and follows him through the deep waters of inferential reasoning can in fact justify neither (1) nor (4) and, by adding further premises, would also find themselves at best in a trilemma. This knowledge has been around since Pyrrhonian skepticism, Agrippa, Jakob Friedrich Fries, and finally Hans Albert (cf. most recently: M. Williams 2001, chapter 5).

16 Emphasis added by the author. John Finnis shares the view that his so-called "operationally self-refuting" propositions "cannot be coherently asserted, because they are inevitably falsified by *any* assertion of them" (Finnis 2011, p. 66).

17 Niquet speaks less clearly of a "performative-pragmatic contradiction" from which he withdraws a meaning-critically effective, "strictly performative contradiction" (Niquet 1999, p. 87).

sertion, and at the same time produce a meaningfully valid assertion (a meaningfully valid argument)." And: "The empirical enabling condition of sufficient cognitive consciousness seems to be considered [...] even less than my own existence as a state of affairs of transcendental presuppositionality." (Niquet 1999, p. 91)[18] A pragmatically or performatively contradiction-free denial of *another* speaker would be, for instance: (δ) 'N.N. asserts that I do not exist!' A corresponding assertion from my perspective would be: (ε) 'I assert that N.N. does not exist!' Both assertions are not performatively contradictory[19] and are thus meaningfully valid. Even if only (ε) can be true at the point in time when both assertions are expressed, the decisive objection still remains: It seems that by demonstrating the presupposition of my (N. N.'s) empirically coincidental, singular existence or consciousness with help of the concept of empirical-pragmatic contradictions, we fail to reach the goal of uncovering uncircumventable presuppositions *of the argumentation in general*. We thus remain with two objections:

O_1: An empirically-pragmatically understood concept of self-affirmation cannot warrant a doubtless empirical identification of the performative subject of third party statements.

O_2: The empirical reading of the concept of pragmatic contradictoriness is inadequate for uncovering argumentatively uncircumventable presuppositions of the argumentation.

As a first response we can call our adversary's attention to the fact that she herself cannot help but taking on the performative subject position of those statements with which she raises her objection. As an arguing party she presupposes the existence of not just *any* person that must take on this position, but of *herself*. However, she may still concede this point without considering her objections to be refuted. Indeed, I think the adversary is right on both counts: *De facto*, I can never be absolutely sure who is the source of a third-party-statement. And the knowledge regarding my own indispensability and irreplaceability—although performatively self-verifying—would have at best the status of empirical knowl-

---

18 Emphasis added by the author; cf. Niquet (1999, pp. 86–7).
19 Admittedly, this only applies with an important restriction: As soon as N. N. tries to assert (δ) in *direct* communication with me or I address myself directly to him (whoever N. N. may be) with the statement (ε), we produce performatively inconsistent statements which are not to be understood as assertions. The following objection could be raised here: N. N. can address himself to me with the assertion (ε)—"J. P. B. does not exist!"—and still be performatively consistent while asserting falsely—assuming that he does not mistakingly identify me as somebody else or that he knows somebody else by the name J. P. B. who had recently passed away.

edge. As an *empirical* premise for the existence of one's own statements, the performative 'I' is coupled with a time index (cf. Illies 2003, p. 53) so that we could hardly go past the observation that each factual statement also needs *some* concrete empirical subject as the originator of this statement.

3 A sense-critical look at the empirical reading of the concept of performative self-contradictoriness

Of course, the empirical reading of the pragmatic contradiction is not the type that transcendental pragmatics like Apel or Kuhlmann would advocate. Their concept of performative self-contradiction is not a matter of proof that an assertion performatively produces empirical falsification evidence for that assertion's *propositional* part,—an assertion that is, in other words, supposed to be 'self-falsifying'—which, as we will see in a moment, does not apply anyway in the case of empirical-pragmatic contradictions. For them—as I understand—it is rather about a logically preceding '*sense critique' of the validity status* of argumentation acts. To their mind, the sense-critical point of demonstrating a performative self-contradiction would be to annihilate the performative (illocutive) sense of those statements convicted of the contradiction. It is, then, not at all clear whether a statement can be deemed as (or considered to be) an assertion. Without validity at the level of (intended) sense, that is, intersubjective *comprehensibility* as an assertion, such a statement's propositional component is not nominated for a truth value: It cannot be a candidate for falsification. Accordingly, the utterances (α'), (β'), and (γ') should be rephrased:

(α") "I assert [and by doing so performatively presuppose *for the intersubjective comprehensibility of this statement as assertion* that I am the subject of this statement] that the performative subject position of this assertion is not taken on by me!"

(β") "I assert [and by doing so performatively presuppose *for the intersubjective comprehensibility of this statement as assertion* that I exist] that I do not exist (now)!"

and

(γ") "I assert [and by doing so performatively presuppose *for the intersubjective comprehensibility of this statement as assertion* that I am not unconscious] that I am unconscious (now)!"

Now, it is important to note: if the performative presupposition of each subject's (current) existence and each subject's (current) consciousness *constitutes intersubjective comprehensibility* for one's own current statements as statement of this or that kind, then with my performatively presupposed existence and consciousness, presuppositions are revealed that are not only empirically but *necessary* for my discourse contributions as well as for others' discursive reactions to these contributions. The withdrawal of these presuppositions in the propositional component of statements β'' and γ'' leads to performative self-contradictions that prevent me and other possible discourse partners from understanding or identifying β'' and γ'' as my assertions. And this assumption still seems to be logically behind any person who, from the *observing* perspective of a third party, wants to infer from the symbolic 'occasions' of statements (β'') and (γ'') the verifying *empirical evidence* for my existence and consciousness at the moment of uttering those statements. For this person must presuppose that the performative subject positions of the statements observed by her are not just taken on by *anyone*, but rather that they are taken on by *me* so that what she considers as empirical evidence of my existence and consciousness could be verified. Likewise, she must presuppose that the performative subject position of the observing person is taken on by *her* so that the performative-propositional unity of her observations is maintained in a way that her observations can be attributed to her by others (for example, me).

What would this mean for the empirical reading of pragmatic contradiction and thus for the objections O_1 and O_2? I think, from a transcendental-pragmatist view, there are two appropriate responses: The thesis that someone who makes any statement and thereby produces an empirical falsification instance for the *assertion* (not made by him) of the proposition "that he does not take on the performative subject position of his statement" (= p_1) [or "that he does not exist" (= p_2) ; or that he is unconscious" (= p_3)], remains unaffected—with a *crucial constraint:* The proposition p_1 [p_1, p_2] *cannot originate from him* or from any discourse partner who wants to *address him directly* from the 1st/2nd person standpoint.

It is true that in these cases an empirical instance is produced, but this instance cannot be applied as a falsification instance to the propositional component of the statement *qua* intersubjective comprehensible assertion: there is nothing here that could be comprehended *as falsifiable*. In short, the second response to our adversary from a transcendental-pragmatist view is likely as follows:

R₁: As long as the statement is performatively self-contradictory, it cannot be construed as having a valid sense [to be "sinngültig"], let alone as a self-falsifying *assertion*.[20]

According to this interpretation, the statements (α), (β), and (γ) as well as the corresponding (α'), (β'), and (γ') are by no means about empiric-pragmatic *self*-contradictions in the sense of self-falsification. However, if we would truthfully assert of a third party, who factually does not take part in the discourse, that she does not exist (now), is (now) unconscious, or does not take on the performative subject position of statements, then these statements are understood as assertions, i.e. pragmatically unproblematic, and can be true or false. You would not contradict yourself by making such assertions, as long as you refrain from addressing them to those whom you speak about,—refrain from taking up the second-person standpoint (Darwall).

Actually, the discussion and rejection of the empirical reading of pragmatic self-contradictions seems to demonstrate even more: Alter Ego (from whom the original objections *de facto* stems) and I have not only mutually presupposed each other as performative subjects, but also mutually treated each other as addressees of comprehensibility claims. Therein lies a confirmation of both my and the other person's claim on autonomy of judgment—and this confirmation is completely independent from whether the objection comes from Alter Ego or another person. Just as I cannot, within the discourse, reify myself entirely or "use merely as a means" of discursive intention, i.e. completely turn myself into the propositional 'means' of an intentional verbal statement, nor can I make others, on whose free judgment I rely for securing the meaning and validity of my statements, into the *bare* medium of testing sense [intersubjective comprehensibility] and validity, without compromising my statements' comprehensibility and validity. The same way I presuppose *my autonomy of judgment in the role of a discourse partner*, I also recognize their autonomy of judgment as constitutive for meaning and validity—and *vice versa*.[21] Whoever denies this would, merely by

---

20 However, this argument presupposes what I have tried to demonstrate in Brune (2010, chapter I, section 4): that mere propositions *qua* naked locutions (in the Austinian sense) or in other words, *discursively unsituated* assertoric sentences cannot have truth value because they cannot be thought.

21 In view of the pending debate between K.-O. Apel and J. Habermas about the dependency of openly strategic language use on language use oriented to mutual understanding, I have tried to demonstrate that openly strategic (speech-)acting is dependent on meaning and validity assurance, which cannot be conceived as a result of mutual instrumentalisation (cf. Brune 2010, chapter II, esp. section 3.3).

attempting to refer to their own or others' statements, find themselves embracing a cloud instead of Juno (Kant). I therefore assert:

> R_2: The actual 'point of departure' of transcendental-pragmatic reconstruction of the concept of human dignity is our *role or status in discourse*, already taken on by us here and now and possibly taken on by all (potentially) discourse-capable subjects; and in this role or status an indispensability and irreplaceability as well as a mutually recognized judgment autonomy (with its inherent moments of equality and co-responsibility) are already embedded. And we cannot—within discourse—deny or leave this role or status for others in a comprehensible way since we had to have laid claim to it all along for this purpose.

4 Conclusion: Mutual respect transcends the issue of value

So what are the consequences for the *value-theoretical* line of interpretation mentioned at the outset of this paper? If I am not mistaken, the following objection must obtain from this viewpoint: Admittedly, on the basis of your "sense-critical" interpretation, you have demonstrated performative self-contradictoriness that entails a discursive or even a dialogical connection between the performative consistency of our statements and the mutual respect of discursive status (as performatively indispensable and irreplaceable subjects of all argumentation acts possible to us). Even if this connection should be constitutive for our discursive praxis, there is still not much gained by this insight, as:

> O_3: Why should I, on the basis of the fact that such a connection exists, attribute an *absolute* value to anyone? There is a lack of evidence than my *respect* of your status as a discourse partner is based on the condition that I must *value* you in this sense (and vice versa). The morally relevant point is lacking without such evidence.

The adversary's formulation of O_3 hereby brings the value-theoretical standpoint initially into play, requiring that she ascribes a value judgment on her respect of my status. Assuming we take such a value judgment as fact and follow this line of sight for a moment, questions emerge such as these: Is her attribution of value based on her valuing a quality that I possess, i.e. "humanity," my "rational nature," or my "power of rational choice," completely independent of her own choices or attitudes? Is it that these qualities are objectively valuable? Or does she see herself compelled to ascribe value on the grounds that she understands herself to be a being with the "power of rational choice," who must at least implicitly value this "power" and thereby cannot deny me, as a relevantly equal being, such a value?

Regardless of how one answers such questions, the fact remains that with the claim that evidence remains lacking and that respect, for her part, is once again based on a valuation (a value judgment), the adversary has already (again) recognized my status as a discourse partner. This leads to a third reply:

> R₃: It is interesting that you subsequently ask if you must somehow value me. I would like to pose the question from my point of view: Must I value you (in some manner)—be it that this valuation is due to a quality you possess or is implicit within my power of rational choice? I am still not clear as to where exactly I should allocate this "value" of humanity. At this point, I only know that I am to respect you. Whether, over and above this, there are good reasons to ascribe to you an (absolute) value is a question that we could gladly continue to discuss on the basis of the already *assumed* mutual respect of our discursive status.

The mutual respect of the discursive status of those encountered in a first and second person constellation transcends all considerations that might relate to a one-sided or even a mutual attribution of value. As such, it seems to me that the approach of taking the *respect of discursive status* as the starting point for a theory of mutually respected dignity is much more promising than an approach focused on the value of the other—regardless of whether this *value* can be comprehended only realistically or non-realistically. To deem this respect as therefore morally irrelevant just because it remains unclear if and how it should be supplemented, if necessary, by a mutual *attribution of value* seems to me to be nothing more than a stipulation.

Bibliography

Apel, Karl-Otto (1987): "Fallibilismus, Konsenstheorie der Wahrheit und Letztbegründung." In: Apel 1998, pp. 81–193.

Apel, Karl-Otto (1998): *Auseinandersetzungen in Erprobung des transzendentalpragmatischen Ansatzes*. Frankfurt a. M.: Suhrkamp.

Apel, Karl-Otto (2001): *The Response of Discourse Ethics to the Moral Challenge of the Human Situation as Such and Especially Today*. Leuven: Peeters.

Bagnoli, Carla (Ed.) (2013): *Constructivism in Ethics*. Cambridge: Cambridge University Press.

Brune, Jens Peter (2003): "Mitverantwortung und Selbstverantwortung im argumentativen Dialog." In: D. Böhler/M. Kettner/G. Skirbekk (Eds.): *Reflexion und Verantwortung.* Frankfurt a. M.: Suhrkamp, pp. 97–112.

Brune, Jens Peter (2010): *Moral und Recht. Zur Diskurstheorie des Rechts und der Demokratie von Jürgen Habermas.* München/Freiburg: Alber.

Darwall, Stephen (2006): *The Second-Person Standpoint. Morality, Respect and Accountability.* Cambridge: Harvard University Press.

Dean, Richard (2006): *The Value of Humanity in Kant's Moral Theory.* Oxford: Clarendon Press.

Finnis, John (1977/2011): "Scepticism's Self-Refutation" (1977). In: *Reason in Action. Collected Essays: Vol I.* Oxford: Oxford University Press 2011, pp. 62–80.

FitzPatrick, William J. (2005): "The Practical Turn in Ethical Theory: Korsgaard's Constructivism, Realism, and the Nature of Normativity." In: *Ethics* 115 (4), pp. 651–691.

Habermas, Jürgen (1971): "Theorie der Gesellschaft oder Sozialtechnologie? Eine Auseinandersetzung mit Niklas Luhmann." In: J. Habermas/N. Luhmann (Eds.): *Theorie der Gesellschaft oder Sozialtechnologie—Was leistet die Systemforschung?* Frankfurt a. M.: Suhrkamp, pp. 142–290.

Hill, Thomas E. Jr. (1980): "Humanity as an End in Itself." In: *Ethics* 91 (1), pp. 84–99.

Hills, Alison (2008): "Kantian Value Realism." In: *Ratio* XXI, pp. 182–200.

Illies, Christian F. R. (2003): *The Grounds of Ethical Judgment. New Transcendental Arguments in Moral Philosophy.* Oxford: Clarendon Press.

Kant, Immanuel (GMS): "Groundwork of The Metaphysics of Morals (1785)." In: Immanuel Kant: *Practical Philosophy.* Trans. and ed. by Mary J. Gregor. Cambridge: Cambridge University Press 1996. [Page references cite the volume and page number of *Kants Werke. Akademie-Textausgabe.* Preussische Akademie der Wissenschaften (Ed.). Berlin: De Gruyter 1900 ff. Vol 4].

Kant, Immanuel (1798): "Anthropologie in pragmatischer Hinsicht." In: *Kants Werke. Akademie-Textausgabe.* Preussische Akademie der Wissenschaften (Ed.). Berlin: De Gruyter 1900 ff. Vol. 7.

Kettner, Matthias (1993): "Ansatz zu einer Taxonomie performativer Selbstwidersprüche". In: A. Dorschel/M. Kettner et al. (Eds.): *Tanszendentalpragmatik.* Frankfurt a. M.: Suhrkamp, pp. 187–211.

Korsgaard, Christine (1996a): *Creating the Kingdom of Ends.* Cambridge: Cambridge University Press.

Korsgaard, Christine (1996b): *The Sources of Normativity.* Cambridge: Cambridge University Press.

Korsgaard, Christine (2008): *The Constitution of Agency: Essays on Practical Reason and Moral Psychology.* Cambridge: Cambridge University Press.

Kuhlmann, Wolfgang (1985): *Reflexive Letztbegründung. Untersuchungen zur Transzendentalpragmatik.* Freiburg/München: Alber.

Leist, Anton (2000): *Die gute Handlung. Eine Einführung in die Ethik.* Berlin: Akademie Verlag.

Niquet, Marcel (1999): *Nichthintergehbarkeit und Diskurs. Prolegmomena zu einer Diskurstheorie des Transzendentalen.* Berlin: Duncker & Humblot.

Øfsti, Audun (1994): *Abwandlungen: Essays zur Sprachphilosophie und Wissenschaftstheorie.* Würzburg: Königshausen & Neumann.

Sensen, Oliver (2009a): *Kant on Human Dignity.* Berlin/Boston: De Gruyter.

Sensen, Oliver (2009b): "Kant's Conception of Human Dignity." In: *Kant-Studien* 100, pp. 309–31.

Sensen, Oliver (2015): "Kant on Human Dignity Reconsidered. A Reply to my Critics." In: *Kant-Studien* 106, pp. 107–29.

Steigleder, Klaus (2002): *Kants Moralphilosophie. Die Selbstbezüglichkeit reiner praktischer Vernunft.* Stuttgart/Weimar: J. B. Metzler.

Stern, Robert (2010): "Moral Scepticism and Agency: Kant and Korsgaard." In: *Ratio* XIII, pp. 453–474.

Stern, Robert (2011): "The Value of Humanity: Reflections on Korsgaard's Transcendental Argument." In: J. Smith/P. Sullivan (Eds.): *Transcendental Philosophy and Naturalism.* Oxford: Oxford University Press, pp. 74–95.

Stern, Robert (2013): "Moral Skepticism, Constructivism, and the Value of Humanity." In: C. Bagnoli (Ed.) (2013), pp. 22–40.

Stroud, Barry (1968): "Transcendental Arguments." In: *Journal of Philosophy* 65 (9), pp. 241–56.

Williams, Michael (2001): *Problems of Knowledge.* Oxford: Oxford University Press.

Wingert, Lutz (1993): *Gemeinsinn und Moral.* Frankfurt a. M.: Suhrkamp.

Wood, Allan W. (1999): *Kant's Ethical Thought.* Cambridge: Cambridge University Press.

Wood, Allan W. (2008): *Kantian Ethics.* Cambridge: Cambridge University Press.

Sami Pihlström
Transcendental Anti-Theodicy

Abstract: This essay examines the possibility of arguing transcendentally for anti-theodicism, i.e., the view that theodicies seeking to justify or excuse God's allowing the world to contain evil and suffering ought to be rejected. In particular, it will be suggested that a certain kind of moral criticism of theodicies can be given a transcendental formulation. The occasionally shifting roles of the transcendental, the empirical, and the transcendent will thereby also be discussed. Finally, the question of truth—a general issue in transcendental argumentation—will be briefly explored from a pragmatist perspective in relation to the possibility of moral testimony and the acknowledgment of others' suffering.

1 Introduction

This essay examines the ways in which transcendental arguments—or, more generally, transcendental reflection and inquiry—can be put to work in philosophical attempts to understand the conditions for the possibility of appropriately acknowledging human suffering and its moral relevance. In particular, I will suggest that the opposition between *theodicy* (religious or secular) and *anti-theodicy*—i.e., what can be regarded as the main opposition in attempts to explore the problem of evil and suffering—ought to be investigated from a transcendental point of view. It will be argued that theodicies should be rejected not only for straightforwardly ethical but, at the meta-level, for transcendental (conceptual and even metaphysical) reasons and that *a commitment to anti-theodicy is a necessary (transcendental) condition for the possibility of seriously occupying the moral perspective itself.* Hence, my essay joins the tradition of moral criticism of theodicies that can be traced back to Immanuel Kant's "Theodicy Essay" (1791), and even all the way back to the Book of Job, which Kant comments upon, with more recent representatives among, e.g., post-Holocaust ethical thinkers developing Jewish responses to the Holocaust (such as Emmanuel Levinas, Hans Jonas, and Richard Bernstein), Wittgensteinian moral philosophers and philosophers of religion (such as Dewi Zephaniah Phillips), and even pragmatists (especially William James). These Kantian anti-theodicies cannot be discussed in any great detail here, but I will try to identify a relatively widely shared albeit usually merely implicit transcendental strategy of argumentation at work in such moral criticisms of theodicies.

DOI 10.1515/9783110470215-017

Generally, we may say that theodicies seek a justification, legitimation, and/ or excusing of an omnipotent, omniscient and absolutely benevolent God's allowing the world (His creation) to contain evil and suffering. Classical formulations can be found, e. g., in Augustine's appeal to God's having created human beings with the freedom of the will as the reason why there is moral evil, and in G.W. Leibniz's *Theodicee* (1710), according to which God could not have created any better world than the one that he, choosing from among all possible worlds, did create; hence we live, according to Leibniz, in the best possible world, and while there may be some evil there, it is necessary for the overall good. In the Platonic tradition, the very existence of evil is typically denied, or at least its full reality is restricted: evil is merely the absence of goodness, rather than enjoying any positive reality in itself. Even though Platonism is unpopular today, various free will and "soul-making" theodicies and "defenses" thrive in scholarly literature (cf. Plantinga 1977, Hick 1978, van Inwagen 2006, Stump 2010).

The mainstream approach to the problem of evil in contemporary Anglo-American (broadly analytic) philosophy of religion is, indeed, strongly *theodicist* in the sense that providing a theodicy or a defense is regarded as a requirement for any acceptable form of theism.[1] Conversely, by *anti-theodicism* we may designate the rejection of the very project of theodicy and of the theodicist desideratum—typically for moral reasons. Theodicist reactions to evil and suffering usually seek to respond to what is called the "argument from evil", i. e., the case against theism appealing to the empirical reality of evil as a premise in an evidential argument that needs to be defeated by the rational theist. What I am calling anti-theodicism does not simply maintain that such theodicist responses fail but that there is something wrong with the theodicist requirement itself, and this calls for a transcendental investigation.

While the anti-theodicist philosophies and philosophers mentioned above cannot be discussed in detail in a brief essay, it needs to examined at a general level whether, and in what sense, the ethical arguments against theodicies presented by such post-Kantian thinkers and traditions—arguments seeking to determine the deep moral inappropriateness of theodicies—are, or could be reconstructed as, transcendental arguments. The basic structure of a successful anti-theodicist transcendental argument will therefore have to be sketched. In addition, the question of what degree of *truth* can be achieved by employing tran-

---

1 The difference between a theodicy and a defense is that the latter only claims that, for all we know, God could have morally acceptable reasons to allow evil and suffering, without claiming that he in fact has those reasons in the actual world, while theodicies claim to tell a true story about the reasons God has for allowing evil and suffering. See, e. g., van Inwagen (2006).

scendental arguments will be approached by proposing that in this context the relevant notion of truth should be rearticulated in *pragmatist* terms covering not only the notion of propositional factual truth but more broadly something that can be called "moral truth" (and truthfulness).[2]

Thus, my discussion will, by examining the specific case of transcendental arguments concerning the appropriate ethical acknowledgment of suffering (and of the moral truth of experiences of suffering), contribute to the more general re-evaluation of the possibility of transcendental argumentation within an overall pragmatist philosophical framework (which, however, I cannot articulate in any detail here). I therefore also hope to reach metaphilosophical results concerning what I propose to call the contextual relativity, or the *perspectival* character, of the distinctions between the transcendental and the empirical on the one hand, and between the transcendental and the transcendent on the other hand. We may also speak about the (pragmatically) *shifting roles* of the empirical, the transcendental, and the transcendent. To address these issues, the argument of the paper will unfold in four sections (sections 2–5 below), before a brief concluding section will tie the threads together.

One of the implicit aims of this essay is to show that a transcendental criticism of theodicies is significantly stronger than the "merely" straightforwardly moral critique we find in some recent "meta-theodical" literature (e. g., Tilley 1991, Trakakis 2008) emphasizing the ways in which theodicies are morally problematic because they may sanction evil instead of contributing to fighting evil in the contemporary world. Those (non-transcendental) moral arguments against theodicies are highly important and welcome, but they do not seek to show that the very *possibility* of a moral perspective on reality and on other human beings becomes threatened if we adopt a theodicist worldview.[3] It is right here that

---

2 It might seem that the issue of *truth* is not as urgent when we are considering transcendental arguments in the *moral* realm as it is in the "theoretical" (epistemological) realm focusing on external world or other minds skepticism (with the challenge of Stroud 1968 still on the agenda; cf. Stern 1999). In a sense this is so, as we are definitely not interested in any (challenged) inference from how we must think to how the world actually is independently of our thought. It is not clear that such a distinction makes much sense in the moral sphere, which is based on human thought. However, anti-theodicy is a deeply metaphysical topic, too, and I will argue that in this case we should draw metaphysical conclusions from an ethical argument. The general entanglement of ethics and metaphysics I would be willing to defend (e. g., Pihlström 2009) cannot be explored here, though.

3 Note that a theodicist worldview need not be committed to theism or even to a theological exploration of the problem of evil and suffering. There are secular theodicies, and we may in a broad sense understand theodicism as a commitment to any project of excusing or legitimizing

transcendental anti-theodicism, as we may call it, emerges as a considerable strengthening of the case for *moral anti-theodicism*. It needs to be examined, however, in what sense exactly moral arguments against theodicies can be transcendental. I will also try to show that a proper appreciation of their transcendental character is facilitated by our seeing the transcendental and pragmatic strategies as working in close collaboration.

2 In what sense can anti-theodicist arguments be transcendental?

Let me first examine the sense in which arguments focusing on the moral inappropriateness of theodicies might be regarded as transcendental arguments. First, it may seem that moral anti-theodicism is typically based on the following kind of basic argument taking different forms in different specific anti-theodicist positions:

(i)   The morally adequate acknowledgment of other human beings' experiences (especially their experiences of suffering) is a moral duty (for all moral agents).

(ii)   Theodicies do not appropriately acknowledge experiences of suffering. (More specifically, theodicies are a form of ethical non-acknowledgment of another suffering human being.)

(iii)   Therefore, theodicies prevent us from performing our moral duty.

(iv)   Therefore, theodicies are ethically inappropriate and ought to be rejected (for moral reasons).

However, this is hardly a proper transcendental argument referring to the necessary conditions for the possibility of the moral point of view. A truly transcendental form of anti-theodicism could, rather, be based on something like this:

---

apparently meaningless suffering—if not in a theistic context, then possibly in the context of some kind of historical teleology or other secular overarching scheme.

(i)   Adopting a moral point of view on other human beings (or the world in general) is possible only if others' suffering (or their experiences of suffering, or the truthful communication of such experiences) is recognized (or acknowledged).[4]

(ii)   Recognizing (acknowledging) the other's suffering presupposes that suffering sincerely experienced as meaningless and/or absurd is not explained away or justified in terms of any externally imposed (e. g., narrative) structure of meaningfulness.

(iii)   Theodicies justify, or explain away, (all) suffering as part of an externally imposed, allegedly harmonious (either theological or secular) total narrative, thus giving suffering a meaning or function not manifested—and not recognized—in the experience of suffering.

(iv)   Therefore, theodicies do not enable us to recognize (acknowledge) others' suffering. In particular, they fail to recognize the sufferer's inability to recognize any meaning or function in her/his suffering.

(v)   Therefore, theodicies prevent us from adopting (occupying) a moral point of view.

(vi)   It is possible for us to adopt a moral point of view (because we actually do so).

(vii)   Therefore, theodicies must be rejected (not only for moral but for transcendental reasons).

In brief, insofar as we do occupy a moral perspective at all, or are even able to do so, we cannot coherently subscribe to any theodicy. The conclusion (vii) follows for (meta)ethical and transcendental reasons, not for moral reasons alone (though these are inseparable here). The key premises, requiring lengthy elaboration (impossible in this essay), are, arguably, premises (ii) and (iii), which basically claim that theodicies are forms of ethical non-acknowledgment, failures to recognize others' suffering, especially the sufferers' sincere experiences of the utter meaninglessness of their suffering.

This argument takes different forms depending on whether we locate it in the writings of post-Holocaust Jewish philosophers like Levinas (2006), Bern-

---

4 In this essay, I will skip the questions concerning the relation between recognition and acknowledgment, except for the brief remarks below in section 5.

306 — Sami Pihlström

stein (2002), or Jonas (1996), who frequently refer to the moral scandalousness or even obscenity of theodicies—to the sheer "disproportionality" (as Levinas puts it) of theodicies in comparison to the sufferings of the twentieth century—or in those of Wittgensteinians like Phillips (2004), examining the "grammar" of moral and religious language-games; or in the pragmatist tradition, e.g., James, who emphatically rejects especially Hegelian philosophers' denials of the full reality of evil in *Pragmatism* (1907).[5] All these different anti-theodicists, I am suggesting, provide us with some version of the same argument, maintaining that it is morally problematic at best, and immoral or obscene at worst, and therefore morally impossible, to even try to offer a theodicy. It is not only a moral duty to reject theodicies but, more strongly, theodicies lead us out of the moral sphere.

In some thinkers, especially Jonas and James, we may find quite explicitly metaphysical conclusions based on a transcendental argument starting from ethical premises: both, for instance, are willing to radically rethink the concept of God—to defend an idea of a finite or (in Jonas's terms) "self-contracting" God —on the grounds of the undeniable reality of meaningless suffering (see James 1907; Jonas 1996; cf. Pihlström 2014, chapter 3). James (1907, chapter 4) also defends pluralism and attacks monism for ethical reasons, arguing that the latter, unlike the former, leads to the irresolvable theodicy problem. In this sense, for these very different philosophers, metaphysics can in the end be based on ethics, rather than the other way round (cf. Pihlström 2009). In particular, it is impossible to deny at a metaphysical level the full, shocking reality of evil; there is, as Jonas puts it, "nothing more real" than the wasted humanity of the camps of the twentieth century.

The fate of transcendental arguments of the kind sketched here depends on the more general question concerning the relation between ethics and metaphysics. I have argued elsewhere not only for the view that pragmatism may yield a grounding of metaphysics in ethics both generally (cf. Pihlström 2009) and in the philosophy of religion in particular (cf. Pihlström 2013) but also, more specifically, that according to James an anti-theodicist approach to evil and suffering is a necessary condition for the possibility of adopting the moral point of view in the first place (for pursuing what James called the "strenuous mood"), and thus even for the employment of his pragmatic method, which seeks to analyze the proper meaning of metaphysical and other theoretical concepts in terms of their potential ethical relevance (cf. Pihlström 2016). We may even say that for James the pragmatist entanglement of ethics and metaphysics is based on a "framing" of

---

5 For some more detailed discussions, see, e.g., Pihlström (2013), chapter 5; (2014); and (2016).

the pragmatic method by the problem of evil and suffering. The ethical point of view on the world is not even *available* to us unless we take the reality of evil and suffering seriously—that is, unless we are willing to acknowledge our fellow human beings' experiences of suffering (including their experiences of being victims of deliberate moral evil) and willing to abandon all theodicies.

Now, why doesn't an argument like this generalize to *anything* morally problematic? Imagine that someone argues—perhaps quasi-transcendentally—from there being something (deeply, seriously) morally problematic about some particular way of thinking, X, to non-X being a necessary condition for the possibility of occupying a (deep, serious) moral perspective at all. This would be parallel to the argument for anti-theodicy as a condition for the possibility of morality. Why doesn't anything immoral turn out to be a violation of the conditions for the possibility of morality? Can we no longer draw a distinction between morality and immorality *within* the moral sphere, or from the moral perspective; is the very possibility of that perspective inevitably at issue as soon as we adopt a transcendental approach to these questions?

Well, the short answer is that in some sense it is. This is, we might say, what morality is like for us—or more precisely what its *foundationlessness* and *overridingness* are like in our lives and our moral vocabularies. In considering what an appropriate moral response to some situation is, we are in a sense inevitably, though usually implicitly, also considering what it means, or is, to respond morally to anything. Morality, moreover, *is* largely (though not exclusively) about dealing with evil and suffering. The problem of evil and suffering (as I have suggested in more detail in James's case) *frames moral philosophy generally*, or even philosophy generally. This is why it is crucially important to investigate it in transcendental terms characterizing the conditions for the possibility of ethically responsible thought in general. I would be willing to extend this suggestion to the metaethical proposal that moral philosophy is about "negativities" more generally—evil, suffering, death, guilt, and the contingent, finite, limited, vulnerable, and incomplete overall condition of the human being. At least we might say (quasi-transcendentally again) that an appropriate acknowledgment of such negativities is a necessary presupposition for us to be able to engage in moral argumentation and serious moral deliberation.

It is also important that we speak about *our ability to occupy a moral perspective*, or *the availability of the moral perspective for us*, rather than about the possibility of the moral perspective itself in neutral terms. What we are interested in here is the way in which *we* – as the kind of finite, vulnerable creatures for whom suffering is a reality that cannot be wiped away—are able to view the world we live in (our own lives and those of others) from a moral perspective. We are *not* primarily interested, for instance, in the metaphysics of "moral facts" independently of human experience. This is not to say that we would have to reject moral realism; on the contrary, we might very well be committed to a (say) pragmatically grounded form of moral realism (cf. Pihlström 2005), according to which the objectivity of moral values is a humanly given element of the reality we live in. Any transcendental argument in this area of life and reflection must, however, examine the constitutive conditions of *our ability* to be involved in moral thought and deliberation, that is, of our ability to occupy the moral perspective (or to be seriously committed to the requirements of morality), rather than (*per impossibile*) the metaphysical structures of any humanly neutral moral reality.

My proposal to view anti-theodicism as transcendental in a way contains an invitation to think about ethics in general *not* primarily as a system of moral rules or principles that could be applied to moral disagreements and employed in order to categorize actions, ideas, or practices as morally good or bad, or right and wrong, *but rather* as an unending search for an appropriate way of speaking about the world (or life, which, as we recall, are one and the same thing according to Wittgenstein's *Tractatus*, § 5.621), especially about other human beings and their experiences—that is, as a continuous search for a proper moral language-use and an examination of its (transcendental) conditions and limits.[6] Suffering clearly lies in the core areas of moral language. Our attitude to (actual or possible) suffering, manifested in our ways of speaking, largely determines the status of our moral language-use. Insofar as the transcendental argument proposed above is plausible, theodicist language is not simply morally inappropriate but leads us to a perspective from which we can no longer so much as occupy the moral point of view characterized by its distinctive language-use enabling us to distinguish between moral appropriateness and inappropriateness. We are, then, in a constant danger to step outside morality in our thought, talk, and actions (even though, paradoxically, there is a sense in which this is impossible, as any attempt to move beyond morality can only be morally judged). It is a crucial part of our search for an appropriate moral language to be aware of this danger and try to avoid it.

The transcendental anti-theodicy argumentation sketched here can be compared to Kant's (1781/1787) arguments in the "transcendental dialectic" of the

---

6 Note, however, that nothing here is intended to provide us with any reductive definition of ethics; on the contrary, my characterization of ethics as a search for an appropriate language-use is rather explicitly circular in the sense of employing the notion of moral appropriateness. Note also that this way of thinking about ethics does not follow any neat separation between ethics and metaethics. In trying to think ("metaethically") about what ethics is or means for us we are always already engaged in an ethical task.

First Critique, examining the transcendental illusions of human reason (i. e., the paralogisms, the antinomies, and the ideal of pure reason). These are, from Kant's critical point of view, desperate albeit humanly natural or even unavoidable attempts to think about the world as a totality, from a *theocentric* perspective. So are theodicies: they are attempts to interpret the meaning of suffering from an imagined yet humanly unattainable divine perspective. In contrast, Kantian critical philosophy—and transcendental anti-theodicism—occupies a resolutely human, *anthropocentric* perspective.[7] From this finite human standpoint, there can be no overall theocentric justification, explanation, or legitimation for suffering. Moreover, we might say that occupying the anthropocentric perspective and giving up theodicist illusions is a way of "seeing the world aright" in the sense of Wittgenstein's *Tractatus* (1921, § 6.54). Anti-theodicism incorporates a change of perspective, an essentially new way of seeing *everything* (in contrast to theodicist attempts to provide meaning for suffering). It is in this sense that it can be considered transcendental. This "seeing the world aright" is itself an unending ethical quest, perhaps comparable to the Levinasian idea of the infinity of one's (my) ethical responsibility for the other.

In making us unable to "see the world aright" in this ethically demanding sense, theodicies violate the necessary conditions for the possibility of the moral point of view in a manner resembling the way in which the transcendental illusions of reason analyzed by Kant violate the transcendental conditions for the possibility of cognitive experience outlined and defended in the "transcendental analytic" of the First Critique. The illusory theodicist way of viewing the world "wrongly" is precisely the way of viewing it from a God's-Eye-View unavailable to us (or attempting, in vain, to do so).[8]

3 The relativity of the transcendental vs. empirical distinction

Ludwig Wittgenstein famously writes in the *Tractatus Logico-Philosophicus* (1921, § 6.421): "Ethics is transcendental." This should be read in the context of another

---

7 On the distinction between theocentrism and anthropocentrism as a key to Kant's transcendental idealism, see Allison (2004).

8 The importance of Kant for the rejection of theodicies has of course been generally recognized (see, e. g., Bernstein 2002, Neiman 2002), but the structural similarity between anti-theodicism and Kantian transcendental argumentation (including the criticism of transcendental illusions) has not, as far as I know, been emphasized in the literature.

important statement in the same book, the one about logic being transcendental and "pervading the world" (§ 5.61)—and of course also in the context of the equally famous yet puzzling identification of ethics with aesthetics (§ 6.421). Qua transcendental, ethics (like logic) is, we might say, constitutive of our relation to and engagement in the world in general, including any ontology or metaphysics we are able to develop—this, indeed, is what the kind of transcendental argument imagined in section 2 above incorporates as its key idea and presupposition. This view could be compared to Levinas's (1974) well-known suggestion that ethics, primarily consisting in the infinite duty toward the Other, is a "first philosophy", preceding ontology and epistemology, or indeed subjectivity itself (without taking here any stand on the very interesting interpretive question concerning the availability of a transcendental reading of Levinas's moral thought).

The anti-theodicist argumentation defended here obviously presupposes that we can ask the further question about the constitutive or necessary conditions for the possibility of ethics itself. What makes ethics possible, or what do we have to presuppose in order for ethics to be possible (for us, as the kind of beings we are)? This question must make sense insofar as it is plausible to claim, as I just did, that the very possibility of occupying the moral point of view necessarily presupposes anti-theodicism—and thus taking evil and suffering seriously. However, there could be other constitutive presuppositions, too. There may, indeed, be an indefinite number of constitutive criteria or transcendental conditions that ethics itself—or the seriousness of the ethical, or the possibility of occupying a moral point of view—presupposes, such as the possibility of experiencing guilt and remorse, the possibility of forgiveness, or, of course, anti-theodicism. We may say that ethical seriousness presupposes that we do not adopt any too easy "happy end" view on evil and suffering but take them seriously in a proper ethical sense—which also entails taking them *ontologically* seriously. Therefore, ethics does not simply precede ontology but is entangled with it in a relation of reciprocal containment or interpenetration. The transcendental thus cuts both ways, or in other words, a condition's being transcendental (in contrast to its being merely factual or empirical, or being itself "conditioned") *depends on our perspective of inquiry*. From a certain perspective, ethics is transcendental, i.e., a condition necessary for the possibility of our engagement in any ontological structuring of reality (or, arguably, for any other genuine engagement in human practices whatsoever),[9] while from another perspective,

---

9 For a pragmatist transcendental philosopher, it would be important to characterize the notion of engagement in more detail. Here the key point is that even the most theoretical practices require engagement, which in turn requires an ethical perspective.

ethics itself presupposes an ontology in which the reality of evil and suffering is not denied but is duly acknowledged. This is a (paradoxically) fundamentally antifoundationalist view in the sense that there is no final transcendental or metaphysical bedrock for our views on the transcendental status of ethics. It is the kind of understanding of the transcendental that we might develop within a pragmatist transcendental philosophy (cf. Pihlström 2003, 2013).

Let us, in order to more clearly see the depth of this issue, consider a reflexive question: insofar as anti-theodicism is a transcendental condition for the possibility of morality, how can we *argue ethically* for anti-theodicism itself (against what we may take to be the moral corruption involved in theodicies)? We must *already occupy a moral perspective*—the perspective we are simultaneously arguing to be possible only due to anti-theodicism, the outcome of our argument—in order to be able to do so. We need such a moral perspective in order to be able to offer support for the crucial premises of our transcendental argument, (ii) and (iii). We must, hence, be committed to the moral point of view and its seriousness in order to be able to argue for morally grounded anti-theodicism, or (at a higher meta-level) for the view that such anti-theodicism is itself a necessary condition for the possibility of the moral point of view that we are (already) occupying. Anti-theodicism and the moral perspective are, thus, *co-constitutive*. There is a kind of circularity at work here, which can, however, be considered benign, or self-strengthening, rather than vicious. Anti-theodicism and the (possibility of occupying the) moral perspective presuppose each other; neither can be regarded as more fundamental or primary in relation to the other. (Compare the basic Kantian idea that there must already be experience in order for us to be able to show transcendentally *how* it is possible. Similarly, we must already be able to occupy a moral perspective on reality in order for us to be able to show transcendentally—reflexively, through a moral argument —how that perspective is available for us.)

The leading idea in developing a transcendental argumentation strategy in this context in the first place is that we may view an anti-theodicist response to the reality of evil and suffering as necessary for our capability of occupying a moral perspective. Theodicism allegedly justifying innocent suffering could, thus, be argued to violate the necessary conditions that make morality itself possible for us, and thus to step out of the moral language-game.[10] Hence, in developing this transcendental argument and the resulting transcendental anti-theodicism, we must critically examine the challenge of co-constitutivity. We have to

---

[10] As well as, arguably, out of genuinely religious language-games, at least according to Wittgensteinians like Phillips (2004).

make sense of the fact that anti-theodicist argumentation is itself essentially ethical, appealing to ethically appropriate acknowledgment of suffering, and therefore dependent on the availability of the moral point of view that is at issue here, while simultaneously reflexively constituting the possibility of engaging in any such ethical argumentation at all.

Now, my proposal here, very briefly, is that only a *pragmatically enriched transcendental method* can make sense of the idea that anti-theodicism transcendentally constitutes the moral point of view while itself constitutively depending on moral argumentation emerging from that point of view (whose availability must therefore have already been presupposed). A *pragmatically pluralist* argumentation strategy enabling us to switch the (transcendental) perspective or "direction" of argumentation is needed to make sense of this. The co-constitutivity of anti-theodicism and morality requires us to be able to change the direction of our transcendental argumentation. This requires, in turn, a pragmatically *perspectivalist* understanding of the method of transcendental argumentation. Such a methodological position thus in a sense emerges as a *meta-level transcendental condition* for the possibility of transcendental moral anti-theodicism.

The kind of foundationlessness relevant here may be illuminated by another remark we find in Wittgenstein. In *Culture and Value*, he says that life can lead us to believe in God—and he adds that by "life" he means certain experiences of life, such as sufferings of a certain kind (Wittgenstein 1980). Now, sufferings, or the mere awareness of the evil and suffering there is in the world, may also lead us to lose religious faith, though not as a conclusion of an argument. From the Wittgensteinian point of view, the issue is hardly one concerning what the mainstream analytic theodicy discourse calls the "argument *from* evil"; sufferings would not lead us either to God or away from God because of the success or failure of such theoretical arguments. Yet, the empirical reality of suffering could play a transcendental role in relation to religion and ethics (and thus act as an element of transcendental arguments).

The metaphilosophical moral of this is that there is no fundamental unchanging a priori structure of the transcendental. Something (e. g., ethics) is transcendental relative to something else (e. g., ontology), and something (e. g., anti-theodicism) may in turn be transcendental relative to ethics itself, while on the other hand transcendentally depending on our already occupying the moral perspective from which we may be able to argumentatively defend it. Everything depends on our pragmatically established perspective of inquiry. In this sense, transcendental philosophy is here subordinated to a certain kind of perspectival pragmatism allowing a critically self-reflective plurality of perspectives guiding our inquiries—and our lives. As the co-constitutivity of morality and anti-theodicism briefly discussed here requires us to be able to switch our perspective of transcendental argumentation, such a pragmatic perspectivalism itself emerges as a meta-level condition for the possibility of transcendentally establishing ethical anti-theodicism.[11]

4 The transcendentality of the transcendent

Not only do the roles of the empirical (or factual) and the transcendental occasionally shift, as they do, e. g., in Wittgenstein's *On Certainty* (1969), where empirical-sounding propositions such as "I have two hands" or "I have never been very far from the surface of the earth" may take the role of grammatical rules, resembling transcendental principles governing meaningful language-use within a certain form of life, while remaining in principle open to historical transformation and reinterpretation. Another key distinction relevant here, the one between the transcendental and the transcendent (highly central in Kant) may also become shifting and perspectival in an analogous way. Insofar as the transcendental boundaries of human experience and meaningfulness are not categorically fixed once and for all, ahistorically and immutably—that is, insofar as the transcendental may itself be "conditioned" from a different point of view—then the transcendent, which by definition lies beyond the boundaries of the empirical or factual (beyond their transcendental limits, that is), might also in some special cases be drifted into the realm of non-transcendence, when seen from an appropriate perspective.

Analogously and perhaps more importantly, something empirical or transcendental may in some special cases even take the role of the transcendent. In particular, the shocking reality of meaningless human suffering may not only play a transcendental role demanding us to adopt a moral perspective on the world but even a transcendent role demonstrating that the world, as experienced by us, is not at all under our control, perhaps not even categorizable by us, i. e., that there is ineffability and mystery in it. We might say that Gregor Samsa's turning into an insect breaks the boundaries of the empirical, the transcendental, and the transcendent in Franz Kafka's *Die Verwandlung*. Or consider Kafka's *Der Prozess*, particularly the parable about the man waiting outside the Law ("Vor dem Gesetz"). He just waits and waits, until the door is finally closed in

---

11 Subordinating transcendental argumentation to a meta-level pragmatism requires that we view transcendental arguments as in principle fallible. Much more would have to be said here about the "pragmatic a priori" and contextualized, relativized transcendental principles that have been discussed in the context of epistemology and philosophy of science (cf. Pihlström 2003).

front of him. We might say that here his remaining (forever) outside the law amounts to his being in a transcendent sphere where law and its immanent norms are not operative but where there is only room for something like transcendental guilt (cf. Pihlström 2011), as distinguished from empirical or factual (e. g., legal) guilt, i. e., for the kind of metaphysical truth about one's "case" (i. e., the truth about which crime one is actually guilty of) that Josef K. in *The Trial* desperately seeks to find out but inevitably fails.[12]

The horizon of transcendence is crucial here, as no law or legal punishment or even any conventional moral condemnation applied to the perpetrators *could* be morally sufficient or even appropriate as a recognition (acknowledgment) of the sufferings of the victims of a crime of the magnitude of, say, the Holocaust. Even so, it could still be meaningfully asked whether there is, e. g., a possibility for *forgiveness* even in such cases. Such forgiveness reaching for the transcendent (which, by definition, can never actually be reached from an immanent perspective) is not, and cannot be, any kind of moral or political duty for us in the empirical world, either the sufferers or the bystanders, and it can even be argued, with Fjodor Dostoyevsky's character Ivan Karamazov, that we have no right to forgive the most horrible crimes; what is at issue here can, then, only be a radical *transcendent* forgiveness in Vladimir Jankélévitch's (2005) sense, a forgiveness that goes beyond the immanent sphere of space and time entirely and cannot have any reasons. Indeed, the suggestion that we should or even could forgive the most horrible wrongdoers—or forgive God the fact that the world contains evil and suffering in the way it does—could be regarded as verging on the obscenity of a theodicy. In my view, it makes sense to think of the Holocaust as a crime and evil beyond any conceivable laws, norms, principles, punishment, trials, etc.—and hence as something transcendent—but not beyond the possibility of transcendent forgiveness. The philosophically striking point here is that an empirical event or process, which the Holocaust undeniably is, can come to play not only a transcendental but a transcendent role in our attempts to reflect on the (transcendental) limits of what we can meaningfully say and do. Our relation to such transcendence, manifested in our practices of ethical language-use and moral deliberation, can then in turn come to play a transcendental role in conditioning the possibility of our moral responses to suffering.

The moral of these reflections is that the postulation of (the possibility of) transcendence may itself be a transcendental condition for a certain understand-

---

12 Analogously, there is, then, perhaps also room (only) for something like transcendent forgiveness in the sense of Vladimir Jankélévitch's theory of radical forgiveness, which is beyond any reasons and norms (as articulated in Jankélévitch 2005).

ing of the ethical (cf. again Pihlström 2011). The distinction between the transcendental and the transcendent may therefore itself be as perspectival as the one between the transcendental and the empirical. There is no more absoluteness in this distinction than there is in the "direction" of transcendental arguments, which may shift depending on our perspective of inquiry (cf. section 2 above).

5 Testimony, truth, and the transcendental impossibility of full acknowledgment

These issues, also invoking the notions of truth and truthfulness in relation to the acknowledgment of the suffering of other human beings, should be further connected with the (possibility of) testimony, especially *moral testimony* (as analyzed, e. g., in Margalit 2002) and *martyrdom*. Both moral testimony and martyrdom, as has sometimes been remarked, were in a sense rendered impossible in the Holocaust, in which people were murdered anonymously, deprived of any reason to die for anything, and of course of the possibility of testifying about what happened. We have to be careful in analyzing the way in which the concept of truth comes into the picture here. The witness, especially the moral witness, when delivering a testimony about the suffering of her/his fellow human beings (who no longer can testify) testifies of something whose actual (factual) propositional truth corresponding to an actual historical occurrence is, though not irrelevant, not the most important issue. The *moral truth* of what happened is what really matters in such cases of interpreting and acknowledging suffering. Therefore, we also need to examine the relation between truth and truthfulness (cf. Williams 2002), as this kind of moral truth may have more to do with what is known as the moral quality of truthfulness than with the propositional truth of ethical statements that philosophers contributing to the standard metaethical disputes over moral realism and antirealism focus on. The notions of moral truth and truthfulness may seem to be less clear and messier than the straightforward notion of propositional truth, but the moral world—the world in which transcendental arguments exploring the availability of the moral point of view are relevant—is rather messy.

What do I mean by speaking about "moral truth" in contrast to (mere) propositional truth? The kind of moral truth (truthfulness) relevant here is, again, a matter of developing a general attitude to the world, not confined to true beliefs about facts or propositional truths about any particular historical event.[13] Our adopting an anti-theodicist way of thinking about suffering, and about other people's experiences in general, *changes everything* in the way we think about, or relate to, the world in general; nothing regarding our attitude to the world remains unchanged, and it is precisely in this sense that we are here dealing with a transcendental matter that can only be adequately thematized in terms of transcendental arguments and inquiries. The transcendental, precisely, pertains to the general framework through which we have to experience and conceptualize anything whatsoever we are able to experience and conceptualize at all.[14] Acknowledging, in an anti-theodicist manner, the moral truth of survivor testimonies of atrocities such as the Holocaust (to which I am here referring metonymically, letting it stand for any deliberate moral evil inflicted on innocent human beings) plays a transcendental role in being constitutive of our ability to adopt a moral perspective in the first place.

In any case, even then we still need a notion of truth, even if we reach the limits of testimony, or the impossibility of bearing witness—something that Holocaust writers and philosophers investigating the Holocaust (e.g., Primo Levi) have emphasized in different ways (cf. Agamben 2002, Alford 2009). Even the non-testifiability and non-martyrdom of Auschwitz will not, and cannot, destroy the concept of truth. On the contrary, the relevant notion of truth needed here is, I would like to suggest, open to a pragmatist articulation *à la* William James (1907), precisely because we need to (re)connect the notion of truth—the kind of truth at issue in a transcendental argument addressing our ability to occupy a moral point of view—with the notion of moral truth inextricably entangled with the concept of ethically appropriate acknowledgment of another's experience. However, a problem continues to haunt us: what if the concept of truth *is* destroyed in the manner imagined in George Orwell's novel, *Nineteen Eighty-Four* (1949), i.e., in the novel's torturer's, O'Brien's, manner? Famously, the protagonist of the story, Winston, is led to believe obvious falsehoods, including 2

---

13 Note that Williams (2002), though emphasizing the moral virtues of truthfulness and their essential connection to the concept of truth, does not really believe in "moral truth" in a sense comparable to scientific truth.

14 Recall what was said about the Wittgensteinian notion of "seeing the world aright" in section 2 above. Compare this also to the medieval notion of *transcendentalia* still partly at work in the Kantian conception of the generality of transcendental conditions and principles: what the "transcendentals" transcend is not, of course, the boundary of experience (they do not transcend but set it) but the boundaries between all specific ontological and other categories; they concern *everything*, generally. In this sense ethics is transcendental: it concerns everything in the human world, just like the Kantian categories, for example, cover phenomena generally, all objects and events of possible experience.

+2=5, due to indescribable torture as well as the systematic destruction of historical documents and any objective evidence about truths he takes to be true. Then, arguably, the very idea of a moral witness or moral testimony becomes obsolete, or even impossible. We can fully acknowledge the limits and fragility of testimony and the moral witness only by acknowledging this fundamental insecurity and foundationlessness of the (or any) moral truth(s) that we (can, or could) testify about.

Even anti-theodicy itself in the Kantian sense based on the idea of sincerity or truthfulness, thematized (according to Kant 1791) in the Book of Job (cf. Kivistö and Pihlström 2016a, 2016b), will be vulnerable if the notion of truth is in danger. Kant (1791) praises the Book of Job for highlighting the moral virtues of sincerity and truthfulness (*Aufrichtigkeit*), which, in contrast to the traditional virtue of patience, he regards as Job's key virtues in contrast to his friends' theodicist speeches that seek to justify Job's meaningless suffering by arguing that God must have had a good reason to let him suffer. Such truthfulness can, arguably, be regarded as the point of departure of any anti-theodicy worth the name: we have to—it is our moral obligation to—avoid rationalizing speculations about the alleged meaning or justification of others' sufferings. But insofar as the notion of truthfulness presupposes the notion of truth, albeit in a pragmatic sense, the challenge of Orwell's *1984* strikes us with full force. These notions could lose their meaning in a world that would be based on systematic torture and totalitarianism. We can never be fully certain about our ability to continue to acknowledge the other's perspective on her/his unique individual (or social) suffering. *This* is also transcendentally constitutive of our moral commitment to "seeing the world aright".

The impossibility of ever fully acknowledging the "whole truth and nothing but the truth" about the non-testifiable suffering of the martyr, or of any suffering individual, or any moral witness, is a crucial part of the anti-theodicist acknowledgment of others' suffering in general. I would like to suggest, though I won't be able to develop the idea any further here, that the relevant notion of truth needed here for a proper communication of moral witnessing or testimony, viz., a notion of truth incorporating truthfulness, is the broader pragmatic (Jamesian) notion, not the correspondence notion of truth narrowly restricted to propositional truth.

We may speak about acknowledging such truths or facts as the reality of the world, the existence of God—or another's suffering. These are "transcendent" in the sense that we can hardly *know* what exactly they are, or even that they are there to be acknowledged.[15] Within the immanent sphere of human experience (made possible by its transcendental limiting conditions), we may easily speak about our recognizing people, truths, norms, principles, etc., *as* something— but this recognizing "as" may not be available to us in the case of the world, God, or evil and suffering.[16] There is a kind of transcendent infinity in these objects of acknowledgment that we can never fully control or adopt within the sphere of immanence. The other's suffering, in particular, demands infinite responsibility (cf. again Levinas 1974, 2006), and this demand can, again, be regarded as a transcendental condition for the possibility of ethics. Somewhat paradoxically, acknowledgment—in contrast to knowledge, or even recognition (which may be argued to require knowledge about the "as" clause in "recognizing as")—is the morally appropriate notion precisely where it cannot be overarching, precisely when we are invited to observe that there can be no such thing as full acknowledgment. (What would it even mean to "fully acknowledge" the reality of the world, the existence—or non-existence—of God, or the suffering of another human being?) The paradox lies in the fact that acknowledgment is most needed when it is also impossible. It would be a colossal failure of acknowledgment to believe that one could completely acknowledge the other's suffering, or more generally the other's unique human perspective on the world (including *its* various challenges for appropriate acknowledgment).

However, the impossibility of full acknowledgment does not mean that we would not have the duty to continuously try to develop a truthful and sincere attitude to the other's suffering. On the contrary, the key insight of a pragmatist view of truth may be exactly here: it is by giving up the primacy of (mere) truth (and the mere knowing of the truth) that we can (only) open the space for acknowledgment and truthfulness. This "can" refers to a transcendental presuppositional condition opening up a certain way of viewing, sharing, and re-

---

15 This is also why it is better to focus on negative examples of failures of acknowledgment rather than positive examples of successful acknowledging of others' suffering. As Margalit (2002) reminds us, cases of non-acknowledgment, rather than acknowledgment, "hurt us into" ethics and politics.

16 See Cavell (1979) for an influential discussion of the distinction between knowledge and acknowledgment; from the Cavellian point of view, our basic relation to other human beings ("other minds" or souls) and the world we live in is one of acknowledgment rather than knowledge. Furthermore, on acknowledgment and recognition, see Kovalainen (2015). It could be argued that recognition (*Anerkennung*) in the standard sense requires knowledge, because one has to know "as" what the other party is to be recognized, whereas acknowledgment in the Cavellian sense does not require this but respects (recognizes, acknowledges) the other's otherness more openly than recognition. This could be a highly important difference when we deal with issues of evil, suffering, and (anti-)theodicy; cf. also Pihlström (2014).

sponding to the world in general. As explained above, adopting anti-theodicism changes everything in the way we view ourselves, others, and the world we live in. Nothing remains untouched by the realization that there is no excusing of meaningless suffering, no justification for the absurdity of evil. In particular, everything changes as soon as we acknowledge the impossibility of fully acknowledging the utter *meaninglessness* of others' suffering, the duty to avoid constructing apparently meaning-bestowing "happy end" stories to account for human catastrophes. Such a transformed attitude to our fellow human beings' lives may, and should, fundamentally transform our existence as such, our way of being in the world with other people.

This impossibility of full acknowledgment and its world- and life-changing character may be comparable to the way in which the loss of a person—for example, the death of a loved one, some concrete and unique individual who has been present in one's life but no longer is—changes one's entire world into something different. It is also comparable to the way in which, according to Wittgenstein's *Tractatus*, the world can "wax and wane" as a totality. The good or evil will, Wittgenstein maintains, cannot change the states of affairs the world consists of, but it can change the *limits* of the world, and as these limits *are* the transcendental subject itself—because the metaphysical (transcendental) subject is not an entity in the world but a limit of the world (cf. § 5.632)—one's anti-theodicist attitude of acknowledgment (including the meta-level acknowledgment of the impossibility of full acknowledgment) changes its world, and thus *the* world, in a fundamental manner.

However, there is one reflexive reflection to be added. Is the meta-acknowledgment of the impossibility of full acknowledgment itself an ethically appropriate anti-theodicist attitude to suffering? Or does it, in the end, run the risk of collapsing back into a theodicy by other means? Does it, more specifically, lead to an infinite regress or question-begging: are we trying to acknowledge others' suffering fully and completely, after all, when acknowledging the impossibility of full acknowledgment? Is there any place to stop here? Perhaps the honest and sincere response here is *no*. We must self-reflectively and transcendentally examine our own practices and processes of acknowledgment (and meta-acknowledgment) themselves, being prepared to revise them continuously, not being blind to those sufferers' experiences that actually or potentially question our acknowledgment attempts as insincere, incomplete, or hubristic in their attempted or alleged modesty. (We may, in the end, be like Job's "friends" precisely when we try to avoid their theodicist vocabularies.) Our *failures* of proper acknowledgment should be in our focus, not the successes—and this is, again, a transcendental claim about the necessary conditions for the possibility of morally responding to others at all.

Perhaps somewhat surprisingly, then, all this is intimately connected with the project of engaging in transcendental argumentation (or, more broadly, transcendental reflection) in moral philosophy. This is, we may say, transcendental moral philosophy pragmatically naturalized through the fundamental ethical need to take empirically real evil and suffering seriously while maintaining the philosophical focus in an analysis of the necessary conditions for the possibility of a certain kind of human actuality, namely, the ability to occupy a moral perspective on other human beings, their experiences of suffering, and the world in general. In a quasi-Wittgensteinian sense, we may say that we are here interested in the necessary conditions for the possibility of (a certain kind of) meaningful language-use.[17] It is precisely by emphasizing this that we may come to appreciate the transcendental character of the anti-theodicist account of acknowledgment defended here.

6 Conclusion

This essay has addressed several topics that are all deeply interconnected as features of an analysis of what it means to engage in ethically adequate (truthful) acknowledging of others' suffering, or a pragmatic-cum-transcendental analysis of the conditions enabling us to appropriately recognize such suffering. We also saw, at the meta-level, that there is something like a transcendental impossibility of *full* acknowledgment at work in the dialectical situation we are examining. That is, it is part of (or even transcendentally constitutive of) our ethically adequate acknowledgment of otherness, especially of the suffering other and the moral truth of her/his suffering, that we admit that we can never fully acknowledge it—let alone recognize it as something specific, claiming to "know" what it is like—i.e., that we duly recognize the limits of even our most sincere attitudes of recognition and acknowledgment.[18] This is comparable to our being committed to adopting a Wittgensteinian attitude to another human being as an "attitude to a soul" (*eine Einstellung zur Seele*), without claiming to know that the other "has" or possesses a soul (cf. Wittgenstein 1953, Part II, iv), or without claiming to know what kind of *qualia* s/he experiences. This reflection thus

---

17 A Wittgensteinian caveat here would be that moral language is in a sense not meaningful language at all but goes beyond the limits of language. It might be better to say that moral language-use is, primarily, a *continuous search for meaning*.
18 Thus, we should even acknowledge the necessary limits of our own anti-theodicist project of acknowledgment, including the fact that in some sense even theodicies could be (morally failed yet at least possibly sincere) attempts at acknowledgment.

also invokes the *transcendental impossibility* of knowing the truth about another's inner experience; this is what (according to Cavell) amounts to the "truth in skepticism" (or what might also be considered the "truth of solipsism", according to the early Wittgenstein).[19] The unavailability of any (full) propositional truth about others' suffering (or any full knowledge about such truths) is precisely something that a truthful, "morally true" acknowledgment of otherness needs to emphasize, and as philosophical resources to highlight this metaphilosophical moral we need both an enriched, pragmatically perspectival conception of transcendental argumentation and a pragmatic notion of truth rich enough to cover the intuitive ideas of moral truth and truthfulness.

I started from a rather sketchy analysis of the way in which a certain kind of argument seeking to establish the moral *inappropriateness* of theodicies is, or can be interpreted as, a transcendental argument establishing the *impossibility* of a theodicy given our ability to occupy a moral point of view. I ended up, however, discussing broader transcendental issues bringing these reflections onto a metaphilosophical level. In a sense, this inquiry is inevitably metaphilosophical, as what is at stake is the availability of a moral perspective and hence also the possibility of ethical inquiry.

My general conclusion is, then, that mere transcendental *argumentation* cannot morally appropriately account for our need to respond to human suffering, or to acknowledge the suffering other and her/his experiences. Yet, a transcendental *perspective* on ethics is vitally needed in this area. In investigating anti-theodicy as a moral response to suffering and evil we are engaging in a transcendental *reflection* on the constitutive features of moral seriousness. Therefore, also the anti-theodicist argumentation sketched above can be regarded as an instance of post-Kantian transcendental anti-theodicy. Pragmatic perspectivalness, moreover, shows us how transcendental anti-theodicism and its ethical grounding mutually "condition" each other.[20]

---

19 As noted above, Cavell (1979) suggests that a fundamental distinction should be made between knowing and acknowledging. See also the famous passages on solipsism (and its inexpressible "truth") in Wittgenstein's *Tractatus* (1921, especially §§ 5.62–5.64).

20 This paper was partly presented as a guest lecture at FEST in Heidelberg, Germany (February, 2015). Special thanks to Magnus Schlette, Philipp Stoelger, and, as always, Sari Kivistö. The topic of this essay is more comprehensively discussed in Kivistö and Pihlström 2016b. See especially chapter 6.

References

Agamben, Giorgio (2002): *Remnants of Auschwitz*. New York: Zone Books.

Alford, C. Fred (2009): *After the Holocaust: The Book of Job, Primo Levi, and the Path to Affliction*. Cambridge: Cambridge University Press.

Allison, Henry E. (2004): *Kant's Transcendental Idealism: An Interpretation and Defense. A Revised and Enlarged Edition*. New Haven, CT and London: Yale University Press. (1st ed. 1983.)

Bernstein, Richard (2002): *Radical Evil: A Philosophical Interrogation*. Cambridge: Polity Press.

Cavell, Stanley (1979): *The Claim of Reason*. New York: Oxford University Press.

Hick, John (1978): *Evil and the God of Love*. Rev. ed. San Francisco: Harper & Row.

van Inwagen, Peter (2006): *The Problem of Evil*. Oxford: Clarendon Press.

James, William (1907): *Pragmatism: A New Name for Some Old Ways of Thinking*. Ed. by Frederick H. Burkhardt, Fredson Bowers, and Ignas K. Skrupskelis. Cambridge, MA/London: Harvard University Press, 1975.

Jankélévitch, Vladimir (2005): *Forgiveness*. Trans. by Andrew Kelley. Chicago/London: The University of Chicago Press. (French original: *Le Pardon*, 1967.)

Jonas, Hans (1996): *Mortality and Morality*. Ed. by Lawrence Vogel. Evanston, IL: Northwestern University Press.

Kant, Immanuel (1781/1787): *Kritik der reinen Vernunft*. Ed. Raymund Schmidt. Hamburg: Felix Meiner, 1990.

Kant, Immanuel (1791): "Über das Misslingen aller philosophischen Versuche in der Theodicee". In: Wilhelm Weischedel (Ed.): *Immanuel Kant: Werke in zehn Bänden*. Darmstadt: Wissenschaftliche Buchgesellschaft, 1983, vol. 9. English translation: "On the Miscarriage of all Philosophical Trials in Theodicy." In: Immanuel Kant, *Religion and Rational Theology*. Trans. and eds. A.W. Wood & G. Di Giovanni. Cambridge: Cambridge University Press, 1996, pp. 20–37.

Kivistö, Sari; Pihlström, Sami (2016a): "Kantian Anti-Theodicy and Job's Sincerity". Forthcoming in *Philosophy and Literature*.

Kivistö, Sari; Pihlström, Sami (2016b): *Kantian Antitheodicy: Philosophical and Literary Varieties*. Basingstoke: Palgrave Macmillan.

Knepper, Timothy (2013): *The Ends of Philosophy of Religion*. Basingstoke: Palgrave Macmillan.

Kovalainen, Heikki A. (2015): "Recognition and Acknowledgment: Remarks on Cavell and Laitinen", paper presented at the conference, *Issues of Recognition in Pragmatism and American Transcendentalism* (University of Helsinki, December, 2015).

Levinas, Emmanuel (1974): *Totality and Infinity*. Trans. by Alphonso Lingis. Pittsburgh, PA: Duquesne University Press. (French original: *Totalité et infini*, 1961.)

Levinas, Emmanuel (2006): "Useless Suffering". Trans. by M.B. Smith. In: Levinas, *Entre-nous: Thinking-of-the-other*. London: Continuum, pp. 78–87.

Margalit, Avishai (2002): *The Ethics of Memory*. Cambridge, MA and London: Harvard University Press.

Neiman, Susan (2002): *Evil in Modern Thought: An Alternative History of Philosophy*. Princeton, NJ: Princeton University Press.

Orwell, George (1949): *Nineteen Eighty-Four*. London: Penguin, 1982.

Phillips, Dewi Zephaniah (2004): *The Problem of Evil and the Problem of God*. London: SCM Press.

Pihlström, Sami (2003): *Naturalizing the Transcendental: A Pragmatic View*. Amherst, NY: Prometheus/Humanity Books.

Pihlström, Sami (2005): *Pragmatic Moral Realism: A Transcendental Defense*. Amsterdam: Rodopi.

Pihlström, Sami (2009): *Pragmatist Metaphysics: An Essay on the Ethical Grounds of Ontology*. London and New York: Continuum.

Pihlström, Sami (2011): *Transcendental Guilt: Reflections on Ethical Finitude*. Lanham, MD: Lexington Books.

Pihlström, Sami (2013): *Pragmatic Pluralism and the Problem of God*. New York: Fordham University Press.

Pihlström, Sami (2014): *Taking Evil Seriously*. Basingstoke: Palgrave Macmillan.

Pihlström, Sami (2016): "The Cries of the Wounded in *Pragmatism*". In: Jacob Goodson (Ed.): *William James, Moral Philosophy, and the Ethical Life: The Cries of the Wounded*. Lexington (forthcoming).

Plantinga, Alvin (1977): *God, Freedom, and Evil*. Grand Rapids, MI: Eerdmans.

Stern, Robert (Ed.) (1999): *Transcendental Arguments: Problems and Prospects*. Oxford: Oxford University Press.

Stroud, Barry (1968): "Transcendental Arguments". *The Journal of Philosophy* 65. No. 9, pp. 241–56.

Stump, Eleonore (2010): *Wandering in Darkness*. Oxford: Oxford University Press.

Tilley, Terrence W. (1991): *The Evils of Theodicy*. Washington, DC: Georgetown University Press.

Trakakis, Nicholas (2008): *The End of Philosophy of Religion*. London: Continuum.

Williams, Bernard (2002): *Truth and Truthfulness*. Cambridge: Cambridge University Press.

Wittgenstein, Ludwig (1921): *Tractatus Logico-Philosophicus*. Trans. by David F. Pears and Brian F. McGuinness. London: Routledge and Kegan Paul, 1974.

Wittgenstein, Ludwig (1953): *Philosophical Investigations*. Trans. by G.E.M. Anscombe. Eds. G.E.M. Anscombe and G.H. von Wright. Oxford: Basil Blackwell, 1958.

Wittgenstein, Ludwig (1969): *On Certainty*. Trans. by Denis Paul. Eds. G.E.M. Anscombe and G.H. von Wright. Oxford: Basil Blackwell.

Wittgenstein, Ludwig (1980): *Culture and Value*. Trans. by Peter Winch. Chicago and London: University of Chicago Press.

Matthias Kettner
Argumentative Discourse: The Transcendental Starting Point of Apelian Discourse Ethics

Abstract: This paper deals with the question whether some morally normative content is grounded in the dialogical practice that both Apel and Habermas call argumentative discourse, and, if so, how to demonstrate that it is so grounded. Apel (unlike Habermas) claims that discourse has rationally necessary conceptual presuppositions; that morally normative content is part of such presuppositions; and that this can be ascertained in transcendental reflection, i.e. by a kind of transcendental argument. I argue that these claims can be charitably interpreted but require clarifications of their key concepts, i.e. "discourse", "validity claims", "performative self-contradiction", and "community of communication". I argue that discourse as a practice of reason-sensitive agents who are communicatively connected via argumentation can be explained by its normatively constitutive aim, namely fixing the true values of our reasons; that the primary level of validity claims are claims concerning good reasons; that performative self-contradictions are pragmatic-cum-logical inconsistencies that we can know *a priori* to be incompatible with discourse's constitutive aim; and finally, that competent discourse participants can know *a priori* that they would be performatively inconsistent if they flouted a moral kernel that is intrinsic in discourse.

Karl-Otto Apel is known for his philosophical approach of a Transcendental Pragmatics of Communication ("*Transzendentale Sprach-Pragmatik*", hereafter abbreviated as TPC). TPC has profound implications for a gamut of issues in theoretical and practical philosophy amounting to a "transformation" of a number of foundationalist projects that have been elaborated in the venerable tradition of ontological metaphysics and had already been thoroughly transformed via Kant's new paradigm of transcendental reflection.[1] The "T" in the somewhat unwieldy label of Apel's mature philosophical position signals Apel's intention to defend and revise Kant's paradigmatic shift from ontological to transcendental

---

1 Cf. Apel 1976; 1978; 1994; 1998; 2001a. For Apel's theory of paradigms of first philosophy see Apel 1998c and 2011.

DOI 10.1515/9783110470215-018

reflection (Apel 1998b). The "C" indicates the disclosure of a communicative dimension within transcendental reflection (Apel 1976a). The "P" refers to the pragmaticist background of Apel's position (Apel 1981).

TPC assigns to "genuine argumentative discourse" and its essential presuppositions a foundational role as well as critical role within all other philosophical inquiries in which universal validity claims are being raised and appraised (e.g. ontology, epistemology, philosophical theories of rationality, ethics). If there are such essential presuppositions then any interlocutor's communicative intention to waive them, when involved in an instance of argumentative discourse, must clash with the construal of that instance as rationally meaningful, since it involves the interlocutor in a philosophically interesting kind of inconsistency: "performative self-contradiction". This notion, Apel contends (2001a:156), is the "post-linguistic-turn equivalent to what Kant considered a violation of the 'self-consistency of reason' (*Selbsteinstimmigkeit der Vernunft*)". The way Apel thinks about transcendental arguments is intimately linked with the way he understands performative self-consistency, i.e. the principled avoidance of performative self-contradictions.

In the first section of the present paper I characterize how Apel, unlike Kant, relates transcendental arguments to rational agents who are communicatively connected via argumentation. Section 2 introduces the normatively constitutive aim of argumentative discourse, section 3 develops a real definition of the latter. On the basis of these clarifications of the nature of argumentative discourse, section 4 elaborates the sense in which discourse ethics' starting point is transcendental. Section 5 illustrates what necessary presuppositions of argumentative discourse are and distinguishes ontological and deontological conceptual elements, section 6 clarifies how their "rational necessity" can be demonstrated. In order to do so, Apel's concept of a performative self-contradiction has to be analysed. Section 7 highlights the principal importance of performative self-consistency. In the final section, I return to Apelian discourse ethics and distinguish a thin but universally valid morality that is intrinsic in argumentatively disciplined discourse from an ethos of argumentative discourse that is a particular moral stance contingent on the former but not implied by it.

1 Apel on arguing transcendentally

A long and winding search for specifically transcendental arguments as a distinct form of arguments has not really produced any philosophically encouraging results.[2] Candidate skeletal forms for transcendental arguments that have been proposed do not differ from the standard format of reasoning by modus ponens except perhaps in the content of the premises.[3] An altogether not implausible interpretation of the meagre results is that the hope of locating the very point of Kantian style transcendental reflection in a clearly distinct inferential format is misguided (Westphal 2003).

For Kant, transcendental reflection is reflection on the epistemic and ontological implications of the unity of the First-person perspective in whatever cognitive activity that produces intersubjectively valid cognitive products. For Apel, transcendental reflection is reflection that discloses ontological and deontological commitments that are part and parcel of the reciprocally shared self-understanding of argumentative discourse-participants and that are indispensable for the rational powers of their argumentative discourse. Any argument that articulates transcendental reflection so conceived we can call, relative to the background of Apelian TPC, a "transcendental" argument.

Apelian transcendental arguments are arguments that establish that there are some commitments that are rationally necessary by demonstrating that a justificatory move towards them no less than a sceptical move away from them is impossible without endorsing the commitments in question. Without them, success of the justificatory move towards backing the corresponding validity claim no less than success of the sceptical move away from the corresponding validity claim is not conceivably possible. That is why the sceptical move away from them is, and can be demonstrated to be, necessarily unsuccessful.

The sense in which a commitment can be "rationally necessary"[4] refers to Apel's and Habermas' doctrine of communicative rationality. Briefly, they maintain that stock-notions of rationality that account for particular forms of human rationality (e. g. means-ends-rationality) are incomplete unless their nexus to the general form human rationality, communicative rationality, is taken into account. Apel and Habermas place communicative rationality in the ways we more or less successfully deal with three (or in the case of Apel: four) distinguishable types of universal validity claims (truth, moral rightness, truthfulness, and intelligibility) that we have to handle and coordinate in linguistically mediated practices of communication.

---

2 Cf. Stern 2007 and Stern's contribution in the present volume. See also Niquet 1991.

3 Chase and Reynolds (2010), for instance, give the following characterization of a transcendental argument: "(1) Subject-involving state of affairs p obtains. (2) A necessary condition for p obtaining is that q obtain. (C) So q obtains."

4 Note that this is my interpretative terminology, not Apel's own.

Both in Apelian TPC and in Habermasian "Formal Pragmatics" the term *validity claim*, as a translation of the German term *Geltungsanspruch*, connotes a richer idea than speaking of the validity of a truth-preserving argument-form. The term connotes "that a claim (statement) merits the addressee's acceptance because it is justified or true in some sense, which can vary according to the sphere of validity and dialogical context".[5]

Elswhere I have outlined how to provide more content to their views by tying the notion of *communicative rationality* more closely, or perhaps exclusively, to the interrelated notions of *acting for a reason* and of *evaluating reasons as better or worse* (Kettner 1999). The latter two notions are interrelated in that we generally take communicatively connected rational agents (1) to aim at doing what they have good reasons to do, and (2) when they are uncertain what their comparatively best reasons are, to deliberate about their reasons in order to find out what (given their situation) their best reasons would be, and (3) when they are uncertain about what it is that they rationally ought, or are rationally permitted, to do (given how they perceive their situation and what they perceive as their reasons and as their comparatively best reasons) to aim at behaving in ways that would best express what they take to be their best reasons, and (4) to aim at employing for all this (1–3) only procedures that cannot be faulted for irrationality (such as arbitrariness, idionsyncracy, ignorance, self-subversion etc.). In a nutshell, the point of communicative rationality is reproducing and refreshing the stock of reasons that can serve as common grounds in whatever judgmental practices we develop (Kettner 2016a, p. 653).

In what follows I want to analyse how Apelian transcendental arguments depend on the notion of a performative self-contradiction which in turn depends on a specific construal of "discourse" as argumentative discourse. In light of TPC, the philosophically intriguing thing about argumentative discourse is its rational power. The rational power of real argumentatively disciplined discourse consists in its capacity to determine the relative validity of any determinable thought-content that any interlocutors in their roles of proponent and opponent in genuine argumentative discourse can collectively intend to posit, revise, or retract. Under this aspect, TPC differs sharply from Foucault-style construals of "discourse" as symbolic rationalizations of forms of power that are at bottom a-rational.

---

5 As Bohman and Rehg (2014) nicely put it.

2 A constitutive-aim explanation of argumentative discourse

The practice and activity of argumentation, being dialogical, involves more than one social role and normally more than one rational agent for its full realization.[6] Structurally required are thinkers/speakers who are capable of first-, second-, and third-personal thinking, at least one of them in the role of an *author* of a validity claiming utterance or thought, one of them in the role of an *addressee* of that utterance or thought, who has the potential to reciprocate, and a third thinker/speaker in the role of a *reporter* who can report to other thinkers/speakers whatever exactly it is that the author claimed vis-à-vis an addressee and what the latter claimed in response. Any competent thinker will be able to virtually take each of these roles in turn.

Evidently, the activity of argumentation requires suitable dialogical practices in which different rational agents can act, and are willing to act, as communicatively connected rational agents, and to do so while sharing the intention to cooperatively make, probe, contest or defend determinate validity claims.[7] Apel's somewhat monotonously explains the interdependency of dialogical practices, validity and communicative connectedness by repeating the point that to identify with a "virtually unlimited community of communication" is "an *a priori*" requirement for rational agents in order for them to be able to think thought-contents validity claimingly, i.e. to think thought-contents *as* valid (or *as* invalid). Note that Apel's point is not merely a psychological one about mental identification, nor is it merely a sociological one about social facts. Rather, his point about the a priori status of situating ourselves at once in both a finite real community of communication and in a virtually unlimited community of communication is a conceptual point about validity: if it *is* rationally valid to claim *that p* (i.e. a fact-expressing thought) *is true*, or *that n* (i.e. an obligation-expressing thought) *is right*, then the rational validity of so claiming must outstrip the particular set of particular individuals who already share confidence that this is so. For instance, if we think *that the earth is flat* is true, or that *forbidding the killing of in-*

---

6 Argumentation is not an activity that any radically socially isolated individual could learn. Of course, once socially learned, argumentation can be carried out *in foro interno*, i.e. embedded in first-personal thought of a single person.

7 In terms of a distinction that Habermas has made popular one could express this point by saying that rational agents, when involved in argumentative discourse, must be able and willing to act communicatively, not strategically or instrumentally (cf. Habermas 1990, 1993, Cooke 1997).

330 ⎯⎯ Matthias Kettner

nocent people is right, then it would be odd to think that this is so only for us. Rather, it would be natural to think that these claims appear to us (and others) to be rationally valid claims *in virtue of certain reasons* that sufficiently justify the respective claims and make anyone's claiming validity concerning the respective thought-contents for these reasons into rationally valid claimings. Rational validity extends as far as the reasons on which such claiming is based can be shared via argumentation. (Likewise for *dis*claiming that a certain claim that purports to be rationally valid really is so.)

Does argumentative discourse have a constitutive aim? Whenever we are fully engaged in argumentative discourse, do we have to have a constitutive aim by being so engaged, i.e. does discourse have a *normatively* constitutive aim? How would we know?

A non-constitutive aim of a type of practice would be an aim that if dropped would leave the practice in its proper function. A constitutive aim would be an aim that could not be dropped in the practice while leaving its spirit unscathed.[8] A normatively constitutive aim would be an aim that practitioners who are competent in the practice know they all ought to intend to pursue if they collectively intend their practice to go on well and continue to be worthwhile and valuable for them.

How do these distinctions bear on the praxis we call argumentation? Are there any interesting constraints on the multifarious purposes or aims for which we might choose to use dialogical practices of argumentation? For instance, for fighting, for insulting, for keeping the upper hand in a clash of opinions, for persuading or for convincing, for publicly articulating our beliefs and reasons etc. Note that there is one general purpose or aim which we can advance via dialogical practices of argumentation that is excitingly interesting for communicatively connected rational agent. This is the purpose or aim of invoking a non-arbitrary and impartial authority and final arbiter whenever validity claims clash, i.e. whenever people are in doubt or disagreement about what to believe validly.

Being "language animals" (Taylor 2015), the cultural-anthropological fact that humans developed dialogical practices of argumentation is not surprising, whereas the fact that such practices can be tailored to fit our need for a non-ar-

---

8 Whereas the distinction between non-constitutive and constitutive rules concerns fixing the identity of practices, e.g. the identity of the game of chess by fixing the rules of chess, I want the distinction between non-constitutive and constitutive aims to concern fixing the normative essence of practices, i.e. fixing how practitioners of a certain practice P ought to shape P if they want P to be perfect as P. Drop the constitutive aim and you can no longer know how the practice ought to be in order for it to be in good shape.

bitrary and impartial authority and final arbiter concerning conflicting validity claims is a surprising cultural achievement of global importance. In the history of philosophy this achievement is proudly registered as a breakthrough of *logos*. It is associated with the name of Socrates and the invention of "Socratic dialogue".

Practices of argumentative discourse for settling disagreement in judgments concerning what is to be believed validly (rightly) exist today apparently in all cultures. Yet there is evidently dramatic cultural variation in the scopes of proper referents, permitted occasions, and legitimate participants of discourse. The idea that human progress requires maximizing all structural scopes of real argumentative discourse (scope of reference, scope of occasions, scope of participants) is, of course, an enlightenment idea of a collectively good form of life that prioritizes communicative rationality in all human affairs. Yet the notorious cultural specificity of this *socio-political ideal* is compatible with complete cultural generality of the *common sense idea* that we can ground, attack and defend validity-judgments, and can collectively intend to validly resolve conflicting validity claims, by way of argumentatively disciplined discourse. The *philosophical position* (as in TPC) that there is no rationally superior alternative way when it comes to trying to validly resolve conflicting validity claims than by way of argumentatively disciplined discourse of the widest possible scope is a strong and venerable philosophical position (Sintonen 2009). Though the underlying intuition is plain commonsense, its elaboration into a position requires philosophical insight; in TPC specifically, insight into the rational capacities of the community of communication (Apel 1980, Lafont 2002, Mendieta 2002, Taylor 2016).

What is the upshot of these ruminations for our search of a constitutive aim of discourse? We said that a good conjecture of a constitutive aim of argumentatively disciplined discourse is the aim of settling clashes of discrepant validity-judgments in ways that no one concerned can sensibly fault for arbitrariness, unjust partiality, and ignorance. We can express substantially the same point with the help of the TPC-concept of a rational consensus. Here, consensus counts as rational to the extent that a reason-responsive shared conviction of the rightness of a determinate validity claim (i.e. the determinate content of a consensus) is arrived at, or could have been arrived at, in a community of argumentative disciplined discourse. Consensus counts as rational to the extent that it is or could be discursively prompted. Consensus, in this sense, is not an empirical psychological notion that designates interpersonal harmony of mind. It is a normative notion pertaining to the theory of communicative rationality, and it designates collectively shared acceptance of reasons as sufficiently good justifiers of rightness-convictions viz. validity claims. Rational consensus is consensus rational-*ized,* meaning a consensus that is grounded in reasons which no one who is co-responsible for the discursive construction of consensus could not judge to be, and accept as being, good enough reasons.

With these clarifications in place, it seems safe to formulate the normatively constitutive aim of argumentatively disciplined discourse:

(D-Aim): Reaching a reason-responsive consensus about the reason-relative merits of validity claims in as much as these stand in need of revision since they conflict in the perspectives of at least two argumentative discourse participants who are communicatively connected via argumentation.

Note that the fact that D-Aim is the normatively constitutive aim of argumentative discourse explains the latter's general value: Being human, we are frequently in doubt and in disagreement about what to believe validly, therefore we badly need a non-arbitrary and impartial authority and final arbiter in clashes of validity claims.

Why is it safe to think that D-Aim is the constitutive aim of argumentative discourse? Consider: If someone else were to claim otherwise, then in order to take this dissenting opinion seriously, we would have to embark on a practice that already has at its aim that we reach a rational consensus about conflicting claims amongst argumentative discourse participants.

Could we switch to another validity-fixing practice? Are there social practices other than proper discourse that are functionally equivalents relative to D-Aim? The obvious answer is no. As far as we know there is no practical equivalent of argumentation that we can rely on to lead us towards D-Aim. Rational validity claims cannot be fixed, apparently, other than by way of argumentation. Rational validity claims require fully rational ways of fixing them. Dissenting opinions can be thwarted, to be sure, and consensus can be manufactured. But silencing the sceptic, banning the dissent voice, buying the approving voice, suppressing differing rightness-convictions, shunning conflicts about good reasons, prompting consensus by stepping up peer-group social pressure, etc., these are so many ways of deferring the question of rational validity (in older parlance: the *de jure* question). In all pseudo-alternatives mentioned, the fixing of validity boils down either to acceptance that is either unreflectedly motivational (the *de facto* question), e. g. habitual acceptance, or to acceptance that is contingent on reasons whose source is a reflective awareness of conditions of (various forms of) power other than the power of unfettered insight into the validity of the matter. But if we want to fix validity claims rationally, we want a non-arbitrary method that is unconditionally powered by our own unfettered insight, individually and jointly.[9]

---

9 Cf. Rehg (1994, p. 84–87): "The insight itself is genuinely intersubjective in that no single in-

Nothing guarantees, of course, that we can and will actually reach the constitutive aim of argumentative discourse in every single case of real discourse. Nothing guarantees that communicatively connected rational evaluators of reasons will be able to arrive via argumentation at a determinate consensus on every determinate validity claim. D-Aim has the status (unlike Kantian "regulative ideas") of a not altogether unrealizable ideal of communicative rationality. Note that rational consensus does not require unanimity. Rational consensus is a phase of a process in an essentially open (i.e. recursive) activity of reflexively equilibrating reasons for consenting *and* reasons for dissenting to controversial validity claims. In case some determinate community of communication does not reach consensus, at least they will have transformed brute disagreement into reflective disagreement. Disagreement is *brute* if it is unconstrained by any reason-giving aimed at reaching a common understanding of the reasonableness or unreasonableness of a disagreement in light of other factual, evaluative and normative beliefs on which there is currently less or no disagreement. Conversely, disagreement so constrained is *reflective* disagreement (Kettner 2003). Consensus on reflective disagreement can be fully in line with D-Aim and can be a fully rational consensus.

3 Towards a real definition of argumentative discourse

Argumentative discourse is not a type of speech-act (like, e.g., the speech-act of assertion) but a rich and complex practice for which many kinds of speech acts have to be available for this practice to get off the ground. Unlike assertion in contrast to other speech acts within and beyond the class of assertives, argumentative discourse cannot be contrasted with non-argumentative dialogical and non-dialogical practices in terms of norms alone, or effects alone, or commitments alone.[10] Given that argumentative discourse is a dialogical practice on a more complex level than the level on which we distinguish kinds of speech acts, we may expect norms, effects, commitments, and perhaps further determiners to jointly contribute to giving argumentative discourse its characteristic

---

dividual has a rational conviction alone, but only at the moment that it becomes clear to all that on one has any further questions" (ibid, p.87).

10 Brown and Cappelen (2011, p. 1–17) survey various attempts to capture the normative nature of assertions in these terms.

shape. But normatively essential in all this is the *aim* of argumentative discourse which gives argumentative discourse its *proper* shape.

For both Apel and Habermas the term *discourse* means, roughly, that argumentation is carried on under conditions of free and open dialogue. They have surprisingly little to say about how the fixing of validity claims via argumentation actually operates. In this section, I augment Apel's characterization of the essence of argumentative discourse as distinct from non-argumentative discourse or non-discursive dialogical practices. So now more has to be said about what it is like to be "communicatively connected via argumentation", as I formulated in D-Aim.

I propose we conceive of argumentative discourse (D), roughly, as the dialogical practice in which revision or re-evaluation of conflicting reasons is permanently possible. This accords with D-Aim. Furthermore, revision of conflicting reasons in D proceeds by bringing to bear on focussed reasons nothing over and above further reasons. The operation of revising and re-evaluating conflicting reasons has to be enclosed within the space of reasons if this operation is to be governed by fully rational procedures. In order to see why, consider: Changing our evaluation of determinate reasons as a consequence of, say, chance, threats, forgetfulness, social mimesis, distraction or neglect, would not count as *revising* them. In order to revise my and our reasons I have to change my and our evaluation of them by being guided by nothing else than my and our unfettered insight, i.e. in light of other of our reasons whose rational credentials we take, for the time being, as unquestionable or at least as less questionable than the reasons whose value we collectively intend to scrutinize.

Getting from the rough definition to a slightly more refined one and harking back to D-Aim, I propose the following real definition of argumentative discourse:

(D)   *Argumentative discourse is a dialogical practice that is open to all persons in their capacity as reasonable evaluators who collectively intend to revise controversial reasons via less controversial reasons in fully communicatively rational ways, thereby willing to realize D-Aim* (i.e. to reach a reason-responsive consensus about the reason-relative merits of validity claims in as much as these stand in need of revision since they conflict in the perspectives of at least two argumentative discourse participants).

With (D) in view, I want to mention two complex interrelated problems I have to defer given the confines of the present chapter. The first problem that both Apelian TPC and its Habermasian counterpart "Formal Pragmatics" leave unsolved is the problem of a robust taxonomy of validity claims. I leave this aside now.

Technically speaking, Apel's TPC and its Habermasian counterpart strive for a position of alethic pluralism in the theory of truth—that there is more than one truth property across different domains of argumentative discourse, and both are inflationists in that both hold that the concept of truth does not boil down to what is captured in a truth-conditional analysis in the Tarskian vein. But much remains to be clarified.[11]

The second problem is the problem of the proper scope of validity claims. Clearly, the paradigm of a validity claim of maximally *unrestricted* scope is the claim that a logical form (e.g. modus ponens) is logically valid. Neither Apel nor Habermas ever consider logical validity. Instead, their paradigm of a validity claim of unrestricted personal scope is that a fact-stating proposition is true, or false. Consider: A truth claim is unrestricted in scope in the sense that to claim that p is true is to claim that what p states as factually being so really is so no matter whether only some (we here and now) or likewise all others (or, as realists would add: no one at all) grasp the corresponding fact. TPC and "Formal Pragmatics" make this point in terms of universality: if a determinate truth claim is valid, its truth ought in principle to be claimed vis-à-vis any- and everyone, i.e. *universally.* The qualification "in principle" must be added here since it is obviously not the case that every person is able to grasp every fact that every other person is able to grasp, nor are all situations situation in which truth is a paramount consideration.

An advantage of (D) (over formulations found in Apel and Habermas) is that (D) clarifies the operative role of competent participants: To act as competent practitioners of argumentative discourse is to act as reasonable evaluators of reasons. Participants evaluate reasons whose supposed values have come under scrutiny in light of other reasons whose true values they are confident they know, for the time being, without reasonable doubt.

This serves to bring out a continuity between acting for a reason in *all* kinds of situations whatever and acting specifically as a participant in argumentative discourse. Suppose I think that I have reason R for doing A in situation C, and I think that my doing A in C is reasonable in virtue of my doing it for the reason R (instead of different reasons). Suppose you criticize not only what I do but how I understand what I do.[12] Let us assume we act in suitable social conditions that

---

11 For a range of issues that are at stake in the inflationist versus deflationist debate, cf. Wright and Pederson 2010. Apel gives the most detailed statement of his truth-theoretical views in an essay in which he attempts to integrate correspondence, evidence, coherence, and consensus into a comprehensive truth-property, cf. Apel (1998, 81–193).

12 Cf. Koorsgaard (2008, p. 227): "The demand for justification can as easily take the form: *what are you doing?* Or more aggressively and skeptically *what do you think you are doing?* As it can

support the move to D in our situation. Then your putting into question my taking R to be a good enough reason for doing what I do will bring us into argumentative discourse so that we now try to establish R's *true value* by evaluating R, my supposedly good enough reason for doing A in C, by the measure of other reasons R* that we bring in to bear on R as relevant and acknowledged (among reasonable evaluators like us) standards of evaluation. I might for instance justify and defend my action by disclosing to you that I take R to be a perfectly good reason in light of standard (R*1) of *morally permitted prudence.* You might object that moral considerations, in your view, are irrelevant here, and that as soon as we consider and evaluate R's real contribution to properly rationalizing my doing A in C for R by the measure of a different standard reason that you think appropriately applies, namely a standard reason (R*2) of *pure prudence,* then (you maintain) R will no longer count for much. And so on.

Reasoning about arguably good reasons with a view to consensually settling their true value is already reasoning in the mode of argumentative discourse. Reasoning about the rank and relevance of determinate standard-reasons that we want to bring to bear on targeted first-order reasons is part and parcel of what reasonable evaluators of reasons do when fully engaged in argumentative discourse. Claims concerning the relative rational merits or demerits of purportedly "good reasons" apparently are the most elementary format of rationally justifiable validity claims. All rational validity claims boil down to claims about the true values of reasons. Realizing this permits us to compress the formulation of (D) into:

> (D') *Argumentative discourse is a dialogical practice that is open to all persons in their capacity as reasonable evaluators who collectively intend to fix the true value of their reasons in fully communicatively rational ways.*

4 The transcendental starting point of discourse ethics

Apel's project of a discourse ethics starts from the premise that argumentative discourse necessarily involves presuppositions some of which are moral require-

---

why are you doing that? [Footnote omitted] The reason for an action is not something that stands behind it and makes you want to do it: it is the action itself, described in a way that makes it intelligible."

ments to which universal validity must be accorded in every possible discursive world, and cannot successfully be disclaimed in any discursive world. At least this is how I want to interpret Apel's intuition.

The identification specifically of morally charged conceptually normative presuppositions of argumentative discourse and the proof that Apel offers for their unassailable rational credentials both rely on transcendental reflection, as characterized in section 1, and are transcendental arguments in Apel's sense of the term.[13] In the remainder of this section I will elaborate the sense in which discourse ethics has a transcendental starting point.

For any community of reasonable evaluators P1, P2, P3 as author, addressee and reporter in an ongoing practice D, if abandoning a certain conceptual element c would clash with the very possibility for P1, P2, or P3 of construing their joint (i.e. collectively intended) practice D as rationally meaningful, then c is conceptually necessary in the sense of requiring to be used endorsingly in all possible worlds in which argumentative discourse as we know it exists, i.e. in all possible discursive worlds (Kettner 1993). In this sense, all the conceptual elements that we have to operate with in order to understand ourselves as enacting the essence of argumentative discourse (i.e. as collectively intending its normatively constitutive aim) are presuppositions that are rationally necessary in order for (D) to have its normatively constitutive aim (D-Aim).

A list of conceptual elements whose application we must endorse if we collectively intend D to have D-Aim (namely, to fix the true values of our reasons omni-laterally, i.e. for "everyone concerned", by the joint exercise of our communicatively rational capacities of insight) will have many diverse items. For instance, there will be items that articulate existential presuppositions such as the thought "I exist" and "you exist" (for all structural subject-places P1, P2, P3 respectively). These are ontological items. Other items on the list will articulate what it takes to have communicative intentions and attribute them to oneself and others. And so on. Assume that on the list there are also conceptual elements of a *conceptually normative* kind (*cn*), i.e. concepts that when enacted cannot properly be understood otherwise than as *permitting* or *requiring* something of someone in some respect. These are deontological items.

For any set of reasonable evaluators P1, P2, P3 as author, addressee and reporter in an ongoing practice of argumentative discourse, if and only if *the intention to disclaim that cn is valid* (i.e. to disclaim that thinking in terms of *cn* counts as a valid thought in that context) would make it impossible for them to construe their common practice of argumentative discourse, and their activities in this

---

13 I give a more detailed account of Apel on transcendental reflection in Kettner 2016b.

practice, as collectively aiming at a consensus about contested reason-responsive validity claims about the reference of their discourse, then to acknowledge *cn*'s validity (i.e. to think endorsingly or consenting of what *cn* presents as permitted or required) is necessary in all possible discursive worlds.

Having Stroud's consequential criticism of transcendental arguments in mind we might want to insist on a principal difference between *our acknowledging cn's validity* and *cn*'s having validity *simpliciter*, or *being* valid. Yet recall TPC's doctrine of rational validity: Rational validity emerges from communicatively constructed claims and is nothing over and above a qualified intersubjective construction of communicatively related rational agents (Kettner / Öfsti 1997). Call TPC's doctrine of rational validity a species of "discursive constructivism".

If we accept TPC's doctrine of rational validity, we see that no real difference between acknowledging *cn*'s validity-for-us and *cn*'s validity simpliciter can be made in case *cn*'s validity cannot be doubted without by the same token acknowledging *cn*'s validity (since doubting anything requires argumentative discourse and argumentative discourse requires acknowledging that *cn* is valid).

Call this the "retorsive" condition.[14] Note that only in cases where the retorsive condition holds does it not at all make sense to ply apart validity-for-us and validity simpliciter. In all cases where D has content that we call "empirical" as its reference, and not one of D's rationally necessary presuppositions, there will be leeway between validity-for-us and validity simpliciter. Fortunately then, TPC's discourse constructivist explanation of rational validity is immune to the charge of simply equating rational validity with whatever any particular community of argumentative discourse happens to acknowledge as valid.

5 Identifying necessary conceptually normative elements of argumentative discourse

Returning to D, the dialogical practice that is open to all persons in their capacity as reasonable evaluators who collectively intend to fix the true value of their reasons in fully communicatively rational ways. What general requirements

---

14 Cf. Illies' (2003, p. 44 ff.) discussion of "retorsive arguments" as a form of transcendental arguments. An argument that fulfills the retorsive condition "cannot reasonably be questioned and thus it cannot be false. As we might say more metaphorically: the argument 'retorts' or 'turns' the objection the sceptic 'back' against himself (in Latin, *retorquere*)" (ibid, p. 46).

amongst participants can we know *a priori* would, if absent, unhinge our self-understanding as enacting the essence of argumentative discourse?

For a start, (1) we have to attribute to other persons no less of all the generic rational capacities we ourselves think it takes in order to fully engage in D and that we think we ourselves have.[15] This is evident if we imagine we knock out as a normative presupposition the rule that discourse participants ought to take actual and potential others in their capacity as evaluators of reasons neither more serious nor less serious than we do take ourselves. With that normative presupposition gone, we can no longer think of ourselves as aiming jointly at communicatively rational revisions of conflicting reasons since any such conflict could be made to disappear by discounting those who are responsible for bringing it up. For all actual as well as potential reasoners, only if they are on an equal footing can their reasons conflict for them. And only for reasoners on an equal footing can it make sense to aim at fixing the true value of their reasons by way of D, and not by some other way that exploits asymmetries of situatedness amongst participants. Next, any outline of the respective generic rational capacities would definitely be incomplete if it did not contain the following elements of communicative and logical competence:

(2) A sufficient command of certain linguistic and cognitive competences evidently is a conceptually normative presupposition in and for D, since lacking the respective competences we could neither gain nor maintain a self-understanding as enacting the essence of argumentative discourse in our practice.

(3) A sufficient command of elementary logical rules is a conceptually normative presupposition in D. There is no point in drawing upward boundaries here, but there is a minimalist point: Participants in D must reciprocally presuppose that it is required of any and every participant in D to avoid open logical contradictions. For if open logical contradictions were not ruled out in D, then no reasons would ever stand in need of revision, nor would anyone be able to back or defeat, to ground or dislodge, to warrant or criticize, to support or attack *anything* by reasons. Consider: We would find ourselves in a world without common grounds. It is not hard to imagine that such a world, compared to the world as we know it, would be a Hobbesian nightmare; the life of reason, if reason could be at home at all in such a world, would be nasty, brutish, and short.

---

15 In specialized argumentative discourses, e.g. expert discourses, we might want to exclude some reasonable evaluators and rest with the set of those whom we treat as our discursive peers concerning the expert issue at hand. But this selective exclusion can only be rationally valid to the extent that it is grounded in reasons that we can offer them, and that they can accept, as a justification of their exclusion. The exclusion is a partition within, not a fragmentation of, the principally open community of D.

(4) D ought to be and remain essentially open. That this requirement is a rationally necessary presupposition in and for D becomes obvious if we imagine any or all of the structural scopes of D (scope of reference, scope of occasions, scope of participants) were governed by some authority *A* other than D and itself ungoverned by D. Knowing this to be the case we cannot, or can no longer, conceive of the practice that passes as D as a non-arbitrary method that is unconditionally powered by our own unfettered insight, individually and jointly. To the extent that we know how *A* impacts on the scopes of "D", we know that "D" is a deficient variant of D.[16]

With reference to participants, D's openness requirement translates into a general co-responsibility to care for D's openness where and when this is within their power.

Note that D's openness requirement also extends in time: No reason must be unconditionally removed from recursive scrutiny in light of other and perhaps novel reasons, occasions, and persons. This is because once some reason's rational merits have been determined in a particular community of argumentation, removing this reason from further revision is itself a determinate action that stands in need of justification. The removed reason would have to be removed for some (other) supposedly good-enough reason, which in turn cannot be removed from scrutiny except for some further supposedly good-enough reason, and so on. So even "best" reasons are best not in an absolute sense but only relative to a determinate set of reasons, namely the set of all reasons that have been evaluated and found wanting in the ongoing process of D. We might add the temporal scope as a fourth scope to the three structural scopes that we have already discerned in D.

6 Demonstrating the necessity of conceptually normative elements in argumentative discourse

How can we demonstrate that any doubt that could make a difference in argumentative discourse requires that *nc*'s validity be acknowledged by everyone concerned? According to TPC, the most convincing way for demonstrating that

---

16 As was mentioned in section 2, there is dramatic cultural variation in the scopes of D. The status of the requirement that D stay essentially open as a rationally necessary presupposition of D explains why we think of these variations, not as unproblematic variants of D, but as (perhaps tolerable, perhaps pragmatically unvoidable) restrictions on D.

the content of a conceptually normative element *nc* is necessarily valid for D-Aim to be possible (and hence counts as one of D's rationally necessary presuppositions) is by demonstrating (1) that whoever tries to deny that *nc* is valid cannot validly do so (i.e. it is inconceivable for us that we ever could validly do so), and (2) that there is a perfectly good reason, and not intellectual blindness, inability etc., why it is inconceivable for us that we ever could validly reject *nc* as valid, namely the reason that any doubt that could make a difference in D requires that *nc*'s validity be already acknowledged by everyone involved in D.

At this point the notion of a performative self-contradiction becomes crucial. This notion indicates a predicament that rational evaluators like us would basically want to avoid in argumentation. What is a performative self-contradiction, as construed in TPC?

Performative self-contradictions reveal a kind of inconsistency that does not reduce to the logical incompatibility between two or more propositions whose conjunction is logically contradictory. A performative self-contradiction is a logical-cum-practical inconsistency between on the one hand a determinate content *c* that some speaker S posits in D with the intention of claiming validity for it, and on the other hand one or more of those of D's conceptual presuppositions that are rationally necessary for D's normatively constitutive aim.

For instance: We attribute a performative self-contradiction to discourse-participant P1 in case P1 intends as author to claim rational validity for content *c* whereas *c* is such that if *c were* universally valid then we (i.e. P2 and P3 as addressee and reporter) could not sensibly attribute to P1 the very intention to claim rational validity for *c*.

Let *c* be the unqualifiedly general thought *that one is permitted to assert whatever one wants if one perceives this to further one's interests*. If P1 intends to claim rational validity in D for this thought then we cannot take seriously P1's speech-act of asserting *c* (as we would have to if we are to understand P1 and ourselves as jointly enacting the essence of discourse), and the reason why we cannot do so is that if P1 *were* right we all would be allowed to assert or deny whatever we want. Intending to convince someone that some belief is valid and believing its negation invalid would no longer be an intention it would make sense for anyone (including P1) to have.

Let content c be the unqualifiedly general thought *that judging reasons for their merits and demerits is a subjective affair and totally arbitrary*. So P1 appears to open an episode of discourse by asserting: "Judging reasons for their merits and demerits is a subjective affair and totally arbitrary". Placing P1's utterance in the space of discourse, we take P1 as intending to point out something true. Yet, if what P1 apparently intends to point out as true *were* really true then whatever reason P1 could have for being convinced of its truth and for convincing us likewise of its truth could have no determinate true value at all and hence could not make a difference within argumentative discourse. So whatever P1 thinks he is doing by saying what he says, we cannot sensibly attribute to P1 the intention to enact the essence of discourse.

Let's suppose I (P1) address you (P2) with the following eliminatively reductionist belief: "Argumentation and this entire game of giving and taking reasons is nothing but a power-game for winning others over to one's own convictions." You (P2) report to her (P3): "P1 claims that argumentation is nothing but a power game." On the assumption that we are involved in an episode of real discourse, it would be natural for P3 to respond skeptically: "But why should this be true? Why does P1 think *that?*" So P2 asks me which of my reasons for claiming truth for what I say I think he should report to P3 in order to convince P3. However, we all would know that no convincing reason could be forthcoming if what P1 (I) thinks and says *were* really so. The concept of convincing someone by sharing the reasons which one thinks represent one's own unfettered insight will disappear from our (presumed) space of discourse and this will render this space itself vacuous.

The three vignettes that I have outlined are cases where someone gets entangled in a performative self-contradiction, i.e. in a logical-cum-practical inconsistency that *can* de facto occur among communicatively connected agents, but *must not* occur if they are communicatively connected specifically as rational evaluators of reasons, viz. via argumentation. In all three cases, for the person embracing a performative self-contradiction (leaving it unresolved, treating it as permissible) implies dropping out of D (because of intending something incompatible with D-Aim) in the perspective of those who intend to continue D.

In order to see more clearly that performative self-contradictions do involve, but do not reduce to logical contradictions, consider what it is like for me or you to actually contradict myself performatively:

Between us as potential argumentative discourse partners, I present myself such that you (P2, P3) ought to take me to be willing *to make an appropriately reason-grounded validity claim concerning some judgeable content c* such that we should jointly accept this claim as insightfully warranted. But the posited content *c* is such that if what I claim were indeed valid—in a sense in which you in context D must take me to think *c* is valid (e.g. valid in the sense of true, morally right, legitimate, etc.)—then that very intention (viz. *to make an appropriately reason-grounded validity claim concerning c*) would not be available to me as my intention. So now you have to attribute to me a logically inconsistent pair of beliefs: that I do believe *and* that I do not believe that I intend *to make an appropriately reason-grounded validity claim concerning c*. My practical move within the practice of argumentative discourse creates good reasons that *a priori* cancel my position as a competent participant in the practice of argumentative discourse.

7 Performative self-consistency as a principle of reason

Is the very requirement to avoid performatively contradicting oneself one of D's rationally necessary conceptually normative presuppositions? Is it a "principle of reason" much like the requirement to avoid logically contradicting oneself is a principle of reason? Certainly, provided we understand reason as involving communicative rationality. Again, the principle's point is that one cannot consistently will within D to principally allow performative self-contradictions while at the same time intending uptake of one's speech-acts as being authored by a reasonable evaluator of reasons who intends to enact the essence of discourse, i.e. who intends communicative uptake as a move within D in accord with D-Aim.

But why care about being a discursive agent (rather than a discursive "schmagent" (Enoch 2006))? What is bad about actually contradicting oneself performatively? Compare: What is bad about actually contradicting oneself logically? A plausible answer will have to specify a loss. Willingly going against the respective principles will cancel your status as an interlocutor that we ought to respect as a co-equal within argumentation. In other words: You count yourself out as a communicatively rational evaluator of reasons.

If this loss does not impress schmagents, the following agent-neutral general answer might do. Permitting performative self-contradictions instead of requiring their avoidance would make something important break down. We would lose argumentation as a non-arbitrary and impartial rational authority and final arbiter in clashes of validity claims. What we stand to lose if argumentation would mutate into schmargumentation is the real possibility of continually improving the stock of reasons that can serve as common grounds in all our judgmental practices. One might be willing to accept this loss. But one can know that one could not will this loss to be acceptable for any good reason.

8 Conclusion: The moral in argumentative discourse

Apel frequently (and somewhat misleadingly) says that the morally normative content of discourse ethics consists in the rules or norms of "an ideal discourse community". Clearly Apel contends that within D it is at least implicitly, if not explicitly, recognized omni-laterally that D (be it a discourse about truth claims or another kind of discourse focussing on another kind of validity claims) necessarily presupposes a minimum of moral rules or norms.

As already said in section 4, the initial plausibility of Apelian discourse ethics (Apel 1976a) depends on the intuition that argumentatively disciplined discourse necessarily involves conceptually normative presuppositions some of which have a recognizably moral content in the form of moral requirements for which validity must be claimed universally and cannot sensibly be disclaimed. The person-scope of these moral requirements encompasses all persons who are reason-responsive agents and who are or could be communicatively connected via argumentative discourse. The requirements are recognizably moral in the sense that by being so connected we all reciprocally expect that we all ought to take seriously how the consequences of our argumentative acts affect all other reason-responsive agents for their good or ill in their capacity as reason responsive agents.

Apel (1976a; 1988; 2011) frequently articulates the moral relevance of some of D's conceptually normative and rationally necessary presuppositions in terms of a "moral co-responsibility" of all actual as well as all possible participants in D. It is their moral responsibility, Apel contends, that they take seriously that all their actions within D should be in accordance with the generic deontic status of free and equal co-subjects. The generic deontic status of free and equal co-subjects ideally requires of whoever is involved in D a complex normative attitude of mutual recognition: the normative attitude of wanting all interlocutors to accept a default stance of mutual recognition as co-valid reversible authors, addressees, and reporters, in D as binding on anyone who is or could be so involved.

These moral requirements are as securely established as the practice of argumentative discourse itself. However, the morality intrinsic in argumentative discourse (MID) is too thin a normative moral system to be on a par with "common sense morality" (Gert 1998). We may of course cherish MID as the focus of a thin but maximally person-inclusive rational ethos. This rational ethos, i.e. MID virtuously and habitually extended beyond contexts of actual argumentative discourse, may properly be denoted by the term "discourse ethos" or "ethos of argumentative discourse". The ethos of argumentative discourse is a morally-normative stance, a particular conception of the moral, one amongst alternative conceptions of the moral.

The ethos of argumentative discourse is the morally-normative stance that all committed proponents of discourse ethics will find congenial and recommendable. All committed proponents of discourse ethics make the moral integrity of the powers of argumentative discourse their foremost moral concern (Kettner 2004), and they extend this moral concern to extant formats and fora of actual communities of argumentation in our actual world.

Bibliography

Apel, Karl-Otto (1976): *Transformation der Philosophie*. Vol. 1, Sprachanalytik, Semiotik, Hermeneutik. Vol. 2, Das Apriori der Kommunikationsgemeinschaft. Frankfurt: Suhrkamp.

Apel, Karl-Otto (1976a): "The A Priori of the Communication Community and the Foundations of Ethics". In: *Transformation der Philosophie. Volume 2, Das Apriori der Kommunikationsgemeinschaft*. Frankfurt: Suhrkamp Verlag, pp. 358–435. (English Translation: *Toward a Transformation of Philosophy*, London: Routledge 1980, reprinted by Marquette University Press 1998.)

Apel, Karl-Otto (1981): *Charles S. Peirce: From Pragmatism to Pragmaticism*. Amherst, Mass.: University of Massachusetts Press.

Apel, Karl-Otto (1987): "The Problem of Philosophical Foundations in Light of a Transcendental Pragmatics of Language". In: K. Baynes, J. Bohman, T. McCarthy (Eds.): *After Philosophy. End or Transformation?* Cambridge, MIT Press, pp. 250–290.

Apel, Karl-Otto (1988): *Diskurs und Verantwortung: Das Problem des Übergangs zur postkonventionellen Moral*, Frankfurt: Suhrkamp.

Apel, Karl-Otto (1994): *Selected Essays. Volume One: Towards a Transcendental Semiotics*. Atlantic Highlands, NJ: Humanities Press.

Apel, Karl-Otto (1998): *Auseinandersetzungen in Erprobung des transzendentalpragmatischen Ansatzes*. Frankfurt: Suhrkamp.

Apel, Karl-Otto (1998a): "Fallibilismus, Konsenstheorie der Wahrheit und Letztbegründung." In: *Auseinandersetzungen. Erprobung des transzendentalpragmatischen Ansatzes*, Frankfurt: Suhrkamp, pp. 81–193.

Apel, Karl-Otto (1998b): *From a transcendental-semiotic point of view*. Manchester: Manchester University Press.

Apel, Karl-Otto (1998c): "Transcendental semiotics and the paradigms of First Philosophy." In: *From a transcendental-semiotic point of view*. Manchester: Manchester University Press, pp. 43–63.

Apel, Karl-Otto (1998d): "Transcendental semiotics and truth: the relevance of a Peircean consensus theory of truth in the present debate about truth theories." In: *From a transcendental-semiotic point of view*. Manchester: Manchester University Press, pp. 64–80.

Apel, Karl-Otto (2001a): "What is Philosophy? The Philosophical Point of View After the End of Dogmatic Metaphysics". In: C. P. Ragland/Sarah Heidt (Eds.): *What is Philosophy?* New Haven: Yale University Press, pp. 153–182.

Apel, Karl-Otto (2001b): *The Response of Discourse Ethics to the Moral Challenge of the Human Situation as Such and Especially Today: Mercier Lectures*. Leuven: Peeters Publishers.

Apel, Karl-Otto (2011): *Paradigmen der Ersten Philosophie. Zur reflexiven—
transzendentalpragmatischen—Rekonstruktion der Philosophiegeschichte.* Frankfurt:
Suhrkamp.

Bohman, James / Rehg, William: "Jürgen Habermas". *The Stanford Encyclopedia of
Philosophy* (Fall 2014 Edition), Edward N. Zalta (ed.), http://plato.stanford.edu/archives/
fall2014/entries/habermas/ (accessed 04.06.2016)

Brown, Jessica / Cappelen, Herman (2011) Eds.: *Assertion. New Philosophical Essays.* Oxford:
Oxford University Press.

Chase, James / Reynolds, Jack (2010): "The Fate of Transcendental Reasoning in
Contemporary Philosophy". In: Jack Reynolds et al (Eds.): *Postanalytic and
Metacontinental: Crossing Philosophical Divides.* London: Continuum, pp. 27–52.

Cooke, Mave (1997).: *Language and Reason: A Study of Habermas's Pragmatics.* Cambridge:
MIT-Press.

Enoch, David (2006): "Agency, Shmagency: Why Normativity Won't Come from What Is
Constitutive of Action." *Philosophical Review,* Vol. 115, No. 2, pp. 169–198.

Gert, Bernard (1998): *Morality. Its Nature and Justification.* Oxford: Oxford University Press.

Habermas, Jürgen (1990): "Discourse Ethics: Notes on a Program of Philosophical
Justification". In: *Moral Consciousness and Communicative Action.* Cambridge: MIT
Press, pp. 43–115.

Habermas, Jürgen (1993): *Justification and Application: Remarks on Discourse Ethics.*
Cambridge: MIT Press.

Habermas, Jürgen (1998): *On the Pragmatics of Communication* (edited by Maeve Cooke).
Cambridge: MIT Press.

Illies, Christian F. R. (2003): *The Grounds of Ethical Judgement. New Transcendental
Arguments in Moral Philosophy.* Oxford: Clarendon Press.

Kettner, Matthias (1993): "Ansatz zu einer Taxonomie performativer Selbstwidersprüche". In:
Andreas Dorschel / Matthias Kettner / Wolfgang Kuhlmann / Marcel Niquet (Hg.):
Transzendentalpragmatik. Ein Symposion für Karl-Otto Apel. Frankfurt: Suhrkamp,
S. 187–211.

Kettner, Matthias (1999): "Second Thoughts about Argumentative Discourse, Good Reasons,
and Communicative Rationality". In: Solveig Boe/ Bengt Molander / Brit Strandhagen
(Eds.): *I foerste, andre og tredje person. Festskrift til Audun Oefsti.* Trondheim: Norges
tekniks-naturvitenskapelige universitetet, pp. 223–234.

Kettner, Matthias (2003): "Gert's Moral Theory and Discourse Ethics". In: Walter
Sinnott-Armstrong / Robert Audi (Eds.): *Rationality, Rules, and Ideals. Critical Essays on
Bernard Gert's Moral Theory.* Lanham: Rowman & Littlefield, pp. 31–50.

Kettner, Matthias (2004): Das Spezifikum der Diskursethik ist die vernunftmoralische
Normierung diskursiver Macht. S. 45–64 in: Peter Ulrich / Markus Breuer (Hg.):
*Wirtschaftsethik im philosophischen Diskurs. Begründung und "Anwendung" praktischen
Orientierungswissens.* Würzburg: Königshausen + Neumann, S. 45–64.

Kettner, Matthias (2006): "Discourse Ethics. Apel, Habermas, and Beyond." In:
Rehmann-Sutter, Christoph / Düwell, Marcus / Mieth, Dietmar (Eds.): *Bioethics in
Cultural Contexts. Reflections on Methods and Finitude.* Berlin: Springer, p. 299–318.

Kettner, Matthias (2016a): "Der Raum der Gründe und die Kommunikationsgemeinschaft der
Begründer". *Deutsches Jahrbuch für Philosophie,* Band 5 (Beiträgen des XXIII.
Kongresses der Deutschen Gesellschaft für Philosophie 2014 in Münster), pp. 637–655.

Kettner, Matthias (2016b): "Raising Validity Claims for Reasons. Transcendental Reflection in
Apel's Argumentative Discourse." In: Halla Kim / Steven Hoeltzel (Eds.): *Transcendental
Inquiry: Its History, Methods and Critiques*. Basingstoke: Palgrave Macmillan (in print).

Kettner, Matthias / Öfsti, Audun (1997): ""Intersubjektivität". Einige Analyseschritte". In:
Georg Meggle (Ed.): *Analyomen 2. Proceedings of the 2nd Conference "Perspectives in
Analytical Philosophy", Volume 3*. Berlin: Walter de Gruyter, pp. 468–477.

Korsgaard, Cristine M. (2008): "Acting for a Reason". In: *The Constitution of Agency. Essays
on Practical Reason and Moral Psychology*. Oxford: Oxford University Press,
pp. 207–229.

Lafont, Cristina (2002): *The Linguistic Turn in Hermeneutic Philosophy*. Cambridge: MIT Press.

Mendieta, Eduardo (2002): *The Adventures of Transcendental Philosophy: Karl-Otto Apel's
Semiotics and Discourse Ethics*. Lanham: Rowman & Littlefield.

Niquet, Marcel (1991): *Transzendentale Argumente. Kant, Strawson und die Aporetik der
Detranszendentalisierung*. Frankfurt: Suhrkamp.

Sintonen, Matti (2009) Ed.: *The Socratic Tradition. Questioning as Philosophy and as Method*.
London: Kings College Publications.

Stern, Robert (2007): "Transcendental arguments: a plea for modesty." *Grazer philosophische
Studien*, 47, pp. 143–161.

Rehg, William (1994): *Insight and Solidarity. A Study in the Discourse Ethics of Jürgen
Habermas*. Berkely: University of California Press.

Taylor, Charles (2016): *The Language Animal. The Full Shape of the Human Linguistic
Capacity*. Harvard: Harvard University Press.

Westphal, Ken (2003): "Epistemic Reflection and Transcendental Proof". In: Glock,
Hans-Johann (Ed.): *Strawson and Kant*. Oxford: Clarendon Press, pp.127–140.

Wright, Cory D. / Pedersen, Nicolaj (2010) Eds.: *New Waves in Truth*. New York: Palgrave
Macmillan.

Notes on Contributors

Dennis Badenhop is research assistant at the Department of Philosophy, University of Greifswald. He is the author of *Praktische Anschauung. Sinneswahrnehmung, Emotion und moralisches Begründen* (2015) and a range of articles on moral theory and metaethics.

Sorin Baiasu is Professor of Philosophy at Keele University. He is the author of *Politics and Metaphysics in Kant* (2011), together with M. Timmons editor of *Kant on Practical Justification: Interpretive Essays* (2013) and published numerous articles on Kant and Kantian Philosophy.

Deryck Beyleveld is Professor of Law and Bioethics at Durham Law School and Co-Director of Durham CELLS (Centre for Ethics and Law in the Life Sciences). His numerous publications span criminology, philosophy of the social sciences, moral and legal philosophy, and many areas of law.

Jens Peter Brune is principal investigator of the research project "Human Dignity and Minimal Subsistence" funded by the German Research Foundation (DFG) at University of Greifswald. He is the author of *Recht und Moral. Zur Diskurstheorie der Moral und des Rechts von Jürgen Habermas* (2010) and of a range of articles on practical philosophy and socratic dialogue.

Marcus Düwell is Professor of Philosophical Ethics at Utrecht University. He is director of the Ethics Institute of Utrecht University and director of the Utrecht Research Institute for Philosophy and Religious Studies. His research interests and publications span bioethics, ethics of climate change and general topics of moral and political philosophy, particular the ethics of human dignity and human rights.

Christian Illies is Professor of Philosophy at University of Bamberg and the author of *The Grounds of Ethical Judgement. New Transcendental Arguments in Moral Philosophy (2003). His research interests and publications cover the fields of anthropology, ethics, biotechnology and philosophy of architecture.*

Wulf Kellerwessel is Adjunct Professor of Philosophy at RWTH Aachen University. He is the author of several books including *Normenbegründung in der analytischen Ethik* (2003) and a great number of articles on ethics, political philosophy, philosophy of language and philosophy of the Enlightenment.

Matthias Kettner is Professor of Philosophy at Witten/Herdecke University. In numerous publication he deals with ethics, in particular discourse ethics, bioethics, medical ethics, but also cultural studies, philosophical questions of psychology, and naturalism.

Wolfgang Kuhlmann is retired Professor of Philosophy at RWTH Aachen. He has authored several books about Transcendental Pragmatics including *Reflexive Letztbegründung* (1985) and published numerous articles on ethics, especially discourse ethics, Kantian philosophy and philosophy of language.

Niels Gottschalk-Mazouz is Professor for Social Philosophy at University of Bayreuth. He is the author of *Diskursethik. Theorien—Entwicklungen—Perspektiven* (2000) and a whole series of articles on philosophy of science and of technology, social philosophy and ethics.

Konrad Ott is Professor for Philosophy and Environmental Ethics at Kiel University. His main research and publications cover discourse ethics, environmental ethics, theories of justice, sustainability, ethical aspects of climate change, nature conservation justifications, and the normative basis for environmental policy.

Sami Pihlström is Professor of Philosophy of Religion at the Faculty of Theology, University of Helsinki, Finland, and the President of the Philosophical Society of Finland. He has published widely on pragmatism, realism, transcendental philosophy, ethics, metaphysics, and philosophy of religion. His recent books include *Pragmatic Pluralism and the Problem of God* (Fordham UP, 2013), *Taking Evil Seriously* (Palgrave Macmillan, 2014), *Death and Finitude* (Lexington, 2016), and *Kantian Antitheodicy: Philosophical and Literary Varieties* (with Sari Kivistö, Palgrave Macmillan, 2016).

Boris Rähme is researcher at the Fondazione Bruno Kessler in Trento, Italy. He is the author of *Wahrheit, Begründbarkeit und Fallibilität* (2010) and various articles in the fields of truth theories, normative ethics and metaethics. His further research interests include the epistemology of disagreement, and theories of argumentation.

Friedrich Reinmuth is research assistent at University of Greifswald. He is author of *Logische Rekonstruktion. Ein hermeneutischer Traktat* (2014). His main research interests and publications cover argumentation theory, logic, hermeneutics and philosophy of language.

Gerhard Schönrich is Professor of Philosophy at Technical University of Dresden. He is the author of *Kategorien und transzendentale Argumentation. Kant und die Idee einer transzendentalen Semiotik* (1981) and numerous books and articles on epistemology, philosophy of language, philosophy of sciences, ontology and philosophy of mind.

Robert Stern is Professor of Philosophy at Sheffield University. He is the author of *Transcendental Arguments and Scepticism* (2000) and *Kantian Ethics: Value, Agency, and Obligation* (2015). He published further books on Kant and Hegel an a large range of articles on epistemology, metaphysics, ethics and political philosophy.

Micha H. Werner is Professor of Philosophy with the focus on practical philosophy. He is the author of *Diskursethik als Maximenethik: Von der Prinzipienbegründung zur Handlungsorientierung* (2003) and published on normative ethics, metaethics, Kantian constructivism and bioethics.

Index

CPSIA information can be obtained
at www.ICGtesting.com
Printed in the USA
BVHW040014031118
532015BV00002B/33/P